The Psychology of Touch

The Psychology of Touch

Edited by

Morton A. Heller
Winston-Salem State University

William Schiff
New York University

LEA LAWRENCE ERLBAUM ASSOCIATES, PUBLISHERS
1991   Hillsdale, New Jersey   Hove and London

Lawrence Erlbaum Associates, Inc., Publishers
365 Broadway
Hillsdale, New Jersey 07642

Cover Illustration by: Faith Heller

Library of Congress Cataloging-in-Publication Data

The Psychology of touch / [edited by] Morton A. Heller, William
    Schiff.
        p.   cm.
    Includes bibliographical references and index.
    ISBN 0-8058-0750-0. – ISBN 0-8058-0751-9 (pbk.)
    1. Touch—Psychological aspects.   I. Heller, Morton A.
    II. Schiff, William.
    BF275.P79   1991
    152.1 '82--dc20   91-14484
                                                        CIP

Printed in the United States of America
10 9 8 7 6 5 4 3 2

To Elsa and Joseph Heller

—M.A.H.

CONTENTS

PREFACE

The *Psychology of Touch* is designed to appeal to a broad audience of experimental psychologists, researchers, graduate students, and advanced undergraduates. Many of the chapters are important reading for educators of people with perceptual impairments, special education students, medical and dental students, nursing students, and other workers in health-related fields. Most chapters require minimal specialized knowledge, because the authors have defined terms and explained methodology for readers outside of the immediate research area. This book is particularly useful as an adjunct to courses in sensation and perception, at the graduate and advanced undergraduate level.

The editors wish to point out that there is no "single theory" of touch. The field has not progressed to the point where we have theoretical conformity, because too many issues remain unresolved. We should note that haptics shares this status with most other fields of perception and psychology. Some researchers have adopted a Gibsonian approach (Epstein, Hughes, Schneider, & Bach-y-Rita, 1989; Solomon & Turvey, 1988). Others have made use of information-processing types of experimental paradigms (e.g., Horner & Craig, 1989; Manning, 1980); still many other researchers do not clearly fit into a single theoretical mold.

There is more to the psychology of touch than "meets the hand." Although many people may not associate touch with philosophy, there is a broad literature encompassing philosophical issues related to tactile perception. Of course, philosophy is only one of many related content areas, that also includes interest in pattern identification, object recognition, sensory physiology, intermodal relations, and developmental issues.

Sensory phenomena can be studied from many points of view, as illustrated in the first part of this volume. The authors of these chapters discuss various psychophysical techniques used to investigate the acuity of our senses, the magnitude of our sensations, and the nature of the tactile qualities we experience. Alternative methods of studying sensory phenomena, addressed in this first part, also include introspection and physiology.

Cholewiak and Collins discuss the sensory and physiological bases of touch: A traditional research concern that has involved attempts to link specific receptor organs in the skin with classes of sensation. The next two chapters, by Stevens and by Rollman, cover thermal sensibility and pain. These areas both involve substantial affective components. Stevens discusses thermal sensibility, and Rollman provides an interesting account of the problems involved in the measurement of pain, as well as covering the major theories of pain sensibility.

The second part is concerned with intermodal relations and the development of touch. Warren and Rossano provide an overview of work on intermodal relations and the influence of vision on touch. In their chapter, Bushnell and Boudreau have focused their attention on intermodal relations in infancy and early childhood.

Tactile pattern perception is covered in the third part of this book. Appelle addresses the influence of motor activity on form perception and the attributes of form. His account is guided by the idea that the nature of our hand movements determines what we perceive. Sherrick provides a perceptive account of the current research in vibrotactile stimulation, an area that has proven extremely useful for communication via the skin. In addition, he describes the application of vibrotactile stimulators to solve problems posed by visual and/or hearing impairment. Finally, Foulke's chapter presents an overview of research on reading braille.

The final part of this book deals with tactile perception in blind people; an area that has fascinated philosophers for hundreds of years. Although some of the research on tactile perception in blind people has been concerned with the solution of applied problems, the chapters in this part are primarily devoted to the empirical evidence on theoretical issues in haptics. Heller provides a general discussion of tactile perception in blind individuals. Kennedy, Gabias, and Nicholls describe the drawing of pictures by blind people. Millar reconciles the drawing ability of blind children with an apparent difficulty in their interpretation of raised line drawings.

ACKNOWLEDGMENTS

The editors wish to acknowledge the contributions of a number of people to this book. First, we are grateful for the guidance provided by our editor at Lawrence Erlbaum Associates, Judi Amsel, and our production editor,

Christopher Pecci. A number of people read portions of the book and provided helpful feedback. We appreciate the input of Lester Krueger, Carl Sherrick, John M. Kennedy, Mark Hollins, David Warren, and Emerson Foulke. Some of the research reported by M. A. Heller in various parts of the book was supported by NIH/MBRS grant 2S06 RR-08040. Although M. A. Heller is grateful for the assistance of a large number of students, too numerous to name individually, he particularly wishes to thank Carl Perry for some of the illustrations in the chapter on blindness, and Aretha Jones, Tamala Joyner, and Keisha Speller for their continued assistance. M. A. Heller wishes to thank Katie Heller for putting up with him while working on this book and Faith Heller for her patience and incisive comments and suggestions on writing. We owe a debt of gratitude to our teachers, who inspired us and spurred our interest in the scientific study of perception. M. A. Heller is grateful to Bill Schiff, who taught a fascinating perception course at City College of New York and has encouraged and supported his efforts over the years.

REFERENCES

Epstein, W., Hughes, B., Schneider, S. L., & Bach-y-Rita, P. (1989). Perceptual learning of spatiotemporal events: Evidence from an unfamiliar modality. *Journal of Experimental Psychology, 15,* 28–44.

Horner, D. T., & Craig, J. C. (1989). A comparison of discrimination and identification of vibrotactile patterns. *Perception & Psychophysics, 45,* 21–30.

Manning, S. K. (1980). Tactual and visual alphanumeric suffix effects. *Quarterly Journal of Experimental Psychology, 32,* 257–267.

Solomon, H. Y., & Turvey, M. T. (1988). Haptically perceiving the distances reachable with handheld objects. *Journal of Experimental Psychology: Human Perception and Performance, 14,* 404–427.

1

INTRODUCTION

Morton A. Heller
Winston-Salem State University

This book is about the sense of touch. Our coverage here runs from details of physiology to matters of communication, cognition, and representation. The psychology of touch includes cutaneous sensitivity, kinesthesis, and haptics. The term haptics incorporates both cutaneous and kinesthetic information (Revesz, 1950). Through haptics, we obtain information about objects by actively manipulating them, with covariant cutaneous and kinesthetic input (Gibson, 1966). The 1980s saw vigorous theoretical debate and challenging empirical findings on touch and the range of perceptions it allows. We will survey contemporary thought on these issues. In some instances, the discussion of the evidence and resolution of controversial issues will await later sections of this book. I beg the reader's indulgence in this matter, and urge patience. The interested reader will take a rewarding intellectual journey through the chapters within this volume.

Touch may involve ways of perceiving and representing reality that many people once thought were the exclusive preserve of vision or audition. Only in recent history have people tried to use touch as a channel for reading, speech signals, pictures, and music (via vibration). Some of these ventures have been amazingly successful.

The hand is a remarkable instrument, but it is not the exclusive organ of the sense of touch. If sensations were the source of perceiving, as many have explicitly and implicitly argued, then we can experience tactile sensations with our entire skin surface. If, on the other hand, touching is a set of activities yielding various sorts of information regarding the structure, state, and location of surfaces, substances, and objects in the environment, we use many sorts of haptic information to guide our activities. The feet, for example, make use of textural information about surfaces while we walk on them. Think of the difficulty one has walking on slippery ice. We change our stride in response to changes in friction, surface texture, hardness, and temperature. Blind pedestrians make use of haptic information from a long cane as they move about in the world. The lips are marvelous instruments for acquiring information regarding form, substance, and perhaps intention, and are a major source of shape information throughout life. Critchley (1971, p. 118) shows a photograph of a blind child reading braille with his nose. This is a further indication of the utility of other skin surfaces for pattern perception. We all rely rather heavily on tactile input over much of our skin while engaged in many perceptual activities. This reliance on the sense of touch often goes unnoticed, but rather than diminish its importance, it should stimulate wonder as to how limited our studies of touch have been.

We may become aware of our dependence on the sense of touch when something causes it to malfunction, and only then do we recognize its significance. Neither the leper nor the victim of diabetes doubts the importance of tactile input. Touch serves to warn us about impending or immediate danger, for example, via pain sensibility. In addition, our ability to maneuver in and explore the world as we do requires tactile input. This is obvious when we observe the relearning process as astronauts first walked on the moon. Even sitting utilizes tactile information, if only to tell us to shift our position. Our reliance on touch often goes unnoticed because of attention to visual perception, and because we tend to think of the performatory role of the hand rather than its sensing function (Gibson, 1962, 1966). We use our hands to obtain tactile information as well as to manipulate objects. However, much of our tactile input comes from parts of the body other than our hands (see Stevens, 1990). The tendency to identify touch primarily with the hands, and the close linkage between performance and perception, may have contributed to this bias.

The historical lack of interest in formally and seriously studying touch should be mentioned. Traditionally, psychologists have tended to emphasize the study of visual pattern perception when trying to resolve epistemological issues. Much of visual research has focused on attempts to understand pattern recognition via form perception. For example, more than a thousand experiments have been performed on visual illusions such as the familiar Müller-Lyer arrows. The sense of touch does not seem to operate as efficiently as vision in detection of outline forms. Touch is far slower, typically scans sequentially, and has a far more limited "field of view." This has led many researchers to think of touch as less important than sight—a more primitive mode of perceiving that plays handmaiden to vision. We should also note that the postulated dominance of vision and audition is only recent, and that historically, touch has been regarded as dominant. Moreover, many would say that touch is still dominant, at least in terms of an existence proof for objects, that is, we test the reality of a mirage or dream image by trying to touch it.

This book has much to offer vision researchers and general students of psychology. It asserts that the investigation of touch is important and valuable. Few of us are willing merely to look at our world. Our lives would be short, indeed, if we could only look and not touch; many species would surely vanish. More to the point, many of the most important events in our lives involve the sense of touch. Touch has a powerful affective component as well as a cognitive one. We feel pain and pleasure, and these seem essential to existence. One can't conceive of human life devoid of the sense of touch. Imagine one's entire skin surface always under anesthesia! Rollman provides a detailed discussion of pain in his chapter in the present volume.

Moreover, the cognitive/affective components of tactile experience seem different from visual experience. We can readily feel that something is hot or cold, soft or hard, rough or smooth, in addition to its spatial attributes. Further, we can feel the sensuality of a very smooth piece of walnut, and the cold, impersonal hardness of steel. A splinter prompts intense emotional reactions that we would do well to attend to, as does immersion of the fingers in sticky substances of unknown origins.

While we depend on our sense of touch, some persons rely much more heavily than most on tactile input. Blind people use tactile information for reading and writing braille, for inspecting maps, and for much of their spatial cognition. Deaf-blind people are even more dependent on tactile information, since they also lack acoustical contact with the world. Touch provides information for friction, motion, and speech patterns. The individual with multiple handicaps and spinal injury may be almost completely limited to tactile input. In his provocative fictional book, "Johnny Got His Gun," Dalton Trumbo (1970) described the plight of a veteran who lost almost all sensory input owing to physical trauma; Johnny could neither hear, nor see, nor speak, but learned to communicate with a nurse by tapping out Morse code with what little remained of his head. The nurse was able to talk to him by printing messages on the skin of his chest with her finger (pp. 197–199). The deaf-blind individual may make use of print-on-palm (POP) to communicate with people who are unfamiliar with manual signing, namely sighted and blind persons (Heller, 1986). Three chapters in this volume discuss perception and drawing in blind adults (Heller, Kennedy et al.) and children (Millar).

WHAT AND WHY VISION RESEARCHERS SHOULD KNOW ABOUT TOUCH

If all senses worked exactly like the visual system, it might not be as important to study the nonvisual senses. We could learn all about perception by just studying vision. The problem is not nearly so simple, however. Many aspects of objects and space can be known equally well through vision or touch, but some cannot (see Warren & Rossano, this volume). Very fine textures or surface variation, for example, are accurately perceived by touch, even when vision fails (Heller, 1989a). Moreover, we can often feel a splinter (to our discomfort!) when the same object is not visible without optical magnification. Touch may be especially suited for perception of such object characteristics as hardness, or softness (see Lederman & Klatzky, 1987) or substances within substances (e.g., grit in food or motor oil). Some aspects of thermal conductivity may be revealed only via touch. The chapter by Stevens provides a discussion of thermal sensation. Of course, we may also gain information regarding the hardness of surfaces by seeing or hearing events involving them.

In addition, touch and vision may not always operate in the same fashion (see Day, 1990; Over, 1968). Some researchers have emphasized limitations in touch, primarily because of the sequential nature of processing (Revesz, 1950; see Balakrishnan, Klatzky, Loomis, & Lederman, 1989). More recently, however, researchers have demonstrated word superiority effects in reading braille (Krueger, 1982b). The effect refers to the faster and/or more accurate detection of a particular letter in a word than in a nonword. As we shall see, this is a current theoretical issue, which is considered in the chapter on reading braille by Foulke.

While vision and touch may yield some equivalent percepts, it is in the realm of sensory experience where differences appear most obviously. There is no doubt that affective reactions are aroused by sight. Many of us have experienced the uplifting emotion elicited by a sunset, a waterfall, or other natural panorama of great beauty. We all have known the emotional impact of the sight of a very attractive person. The affective consequences of touch differ rather dramatically from sight, but are worthy of investigation in their own right. This has prompted the study of tactile sensations and sensitivity. Cholewiak and Collins discuss tactile sensitivity and physiology in their chapter. Rollman provides an interesting account of pain sensibility, in terms of both theory and application.

Finally, it should be pointed out that researchers interested in touch have studied many of the same theoretical issues that have directed research in vision and other areas. Research on touch may provide converging evidence on some very knotty theoretical problems. Tactile research has some unique advantages for the study of basic theoretical issues. Touch is well suited for the investigation of the role of revelatory movement in perception, that is, of what changes in stimulus information are revealed by active manipulation. It is easy to immobilize or control movement of the hand, but such control is at best arduous for sight, unless you limit the field of view as through a slit. However, we should note that the greater mechanical inertia of the hand (versus the eye) may make the hand easier to control and study, but it also makes the hand much more clumsy for the observer. In addition, tactile research permits us to study the relations between vision and another sense. Berkeley (1709/1974, p. 302) claimed that "the ideas of space, out-ness, and things placed at a distance are not, strictly speaking, the object of sight. . . . I neither see distance itself, nor anything I take to be at a dis-tance." He suggested that we learn to associate visual and auditory ex-periences with tangible ideas. This sort of discussion has led some individu-als to believe that touch educates vision and audition (e.g., Diderot). Work-ers in motor behavior have been interested in the influence of visual guidance on skilled performance for some time. Visual guidance can aid touch through the provision of redundant information, and by fine-tuning movement so as to optimize information pickup. Visual guidance of the hand can help one cope with pattern tilt while trying to identify braille (Heller, 1989c).

THEORETICAL ISSUES

Much of the research in touch has been directed toward solution of fundamen-tal theoretical issues. These are the same issues that have proven themselves so difficult for philosophers over many generations. The work encompasses research in perception and cognition, as well as fundamental sensory phenomena. If we examine the general experimental and vision literature (e.g., Kimble, 1990; Townsend, 1990), we find a concern with many of the same issues discussed by authors of chapters within this book. The issues will be described in this chapter, and a more thorough assessment of our current knowledge will be presented in the chapters in this volume.

Intersensory Equivalence

Can the senses of vision and touch give us the same information about ob-jects and events? Is this information obtained automatically, or are transla-tion mechanisms necessary? One version of the empiricist tradition holds that the senses are originally separate and must learn to treat information as equivalent. We may accomplish this when we learn to, say, attach the same response or label to something we touch and feel (see Revesz, 1950). Recent research on memory, especially that assuming an information-processing ap-proach, has tended to stress modality differences. The information-processing view explains cognition by assuming our mental apparatus generates "icons," or modality-specific, literal representations of stimulus configurations.

Gestalt psychologists tended to emphasize the notion that we obtain equiva-lent structures from the modalities of vision and touch (see Marks, 1978). Gib-son's ecological view (1966) has favored amodal percepts, that is, the notion that perception typically transcends modality-specific sensory experience. Attention to atypical sensations, and subjective phenomena such as pain or cold, lead us to notice the differences between modalities. Thus we see color, but feel pain. When we identify objects, however, it may matter little which sense obtains the relevant "information." Warren and Rossano's chapter is concerned with intermodal relations, especially the relationship between vision and touch.

Representation: Visual Imagery, Cognition in the Blind, and Tactile Imagery

Many researchers have been interested in the nature of representation. Revesz (1950) has suggested that sighted individuals tend to visualize when they feel objects in the dark. Introspection of the sighted might lead one to believe that visual experience is important for the development of spatial understanding. This problem has been approached through the study of the sense of touch in the blind (see chapters by Heller, Kennedy et al., and Millar, this volume). Late blind people remember how things look, and retain the ability to represent space in terms of visual images. Congenitally blind people must use the sense of touch for spatial representation. If congenitally blind people use imagery, one would expect that their images must be tactual. Some researchers have compared sighted and blind people's performance on tactile tasks, with the aim being an evaluation of the nature of tactile imagery. This will also provide us with information about vision and visual imagery, should differences appear (see Heller, 1989b, this volume). However, we can't rule out the possibility that congenitally blind people have visual imagery, but do not know what to call it. It is conceivable that we may eventually learn how to access visual imagery in these individuals.

It is theoretically possible, of course, that tactile imagery could provide much the same sort of information as visual images. However, should we discover differences in spatial cognition that could be specifically related to the nature of touch, we might begin to learn how best to structure instruction for the visually impaired. These questions about the nature of representation are clearly linked to issues of intersensory equivalence. Millar's chapter is concerned with the nature of representation in touch.

There can be little doubt that learning plays a major role in the development of tactual skills. One need only observe a person who is skilled in the use of this sense, using braille, or a long cane, to realize the tremendous role that learning must play. Of course, this complicates any examination of the role of representation. The late and early blind may possess sophisticated skills (e.g., reading braille) that go untapped in some experiments.

Development of Touch and the Nature/Nurture Issue

Do the senses alter in relative importance over the life span? Does development change the relative importance of different body sites for information pickup? One might think, for example, that children spend more time and rely more on oral tactile input during the first year of life (see Ruff, 1989). Moreover, some researchers have argued that the senses are originally organized separately, and we come to coordinate information from different modalities through active movement. The intersensory integration notion proposes that we come to treat material from the senses as equivalent as a result of associative learning.

How important is learning for the sense of touch? A related issue has questioned the role of nature versus nurture for touch. We may find it rather difficult to resolve the nature/nurture issue, and some researchers believe that the question may be misguided. Research on touch in infancy requires very inventive experimental procedures and expert observation. Bushnell and Boudreau have focused their chapter on intermodal relations and perceptual salience in infancy, with an emphasis on the infant's use of the hands.

Role of Receptor Movement: Active vs. Passive Touch

Tactile researchers have long been fascinated by the role of movement in perception (Katz, 1989; Revesz, 1950). Gibson (1962, 1966) has been most widely cited for his discussion of the distinction between active and passive touch. According to Gibson, touch is passive when the observer does not move and information is imposed on the skin. Gibson thought that passive touch tended to generate the subjective pole of experience. The "prototypical" example of a subjective sensation is pain (but see Rollman, this volume). Active touch consists of self-produced movement that allows the perceiver to obtain objective information about the world. Gibson argued that passive touch is atypical of "normal" experiences. We most often obtain information about the world via intentional movement. Perceptual error is thus partly a consequence of passivity, and is viewed as "abnormal." In addition, active movement permits the achievement of "amodal" percepts that are not linked to a specific modality, and permits the interpretation that much of what is learned in tactual perceiving is exploratory or manipulatory strategies that reveal more useful stimulus information.

The active/passive issue is discussed at length in the chapters by Appelle and by Foulke in this volume. There is little doubt that the problem has been controversial. The issue is not trivial, and will not readily disappear. Intentionality and the role of movement in perception are central issues in perceptual theory. We should bear in mind that some visually and hearing impaired persons learn to rely on passive touch for communication. Deaf-blind persons, for example, communicate with the sighted with print-on-palm, where words are simply printed on the skin of the palm. In addition, a number of blind persons are able to learn to use an Optacon, a device that translates visual input (letters and numbers) into a vibratory display. These people actively move the Optacon camera with the right hand, but the left index finger is passive on the vibrotactile display. Kennedy believes that information, whether obtained passively or not, is the critical factor here (J. M. Kennedy, personal communication, 1990). It is possible that self-produced movement is especially helpful during initial stages of learning a tactile skill (Heller, Rogers, & Perry, 1990).

Many researchers have emphasized the active nature of touch. From this point of view, perception is an achievement that may depend on skilled performance. This tradition is consistent with a recent trend toward emphasis of the active nature of cognition; although the site of the activity is primarily in the head, rather than in the hand, where it tends to be metaphorically placed by researchers in the Gibsonian tradition.

Whole vs. Part Perception and Serial vs. Parallel Processing

There are several interrelated issues here. First, how large is the field of view of touch? One might consider the fingertip the source of tactile pattern information, and then consider the "field of view" rather small. In part, the issue is complicated by the important consideration of what it is that we are touching. If one feels a large, two-dimensional tactile array, such as a map, then the field of view could be 1, 2, or perhaps 10 fingers. Can we attend to two hands at once? (see Craig, 1985). If the two-dimensional configuration is very large, then spatial information must be acquired sequentially, and over time. If we can wrap our hands or arms around a small, three-dimensional stimulus, we can acquire information much more rapidly, with far less of a burden on memory. This notion of a field of view assumes a "glimpse" theory of pattern perception, instead of information pickup over time.

Do we process tactile input in serial form or in parallel? This issue can take the form of questions about attention to more than one haptic attribute. Alternatively, the issue is very much like the visual concern over word superiority effects in reading. For example, one might wonder if the braille reader takes in one character at a time, or perceives the word as a basic perceptual unit. Of course, the experienced reader of braille or print functions very differently from the novice (see Foulke, this volume).

Sensory Dominance

Which sense do we rely on for information about the world? Warren and Rossano describe the evidence on this issue in their chapter. The senses can sometimes provide us with conflicting information about objects in the world. However,

No one would regard it as contradictory if I were to look at the top of a table and find that it looks smooth, and if at the same time I were to touch its underside and find that this surface feels rough. (Mandelbaum, 1964, p. 126)

We have an intersensory conflict only if we believe we feel a unitary object, but the senses do not tell us the same story about this single object. This can happen if we observe an oar in water, to take John Locke's classic example. The appearance of the oar is distorted by the juncture of the air and water. The oar looks crooked, but feels straight. Which sense do we believe (see Welch & Warren, 1980)?

The question of which sense is dominant in conflict paradigms is different in some ways from other questions about the relative salience and normal functioning of the senses. A sense with greater alerting powers, namely audition, may be dominated by vision during the ventriloquism effect; audition may be ignored when "good" visual information is available (Schiff & Oldak, 1990). Pain sensibility may dominate our awareness and take precedence over visual input. Furthermore, one may interpret the dominance experiments to indicate that it is not a sense that is dominated, rather an attribute, for example, direction. Thus, when we fall victim to the "ventriloquism effect," we err in our belief that the mannequin has said something. This is an error in the source of a statement, not in what was said. Intersensory dominance and salience relationships may change over the course of development. Bushnell and Boudreau discuss some of the evidence derived from research with infants.

Tactile researchers have also concerned themselves with questions about which sense is most appropriate for veridical perception. Klatzky, Lederman, and Metzger (1985) argued that touch is especially suited for the pickup of information about objects that vary along a number of substance-related dimensions, namely hardness, texture, and so on. Klatzky, Lederman, and Reed (1987) have claimed that touch may not be well suited for the pickup of two-dimensional pattern information (see Lederman & Klatzky, 1987). They proposed that substance characteristics may be more salient for the sense of touch. Furthermore, Loomis (1990) has stressed that cutaneous spatial resolution is an important factor limiting tactile pattern perception. It is difficult to know how much one's experience and education influence tactile pattern perception and intermodal relations (Villey, 1930). However, it should be pointed out that touch can be very accurate in pattern identification when letters or numbers are printed on the skin (Heller, 1986, 1987). The role of education is also suggested by the superior speed and high levels of accuracy with which some blind persons read braille (Foulke, this volume), and with which blind observers judge when a noise-emitting object—an automobile—may reach them (Schiff & Oldak, 1990).

Ecological Issues

Neisser (1976) is prominent among those claiming that psychological research often lacks *ecological validity*. However the same critique could apply to mathematics, physiology, chemistry, and so on. Studies may be carefully controlled, but tell us little about normal situations in our environment. The laboratory environment may tell us little of practical value because so many studies limit sensory input to static, brief displays of letters, numbers, and geometrical forms. There is also a tendency to restrict the study of perception solely or primarily to the study of vision. According to Neisser, touch is normally active. Furthermore, researchers have only recently, seriously studied the perception of dynamic, changing events (e.g., Epstein, Hughes, Schneider, & Bach-y-Rita, 1989; Johansson, von Hofsten, & Jansson, 1980; Runeson & Frykholm, 1981).

These issues have led to heated debates. Many tactile researchers have pointed out that there are natural situations in which one feels static objects or patterns. In addition, one may evaluate the effect of stimulus change by comparing perception of static patterns with those that vary over time. Similarly, while passive touch may be unlike some more common forms of experience, if studied with dynamic patterns, it allows us to isolate the role of movement in perception. Also, there are "natural" situations in which people depend on passive touch, for example, the Optacon and printing on the skin of the palm.

Laterality Effects and Hemispheric Specialization

Researchers in touch, as in vision, have been concerned with hemispheric specialization. One might think that the left hand would be better for spatial perception, if the right brain were specialized for that skill. There have been demonstrations of left hand advantages for reading print-on-palm (Heller, 1986). However, the research findings on braille are not clear cut, as the issue is very complex (Millar, 1984). Furthermore, it is important to separate effects of hemispace from laterality (Bradshaw, Nettleton, & Spehr, 1982). Thus, it is possible that performance may vary when stimuli are in the left or right hemispace, that is, to the left or right of the body midline. Bradshaw et al. have argued that laterality effects are most likely with perceptually degraded or unfamiliar material. Many researchers, however, believe that the right hemisphere is specialized for braille and tactile information processing (Harris, 1980; see Heller, et al., 1990; Perrier, Belin, & Larmande, 1988). Of course, there are large individual differences in laterality. Moreover, the literature on reading braille suggests that lateralization may change with intellectual and cognitive experience (Harris, 1980; Karavatos, Kaprinis, & Tzavaras, 1984).

Illusions

Many of us, in our normal lives, tend to think of touch as a "reality sense." We can test the reality of an image by trying to touch the object. One can always tell if he/she is awake or dreaming by using the "pinch test." Furthermore, we may distinguish an artificial flower from a "real" one by making use of tactile information. We know, for example, that it is relatively easy to fool vision. Visual input can be distorted by lenses, and appearances often change with variations in lighting or viewing conditions. We also know that some visual textures are not tangible, as in color or brightness variations in paintings or photographs.

These everyday observations do not mean that touch cannot be fooled. For example, there are haptic figural aftereffects. There are a number of tactual illusions, and many of them occur in vision as well (see Coren & Girgus, 1978). Some illusions can be produced by pressing cardboard cutouts against the passive skin surface (Coren & Girgus, p. 98). However, illusions and error are also evident when touch is active (Day, 1990; Lucca, Dellantonio, & Riggio, 1986). Hatwell (1960, 1985) reported that a number of tactile illusions, such as the horizontal/vertical illusion, were smaller in magnitude than corresponding visual illusions. The study of tactual illusions has certainly received far less attention than that of visual illusions.

BRIEF HISTORY

The sense of touch has historical roots in a number of academic disciplines. Philosophers have long entertained discussions about the reliability of the senses, the relationship among vision, touch, and audition, and the relative contributions of learning and innate factors to perception. Physicians have been interested in pain perception, and disorders of tactile functioning. Biologists have studied the physiology of sensation. More recently, psychologists have devoted considerable effort to an understanding of tactile perception. The present discussion will not be comprehensive, but will focus on the contributions of some selected, major influences and theorists.

Diderot

Diderot's "Letter on the Blind," which originally appeared in 1749, is a fascinating account of perception and cognition in the congenitally blind (much of the letter is reproduced in Morgan, 1977). Diderot belonged to the Age of Enlightenment and was one of the authors of a famous encyclopedia. It is noteworthy that Diderot was imprisoned because of the philosophical con-

tent within this tract (Morgan, 1977). Much of the monograph is devoted to
a discussion of the role of learning in the development of normal perception.
The letter is important for a number of reasons. It provides a detailed account of the influence of experience on perception, and it attempts to detail
the relationship between touch and vision.

Diderot described the high level of tactile skill obtainable by some congenitally blind persons. This became the philosophical basis for the notion
of *sensory compensation,* the idea that touch gains in power owing to its use
by the blind. Diderot ascribed rather remarkable abilities to the sense of touch,

> The example of this illustrious blind man proves that touch can become even
> more discriminating than sight, when it is sharpened by exercise, for in run-
> ning his hands over a series of medals, he could distinguish the true from the
> counterfeit, even though the latter were skillfully enough made to deceive a
> sharp-eyed collector. . . (Morgan, 1977, p. 47)

It is possible that these judgments depended on tactual perception of surface
texture, since this is where touch excels (Heller, 1989a).

Diderot described the importance of memory demands on the sense of
touch, and believed that an impression of form relies on retention of component sensations. He suggested that the sighted are likely to use visual imagery when touching forms. The congenitally blind do not have these sorts
of visual images available, but use tactile images instead. Diderot thought
that touch educates sight, especially in the notion of object permanence. An
interesting discussion entailed an examination of the relative reliability of
the senses. Diderot also provided an early illustration of intersensory conflict. He noted that a mirror or magnifying lens can bring the senses of touch
and vision into conflict, so that tactual and visual impressions of an object
are different.

Sensory Phenomena and Psychophysics

Weber (1834/1978) should be regarded as the father of the systematic study
of the sensitivity of the skin. He devoted considerable time to the investigation of the spatial resolution of the skin surface. In addition, Weber provided
a comprehensive account of variation in sensibility to thermal properties,
weight, and other tactile properties.

In the course of his empirical investigations of cutaneous sensation, Weber formulated what later became his famous "law." Weber's Law states that
one's ability to discriminate differences between a standard and comparison
stimulus is a constant function of the magnitude of the standard. Thus, one
requires a much larger difference between weights to discriminate them successfully when the standard weighs 100 grams than when the standard weighs

20 grams. The proportion, of course, remains constant through a moderate range of stimuli. Fechner later translated these principles into a mathematical formula. We should remember that this important advance in psychology depended in large part on the investigation of the senses of touch and kinesthesis.

Weber's work is significant for a number of reasons. He introduced a systematic set of procedures for the study of sensory phenomena. In addition, Weber's work is interesting, inasmuch as he anticipated a number of more contemporary viewpoints. Based on empirical evidence, Weber suggested that the left hand is more sensitive to the weight and thermal properties of objects (see Harris, 1980; Heller et al., 1990). Furthermore, Weber provided a fascinating discussion of Aristotle's illusion. If one feels a round object, such as a pencil with crossed fingers, one experiences two contacts. Weber pointed out that one feels "two noses" if the crossed fingers touch the ball of the nose, but this may be subject to individual differences. Not all of us may experience a doubling of the nose! Recently, Benedetti (1988) has devoted considerable time to the study of Aristotle's illusion. This distortion presumably results from feeling the objects with the outside of each finger.

Weber revealed a very modern approach to the study of touch in his assertion that touch is better when active:

> Indeed the shape and texture of the objects is not discovered by touch, unless the finger is deliberately moved over the surface of the test object. It is fairly obvious that the tactile perception of objects is greatly enhanced if the touch-organ is moved in a deliberate and appropriate manner. It is not surprising, then, that the tactile recognition of objects is very poor if the test objects are moved over stationary touch organs. Shut your eyes, hold your hand still, and ask someone to bring various objects to your finger-tips—objects such as a piece of paper, glass, sheets of metal, smooth wood, leather, smooth silky fabric and rough fabric, and other unknown objects. You will certainly be surprised at the imprecise quality of the sensation, which does not enable you to recognize the nature of the objects. (pp. 52, 53)

Only recently has there been detailed experimental examination of these assertions. Weber also thought that the perception of hardness, softness, and distances between objects depended on intentional movement (p. 202). The issue of activity in perception is discussed at a later point in this chapter, and in various chapters within the book (see Heller, 1986, 1989a).

Theories of Sensation

Researchers have often tried to link receptors in the skin with specific sensory qualities. An alternative strategy has been to relate nerve fibers to classes of sensation, such as pain. Von Frey took the former tack, and claimed that contact, warmth, cold, and pain are associated with specific receptors (Sinclair, 1967). An alternative was a "pattern theory," which assumed that a particular nerve fiber could signal different sensory qualities through variations in the number of nervous impulses and their spatial and temporal relations (Sinclair, 1967). The problem is that many receptors in the skin can be excited by several kinds of stimuli (Iggo, 1982). However, there is little doubt that future research will lead to clarification of the relationship between specific receptors and sensory experience. For example, we know that the Pacinian corpuscle responds to vibration (see the chapter by Cholewiak & Collins, this volume). Other structures are related to thermal sensation (see Stevens, this volume). Rollman discusses the neural substrate for pain in his chapter.

Henry Head distinguished between epicritic and protopathic sensibility. He thought the two types of sensibility were served by different neural transmission mechanisms. Epicritic sensibility involves light touch, fine discrimination of temperature, and spatial localization (Sinclair, 1967). Protopathic sensation involves different nerve fibers and serves pain and extremes of temperature. The theory may represent an oversimplification, and the physiological evidence did not clearly support all aspects of the theory (Sinclair, 1967).

Clinical Roots

A number of authors have studied touch in a clinical setting. Touch can be susceptible to dramatic perceptual distortion given head trauma or neurological damage. The phantom limb phenomenon, in which a person feels pain in a nonexistent body part, is one of the most striking examples of illusory tactile experience. We are often mistaken about the source of pain, and may refer pain to various body sites. Distortions in the body scheme, or body image, are common symptoms of parietal damage (Critchley, 1971). According to Head, we build up a conception or image of our body as a result of active movement (Sinclair, 1967). This body scheme is part of any subsequent tactile experience (Merleau-Ponty, 1962/1981). An alternative view relates our conception of body-self to innate neural structures that can be modified by experience (Melzack, 1989). Melzack adopted this model since there is evidence that phantom limbs can be present in very early childhood in children born without a limb. People may fail to understand adequately many aspects of their anatomy even when the brain is apparently normal. Thus, the anorexic perceives oneself as obese even when very thin. Just note how slow we are to alter our conception of our body size after weight changes!

Modern History: Katz, Revesz, and Gibson

Katz, Revesz, and Gibson have had a major impact on research on touch. Many modern tactile researchers have been influenced by their writing. A common thread running through their work is the emphasis on the importance of hand movement for perception.

Katz's work is interesting for its detailed experimental and phenomenological analyses of tactile perception. Katz (1989) stressed the essential role of movement for tactile perception. Either movement of the hand or of the stimulus seemed essential for texture perception. Katz noted that the sense of touch was superior to vision for judgments of such attributes as the thickness of paper or the presence of vibration. Touch can certainly surpass vision in judgments of texture (Heller, 1989a). The interested reader is referred to an excellent summary of Katz's work (Krueger, 1982a), and to the recent translation of the *World of Touch* (Katz, 1989).

Revesz (1950) stressed the autonomous nature of haptic space. He believed that both vision and touch (but not audition) develop notions of space. Illusions presumably occur in both vision and haptics, and the congenitally blind certainly have some form of spatial understanding. Haptics in the sighted is quite different, however, from haptics in the congenitally blind person. The sense of touch has been modified by visual experience in the sighted and late blind, according to Revesz. The haptic sense may not develop fully in the sighted, due to the influence of vision, a superior sense for perception of form and space.

Revesz asserted that we can learn to coordinate visual and haptic spatial information through an associative process. This is possible because both vision and touch are spatial senses. He was opposed to a simple notion of the unity of the senses, and asserted that we don't really "see" softness or hardness. This was ascribed to an intellectual process.

According to Revesz, haptics tends toward a general understanding of form, rather than exact configurations (see pp. 66–69 in Revesz, 1950, for a discussion of object recognition and haptic exploratory styles). Static touch promotes rather limited comprehension of form, and is good only for detection of thermal properties. Dynamic touch (touching with a moving hand) was deemed necessary for object recognition, for recognition of form, or material (p. 62). Revesz thought that haptic recognition of objects is not immediate, as it is in vision. We see the whole, and only then notice the parts. However, in haptics, the construction of the whole is a cognitive or intellectual process that follows perception of parts (p. 84). Thus, "blind people aren't interested in form" (p. 75). Moreover, Revesz asserted that the blind are only able to understand relatively simple forms. This was a strange assertion, in the light of all of the illustrations in his book of excellent work by blind sculptors.

While Revesz (1950) emphasized the spatial nature of haptics, he also tended to focus on its limitations. He asserted that haptic space ignores the notions of the vertical and the horizontal. According to Revesz, congenitally blind people have no understanding of the horizontal and vertical (p. 41). Haptics cannot know perspective or interposition (covering). Furthermore, haptics operates through the stereoplastic principle, a tendency to apprehend an object from all sides. This can present a problem when we confront 2-D displays. In addition, haptics depends too heavily on successive processes. We tend to examine forms by means of successive movements, and also imagine objects in terms of images of their component parts. Haptics leads to poor apprehension of proportion, symmetry, or aesthetics, according to Revesz (see Appelle, Gravetter, & Davidson, 1980). It is very possible, of course, that the size of the stimulus array is critical. Nearly simultaneous scanning may be more likely with smaller objects that fit within the hand, or both hands together, or perhaps the arms.

The evidence does not clearly support all of the assertions made by Revesz (see part 5, this volume, on perception in blind people). For example, blind persons may have a good understanding of the vertical. In addition, the idea that touch is limited when confronted by 2-D arrays antedates the theoretical position advocated by Lederman and Klatzky (1987). This somewhat controversial viewpoint is discussed at length in the chapters in this volume on perception and drawing by blind people, where the evidence is presented.

Gibson has been a major influence on research in touch and perception in general. He emphasized the role of movement in perception, and stressed the intentionality of haptics (1962, 1966). For Gibson, after Katz (1989), passivity tended to lead one to experience subjective sensations as opposed to objective percepts (see chapters 7 and 9 in this volume on the active/passive issue). Moreover, the tendency of researchers to study only passive touch leads them to conceive of touch as a consequence of "sensations." Gibson argued that we should focus on the functional role of the senses, and study touch in more naturalistic circumstances, that is, when the hand is moving. Intentional movement generates a more objective relationship to the environment, according to Gibson. Thus, active movement leads the individual to pick up information specifying objects and surfaces in the world, instead of attention to the body surface. If one rests his or her hand on a table surface, palm up, and a screwdriver is placed within it, the individual may notice many sensations of contact on the smooth skin of the fingers and palm. As the individual squeezes the tool's handle, he or she notices one object, rather than many sensations of contact. Furthermore, while one drives a screw, the contact is experienced at the end of the screwdriver and not in the hand.

Passivity promotes sensory experience, while activity, and movement, yield perception of the external object. Passivity can promote the formation of aftersensations, which can interfere with the retention of sequences of numbers or letters drawn on the skin (Heller, 1980). Perceptual experiences, according to Gibson (1966), can be amodal. That is, different senses may yield very different sensations, but the same information about the world. Active movement promotes this "intersensory equivalence." Gibson generally stressed the veridicality of perception, namely the idea that we generally know the world accurately. He also thought that the active haptic system functioned to reveal the nature and layout of the world explored over time, as do the other perceptual systems.

The Gibsonian position has been controversial, partly because of its insistence on ecological validity (see earlier section, this chapter). Further, Gibson (1979) argued that perceptual psychologists should spend more time studying perception, and less time investigating such nonperceptual, "intellectual" processes as memory, imagination, conceiving, and so on. This amounts to a programmatic prescription for the proper subject matter and procedures for perceptual research in haptics. A number of researchers, especially those interested in blindness, have wondered about the relationship between haptics and visual imagery. Needless to say, a great deal of controversy exists within this research area, since the Gibsonian point of view ostensibly proscribes perceptual research on imagery and representation. There is certainly room in the field for a variety of approaches to the understanding of haptics and the sense of touch.

REFERENCES

Appelle, S., Gravetter, F. J., & Davidson, P. W. (1980). Proportion judgments in haptic and visual form perception. *Canadian Journal of Psychology, 34,* 161–174.

Balakrishnan, J. D., Klatzky, R. L., Loomis, J. M., & Lederman, S. J. (1989). Length distortion of temporally extended visual displays: Similarity to haptic spatial perception. *Perception & Psychophysics, 46,* 387–394.

Benedetti, F. (1988). Exploration of a rod with crossed fingers. *Perception & Psychophysics, 44,* 281–284.

Berkeley, G. (1709/1974). *An essay towards a new theory of vision.* In D. M. Armstrong (Ed.), *Berkeley's philosophical writings.* New York: Collier.

Bradshaw, J. L., Nettleton, N. C., & Spehr, K. (1982). Braille reading in the left and right hemispace. *Neuropsychologia, 20,* 493–500.

Coren, S., & Girgus, J. S. (1978). *Seeing is deceiving: The psychology of visual illusions.* Hillsdale, NJ: Lawrence Erlbaum Associates.

Craig, J. C. (1985). Attending to two fingers: Two hands are better than one. *Perception & Psychophysics, 38,* 496–511.

Critchley, M. (1971). *The parietal lobes.* New York: Hafner.

Day, R. H. (1990). The Bourdon illusion in haptic space. *Perception & Psychophysics, 47,* 400–404.

Epstein, W., Hughes, B., Schneider, S. L., & Bach-y-Rita, P. (1989). Perceptual learning of spatiotemporal events: Evidence from an unfamiliar modality. *Journal of Experimental Psychology: Human Perception and Performance, 15,* 28–44.

Gibson, J. J. (1962). Observations on active touch. *Psychological Review, 69,* 477–490.

Gibson, J. J. (1966). *The senses considered as perceptual systems.* Boston: Houghton Mifflin.

Gibson, J. J. (1979). *The ecological approach to visual perception.* Boston: Houghton Mifflin.

Harris, L. J. (1980). Which hand is the "eye" of the blind?—A new look at an old question. In J. Herron (Ed.), *Neuropsychology of left handedness.* New York: Academic Press.

Hatwell, Y. (1960). Étude de quelques illusions geometriques tactiles chez lez aveugles. *L'Année Psychologique, 60,* 11–27.

Hatwell, Y. (1985). *Piagetian reasoning and the blind.* New York: American Foundation for the Blind.

Heller, M. A. (1980). Tactile retention: Reading with the skin. *Perception & Psychophysics, 27,* 125–130.

Heller, M. A. (1986). Central and peripheral influences on tactual reading. *Perception & Psychophysics, 39,* 197–204.

Heller, M. A. (1987). Improving the passive tactile digit span. *Bulletin of the Psychonomic Society, 25,* 257–258.

Heller, M. A. (1989a). Texture perception in sighted and blind observers. *Perception & Psychophysics, 45,* 49–54.

Heller, M. A. (1989b). Picture and pattern perception in the sighted and blind: The advantage of the late blind. *Perception, 18,* 379–389.

Heller, M. A. (1989c). Tactile memory in sighted and blind observers: The influence of orientation and rate of presentation. *Perception, 18,* 121–133.

Heller, M. A., Rogers, G. J., & Perry, C. L. (1990). Tactile pattern recognition with the Optacon: Superior performance with active touch and the left hand. *Neuropsychologia, 28,* 1003–1006.

Iggo, A. (1982). Cutaneous sensory mechanisms. In H. B. Barlow & J. D. Mollon (Eds.), *The senses.* New York: Cambridge University Press.

Johansson, G., von Hofsten, C. & Jansson, G. (1980). Event perception. *Annual Review of Psychology, 31,* 27–63.

Karavatos, A., Kaprinis, G., & Tzavaras, A. (1984). Hemispheric specialization for language in the congenitally blind: The influence of the braille system. *Neuropsychologia, 22,* 521–525.

Katz, D. (1989). *The world of touch.* (L. E. Krueger, Trans.). Hillsdale, NJ: Lawrence Erlbaum Associates.

Kimble, G. A. (1990). Mother nature's bag of tricks is small. *Psychological Science, 1,* 36–41.

Klatzky, R. L., Lederman, S. J., & Metzger, V. A. (1985). Identifying objects by touch; An expert system. *Perception & Psychophysics, 37,* 299–302.

Klatzky, R. L., Lederman, S. J., & Reed, C. (1987). There's more to touch than meets the eye: The salience of object characteristics with and without vision. *Journal of Experimental Psychology: General, 116,* 356–369.

Krueger, L. E. (1982a). Tactual perception in historical perspective: David Katz's world of touch. In W. Schiff & E. Foulke (Eds.), *Tactual perception.* New York: Cambridge University Press.

Krueger, L. E. (1982b). A word-superiority effect with print and braille characters. *Perception & Psychophysics, 31,* 345–352.

Lederman, S. J., & Klatzky, R. L. (1987). Hand movements: A window into haptic object recognition. *Cognitive Psychology, 19,* 342–368.

Loomis, J. M. (1990). A model of character recognition and legibility. *Journal of Experimental Psychology: Human Perception and Performance, 16,* 106–120.

Lucca, A., Dellantonio, A., & Riggio, L. (1986). Some observations on the Poggendorff and Muller-Lyer tactual illusions. *Perception & Psychophysics, 39,* 374–380.

Mandelbaum, M. (1964). *Philosophy, science, and sense perception.* Baltimore: Johns Hopkins Press.

Marks, L. E. (1978). *The unity of the senses: Interrelations among the modalities.* New York: Academic Press.

Melzack, R. (1989). Phantom limbs, the self and the brain. *Canadian Psychology, 30,* 1–16.

Merleau-Ponty, M. (1962/1981). *Phenomenology of perception.* (C. Smith, Trans.). London: Routledge & Kegan Paul.

Millar, S. (1984). Is there a "best hand" for braille? *Cortex, 20,* 75–87.

Morgan, M. J. (1977). *Molyneux's question.* New York: Cambridge University Press.

Neisser, U. (1976). *Cognition and reality.* San Francisco: W. H. Freeman.

Over, R. (1968). Explanations of geometrical illusions. *Psychological Bulletin, 70,* 545–562.

Perrier, D., Belin, C., & Larmande, P. (1988). Trouble de la lecture du braille par lesion droite chez un patient deveue aveugle. *Neuropsychologia, 26,* 179–185.

Revesz, G. (1950). *The psychology and art of the blind.* London: Longmans Green.

Ruff, H. A. (1989). The infant's use of visual and haptic information in the perception and recognition of objects. *Canadian Journal of Psychology, 43,* 302–319.

Runeson, S., & Frykholm, G. (1981). Visual perception of lifted weight. *Journal of Experimental Psychology: Human Perception and Performance, 7,* 733–740.

Schiff, W., & Oldak, R. (1990) Accuracy of judging time to arrival: Effects of modality, trajectory, and gender. *Journal of Experimental Psychology: Human Perception and Performance, 16,* 303–316.

Sinclair, D. (1967). *Cutaneous sensation.* London: Oxford University Press.

Stevens, J. C. (1990). Perceived roughness as a function of body locus. *Perception & Psychophysics, 47,* 298–304.

Townsend, J. T. (1990). Serial vs. parallel processing: Sometimes they look like Tweedledum and Tweedledee but they can (and should) be distinguished. *Psychological Science, 1,* 46–54.

Trumbo, D. (1970). *Johnny got his gun.* New York: Bantam.

Villey, P. (1930). *The world of the blind.* New York: Macmillan.

Weber, E. H. (1834/1978). *The sense of touch* (H. E. Ross & D. J. Murray, Trans.). London: Academic Press. (Originally published 1834 & 1846)

Welch, R. B., & Warren, D. H. (1980). Immediate perceptual response to intersensory discrepancy. *Psychological Bulletin, 88,* 638–667.

I

SENSORY PHENOMENA

In this section the authors begin the analysis of the psychology of touch by considering it in the classical manner, that is, as a *proximal* sense delivering a variety of *sensations* (e.g., pressure, pain, warmth) to the CNS as receptors or sets of receptors are activated by stimulus energies. Such a view of touch conceptualizes the questions surrounding our knowledge of the world via touch primarily as a set of problems concerned with how a neural transduction system constrains and converts energies and events occurring at environment–organism interfaces into neural codes to be analyzed by the brain. While this is not the only possible way to conceptualize the fundamental basis for tactual/haptic perception (e.g., see Gibson, 1966) it is the one adopted by the majority of psychologists, and virtually all sensory physiologists.

Cholewiak and Collins begin this first stage of classical psychophysical analysis in an examination of the anatomy and physiology of the skin, broached by the authors in a fine-grained examination of the skin-structures mediating touch. In so doing, they sometimes depart from a purely "punctate" psychophysical approach to analyze physical forces acting on the skin in a more global form, for example, via a wave model. The somatosensory cortex and its "homunculus" are explored in detail, and we emerge with a fascinating account of an extraordinarily complex set of structures and functions. We realize how complex and resistant to simple formulation and explication the "simple" skin senses really are.

Stevens approaches the topic of thermal sensibility from a functional point of view, that is, the regulation of body temperature so as to avoid harm to the organism, and also in terms of the role of the thermal system in informing us concerning the thermally conductive nature of surfaces and substances. He also examines issues in thermal hedonics. He treats the psychophysics of thermal sensitivity in detail, touching on thermal adaptation phenomena. We thus obtain a detailed picture of how the skin and its various receptor systems may function to signal the CNS concerning thermal changes and differences. This can be extremely important not only in avoiding or minimizing tissue damage, but in discovering other objective or hedonic properties of objects, surfaces, and substances.

Although issues of pain perception are mentioned by authors of other chapters, Rollman takes us deeper into a topic that can be as fascinating as the painful experience can be unpleasant, that is, our sensitivities to pain and painful aspects of certain forms of stimulation. Rollman stresses the impact of cognition and emotional factors in the description and evaluation of stimulation as painful, and their roles in pain alleviation. He also examines receptors and their physiology, as well as the relevant spinal tracts, subcortical and cortical areas of the brain in pain. His discussion amplifies the questionable aspects of simple one-to-one models of punctate skin sensitivity, or even sensation-receptor specificity, in the context of a voluminous catalog of receptor types and their relationship to pain. Any strong tactile sensation can be experienced as pain, including those derived from thermal stimulation, pressure, and chemicals. A further difficulty in pain research has been to clarify the relationships between stimulation and CNS transmission lines (e.g., spinal mechanisms), and it is here that specificity has failed to provide all of the answers. Clinical topics relating to pain alleviation are discussed in detail from both methodological and practical standpoints, with specific attention to various sources of pain.

Researchers on pain are confronted with difficult, but important paradoxes. Pain is a "subjective" phenomenon, but we often try to measure it "objectively." Rollman has tried to come to grips with a number of important theoretical and applied issues in pain perception.

We should point out that there are alternative ways to conceptualize touch, and active movement can modify sensory experiences (Coquery, 1978). It is rather difficult to tickle oneself! In addition, movement may help to organize sensory experience.

REFERENCES

Coquery, J. (1978). Role of active movement in control of afferent input from skin in cat and man. In G. Gordon (Ed.), *Active touch*. Oxford, England: Pergamon Press.

Gibson, J. J. (1966). *The senses considered as perceptual systems*. Boston: Houghton Mifflin.

2

SENSORY AND PHYSIOLOGICAL BASES OF TOUCH

Roger W. Cholewiak
Amy A. Collins
Princeton University

INTRODUCTION

Touch has been defined as the variety of sensations evoked by stimulation of the skin by mechanical, thermal, chemical, or electrical events. Even Aristotle, in dividing our contact with the world into the five senses, was doubtful that "touch" described but a single sense. Because there is such a variety of sensations aroused by stimuli interacting with the skin, it might be more appropriate to describe this modality as the "senses of touch." And, as befits such a symphony of sensations, there are a multitude of instruments contributing their voices, each in its own fashion. The mechanical and physiological characteristics of the skin and these receptor structures, as with those in other senses, define and limit the sensitivity of the skin to stimuli. In most of this chapter we will be describing the anatomy and morphology of those structures, both visible and below the surface, that constrain and define the events that eventually will evoke a tactile sensation. In the remainder of the chapter, there will be a discussion of the most basic measures of the skin's sensitivity. The issues involved with the processing of more complex tactile stimuli will be presented in other chapters in this volume.

Touch, for the most part, is a proximal sense. That is, we feel those things that either are close to us or actually contact us. There are exceptions to the strict interpretations of this notion: We feel radiant heat, for example, as well as the deep bass of the opening chords of *Also Sprach Zarathustra* (the *2001* movie theme) or heavy metal rock music! These events produce changes in the skin that are transduced to evoke sensations of warmth or movement, respectively. We can also extend touch beyond its normal bodily limits with special tools just as vision can be extended through the use of tools, such as the telescope. The long cane, for example, provides vibratory and pressure information that can tell a blind person about the roughness of a sidewalk, or the presence of a wall. More commonly, though, for a stimulus to be perceived it must actually come in contact with the skin. You run your fingers over the pages of a book such as this one, feeling the smoothness of the paper, perhaps roughened a bit by the ever so slightly raised imprint of the text. If the paper is glossy ("enameled"), it may feel cool to the touch. The pencil you hold vibrates the fingers slightly as it scratches the rough surface of your notepad. Soon, however, you may even stop being aware that you are holding the pencil. Similarly, the constant pressure of clothing fades from constant perception, unless there is movement or change. The sensations produced by these events are a function of the underlying morphology (form and structure) and physiology (biological functioning) of the neural end organs that lie within and under the skin.

THE ANATOMY AND PHYSIOLOGY OF THE SKIN

Characteristics of the Skin

The skin itself is a multilayered sheet some 1.8 m² in area and 4 kg in weight on the average adult (Montagna, 1956; Quilliam, 1978). It is the body's largest organ, protecting the rest of the body from dehydration (because it is waterproof), physical injury, and ultraviolet radiation. In addition, it is intimately involved in the homeostatic mechanisms that regulate body temperature and blood pressure. Furthermore, contained within its layers are the structures responsible for our ability to "feel." Depending on the body site under examination, skin might be flat or furrowed, loose or tight, hairy or smooth (glabrous), thick or thin. On the fingertip, ridges and valleys of skin form intricate patterns of whorls and loops. These distinctive patterns, fingerprints, develop in the third or fourth month of fetal life and reflect the infinite variety of random undulations in the papillary layer of the dermis, deep below the skin's surface (Quilliam, 1978). Parenthetically, these ridges have been implicated in texture perception (LaMotte & Whitehouse, 1986; Lederman, 1978) and stereognosis (tactile identification of objects: Quilliam, 1978; Loomis & Lederman, 1986).

The outermost layer of skin is called the epidermis, which can be subdivided into several other layers (see Fig. 2.1). The surface of the skin, the corneum, is made up of dead or keratinized cell bodies from the deeper

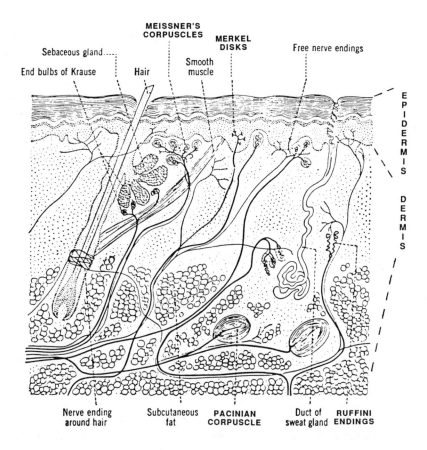

FIG. 2.1. A schematic section of human skin, showing the locations of cutaneous end organs. This section, through a typical portion of hairy skin, is also representative of glabrous skin with only a few exceptions: There are no hairs in glabrous skin, the overall density of end organs is greater, and the surface of glabrous skin is ridged as a result of dermal intrusions, called "plugs," into the epidermis. The presence of these ridges and the Merkel's disks found at their base, might provide a heightened sensitivity to surface textures. From *Fundamentals of Neurology*, 5th ed., p. 137; E. P. Gardner (Ed.), 1968; Philadelphia: Saunders. Copyright 1968 by W. B. Saunders Company; reprinted by permission.

subdivisions of the epidermis that have migrated outward as the skin renews itself from the inside out. A piece of clear cellophane tape stuck to the skin will be found, when removed, to have become cloudy. Embedded in its adhesive are the loosest of these superficial cell bodies. Immediately below this protective layer of cellular ghosts is the epidermis proper, and below that is the dermis, a layer of nutritive and connective tissues. Cutaneous end organs, the structures that are suspected of being responsible for transducing mechanical, thermal, chemical, or electrical energy into neural signals lie within the dermal layer or at the epidermal-dermal interface. In addition, the sweat glands (numbering more than 2 million) are found here, as are fine nerve findings that also seem to be involved in cutaneous sensation. In hairy skin, hair follicles and the structures associated with them are embedded in the dermis. These include the fine muscle filaments (erector pilorus) that reveal their presence in "hair-raising" experiences by the presence of "goose bumps." Finally, below the dermis we find layers of connective tissue (superficial fascia) and subcutaneous fat that lie between the skin and the supportive formations of muscle and bone.

The Biophysics of the Skin

A common experimental procedure involves pushing on the skin—mechanically deforming it, either with infrequent pressure pulses or repetitive vibration. However, these simple stimuli are acting on a complex structure that can be best understood if we examine some of its biophysical characteristics. The layers of skin deformed by a stimulus are, technically speaking, "viscoelastic." This means that when the skin is touched, the energy imposed on it at that point will be transmitted through the medium (it is "viscous"). Some of the energy, however, will be absorbed and stored, and is used to return the skin to its original state (therefore, the skin is also "elastic"; Lamoré & Keemink, 1988; Tregear, 1966).

As energy moves in a wave into the skin, it produces shearing forces that dissipate with distance from the source according to the inverse square law. The form of the displacement wave, as breakers on a beach, changes as it passes through different tissue layers or encounters obstacles, such as blood vessels or bone. These obstructions may reflect, refract, absorb, or otherwise distort the wave front in one way or another. The events that are "witnessed" by the sensory nerve ending within the skin, therefore, may be quite different from those originally presented at the surface. Thus, the location and depth of a cutaneous receptor (a structure that converts mechanical, thermal, or chemical energy into neural signals) within the skin can affect how the stimulus acts upon it. The ways in which these tissue factors may influence tactile perception has been discussed in elaborate models involving tissue mechanics by Johnson and Phillips (1981) and Van Doren (1989).

Mechanical vibration can also generate traveling waves of energy across the surface of the skin that may be transmitted over long distances. Vibration on the finger, for example, can be seen traveling well up the arm, given the appropriate viewing apparatus (Békésy, 1960, pp. 540–556; Keidel, 1968).

These surface waves allow for the possibility that a greater number of receptors from distant locations might respond to vibration on the finger. In some experiments, it is desirable to restrict the vibratory stimulus to a specific region in order to limit the receptor population that can respond. Surface waves may be reduced by placing a static ring (surround) around the moving contactor. This is a technique that has been widely used in studies of tactile sensitivity (Gescheider, Capraro, Frisina, Hamer, & Verrillo, 1978; Verrillo, 1962), but deeper waves may still tend to spread laterally (Lamoré & Keemink, 1988, p. 2348; Moore & Mundie, 1972). Thus, the use of a surround may restrict the number of the most superficial receptors stimulated, but might not have an effect on the involvement of deeper ones. Similarly, chemical or electrical stimulation will tend to spread laterally through whatever available paths might exist. Electrical stimuli may find paths of least resistance through the salty and electrically conductive exudate in the pores of sweat glands. Attempts to stimulate the skin with thermal stimuli have analogous problems with stimulus control. Any attempts to move the skin's temperature above or below its normal level results in activation of local and central homeostatic mechanisms that strive to offset its heating or cooling.

Cutaneous "Receptors" and their Distribution

There are several cutaneous end organs that are suspected of being responsible for transducing tactile stimuli into neural signals. Merkel's disks, Ruffini cylinders, and Meissner's corpuscles (named after their discoverers), have all been implicated in the senses of touch and are found in the upper regions of the dermis. Even deeper than these are the Pacinian corpuscles, found in the subcutaneous connective and fatty tissues. Fig. 2.1 is a generalization that illustrates the locations of some of these structures in relation to one another. Depending on the skin site being examined, the number and types of these structures vary considerably (for example, there are no hair follicles in glabrous skin, nor Pacinian corpuscles in the skin of the cheek).

At this point, we are reluctant to label these end organs as "receptors" because we wish to reserve the use of the term to refer specifically to structures that, when stimulated, are *known* to produce tactile sensations. For example, it is known that pain can be felt everywhere on the body and that free nerve endings are also present throughout the body. For these reasons, physiologists suspect that free nerve endings operate as pain receptors (nociceptors) in many regions (Burgess & Perl, 1973). However, this is a correlation and only provides circumstantial evidence of a relationship. A more informative technique is to establish the intermediate relationships. First, we must determine which end organ produces a specific neural response to tactile stimuli: This is classification by structure. The best method currently available is called single-unit recording, in which a fine electrode is used to pick up the response of a single nerve fiber. This method, however, can only establish how a unit responds to tactile stimuli, not which end organ produces the response (Sherrick & Cholewiak, 1986a, p. 12–9). Thus, a unit is classified as being "slowly adapting" or as having "a punctate receptive field" rather than as being the response of a free nerve ending, or a Ruffini cylinder. Attempts have been made to tie these response profiles to skin structures by excising and examining the area of skin which, when stimulated, activated a unit of a particular type. Unfortunately, by these histological studies, researchers have not usually been able to identify which structure in the skin sample was the one that caused the response because more than one was present or other such problems.

Second, the relationship between those single unit responses and sensations has to be established: classification by function. Microneurography, a relatively new method, is providing the most direct measure possible of this second relationship through simultaneous recording of single-unit activity and human sensation (see reviews by Johannson, Landström, & Lundström, 1982; Vallbo, Hagbarth, Torebjörk, & Wallin, 1979). In this case, recording is done in awake humans with percutaneous (through the skin) microelectrodes instead of by dissection. The power of this technique was realized when these workers were able to correlate the neural responses that they were recording with the actual sensations that their observers could report (Schady & Torebjörk, 1983; Vallbo & Johansson, 1984). Also, with this method they demonstrated that they could electrically stimulate a single-unit nerve fiber and evoke tactile sensations that were localized to a particular region of skin. These were the same sensations that were evoked when that neural unit was driven with mechanical stimulation. In general, the relationships revealed by all of these techniques have not been as clear-cut as one might wish. As a result, none of them has provided us with definitive structure–sensation relationships. In summary, we assume that the complex neural structures that we identify histologically in the skin *do* produce responses, and that the central nervous system interprets these as sensations. At this point, however, the exact correspondence between these structures and their function is not known.

These end organs, the presumed receptors, are scattered throughout the depth and breadth of the skin. Indeed, the density of innervation varies considerably, depending on the location of the body that is examined. One consequence of this irregular distribution is that the skin is not uniformly responsive to mechanical and thermal stimuli. Take the tip of a pencil and lightly touch the back of the hand, first one place, then the next. What will emerge as the sensations are felt is the distinct appearance of spots where the tip feels cold, contrasting to others where no thermal sensation is apparent. In fact, if this demonstration is done with care, even the most elementary of the skin's sensations, pressure, may be found to be distributed only here and there as one explores the surface of the hand (although the number of sensitive spots appears to be related to the intensity of the stimulus). This demonstration illustrates the punctate nature of tactile sensitivity, a property that researchers in cutaneous sensation have to be constantly aware of.

The distribution of cutaneous end organs appears random when small areas are examined, but a regular gradient of receptor density exists across the body's surface. Cutaneous receptors are found to be tightly packed in regions such as the fingertips, lips, and genitals. As one moves toward the body, away from the fingertips, these become more and more rare as the palm, forearm, upper arm, shoulder, and trunk are examined. Furthermore, as one might guess, sensitivity to tactile stimuli is, in many ways, related to the density of innervation.

In the situation described here, the very nature of the skin changes along with the gradient of receptor density. For example, the mechanical properties of the skin vary as one moves from the fingers to the forearm: The skin becomes softer and more compliant. In fact, the differences between the skin of the hand and that of the forearm are great enough that they fall into two distinct classes. On the fingers, palms, and soles of the feet, the skin is smooth and is referred to as glabrous. The skin found almost everywhere else on the body has hair and is simply and appropriately referred to as hairy skin. Most research has concentrated on these two classes, although other regions have not been ignored (e.g., the tongue (Verrillo, 1968) or the prepuce (Bazett, McGlone, Williams, & Lufkin, 1932). Some cutaneous structures such as Pacinian corpuscles are found primarily in glabrous skin, though they do exist at a much lower density in hairy skin (Verrillo, 1968), as well as in mesentery and joints (Hunt, 1974). Free nerve endings, on the other hand, are found throughout the body, even in body sites that are devoid of any other type of complex cutaneous formation. Such atypical regions include the pinna or outer ear and the cornea of the eye (Ganong, 1977; Lele & Weddell, 1956).

Receptor Anatomy and Physiology

The anatomy of the types of cutaneous end organs found in mammalian skin can be divided into two broad classes: free (bare) nerve endings, as opposed to those endings either associated with or encapsulated within accessory structures. Free nerve endings are fine sensory fibrils, the ends of neurons. These, and some of the encapsulated nerve endings were shown in Fig. 2.1. Common encapsulated types include the Pacinian, Merkel, Meissner, Ruffini, Krause, and Basket endings (found around hair follicles) (Munger, 1971). These sensory endings range in complexity from bare fibers apposed to sensory cells, such as those found in the Merkel cell complex, to the intricately wrapped neurite found in the onion-like Pacinian corpuscle (Hunt, 1974). These endings have been described extensively in the anatomical and physiological literature, particularly from the skin of cats, rabbits (e.g., Brown & Iggo, 1967; Burgess, Petit, & Warren, 1968; Iggo, 1974) and monkeys (e.g., Andres & Düring, 1973; Burgess & Perl, 1973; Merzenich & Harrington, 1969).

We would like to emphasize the earlier caveat concerning the problem of attributing specific function to any of these structures within the skin. As of yet, physiological experiments cannot isolate single cutaneous end organs within the skin. Fig. 2.2 illustrates a typical experiment in which cutaneous receptors are stimulated while the nerve fibers are recorded from. Specifically, the microneurographic procedure is illustrated, in which a percutaneous microelectrode is used to record from an intact nerve fiber of the hand (Fig. 2.2a). In most animal preparations, however, the nerve fiber is dissected out from a cutaneous nerve and then a gross electrode is used to record from it. In either procedure, the skin is stroked, prodded, heated, or cooled with stimuli that would normally evoke touch sensations, while the neural responses are examined. These data do not tell us directly which of the end organs are involved. Instead, the experiment consists of stimulating the skin and then asking "what did you feel?" This question can be asked of the whole person, as is done in the series of psychophysical experiments to be described in the last section in this chapter. It can also be asked of the nerve fibers that serve the skin. In this case, interpreting the response is somewhat more difficult. The receptors that lie within the skin are connected to the rest of the nervous system by the body's telephone line, the nervous system. The physiologist is merely tapping that line. What is at the other end is still a question. Is it a touchtone phone? A cordless remote? By carefully analyzing the signals coming down the line and comparing them with other signals recorded from other lines, we may be able to make some educated guesses about the originator of the information. In any case, however, we have to be careful in our extrapolation of data from these studies to behavioral levels.

Receptor Classification

In the experiment described, the neural responses can tell us volumes regarding the sensitivity of the receptor at the other end. The skin site where, for example, mechanical stimulation evokes neural activity (as opposed to, say, thermal stimulation) defines the receptive field of that "unit." The field may be large (as large as a whole finger, for example), or punctate (a millimeter or so in diameter) as illustrated in Fig. 2.2b. Furthermore, a single neural unit does not have exclusive rights to a given point on the skin. Rather, there is extensive overlap of fields such that a point is represented by many differ-

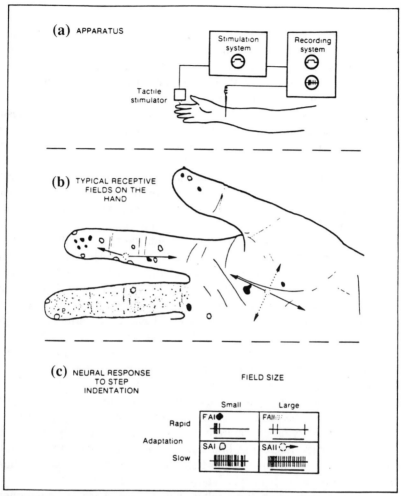

FIG. 2.2. Apparatus and results from a typical single-unit microneurography experiment. Panel (a) shows the apparatus for such an experiment in which a fine tungsten recording microelectrode is inserted into the forearm of an awake human. After the cutaneous nerve has been penetrated, tactile stimuli are presented to various areas of the hand and the responses from the single nerve fiber are recorded to determine its receptive field characteristics. Panel (b) shows representative sizes and locations of fields typically recorded on the hand. There is a wide variety in the sizes of these receptive fields: One may encompass an entire finger while another may be the size of the head of a pin. The type of unit is indicated by the shading pattern, corresponding to the legend in Panel (c). The arrows drawn from the SA II receptive fields illustrate the directions of stretch to which those units will respond. Panel (c) shows the four typical classifications of the responses recorded in this type of experiment to step indentation stimuli. The responses vary on two dimensions: the rate of adaptation and receptive field size. The labels of FA I, FA II, SA I, and SA II are used to identify these four response profiles (also see Fig. 2.6). From "Cutaneous Sensitivity," by C. E. Sherrick & R. W. Cholewiak, in *Handbook of Perception and Human Performance,* p. 12–4; K. R. Boff, L. Kaufman, & J. P. Thomas (Eds.), 1986; New York: Wiley. Copyright 1986 by John Wiley & Sons, Inc.; adapted by permission.

ent types of units. To characterize the unit further, well-controlled bursts of mechanical vibration, taps, or brush strokes are presented to the receptive field, and the responses are recorded. Does the unit respond for the whole duration of the stimulus or just at the onset (i.e., is it rapidly or slowly adapting)? How often does the unit respond to a stimulus? Does it respond better to one frequency of vibration than another? What is the smallest intensity that will evoke a response? How quickly is the neural signal transmitted down the nerve fiber? Is the unit sensitive to temperature? To skin stretch? To noxious stimuli?

These are the kinds of information that we can gather to help classify cutaneous units. There are as many as 20 different unit types found in skin, including motor and sensory fibers. Units in glabrous skin sensitive to noninjurious mechanical stimuli have been classified into four groups. The sensory units vary in the size of their receptive fields (large or small) and in how quickly they adapt to a steady stimulus, either fast (FA) or slow (SA). The responses resulting from indentation of the skin recorded from these groups of "mechanoreceptor" units are illustrated in Fig. 2.2c. Slowly adapting units continue to respond throughout the duration of the stimulus, in contrast to units in which the response dies out quickly. Table 2.1 describes the results of such an analysis on the skin of cats from the work of Burgess, Petit, and Warren (1968). Note that included in the analysis are several other distinguishing physiological measures. The size of the nerve fiber that conducts information from the cutaneous unit can vary considerably, and has a direct relationship to the conduction velocity of the neural "bit" of information, the "action potential." This potential is an electrical event that propagates down the nerve fiber, carrying information from one part of the body to another. Note that the larger the fiber (A-fibers are the biggest, C-fibers the smallest), the faster the rate of conduction. It is thought that two different sizes of fiber carry information about pain, which may be the mechanism for the two kinds of pain ("double pain") sometimes felt with injury: the sharp, fast component versus the dull, slow one.

Physiologists have been able to make some educated guesses about how the response of a unit is related to its proposed structure. The accessory structures of the encapsulated neurites mentioned earlier appear to modify or tune the unit to respond to particular aspects of the mechanical stimulus. The only cutaneous structure that has been carefully examined in this regard is the Pacinian corpuscle. It is not embedded in the dense dermal-epidermal matrix but rather lies in the fatty layers below and is thus much more accessible to isolation and direct manipulation (e.g., Bolanowski & Zwislocki, 1984; Hunt, 1974; Loewenstein, 1971). The lamellated coat of the Pacinian filters out the lower-frequency components of a mechanical stimulus, making the unit particularly sensitive to high-frequency stimuli. If the coat is carefully removed, as was done by Loewenstein (1971), then the nature of the response changes.

TABLE 2.1
Cutaneous Receptor Types in Cat Hairy Skin

Receptor type	Receptive field size (mm2)	Adaptation rate	Velocity threshold (m/ms)	Displacement threshold (m)	Pressure threshold (mg)	Response to cooling	Conduction velocity (m/s)
Pacinian:	focus 2–4	rapid	.02–10	—	—	0	65
Field:	84	variable	.1–1.0	10–80	15–70	variable	55
SAI:	MultiFocal	slow-irregular	—	5–10	8–20	+ +	65
SAII:	UniFocal	slow-regular	—	10–15	10–25	+ +	54
G1 Hair:	66	rapid	20–60[a]	—	—	0	75
G2 Hair:	35	rapid	.01–1.5[a]	5–15	10–25	+	53
D Hair:	42	rapid	—	3–6	5–8	+ +	21

Note: From "Receptor Types in Cat Hairy Skin Supplied by Myelinated Fibers," by P. R. Burgess, D. Petit, & R. M. Warren, 1968; *Journal of Neurophysiology, 31,* p. 837. Copyright 1968 by the American Physiological Society. Adapted by permission.
[a]Two subpopulations noted.

With lamellae intact, a durative pressure stimulus will produce graded local neural responses, called "generator potentials," as well as the propagated action potentials, but only at the onset and offset of the stimulus (see inset labeled "FA II" in Fig. 2.2). Without the coat of many layers, the decapsulated dendrite produces only a generator potential that lasts the duration of the stimulus. Thus the elementary response of the neural core is "slowly adapting," but the layers filter the mechanical stimulus in a way to pass only the transient components. Parenthetically, the size of the generator potential depends partly on the area of the dendrite that is stimulated, so even at this level spatial summation is exhibited.

The question now becomes how the activity of these receptors provides information about the stimulus. The location of a mechanical stimulus would, presumably, be encoded by the location of the responding receptors. The intensity of the stimulus seems to be encoded in both the number of receptors responding, and in their rate and duration of response (see, e.g., Bolanowski & Zwislocki, 1984). Because there is a population of different receptor types in the skin (see, e.g., Table 2.1), it is not necessary to have a single one encode all of the qualities that the observer can identify. It is more likely that, although some overlap exists in the sensitivity of the units to other qualities of the stimulus such as temperature, each unit type specializes in one or another aspect of the stimulus.

The Pacinian, for example, is a receptor that responds to vibratory stimuli. When cooled, it also shows a reduction both in its overall sensitivity as well as in the frequency to which it is most sensitive (Bolanowski & Verrillo, 1982; Green, 1977; Verrillo & Bolanowski, 1986). The response of this unit to mechanical stimuli, however, is much more vigorous and predictable than its responses to temperature changes, so it is an unlikely candidate for a thermal receptor. Iggo (1974, p. 391) lists a half dozen functional characteristics that distinguish true thermoreceptors from receptors that are primarily sensitive to some other modality, but whose response is in some way modulated by temperature ("spurious" thermoreceptors). Physiological recordings indicate that there are thermoreceptors that respond specifically to cold or specifically to warmth. The two populations are distributed differently over the skin's surface (many fewer warm "spots" than cold). Virtually nothing is known about the physical structures of these two receptors, but Hensel (1973) provides an extensive review of the physiological properties of cutaneous thermoreceptors. For example, cutaneous cold receptors produce their highest discharge rate at about 28^0C while warm receptors respond most vigorously to a 43^0C stimulus.

As mentioned earlier, there is a class of receptors called nociceptors, which respond specifically to what would be classified as "painful" stimuli. Again, no unique end organ seems to be implicated as the receptor: "Pain is a sensory modality in search of a sense organ" (Ruch, Patton, Woodbury, & Towe,

1965, p. 313) although free nerve endings seem to be the most likely candidate. The receptors seem to respond to almost all cutaneous stimuli, have extraordinarily high thresholds to these, have tiny receptive fields, have a persistent discharge when adequately stimulated, and seem to be served with the smallest of nerve fibers (Iggo, 1974). Similarly, no specific structure has been tied to chemesthesis, sensitivity to chemical stimuli (Green, 1990).

The Spinal Cord and Cutaneous Information Processing

All of the information from the periphery (the skin) is carried to the spinal cord on individual nerve fibers—some longer than a meter. As they approach the spine, the nerve fibers join at each vertebral level to form a single nerve trunk before they enter the spinal cord. The cell bodies of these fibers clump together in the dorsal root ganglion of the spine. The ganglia from every level in the body form chains on either side of the spinal cord, one to each of the vertebrae. These also happen to be the places where the herpes virus rests until awakened by some insult to the body, then to wreak havoc on the peripheral fields of the cell bodies contained therein. The interesting aspect of this infection, called herpes zoster, or shingles, is that the area of skin affected by the infection will define the band of skin served by that spinal root. This band is called a dermatome, and there is a pair (one on each side of the body) at every spinal level (see Fig. 2.3).

Within the spinal cord, the proximal ends of the first-order cutaneous sensory fibers divide into two major groups, based not on body site, but rather upon function. The smaller fibers, apparently responsible for pain and temperature, form one bundle (sometimes called the spinothalamic system), while the other (the leminiscal system) is made up of larger fibers carrying mechanoreceptor information. The bundles of fibers divide into tracts and send branches up and down the cord. There are afferent (to the brain) and efferent (from the brain) tracts. Afferent fibers are sensory while efferent fibers are typically motor fibers, controlling muscles and glands. The spinal cord is the first place that connections can be made between and among nerves (through synapses). Here, the first-order sensory fibers make contact with one or more second-order neurons. These, in turn, can interact with other neurons (including motor nerve fibers) to either enhance or inhibit neural activity. Because of the variety of these connections, many simple events can occur at the spinal level without any cortical involvement. The simple reflex arc (best known in the knee-jerk reflex) occurs completely within the spinal cord, involving as few as three neurons: a sensory neuron, a second-order interneuron, and a motor fiber. Indeed, even walking may be controlled entirely within the spinal cord in the cat! (e.g., Forssberg & Grillner, 1973). Fig. 2.4 shows representative connections within, up, and down the spinal cord.

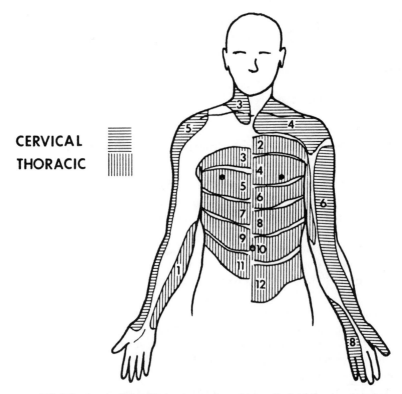

CERVICAL

THORACIC

FIG. 2.3.   Areas of the skin known as dermatomes. Each of these regions is served *primarily* by one of the cervical or thoracic posterior spinal nerve roots, as indicated in the legend, with even-numbered roots shown on the right, odd numbers on the left. A considerable degree of overlap exists between derma-tomes, as shown. This organization only exists at the spinal level; organization in somatosensory cortex is based on functional regions, like the forearm, which cut across dermatomal boundaries. From "Cutaneous Sensitivity," by C. E. Sher-rick & R. W. Cholewiak, in *Handbook of Perception and Human Performance* (p. 12–6); K. R. Boff, L. Kaufman, & J. P. Thomas (Eds.), 1986; New York: Wiley. Copyright 1986 by John Wiley & Sons, Inc.; reprinted by permission.

Somatosensory Cortex and
Cutaneous Information Processing

Eventually the ascending information arrives at the brain through intermedi-ate and direct pathways to be processed further in the somatosensory cor-tex. What has happened to the information that was encoded within the recep-tive field of a single unit? First, it has been combined with that from other first-order units and has been distributed among many other second-order units in the spinal cord. This convergence and divergence continues in the higher centers to produce finally a representation of the body's surface at the cortex (but on the opposite hemisphere). In fact, there are several differ-

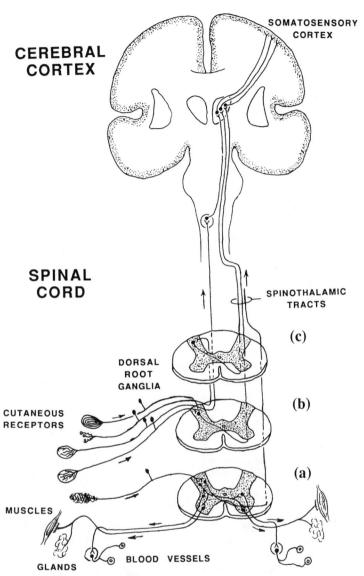

FIG. 2.4. Several cross-sections of the spinal cord are shown, along with examples of how neuronal interactions occur at and between levels on the way to the cerebral cortex. Specifically, (a) shows how information from a temperature receptor can activate smooth muscles in the blood vessels for thermoregulatory functions completely within the spinal cord. Some possible paths for Pacinian, Meissner and joint receptors are shown in (b) with the associated ascending tracts. In addition, the manner in which paths change location within the cord as they course to higher or lower levels is shown in (c). Adapted from *Fundamentals of Neurology* (5th ed., pp. 176 & 227), E. Gardner (Ed.), 1968; Philadelphia: W. B. Saunders Company.

ent areas on the sensory cortex where tactile information is represented, the most important of which are named Somatosensory I and II (SI and SII; Kaas, Nelson, Sur, & Lin, 1979). As early as 1937, Penfield had reported somatosensory sensations in awake humans when such cortical areas were stimulated electrically (Penfield & Boldrey, 1937). Similarly, a map of the body can be charted by placing an electrode on different points on the surface of the cortex, then noting the sites where stimulation of the skin evokes activity. When these points are connected, a systematic topographic projection is seen (Fig. 2.5). This pattern of representation, called a homunculus, appears grotesque at first. Upon closer examination, it can be seen that the surface area of the body site is less important than innervation density in determining the amount of cortex on which it is represented. Areas of the body that are highly innervated, such as the lips, genitals, and fingertips, are represented by large areas, while body sites that are less sensitive, with poorer innervation, are in turn poorly represented. The relationship between the size of the cortical area and the area of the periphery so represented has been called cortical magnification. The magnification factor has been found to vary from body site to body site, but is greatest for body sites such as the fingertips that are highly innervated (Merzenich & Kaas, 1980; Sur, Merzenich, & Kaas, 1980). In the monkey, for example, the glabrous skin of the hand occupies 100 times more cortical tissue per unit body-surface area than the trunk or upper arm.

The receptive fields in the cortex are larger than those recorded peripherally, partly owing to the convergence of information on each of the cortical units. The size of the field is inversely proportional to the sensitivity of the site (Sur et al., 1980). As a result, the number of cortical cells processing information from sites such as the fingertip is considerably greater than for sites such as the back. Another way in which the information contained in cortical receptive fields differs from that represented in peripheral receptive fields is that some cortical cells have fields that are sensitive to specific features of the stimulus. For example, a cell in the cortex might only be sensitive to stroking the surface of the forearm in a single direction (Gardner, Hamalainen, Palmer, & Warren, 1989), or to stimuli of a specific frequency or modality (Clark, Allard, Jenkins, & Merzenich, 1988; Jenkins, Merzenich, Ochs, Allard, & Guíc-Robles, 1990). This specialization, called "feature detection," when found in visual cortex, results from the convergence of information of a specific kind on cortical cells. In examining other types of cortical information processing, Libet and his coworkers (Libet, 1973; Libet, Alberts, Wright, Lewis, & Feinstein, 1975) have found that even illusory sensations resulting from complex spatiotemporal patterns of stimulation at the periphery, such as shifts in apparent skin locus, were mirrored in changing patterns of cortical activity.

Another organizing principle found to exist within the cortex is segregation based on receptor type (Favorov & Whitsel, 1988; Werner & Whitsel,

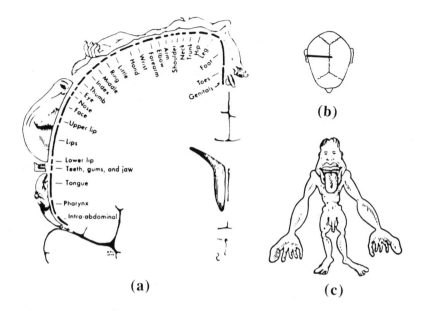

(b)

(a)   (c)

FIG. 2.5.   The amount of cortical area devoted to different body sites is shown in a sagittal section of the brain through somatosensory cortex (a) with an inset (b) indicating the plane of the section. In (c) is shown a representation of the body as it might appear if the surface area was proportional to cortical area. This representation is called a sensory homunculus. In fact, the amount of cortical area is a function of the degree of innervation, not surface area. From *Sensation and Perception: An Integrated Approach* (3rd ed., p. 124), H. R. Schiffman, 1990; New York: Wiley. Copyright 1990 by John Wiley & Sons; adapted by permission.

1973). One of the most exciting recent findings in cutaneous physiology and anatomy is that the size of these cortical receptive fields, and the number of cortical cells responding to stimuli of one type or another might not be fixed but rather appear to be plastic. Merzenich and his colleagues (e.g., Clark et al., 1988; Jenkins et al., 1990), and Whitsel and his colleagues (1989) have been examining the changes in cortical organization that occur with experience. Through their work it now appears as though significant changes in the functional organization of somatosensory cortex can occur as a result of experience with one type of stimulation or another. Furthermore, there is the strong implication that these changes might, in turn, influence tactile perception.

Models of Tactile Mechanosensitivity

Four general classes of mechanoreceptive units, illustrated earlier in Fig. 2.2, have been described in the glabrous skin of humans. Additional characteristics of these four are shown in Fig. 2.6 (from Vallbo & Johannson, 1978, 1984).

A number of other categories of units have also been described using microneurographic techniques in humans that are similar to those recorded from animals. These included several classes of units sensitive to movements of hairs in the skin, units sensitive to noxious stimuli, and units responsive to thermal stimuli. Physiologists have proposed that the four mechanoreceptive units are subserved by specific end organs. It is believed that the FA I response is generated by Meissner corpuscles, the FA II by Pacinian corpuscles, the SA I by Merkel disks, and the SA II by Ruffini cylinders.

Historically there have been many attempts to correlate these physiological responses with behavioral measures. Békésy (1939), Merzenich and Harrington (1969), and Talbot, Darian-Smith, Kornhuber, and Mountcastle (1968) are but a few researchers who have related varieties of conscious experience to underlying cutaneous structures. Perhaps the most ambitious and complete description has been that of Verrillo and his colleagues (Bolanowski, Gescheider, Verrillo, & Checkosky, 1988; Capraro, Verrillo, & Zwislocki, 1979; Verrillo, 1968). In their attempts to describe the vibrotactile receptor system, they have used psychophysical methods that have disclosed the operation of several subsystems. These methods were designed to take advantage of the distinguishing characteristics of tactile receptors, such as their unique frequency sensitivities, the differences in their thresholds, and the differences in their sensitivity to the spatial properties of the stimulus. Through manipulation of stimulus conditions, these workers have performed a sort of "psychophysical dissection," in which one or more of these subsystems are sensitized or desensitized. The net result is that one subsystem can, in effect, be isolated by increasing its sensitivity relative to that of the others (see especially Bolanowski et al., 1988).

The reason that these psychophysical methods have had to be used is that in the "intact" preparation (that is, the observing human) we cannot readily isolate a single receptor system. All of the physiological data described earlier were collected from single-unit preparations that only inform about single cutaneous receptors. Thus, for example, no matter how large or small the contactor was, and no matter how far the stimulus spread, data were obtained only from the unit whose nerve fiber was on or under the electrode. This is in contrast to the psychophysical data that we will now be examining. A stimulus of any kind presented to the surface of the skin will activate a whole population of receptors whose receptive fields happen to overlap at the point of contact. Furthermore, it is likely that the stimulus will have qualities that may appeal to receptors in which we might not be interested. For example, a mechanical stimulus presented with a metal contactor could also activate cold receptors. Similarly, a chemical stimulus carefully applied to the skin of the arm or tongue may also stimulate pressure receptors (as well as cold receptors, if its vehicle, or carrier, evaporates). Consequently, other methods have to be used to be able to describe the operation of a single one of the presumed receptor populations.

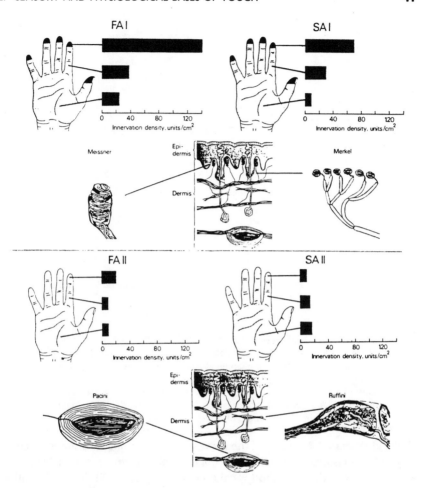

FIG. 2.6. The gradients of density of FA I, FA II, SA I, and SA II units over the surface of the hand are illustrated along with the presumed receptor structures. From "Properties of Cutaneous Mechanoreceptors in the Human Hand Related to Touch Sensation," by Å. B. Vallbo & R. S. Johansson, 1984; *Human Neurobiology, 3, 6 & 8.* Copyright 1984 by Springer-Verlag; adapted by permission.

The Four-channel Model of cutaneous mechanoreception, resulting from psychophysical dissection, attempts to account for the operation of the receptor populations in glabrous skin studied on the palm of the hand (Bolanowski et al., 1988). The model correlates the responses from the psychophysically defined subsystems with the physiological data, recorded either with single-unit analysis from animal preparations or microneurographic single-unit data from humans. In Fig. 2.7, threshold measures from the palm of the hand under normal conditions are plotted as a function of frequency. The Four-channel

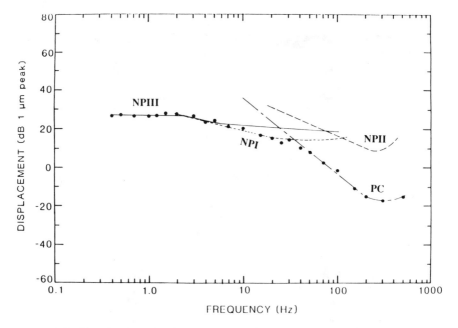

FIG. 2.7. Threshold for vibration on the palm of the hand as a function of frequency showing the threshold response for each of four receptor populations, according to the Four-channel Model of mechanoreception. See Table 2.2 for details regarding the response characteristics of each channel. From "Four Channels Mediate the Mechanical Aspects of Touch," by S. J. Bolanowski et al., 1988; *Journal of the Acoustical Society of America, 84,* 1691. Copyright 1988 by the American Institute of Physics; adapted by permission.

Model identifies each section of the curve as corresponding to a different channel of tactile information. The results of this analysis are shown in Table 2.2, which describes the psychophysical channels (PC, NP I, NP II, and NP III) in terms of their characteristic responses to several stimulus qualities. The correlated receptor systems are also listed, along with their associated physiological characteristics. Finally, the best methods by which these channels can be psychophysically dissected are listed.

TACTILE PSYCHOPHYSICS

In this next section of the chapter, we wish to examine the dimensions of tactile sensitivity as measured behaviorally in typical experiments in sensory psychology. After briefly discussing methodological issues, there are three broad areas we will concentrate on: how the skin responds to the intensitive characteristics of stimuli, how it encodes the spatial aspects of stimuli, and how it responds to the temporal aspects. We will also briefly discuss the in-

TABLE 2.2a
Four-channel Model of Mechanoreception

Psychophysical characteristics of channels: (a, b, c, d, h, i)

	P Channel (a, b, d, & h)	NP I Channel (a, c, d, & i)	NP II Channel (a, c, d, & i)	NP III Channel (a)
Sensation quality:	"vibration"	"flutter"	unknown	"pressure"
Frequencies over which threshold defined				
small contactor (.008 cm²):	none	3–100 Hz	80–500 Hz	.4–3 Hz
large contactor (2.9 cm²):	35–500 Hz	3–35 Hz	none	.4–3 Hz
Shape of frequency response function:	U-shape	flat (slight dip at 30 Hz)	U-shape	flat
Slope of "tuning curve":	−12 dB/oct	−5.0 dB/oct	−5.5 dB/oct	unknown
Best frequency (bf) varies with temperature:				
low temperature (15–25 deg C):	yes	no	yes	no
high temperature (30–40 deg C):	bf: 150–250 Hz	—	bf: 100–150 Hz	—
	bf: 250–400 Hz	—	bf: 225–275 Hz	—
Temperature sensitivity:	yes	slight	yes	slight
Temporal summation:	yes	no	yes	indeterminate
Spatial summation:	yes	no	unknown	no

Physiological characteristics of presumed receptor units: (e, f, & g)

	FA II (PC)	FA I (RA)	SA II	SA I
Adaptation rate:	fast	fast	slow	slow
Type of skin:	glabrous	glabrous	glabrous/hairy	glabrous/hairy
Receptive fields: size/borders:	large/indistinct	small/well defined	large/indistinct	small/well defined
Associated neural structures:	Pacinian corpuscle	Meissner corpuscle	Ruffini cylinders	Merkel disks
Special stimulus attribute responded to:	high frequency	edges	skin stretch	edges

(Continued)

TABLE 2.2b
(Continued)

Psychophysical procedures (a, b, c, d, & h):

To lower threshold:	Best frequency	Surround presence	Contactor size	Skin temperature	Stimulus duration
P Channel:	250–300 Hz	no	large (> 2.9 cm²)	> 32 deg C	> 500 ms
NP I Channel:	25–40 Hz	yes	any	15–40 deg C	> one cycle
NP II Channel:	150–400 Hz	unknown	very small (< 0.02 cm²)	> 32 deg C	> 500 ms
NP III Channel:	.4–1 Hz	yes	any	15–40 deg C	> one cycle

To elevate threshold:	Frequency of masker/adaptor	Surround presence	Contactor size	Skin temperature	Stimulus duration
P Channel:	250–300 Hz	yes	very small (< 0.02 cm²)	cold (15 deg C)	< 200 ms
NP I Channel:	25–40 Hz	no	any	any	any
NP II Channel:	150–400 Hz	unknown	unknown	unknown	< 200 ms
NP III Channel:	.4–10 Hz	no	any	any	any

Note: The information in this table is limited to the palm of the hand and is based upon the studies referred to by letter: (a) Bolanowski et al., 1988; (b) Bolanowski & Verrillo, 1982; (c) Capraro, Verrillo & Zwislocki, 1979; (d) Gescheider et al., 1985; (e) Iggo & Muir, 1969; (f) Talbot et al., 1968; (g) Vallbo & Johansson, 1984; (h) Verrillo, 1968; (i) Verrillo & Bolanowski, 1986 (see full citation in references).

teractions of the latter two, since the most common tactile stimulus changes over time: It is "spatiotemporal." In these discussions, we will generally limit ourselves to vibrotactile or pressure (mechanical) stimuli, leaving the psychophysical aspects of thermal and pain stimuli to other chapters in this volume.

Methodological Considerations

Touch stimuli that produce sensations of pressure, taps, or vibration are delivered to the skin in the experimental setting by devices, such as von Frey hairs, solenoids, shakers, piezoceramic benders, arrays, or even air puffs. Von Frey hairs are used for constant-pressure stimuli because these calibrated hairs bend when a given force is reached as they are pressed into the skin. Solenoids or bell-ringer coils can be used for durative pressure pulses because they will indent the skin for the duration of the applied voltage. Shakers and piezoceramic reed benders can present vibratory stimuli to the skin over the frequency range of .1 Hz to 200 Hz or more. The shakers, however, are able to deliver a wider range of intensities than the benders because they are somewhat independent of the impedance of the skin, and are less susceptible to damping. Electrostatic forces have been used to produce contactless mechanical stimulation of the skin (Moore, 1968). Even air puffs have occasionally been used to provide a noncontacting mechanical stimulus. Arrays, such as that from the Optacon (a reading machine for blind persons), are useful for presenting two-dimensional patterns of stimuli to the skin. However, the Optacon is not always an appropriate device for such applications because its mechanical design prevents the experimenter from having precise control of stimulus amplitude and waveform. Electrocutaneous stimuli (which can produce sensations indistinguishable from mechanical taps) are typically presented to the skin with simple electrodes, either concentric or paired, with electrolytic pastes to provide the conductive interface through the keratinized skin layers. Finally, chemical stimulation occurs when solutions carry the substance of interest onto or under the outer layer of skin.

Intensitive Information Processing

One of the most emergent properties of a tactile stimulus is its perceived intensity or "loudness." The minimal energy that can be felt is called the absolute threshold (RL). Owing to individual differences across observers, this value varies from person to person, and from test to test. A variety of methods can be used to determine threshold, such as gradually increasing or decreasing the intensity and asking the observer when he or she just notices the stimulus or its disappearance. Measurement of threshold, while interesting in and of itself, also provides a reference point that allows us to set stimulus levels in a consistent way across observers. For example, in many vibrotactile experiments the stimulus is set to 5–10 times above threshold (in log units, about 14–20 dB with reference to threshold, or dB SL). The physical intensity of this signal varies from observer to observer, depending on their threshold, but the loudness is the same for all.

Tactile thresholds can be extraordinarily small. Given the appropriate set of conditions, a person can feel a vibratory stimulus that has an amplitude as low as 0.2 microns (250 Hz on the palm of the hand (Gescheider et al., 1978)). Pressure thresholds are as low as 5 mg (on the face), which has been likened to having a wing of a fly dropping from about 3 cm onto the skin. Khanna and Sherrick (1981) have calculated that approximately 2×10^{-8} watts must be expended to stimulate a single Pacinian corpuscle. LaMotte and his colleagues have similarly determined that the careful observer can feel microscopic bumps (or asperities) in an otherwise smooth surface as small as 1–3 microns in height (LaMotte & Whitehouse, 1986). Many of these thresholds have been found to vary over the surface of the body, owing both to the differences in innervation density as well as the variation in the complement of receptors (J. C. Stevens, 1990, and his chapter in this volume). Fig. 2.8 illustrates the variation in threshold over the surface of the body to bursts of 200-Hz sinusoids and pressure stimuli. Females are slightly more sensitive at all body sites by 0.4 to 0.6 log units, although the overall pattern of sensitivity is similar to that of males, shown here (after Weinstein, 1968).

The threshold for a vibratory stimulus depends on its frequency and temperature. As we saw in Fig. 2.7, threshold can vary considerably with frequency, at least over certain ranges. If, on the other hand, the stimulus is a train of pulses, other conditions begin equal, threshold (and suprathreshold loudness) is much less dependent on the rate at which the pulses are presented. A number of laboratories have found that threshold varies by less than 3 dB per octave (doubling) of frequency, whereas the change can be as much as 12 dB per octave for sinusoids (Bernstein, Schecter, & Goldstein, 1986; Rothenberg, Verrillo, Zahorian, Brachman, & Bolanowski, 1977; Sherrick, 1985). Temperature can also effect threshold by inhibiting or exciting individual receptors that are sensitive to both touch and thermal stimuli such as the Pacinian (see earlier).

Other factors that affect threshold include the area of the contactor, the duration of the stimulus, the static force of the stimulus, the presence of a surround (Gescheider et al., 1978), the age of the observer (Verrillo, 1982), and even hormone levels (Gescheider, Verrillo, McCann, & Aldrich, 1984). With regard to contactor area, the larger the contactor, the lower the threshold (Craig, 1968; Verrillo, 1968). This rule has been found to hold, if the receptor system that determines absolute threshold for the tested frequency, exhibits spatial summation (see Table 2.2). However, static force increases with area, too, and this variable has not been factored out in most studies.

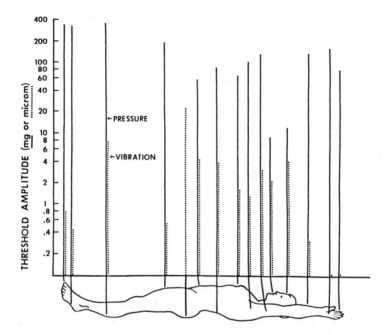

FIG. 2.8. Threshold responses for pressure (bars) and vibration (dots) as a function of body site. Pressure thresholds were evaluated with von Frey hairs, while vibratory thresholds were determined with 200-Hz stimuli. From "Cutaneous Sensitivity," by C. E. Sherrick & R. W. Cholewiak, in *Handbook of Perception and Human Performance* (p. 12–12), by K. R. Boff, L. Kaufman, & J. P. Thomas (Eds.), 1986, New York: Wiley. Copyright 1986 by John Wiley & Sons, Inc.; adapted by permission.

How the intensity of the stimulus is encoded is still not completely understood. At the level of the first-order afferent, intensity appears to be encoded in the rate of neural response or the number of neural action potentials in a given period of time. Psychophysically, the "loudness" (the apparent intensity) of a tactile stimulus is related to its intensity in a power–law relationship (S. S. Stevens, 1970, 1975). This is not unlike the relationship between stimulus and response in other sensory systems (even at the electrophysiological level, see, e.g., S. S. Stevens, 1970; Zwislocki, 1973). Gardner and her colleagues have examined the relationship between parallel psychophysical responses and physiological responses recorded at the cortex. Their data suggest that increasing sensation magnitudes are well correlated with increases in activity of cortical neurons (e.g., Gardner & Tast, 1981).

The exponent of the psychophysical power function depends on many of the same factors that affect threshold. For example, when the site of stimulation is moved from the fingertip to the forearm, the slope of the loudness function increases from 0.90 to about 1.30 (Verrillo & Chamberlain, 1972).

These effects have been attributed to the changing density of neural innervation. Other factors that also affect the loudness of stimuli include the age of the observer (Verrillo, 1982) and the area of the contactor. Suprathreshold stimuli show a dependence on contactor area, if a receptor system that exhibits spatial summation is excited, such that: The larger the stimulus, the greater the apparent intensity. In single-contactor situations, loudness grows with the square root of contactor area (Craig, 1966), whereas in multipoint arrays, the relationship between number of active elements and loudness is 1:1 (Cholewiak, 1979). On the other hand, the growth of loudness is unaffected by changes in other factors such as frequency. To illustrate this point, the growths of loudness of 250 Hz and 60 Hz vibrotactile stimuli presented to the glabrous skin of the palm are plotted in Fig. 2.9. In both cases, loudness increases with signal strength at the higher intensities with a slope of about 0.92 (Verrillo & Capraro, 1975). The slope of the loudness function has been found to be almost invariant over a range of 25 Hz to 350 Hz (Verrillo, Fraioli, & Smith, 1969).

Temporal factors can have an effect on the perceived intensity of tactile stimuli, but in two different ways depending on the duration of the stimulus. For example, temporal summation is said to occur when either threshold decreases or the loudness of the stimulus increases with duration, at least up to about 300–500 ms. Temporal summation has been found in vision, in audition, as well as in touch (Green, 1976; Verrillo, 1965; Zwislocki, 1960). As shown in Table 2.2, thresholds from P and NP II systems in glabrous skin are reduced with increasing stimulus duration, up to a point. On the other hand, if the stimulus is on for an even longer time, adaptation may occur. Adaptation may be defined as the increase in threshold or the reduction in the apparent intensity of a stimulus with prolonged stimulation. Hahn (1966) and Hollins (Hollins, Goble, Whitsel, & Tommerdahl, 1990) have shown that there is a considerable reduction in loudness with stimuli that last hundreds of *seconds*. Furthermore, the time course of adaptation follows a regular growth function, and recovery progresses quickly when the adapting stimulus is removed (see Fig. 2.10). It has also been shown repeatedly that adaptation within one of these vibrotactile channels (described in Table 2.2) will not necessarily raise thresholds in another channel, supporting the notion of their independence (Hahn, 1968). The sensations produced by pressure stimuli also adapt, although the time course has not been established (Nafe & Wagoner, 1941).

The mechanisms involved in adaptation are not readily apparent. At the physiological level, if the skin is driven with a step stimulus lasting hundreds of milliseconds, some receptor types will respond only to the onset then cease firing altogether, as shown in Fig. 2.2. On the other hand, if these same units are driven with sinusoidal stimuli, they may respond for hundreds of milliseconds *without* showing a significant drop in output, owing to their tendency

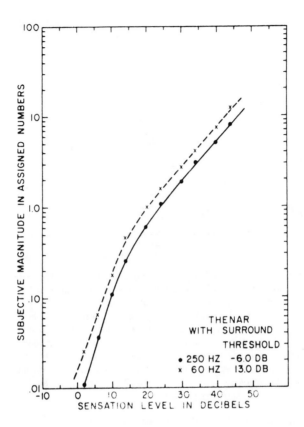

FIG. 2.9. Perceived intensity of vibrotactile stimuli on the palm of the hand is shown as a function of sensation level in decibels with frequency as the parameter. Judgments were by the method of magnitude estimation in which observers generated numbers that corresponded to the magnitudes of their sensations. The slopes at high intensities of both functions are 0.92. The slight bend is often found in psychometric functions of vibrotactile stimuli. From "Effect of Stimulus Frequency on Subjective Vibrotactile Magnitude Functions," by R. T. Verrillo & A. J. Capraro, 1975, *Perception & Psychophysics, 17*, 92. Copyright 1975 by Psychonomic Society; reprinted by permission.

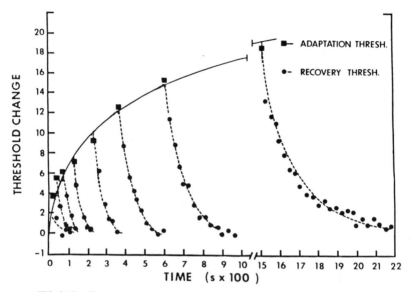

FIG. 2.10. The time course of adaptation of a stimulus presented to the index finger. A 60-Hz stimulus was presented at about 50 X threshold for 8 durations ranging from 10 to 1500 s. At the end of the period, thresholds were measured at roughly 15-s intervals to track the course of recovery. Threshold increased to a maximum of about 20 dB above preadaptation levels after 15 min of steady stimulation, with recovery to initial levels occurring more rapidly than the time needed to adapt to that level. From "Vibrotactile Adaptation and Recovery Measured by two Methods," by J. F. Hahn, 1966, *Journal of Experimental Psychology, 71,* 657. Copyright 1966 by the American Psychological Association; adapted by permission.

to respond on each cycle, and then recover before the next cycle occurs. Any explanation of the mechanisms of adaptation will have to bridge the two different mechanisms that appear to be operating, depending on whether one is dealing with data obtained psychophysically or physiologically.

Finally, we will address masking, another time-dependent phenomenon that can be found to influence either the threshold or the suprathreshold loudness of a tactile stimulus. Masking can occur when a second event either precedes or follows the stimulus of interest within a short period of time resulting in a reduction in perceived intensity or elevation of threshold. Other conditions may have to be met as well. For example, stimuli often have to be presented close together spatially as well as temporally. Sherrick (1964) has shown how separating stimuli in both time and space will reduce the amount of masking (in Fig. 2.11). Furthermore, in the case of vibrotactile stimuli, they appear to have to be presented within the same channel. That is, a 250-Hz stimulus will not mask a 20-Hz stimulus except under conditions of very high stimulus intensities, demonstrating channel independence (Gescheider, O'Malley, & Verrillo, 1983).

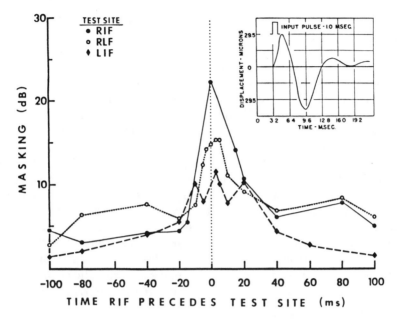

FIG. 2.11. Masking of a 1-ms tap presented to the fingertip by a second tap, presented just before or just after the test, at different sites. The masking stimulus (at 20 dB above threshold) was at the right index finger (RIF) in all cases, while the test site varied. Even when the test site was on the opposite hand (left index finger-LIF), threshold was raised by as much as 10 dB with short interpulse intervals. Note how the stimulus pulse waveform is transformed (inset) when driving the skin. From "Effects of Double Simultaneous Stimulation of the Skin," by C. E. Sherrick, 1964, *American Journal of Psychology, 77,* pp. 45, 46. Copyright 1964 by the University of Illinois Press; adapted by permission.

Spatial Information Processing

Tactile spatial information processing is typically evaluated with von Frey hairs, calipers, or similar devices (Boring, 1942; Weinstein, 1968). One measure, the separation at which two points are in fact perceived as distinct, is called the two-point limen. The two-point limen provides an indication of the spatial resolution of the skin. One or two points are presented to the skin, and the observer is asked to indicate the number of points felt. Below a certain separation, only a single one is reported. Fig. 2.12 illustrates how this measure changes over the body's surface, which is well correlated with receptor density (see also Fig. 2.13 and J. C. Stevens, 1990). Another measure of spatial acuity is the error of localization, which is both a test of spatial acuity and spatial memory. In this case a point is touched, and some time later, either the same or another point is touched, and the observer is asked to report "same" or "different." These values are also shown in Fig. 2.12. The less-than-perfect correspondence between the two measures of spatial acuity reflects the differences in the task demands as well as differences in the neural activity evoked by the stimuli (Békésy, 1960, 1967). The manner in which task demands can influence the results is illustrated by the finding that a two-alternative, forced-choice technique can produce extremely small thresholds relative to other procedures (Loomis & Collins, 1978). In addition, practice has been shown to reduce the size of the two-point limen considerably (Boring, 1942, p. 480).

Spatial acuity for other tactile stimuli such as thermal or chemical events is typically not as good as for mechanical stimuli. Extraordinarily poor localization of radiant heat has been occasionally reported, with confusions as dramatic as localizing a stimulus on the back when it was presented to the front of the body (see the chapter in this volume by J. C. Stevens). The localization of·chemical stimuli is also poor, relative to mechanical stimuli. Recently, Green and Flammer (1989) have compared the abilities to localize mechanical and chemical stimuli applied to the hairy skin of the forearm. The error of localization for a 7.5-mg pressure stimulus on the forearm was 1.4 cm. The error

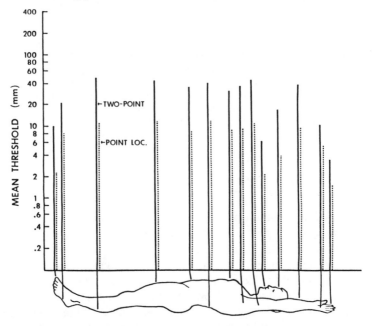

FIG. 2.12. Measures of spatial acuity on different body sites. Two-point thresholds (bars) and errors of localization (dots) are shown for 14 body sites. From "Cutaneous Sensitivity," by C. E. Sherrick & R. W. Cholewiak, in *Handbook of Perception and Human Performance* (p. 12–24), by K. R. Boff, L. Kaufman, & J. P. Thomas (Eds.), 1986, New York: Wiley. Copyright 1986 by John Wiley & Sons, Inc.; adapted by permission.

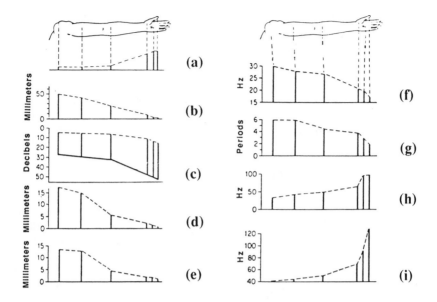

FIG. 2.13.   The influence of body site on a variety of measures of tactile sensitivity: (a) the relative size of area on the cortex, (b) two-point threshold, (c) equal loudness and threshold curves, (d) magnitude of sensation area produced by a vibrating needle (80 cps), (e) magnitude of sensation area produced by an ac current of 80 cps, (f) fusion frequency, (g) number of periods necessary to produce a pitch sensation at 60 cps, (h) apparent pitch of a vibration of 100 cps, and (i) apparent pitch of the sensation produced by striking the surface of the skin with a blunt needle. Both threshold and suprathreshold responses follow the pattern of innervation density, with thresholds being lowest (and suprathreshold stimuli feeling the loudest) at the fingertips. From *Experiments in Hearing* (p. 608), by G. von Békésy, 1960, New York: McGraw-Hill. Copyright 1960 by McGraw-Hill; adapted by permission.

for a 1.0% solution of capsaicin (the compound responsible for the "burn" in chili peppers) was significantly greater, measuring 2.5 cm. Sherrick, Cholewiak, and Collins (1990) discuss the psychophysical and physiological bases of localization of cutaneous stimuli, including the possible underlying mechanisms.

There have also been many attempts to examine the processing of spatial patterns that are elaborated over time on the skin. Other chapters in this volume will deal with the ability to apprehend such patterns, so here we will mention briefly only some of the studies that reflect upon basic measures of tactile sensitivity. Spatiotemporal judgments can be of stimuli as simple as a moving pencil (Langford, Hall, & Monty, 1973) or a brush stroking the skin (Essick, 1991). Alternatively, the tasks can be more complex, with stimuli generated with arrays of contactors, such as three-point localizations (Gardner & Spencer, 1972) or judgments of perceived separation of points presented at different times and locations (Sherrick & Cholewiak, 1986b). The interactions between spatial and temporal information from the skin can, under certain conditions, produce illusions. Examples of these include sensations of apparent movement produced by static displays or distortions of either space or time by similar patterns. Békésy (1960) examines some of these and Geldard (1975) reviews more recent findings in his book on sensory saltation. Even temperature can interact spatially with touch to produce an illusion in which cold is referred to a thermally neural site (Green, 1979).

Temporal Information Processing

Temporal information is processed quite well by the skin. When two events are presented to the skin close in time, one might ask the question "Did you feel one or two stimuli?" The limen, or threshold for successiveness (being able to tell that not one but two events occurred) is about 5 ms (Gescheider, 1974). The ear on the other hand, can resolve clicks separated by 0.01 ms, while the eye is sluggish, requiring as much as 25 ms (Sherrick & Cholewiak, 1986a, pp. 12–21). The ability to count stimuli (numerousness) follows a similar ordering over the senses, with the skin falling between the eye and ear (Lechelt, 1975). In contrast, the perception of order (determining which came first) for the skin requires about the same interval (20 ms) as is necessary for vision and audition (Hirsh & Sherrick, 1961), implying similar order-processing mechanisms in the three modalities.

In summary, Békésy's illustration (1960, Fig. 13-74) describes how a variety of measures of cutaneous sensitivity vary from the fingertips to the arm (reproduced in Fig. 2.13). This figure illustrates the large differences in these measures even over an area of the body as restricted as the arm. Note how most measures show their highest sensitivity at the fingertips, decreasing with innervation density, producing an overall pattern of results that emphasizes the intimate relationship between the sensory and physiological bases of touch.

CONCLUSIONS

Psychophysical measures of the skin's sensitivity can be affected by factors other than its physiology or stimulus conditions. Cognitive factors such as attention, motivation, learning, or task demands also have to be taken into account. To illustrate, there is a popular misconception that the skin of blind persons is more sensitive, as if the disability somehow increased the number or nature of the receptors in the skin. Tests of pressure sensitivity and two-point thresholds, however, show no significant differences owing to the disability itself (Axelrod, 1959). Although no differences exist in these measures of sensitivity, blind persons do excel in certain types of complex tactile form perception, indicating that basic measures do not necessarily predict performance on more cognitively demanding tasks. In fact, what appears to be the case is that blind persons are simply more attentive to this communication channel than those of us who are sighted (Hollins, 1989, pp. 45–47). These issues will be dealt with elsewhere in this volume.

The following chapters will build on these data, discussing in more detail how tactile information is perceived in displays, natural and artificial, simple and complex. The skin can provide a rich alternative input channel for those whose visual and auditory sensory channels are either overloaded (as in the case of jet fighter pilots) or disabled (as in the case of blind or deaf persons). The chapters will illustrate the richness of sensations available through this oft-ignored communication channel, which allows us to keep in touch with the world around us.

ACKNOWLEDGMENT

The preparation of this manuscript was supported by Grant NS–04775–26 from the National Institutes of Health to Princeton University.

REFERENCES

Andres, K. H., & Düring, M., von (1973). Morphology of cutaneous receptors. In A. Iggo (Ed.), *Handbook of sensory physiology: Somatosensory system* (Vol. 2, pp. 3–28). New York: Springer-Verlag.

Axelrod, S. (1959). *Effects of early blindness: Performance of blind and sighted children on tactile and auditory tasks.* New York: American Foundation for the Blind.

Bazett, H. C., McGlone, B., Williams, R. G., & Lufkin, H. M. (1932). Sensation. I. Depth, distribution, and probable identification in the prepuce of sensory end-organs concerned in sensations of temperature and touch; thermometric conductivity. *Archives of Neurology and Psychiatry, 27,* 489–517.

Békésy, G., von (1939). Über die Vibrationsempfindung. *Akustische Zeitschrift, 4,* 316–334.

Békésy, G., von (1960). *Experiments in hearing.* New York: McGraw-Hill.

Békésy, G., von (1967). *Sensory inhibition.* Princeton, NJ: Princeton University Press.

Bernstein, L. E., Schecter, M. B., & Goldstein, M. H., Jr. (1986). Child and adult vibrotactile thresholds for sinusoidal and pulsatile stimuli. *Journal of the Acoustical Society, 80,* 118–123.

Bolanowski, S. J., Jr., Gescheider, G. A., Verrillo, R. T., & Checkosky, C. M. (1988). Four channels mediate the mechanical aspects of touch. *Journal of the Acoustical Society of America, 84*(5), 1680–1694.

Bolanowski, S. J., Jr., & Verrillo, R. T. (1982). Temperature and criterion effects in a somatosensory subsystem: A neurophysiological and psychophysical study. *Journal of Neurophysiology, 48*(3), 836–855.

Bolanowski, S. J., Jr., & Zwislocki, J. J. (1984). Intensity and frequency characteristics of Pacinian corpuscles: I. Action potentials. *Journal of Neurophysiology, 51*(4), 793–811.

Boring, E. G. (1942). *Sensation and perception in the history of experimental psychology.* New York: Appleton-Century.

Brown, A. G., & Iggo, A. A. (1967). A quantitative study of cutaneous receptors and afferent fibres in the cat and rabbit. *Journal of Physiology (London), 193,* 707–733.

Burgess, P. R., & Perl, E. R. (1973). Cutaneous mechanoreceptors and nociceptors. In A. Iggo (Ed.), *Handbook of sensory physiology: Somatosensory system* (Vol. 2, pp. 29–78). New York: Springer-Verlag.

Burgess, P. R., Petit, D., & Warren, R. M. (1968). Receptor types in cat hairy skin supplied by myelinated fibers. *Journal of Neurophysiology, 31,* 833–848.

Capraro, A. J., Verrillo, R. T., & Zwislocki, J. J. (1979). Psychophysical evidence for a triplex system of cutaneous mechanoreception. *Sensory Processes, 3*(4), 334–352.

Cholewiak, R. W. (1979). Spatial factors in the perceived intensity of vibrotactile patterns. *Sensory Processes, 3,* 141–156.

Clark, S. A., Allard, T., Jenkins, W. M., & Merzenich, M. M. (1988). Receptive fields in the body-surface map in adult cortex defined by temporally correlated inputs. *Nature, 332,* 444–445.

Craig, J. C. (1966). Vibrotactile loudness addition. *Perception & Psychophysics, 1,* 185–190.

Craig, J. C. (1968). Vibrotactile spatial summation. *Perception & Psychophysics, 4,* 351–354.

Essick, G. K. (1991). Human capacity to process directional information provided by tactile stimuli which move across the skin: Characterization and potential neural mechanisms. In O. Franzen & J. Westman (Eds.), *Information processing in the somatosensory system.* Wenner-Gren Center International Symposium Series (Vol. 57, pp. 329–339). New York: Macmillan.

Favorov, O. V., & Whitsel, B. L. (1988). Spatial organization of the peripheral input to area 1 cell columns. I. The detection of "segregates." *Brain Research Reviews, 13,* 25–42.

Forssberg, H., & Grillner, S. (1973). The locomotion of the acute spinal cat injected with clonidine i.v. *Brain Research, 50,* 184–186.

Ganong, W. F. (1977). *The nervous system.* Los Altos, CA: Lange Medical Publications.

Gardner, E. P. (1968). *Fundamentals of neurology.* Philadelphia: W. B. Saunders.

Gardner, E. P., Hamalainen, H. A., Palmer, C. I., & Warren, S. (1989). Touching the outside world: Representation of motion and direction within primary somatosensory cortex. In J. S. Lund (Ed.), *Sensory processing in the mammalian brain: Neural substrates and experimental strategies* (pp. 49–66). New York: Oxford Press.

Gardner, E. P., & Spencer, W. A. (1972). Sensory funneling. I. Psychophysical observations of human subjects and responses of cutaneous mechanoreceptive afferents in the cat to patterned skin stimuli. *Journal of Neurophysiology, 35,* 925–953.

Gardner, E. P., & Tast, J. M. (1981). Psychophysical measurements of perceived intensity of single-point and multiple-point cutaneous stimuli in humans and sub-human primates. *Journal of Neurophysiology, 46,* 479–495.

Geldard, F. A. (1975). *Sensory saltation: Metastability in the perceptual world.* Hillsdale, NJ: Lawrence Erlbaum Associates.

Gescheider, G. A. (1974). Temporal relations in cutaneous stimulation. In F. A. Geldard (Ed.), *Cutaneous communication systems and devices* (pp. 33–37). Austin, TX: Psychonomic Society.

Gescheider, G. A., Capraro, A. J., Frisina, R. D., Hamer, R. D. & Verrillo, R. T. (1978). The effects of a surround on vibrotactile thresholds. *Sensory Processes, 2*(2), 99–115.

Gescheider, G. A., O'Malley, M. J., & Verrillo, R. T. (1983). Vibrotactile forward masking: Evidence for channel independence. *Journal of the Acoustical Society of America, 74,* 474–485.

Gescheider, G. A., Sklar, B. F., Van Doren, C. L., & Verrillo, R. T. (1985). Vibrotactile forward masking: Psychophysical evidence for a triplex theory of cutaneous mechanoreception. *Journal of the Acoustical Society of America, 74,* 534–543.

Gescheider, G. A., Verrillo, R. T., McCann, J. T., & Aldrich, E. M. (1984). Effects of the menstrual cycle on vibrotactile sensitivity. *Perception & Psychophysics, 36*(6), 586–592.

Green, B. G. (1976). Vibrotactile temporal summation and the effect of frequency. *Sensory Processes, 1,* 138–149.

Green, B. G. (1977). The effect of skin temperature on vibrotactile sensitivity. *Perception & Psychophysics, 21,* 243–248.

Green, B. G. (1979). Thermo-tactile interactions: Effects of touch on thermal localization. In D. R. Kenshalo (Ed.), *Sensory functions of the skin of humans* (pp. 223–240). New York: Plenum Press.

Green, B. G. (1990). Preface. In B. G. Green, J. R. Mason, & M. R. Kare (Eds.), *Chemical senses. Vol. 2: Irritation* (pp. v–vi). New York: Marcel Dekker.

Green, B. G., & Flammer, L. J. (1989). Localization of chemical stimulation: Capsaicin on hairy skin. *Somatosensory and Motor Research, 6,* 553–566.

Hahn, J. F. (1966). Vibrotactile adaptation and recovery measured by two methods. *Journal of Experimental Psychology, 71,* 655–658.

Hahn, J. F. (1968). Low-frequency vibrotactile adaptation. *Journal of Experimental Psychology, 78,* 655–659.

Hensel, H. (1973). Cutaneous thermoreceptors. In A. A. Iggo (Ed.), *Handbook of sensory physiology: Somatosensory system* (Vol. 2, pp. 79–110). New York: Springer-Verlag.

Hirsh, I. J., & Sherrick, C. E. (1961). Perceived order in different sense modalities. *Journal of Experimental Psychology, 62,* 423–432.

Hollins, M. (1989). *Understanding blindness. An integrative approach.* Hillsdale, NJ: Lawrence Erlbaum Associates.

Hollins, M., Goble, A. K., Whitsel, B. L., & Tommerdahl, M. (1990). Time course and action spectrum of vibrotactile adaptation. *Somatosensory and Motor Research, 7,* 205–221.

Hunt, C. C. (1974). The Pacinian corpuscle. In J. I. Hubbard (Ed.), *The peripheral nervous system* (pp. 405–420). New York: Plenum Press.

Iggo, A. A. (1974). Cutaneous receptors. In J. I. Hubbard (Ed.), *The peripheral nervous system* (pp. 347–404). New York: Plenum Press.

Iggo, A. A., & Muir, A. R. (1969). The structure and function of a slowly adapting touch corpuscle in hairy skin. *Journal of Physiology, 200,* 763–796.

Jenkins, W. M., Merzenich, M. M., Ochs, M. T., Allard, T., & Guíc-Robles, E. (1990). Functional reorganization of primary somatosensory cortex in adult owl monkeys after behaviorally controlled tactile stimulation. *Journal of Neurophysiology, 63,* 82–104.

Johansson, R. S., Landström, U., & Lundström, R. (1982). Responses of mechanoreceptive afferent units in the glabrous skin of the human hand to sinusoidal skin displacements. *Brain Research, 244,* 17–25.

Johnson, K. O., & Phillips, J. R. (1981). Tactile spatial resolution. I. Two-point discrimination, gap detection, grating resolution, and letter recognition. *Journal of Neurophysiology, 46,* 1177–1191.

Kaas, J. H., Nelson, R. J., Sur, M., & Lin, C. S. (1979). Multiple representations of the body within the primary somatosensory cortex of primates. *Science, 204,* 521–523.

Keidel, W. D. (1968). Electrophysiology of vibratory perception. In W. D. Neff (Ed.), *Contributions to Sensory Physiology* (Vol. 3, pp. 1–79). New York: Academic Press.

Khanna, S. M., & Sherrick, C. E. (1981). The comparative sensitivity of selected receptor systems. In T. Gualtierotti (Ed.), *The vestibular system: Function and morphology* (pp. 337–348). New York: Springer-Verlag.

Lamoré, P. J. J., & Keemink, C. J. (1988). Evidence for different types of mechanoreceptors from measurements of the psychophysical threshold for vibrations under different stimulation conditions. *Journal of the Acoustical Society of America, 83,* 2339–2351.

LaMotte, R. H., & Whitehouse, J. (1986). Tactile detection of a dot on a smooth surface: Peripheral neural events. *Journal of Neurophysiology, 56,* 1109–1128.

Langford, N., Hall, R. J., & Monty, R. A. (1973). Cutaneous perception of a track produced by moving a point across the skin. *Journal of Experimental Psychology, 97,* 59–63.

Lechelt, E. C. (1975). Temporal numerosity discrimination: Intermodal comparisons revisited. *British Journal of Psychology, 66,* 101–108.

Lederman, S. J. (1978). Heightening tactile impressions of surface texture. In G. Gordon (Ed.), *Active touch. The mechanisms of recognition of objects by manipulation: A multidisciplinary approach* (pp. 205–214). Oxford: Pergamon Press.

Lele, P. P., & Weddell, G. (1956). The relationship between neurohistology and corneal sensibility. *Brain, 79,* 119–154.

Libet, B. (1973). Electrical stimulation of cortex in human subjects and conscious sensory aspects. In A. Iggo (Ed.), *Handbook of sensory physiology: Somatosensory system* (Vol. 2, pp. 743–790). New York: Springer-Verlag.

Libet, B., Alberts, W. W., Wright, E. W., Jr., Lewis, M., & Feinstein, B. (1975). Cortical representation of evoked potentials relative to conscious sensory responses, and of somatosensory qualities in man. In H. H. Kornhuber (Ed.), *The somatosensory system.* Stuttgart, Germany: Georg Thieme.

Loewenstein, W. R. (1971). Mechano-electric transduction in the pacinian corpuscle. Initiation of sensory impulses in mechanoreceptors. In W. R. Loewenstein (Ed.), *Principles of receptor physiology* (pp. 269–290). New York: Springer-Verlag.

Loomis, J. M., & Collins, C. C. (1978). Sensitivity to shifts of a point stimulus: An instance of tactile hyperacuity. *Perception & Psychophysics, 24,* 487–492.

Loomis, J. M., & Lederman, S. J. (1986). Tactual perception. In K. R. Boff, L. Kaufman, & J. P. Thomas (Eds.), *Handbook of Perception and Human Performance* (Vol. 2, pp. 31-1–31-41). New York: Wiley.

Merzenich, M. M., & Harrington, T. (1969). The sense of flutter-vibration evoked by stimulation of the hairy skin in primates: Comparison of human sensory capacity with the responses of mechanoreceptive afferents innervating the hairy skin of primates. *Experimental Brain Research, 9,* 236–260.

Merzenich, M. M., & Kaas, J. H. (1980). Principles of organization of sensory–perceptual systems in mammals. In J. M. Sprague & A. N. Epstein (Eds.), *Progress in psychobiology and physiological psychology* (Vol. 9, pp. 1–42). Orlando, FL: Academic Press.

Montagna, W. (1956). *The structure and function of skin.* New York: Academic Press.

Moore, T. J. (1968). Vibratory stimulation of the skin by electrostatic field: Effects of size of electrode and site of stimulation on thresholds. *American Journal of Psychology, 81,* 235–240.

Moore, T. J., & Mundie, J. R. (1972). Measurement of specific mechanical impedance of the skin: Effects of static force, site of stimulation, area of probe, and presence of a surround. *Journal of the Acoustical Society of America, 52,* 577–584.

Munger, B. L. (1971). Patterns of organization of peripheral sensory receptors. In W. R. Loewenstein (Ed.), *Principles of receptor physiology* (pp. 523–556). New York: Springer-Verlag.

Nafe, J. P., & Wagoner, K. S. (1941). The nature of pressure adaptation. *Journal of General Psychology, 25,* 323–351.

Penfield, W., & Boldrey, E. (1937). Somatic motor and sensory representation in the cerebral cortex of man as studied by electrical stimulation. *Brain, 60,* 389–443.

Quilliam, T. A. (1978). The structure of finger print skin. In G. Gordon (Ed.), *Active touch. The mechanism of recognition of objects by manipulation: A multidisciplinary approach* (pp. 1–18). Oxford, England: Pergamon Press.

Rothenberg, M., Verrillo, R. T., Zahorian, S. A., Brachman, M. L., & Bolanowski, S. J., Jr. (1977). Vibrotactile frequency for encoding a speech parameter. *Journal of the Acoustical Society of America, 62,* 1003–1012.

Ruch, T. C., Patton, H. D., Woodbury, J. W., & Towe, A. L. (1965). *Neurophysiology.* Philadelphia: W. B. Saunders.

Schady, W. J. L., & Torebjörk, H. E. (1983). Projected and receptive fields: A comparison of projected areas of sensations evoked by intraneural stimulation of mechanoreceptive units and their innervation territories. *Acta Physiologica Scandinavica, 119,* 267–275.

Schiffman, H. R. (1990). *Sensation and perception: An integrated approach.* (3rd ed.). New York: Wiley.

Sherrick, C. E. (1964). Effects of double simultaneous stimulation of the skin. *American Journal of Psychology, 77,* 42–53.

Sherrick, C. E. (1985). A scale for rate of tactile vibration. *Journal of the Acoustical Society of America, 78,* 78–83.

Sherrick, C. E., & Cholewiak, R. W. (1986a). Cutaneous Sensitivity. In K. Boff, L. Kaufman, & J. L. Thomas (Eds.), *Handbook of perception and human performance* (pp. 12-1–12-58). New York: Wiley.

Sherrick, C. E., & Cholewiak, R. W. (1986b). *Princeton Cutaneous Research Project* (Rep. No. 48, Dec. 1986). Princeton, NJ: Princeton University, Department of Psychology.

Sherrick, C. E., Cholewiak, R. W., & Collins, A. A. (1990). The localization of low- and high-frequency vibrotactile stimuli. *Journal of the Acoustical Society of America, 88,* 169–179.

Stevens, J. C. (1990). Perceived roughness as a function of body locus. *Perception & Psychophysics, 47*(3), 298–304.

Stevens, S. S. (1970). Neural events and the psychophysical law. *Science, 170,* 1043–1050.

Stevens, S. S. (1975). *Psychophysics.* New York: Wiley.

Sur, M., Merzenich, M. M., & Kaas, J. H. (1980). Magnification, receptive-field area, and "hypercolumn" size in areas 3b and 1 of somatosensory cortex in owl monkeys. *Journal of Neurophysiology, 44,* 295–311.

Talbot, W. H., Darian-Smith, I., Kornhuber, H. H., & Mountcastle, V. B. (1968). The sense of flutter-vibration: Comparison of the human capacity with response patterns of mechanoreceptive afferents from the monkey hand. *Journal of Neurophysiology, 31,* 301–334.

Tregear, R. T. (1966). *Physical functions of the skin.* New York: Academic Press.

Vallbo, Å. B., Hagbarth, K.-E., Torebjörk, H. E., & Wallin, B. G. (1979). Somatosensory, proprioceptive, and sympathetic activity in human peripheral nerves. *Physiological Reviews, 59,* 919–957.

Vallbo, Å. B. & Johansson, R. S. (1978). The tactile sensory innervation of the glabrous skin of the human hand. In G. Gordon (Ed.), *Active touch. The mechanism of recognition of objects by manipulation: A multidisciplinary approach* (pp. 29–54). Oxford, England: Pergamon Press.

Vallbo, Å. B., & Johansson, R. S. (1984). Properties of cutaneous mechanoreceptors in the human hand related to touch sensation. *Human Neurobiology, 3,* 3–14.

Van Doren, C. L. (1989). A model of spatiotemporal tactile sensitivity linking psychophysics to tissue mechanics. *Journal of the Acoustical Society of America, 85,* 2065–2080.

Verrillo, R. T. (1962). Investigation of some parameters of the cutaneous threshold for vibration. *Journal of the Acoustical Society of America, 34,* 1768–1773.

Verrillo, R. T. (1965). Temporal summation in vibrotactile sensitivity. *Journal of the Acoustical Society of America, 37,* 843–846.

Verrillo, R. T. (1968). A duplex mechanism of mechanoreception. In D. R. Kenshalo (Ed.), *The skin senses* (pp. 139–159). Springfield, IL: Thomas.

Verrillo, R. T. (1982). Effects of aging on the suprathreshold responses to vibration. *Perception & Psychophysics, 32,* 61–68.

Verrillo, R. T., & Bolanowski, S. J., Jr., (1986). The effects of skin temperature on the psychophysical responses to vibration on glabrous and hairy skin. *Journal of the Acoustical Society of America, 80,* 528–532.

Verrillo, R. T., & Capraro, A. J. (1975). Effect of stimulus frequency on subjective vibrotactile magnitude functions. *Perception & Psychophysics, 17*, 91–96.

Verrillo, R. T., & Chamberlain, S. C. (1972). The effect of neural density and contactor surround on vibrotactile sensation magnitude. *Perception & Psychophysics, 11*, 117–120.

Verrillo, R. T., Fraioli, A. J., & Smith, R. L. (1969). Sensation magnitude of vibrotactile stimuli. *Perception & Psychophysics, 6*, 366–372.

Weinstein, S. (1968). Intensive and extensive aspects of tactile sensitivity as a function of body part, sex, and laterality. In D. R. Kenshalo (Ed.), *The skin senses* (pp. 195–222). Springfield, IL: Thomas.

Werner, G., & Whitsel, B. L. (1973). Functional organization of somatosensory cortex. In A. Iggo (Ed.), *Handbook of sensory physiology: Somatosensory system* (Vol. 2, pp. 621–700). New York: Springer-Verlag.

Whitsel, B. L., Favorov, O. V., Tommerdahl, M., Diamond, M. E., Juliano, S. L., & Kelly, D. G. (1989). Dynamic processes governing the somatosensory cortical response to natural stimulation. In J. S. Lund (Ed.), *Sensory processing in the mammalian brain* (pp. 84–116). New York: Oxford University Press.

Zwislocki, J. J. (1960). Theory of temporal auditory summation. *Journal of the Acoustical Society of America, 32*, 1046–1060.

Zwislocki, J. J. (1973). On intensity characteristics of sensory receptors: A generalized function. *Kybernetik, 12*, 169–183.

3

THERMAL SENSIBILITY

Joseph C. Stevens

John B. Pierce Foundation and Yale University

It is well known to scholars that Aristotle classified the human senses into five: vision, hearing, taste, smell, and touch. Less known is Aristotle's qualification that touch may comprise several "submodalities;" and, indeed, by the turn of the 20th century, thanks to the German physiologist Max von Frey, it became widely believed that the skin alone houses four separate senses: touch, pain, warmth, and cold (Boring, 1942; Stevens & Green, 1978a). The issue whether warmth and cold may constitute a single modality, a view championed by von Frey's contemporary, Ewald Hering, rather than two separate modalities, seems to have become largely semantic. Various anatomical and psychophysical considerations argue for independence, others for interaction and continuity. The issue has been brilliantly elucidated by Hensel (1982). Thus, when warmth and cold receive here the labels "thermal senses," it is mainly for convenience rather than from a theoretical stance on their independence.

FUNCTIONAL SIGNIFICANCE
OF THERMAL SENSIBILITY

Broadly speaking, the thermal senses, like pain, taste, and smell, look perceptually and cognitively impoverished compared with vision and hearing. These latter are superbly fit to register spatial and temporal patterns of stimulation, enabling rich processing of information about the world we live in.

No wonder they tend to dominate the sensory interest of psychologist, physiologist, and philosopher. In contrast, pain, smell, taste, and the thermal senses have more to do with regulatory biological functions. Warmth and cold senses may yield only rudimentary information about the external world, but what they tell about our thermal state, both internal and external, is indispensable to body temperature regulation and thereby to personal survival.

Body temperature regulation, is, therefore, the first business of the thermal receptors, and they need to function whether regulation takes place by instrumental *behavioral* escape from, or avoidance of, thermally unpleasant environments, or by *autonomic* behavior such as vasoconstriction, vasodilation, sweating, and shivering. The complexities of both kinds of regulation go beyond this chapter (for reviews, see Gisolfi & Wenger, 1984; Hardy, 1961). We shall see, however, that certain psychophysical properties of the thermal sensory systems relate intimately to regulation. For example, measurements of thermal thresholds and suprathreshold sensation magnitude unveil rich spatial and temporal summation of the neural effects of stimulation over large areas of the skin and over time. This means that to achieve a just-detectable (threshold) or any stronger (suprathreshold) sensation requires a smaller and smaller amount of heating or cooling the greater the area of the skin that is covered (within certain limits). The same principle holds for duration of stimulation: To arouse a given thermal sensation depends on both the level of warming or cooling and how long it lasts (also within certain limits). Thus manifests one general feature of the thermal senses, namely their tendency to register "how much," regardless of the exact spatial and temporal distribution of stimulation over the skin. This very feature precludes good spatiotemporal pattern perception so characteristic of the "higher" senses of sight and sound. A second general feature of the thermal senses also emerges from study of behavioral regulation, namely that they tend to register "how pleasant or unpleasant" nearly as saliently as "how much." The relation of thermal "hedonics" to thermal "magnitude" comes under discussion later.

A second function of thermal sensibility is its role in *avoidance of local damage to the skin.* Damage from freezing usually takes time, and accordingly follows upon the relatively slow onset of aching cold pain (skin temperatures below 15–18⁰C). Damage from burning often imposes so immanent a threat that to avert damage may require response even before pain sets in. Thus, rapid warming of the skin triggers alarm (Hardy, Wolff, & Goodell, 1952) and immediate withdrawal of the affected part, often the fingers. The warmth sense can be thought of as working a compromise between body temperature regulation, which requires summation of low-level thermal signals over large areas of the skin, and avoidance of burning, which requires good ability to *localize* high-level stimulation. Thus, rich spatial summation of warmth and poor localization characterize low-level heating of the skin, and poor summation of warmth and better localization characterize high-level heating, and in the extreme, at the thermal pain threshold (heating the skin to about 45°C), there is little, if any, spatial summation (Green & Hardy, 1958).

The thermal senses also function, albeit poorly, as *thermometers,* signaling, for example, whether substances are safe to touch or ingest. More often their role is to inform not so much "how much" as "what" (Katz, 1925). Thus, in palpating objects we are able to tell by thermal cues, along with other cues from touch, whether an object is made from glass, say, or metal, or wood, for although they could all have the same temperature they may feel warm, cold, or indifferent, depending on their heat-transfer coefficient. Characteristically we ignore the fact that a silver fork, say, feels cold to touch, and perceive instead that what we touch is metal. Thus the very fact that the objects we contact have vastly different thermal conductances and capacities makes the thermal senses unreliable as thermometers. If that is not enough, so do their various psychophysical properties (to be explained further), such as summation (the more skin stimulated, the warmer or cooler the sensation) and adaptation (the longer warm and cold objects are inspected, the more neutral they come to feel).

Notice has already been taken of the propensity of thermal sensation to take on *hedonic value,* from very unpleasant (and usually persistently so until stimulation ceases) to very pleasant (often strong but transient, as when a person is abruptly cooled in a hot environment or heated in a cold one). The pleasure of such abrupt changes often takes place long before thermal neutrality has a chance to be re-established and may be thought of, therefore, as anticipatory in nature (Gagge, Stolwijk, & Hardy, 1967). Hence it is the *transitions* from cold to warm or from warm to cold that please, and these are able to act as the immediate "reinforcement" required for fast instrumental or "operant" learning.

Thermal sensations also tend to furnish or enhance hedonic tone in other sensory experiences, especially in food and drink and perhaps in pleasurable touching and cuddling behavior. Temperature furnishes a whole dimension to food and drink, and sometimes there seems to be no obvious implication for biological well-being other than to enhance their attractiveness and thereby stimulate appetite.

BIOLOGICAL MECHANISMS SUBSERVING THERMAL SENSIBILITY

A variety of receptors near the body surface is responsive to temperature (Darian-Smith, 1984a, 1984b; Perl, 1984). These include *"warm"* and *"cold" receptors.* (Fig. 3.1). Both types exhibit ongoing spontaneous firing at "normal" skin temperature, without arousing appreciable sensation. On heating

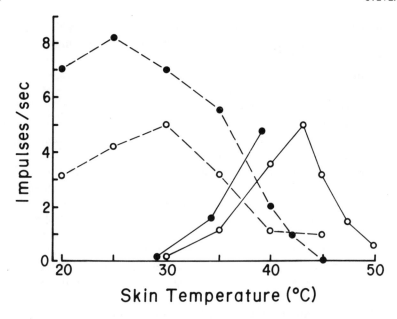

FIG. 3.1. Average rates of firing of cold (left side) and warm (right side) fibers in the hand or foot of the macaque at steady-state temperatures between 20^0 and 50^0C. Open circles: data from Kenshalo and Duclaux, 1977 and Duclaux and Kenshalo, 1980; Filled circles: data from Darian-Smith et al., 1973 and 1979. Redrawn from Darian-Smith, 1984.

above normal the "warm" receptors fire more and more briskly, while the "cold" receptors cease their spontaneous firing; on cooling below normal the cold receptors fire more and more briskly, while the warm receptors cease their spontaneous firing. (In addition, some cold fibers respond "paradoxically" to high temperatures.) The lavish spatial summation observed in psychophysical studies suggests that the outputs of thermal receptors can feed into common integrating neural units in the central nervous system, and indeed, Hellon and Mitchell (1975), for example, have found many neural units in the rat brain and spinal cord whose receptive fields cover large, often bilateral, regions of the body surface. Thus an understanding of the neural mechanisms subserving thermal sensation must include not only the receptors, but also their rich, interactive, central projections.

In addition to warm and cold receptors, the skin also houses *nociceptors* that respond to noxious temperature alone or to noxious temperature plus noxious mechanical stimulation (for a review, see Perl, 1984). These are associated with *pain*. Finally, many so-called SA (slowly adapting) fibers associated primarily with low-threshold mechanical stimulation of the skin, also respond to thermal stimulation (see Darian-Smith, 1984b), and these may reflect psychophysical phenomena (discussed in Part V) involving simultaneous thermal and mechanical stimulation of the skin.

PSYCHOPHYSICAL PROCEDURES FOR EXAMINING THERMAL SENSIBILITY

A variety of psychophysical procedures has been used to assess thermal sensibility—many adaptations of time-honored procedures used to study other sense modalities. These fall into six or so categories.

Absolute Thresholds

Absolute threshold means the smallest stimulus strength that can trigger a sensation of warmth or cold, where stimulus strength may be reckoned either as a change in skin temperature (from what feels thermally neutral) or as radiation of the skin with electromagnetic energy (see Kenshalo, Decker, & Hamilton, 1967, and a later section, for discussion of how these two measures relate). Excluded here are thresholds of pain, even though these have been measured as a function of thermal stimulation. Psychophysical methods have run from classical, that is, those three methods (limits, constant stimuli, and average error) that originate psychophysics (Fechner, 1860, 1966), to modern methods, such as forced-choice and tracking.

The full menu (and details) go beyond present scope, but a word is in order about the philosophy governing choice. In the method of *limits* the subject receives, one by one, a series of brief heat or cold "pulses" presented in ascending and descending order of intensity level; a series ends when a subject's judgments change from "perceived" to "not perceived" (or vice versa), and threshold is defined as the average transition level or "boundary" between perceptible and imperceptible over several series. In the thermal senses, as in other adaptable sense modalities, the series are sometimes confined to ascending ones (e.g., Stevens, Okulicz, & Marks, 1973), in order to prevent the measurement from reflecting too much the effects of ongoing stimulation in the form of adaptation. In *tracking procedures* (used mainly because of their speed and efficiency, but sometimes with reduced accuracy) the subject attempts to adjust the intensity of stimulation so as to maintain a just-noticeable sensation of cold or warmth over time, sometimes in the face of ongoing changes in intensity introduced by the experimental setup (so-called "Békésy tracking"). Thresholds measured this way by Kenshalo (1976) and Kenshalo and Scott (1966) were found to drift systematically upward (warmth) or downward (cold) toward a steady state, reflecting the operation of sensory adaptation. The use of *forced-choice* methods, under the rubric of "signal detection theory," helps to control for *response biases*—the individual personal differences in response criterion that matter. For example, people often respond positively to feigned stimulation ("false alarms") or resist positive response unless entirely certain that a stimulus was given. There are also constraints associated with particular procedures, such as the relative frequencies of real and feigned stimulus presentations (Swets, 1964) that can affect a person's inclination to respond positively or negatively. Forced-choice and adaptive procedures have sometimes been combined in the interest of promoting efficiency and reducing response bias at the same time (for thermal application, see Gray, Stevens, & Marks, 1982; Stevens, 1989).

Absolute thresholds furnish the data for the study of a number of thermal sensory processes. Examples (enlarged on in a later section) include how threshold depends on (1) stimulation mode (contact versus radiant); (2) wavelength of radiation (e.g., infrared versus microwave); (3) rate of change of skin temperature; (4) adaptation temperature of the skin; (5) stimulus area; (6) stimulus duration; (7) body locus; and (8) age.

Difference Thresholds

Although most methods for measuring absolute thresholds can be adapted to difference thresholds, little has been accomplished. Only a few modern data seem to pertain, and without the parametric treatment devoted to absolute threshold. As a result, we are mainly in the dark about differential sensitivity. Seemingly quite lacking, for example, is information about how thermal discrimination depends on areal extent and on body region, or how differential thresholds of warmth depend on increments of stimulus area. The latter holds interest because changes in stimulus area often feel indistinguishable from changes in stimulus intensity when it comes to sensations of warmth and cold. Thus, silence answers such basic questions as: Which is easier to detect, a given percentage change in intensity or the same percentage change in area? and Which part of the body is better at detecting a *change* of warmth (or cold), the head, the trunk, or the extremities? Most of the human senses, especially vision and hearing, have received close scrutiny from the point of view of their capacities to detect not only the *presence–absence* of stimulus events (absolute sensitivity), but also to detect *change–no change* in the intensity of the stimulus (differential sensitivity). Answers to such questions about warmth and cold surely would help to understand how we react and adjust to the thermal environment.

Spot Mapping

The discovery of *sensory spots* was made independently by Blix (1884) in Sweden, Goldscheider (1884) in Germany, and Donaldson (1885) in America. All three investigators, and many since, have reported that when touched with small (punctate) warm and cold stimulators some spots feel warm and/or cold, others do not (see Fig. 3.2). Maps of the skin for warmth and cold spots (pressure and pain have also been mapped) reveal the following: (1) Warmth and cold spots are distributed independently; (2) Cold spots far exceed warm spots (a classic experiment on the forearm [Strughold & Porz, 1931] yielded 7 cold spots per cm², compared with 0.24 warm spots per cm² [ratio of 29 to 1]); (3) the density of spots varies from one body region to another (Rein, 1925; Strughold & Porz, 1931; and see Fig. 3.2); and (4) even when charted with great care, maps reproduce imperfectly (Dallenbach, 1927).

These facts leave unresolved the meaning of spots in general and thermal spots in particular. After first demonstrated it was often assumed (and still is) that spots mark the loci of underlying receptors and that the maps offer compelling evidence that warmth and cold are separate sense modalities. Both conclusions have been doubted or modified, especially on the ground that taken literally they imply that large areas of the skin are insensible (especially to warmth), when in fact these areas can evoke thermal sensations reliably

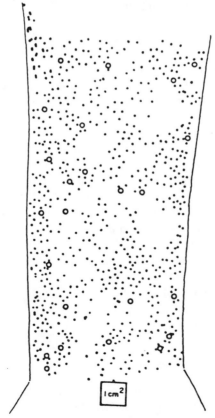

FIG. 3.2. Cold (dots) and warm (circles) spots mapped over 100 cm² of the dorsal side of the right forearm. Redrawn from Strughold and Porz, 1931.

to larger stimulus fields. Critics of mapping agree that in its microstructure the sensitivity of the skin may be punctate, but believe that spot mapping fails to prove a point that may better yield to physiological examination of nerve fiber specificity (see Hensel, 1982). The meaning of sensory spots thus remains cloudy. They could represent high-density *clusters* of spatially summating receptors (Jenkins, 1951), the location of single receptors of superior sensitivity (Stevens & Green, 1978a), or the recruitment of a high-threshold type of receptor, which Head (1920) called "protopathic," (punctiform), as opposed to epicritic (nonpunctiform, spatially summating). Besides, despite the prominent space given to them in handbooks, their functional significance *vis-à-vis,* thermal sensibility remains obscure.

Measures of Spatial and Temporal Acuity

According to a prominent pioneer of the skin senses, 19th-century physiologist E. H. Weber, dermal sensations can be distinguished by means of intensity, temperature, and locus of stimulation (see Weber, 1978). In the laboratory *locus* came to mean for Weber and many thereafter the measurement of the *two-point threshold* and the *error of point localization.* The former is the smallest distance between two points simultaneously touched to the skin that can render them just perceptually "two" rather than "one" (this so-called "compass test" can be modified to the presentation of two edges, rather than points, with little difference in measured threshold); the error of point localization reflects the accuracy with which a point of contact can be localized, for example, the ability to resolve whether two successive contacts fell at the same or at different loci. The two-point threshold always measures a few times larger than the error of point localization, but the two correlate strongly across different body regions, so when one is large (e.g., the upper arm), or small (e.g., the fingertip), so is the other. Measurement of them has provided rich information about the operation of the touch component of the skin senses; but as discussed in a later section, the thermal senses per se have poor spatial acuity, especially at low stimulation levels, that is, give very poor two-field thresholds and errors of localization, compared with touch. More impressively, the thermal environment can act in interesting ways on the touch system, so as to permit good thermal localization and, depending on circumstances, either to enhance touch acuity or to degrade it (these phenomena are explained in a later section).

Direct Psychophysical Scaling

As of thresholds, the treatment here of psychophysical scaling can only highlight this subject (for further information, see Gescheider, 1985; Marks, 1974; S. S. Stevens, 1975). Absolute threshold tells when a person can detect a stimulus, and therefore concerns weak stimuli and sensations. Differential threshold concerns sensations of all magnitudes from weak to strong but limits the question to detectability of *changes* or *differences* in sensation. The question here concerns *how large* one sensation seems relative to another, and how these sensation magnitudes depend on the stimulus magnitudes that arouse them. Thus, the aim of psychophysical scaling is to measure a *psychophysical function,* or, in other words, to learn how the magnitude of thermal sensation depends functionally (mathematically) on the magnitude of thermal stimulation. Sometimes the concern is less with magnitude of warmth or cold than with degree of *pleasantness* or *unpleasantness* associated therewith (called the "hedonic" dimension of sensation—clearly a striking feature of everyday encounter with the thermal environment).

Whether magnitude or hedonics, the goal is to build a scale of some dimension or other of experience and relate it to some dimension of the stimulus. Normally the stimulus dimension of interest is *intensity,* but other dimensions may come into play. For example, in studies of spatial summation one wants to know how sensation magnitude depends not only on stimulus intensity but also on the *areal extent* of skin stimulated. With information of both kinds one can specify the combinations of intensity and area that arouse the same sensation magnitude, or, in other words, to state the rules by which the two variables can be traded for each other to preserve a constant thermal sensation.

Two classes of scaling methods have been used to measure sensory and hedonic magnitudes, in all of the senses but in particular in warmth and cold. These are: (1) *category rating* methods and (2) *ratio scaling* methods. Category rating is simple and pragmatic; the subject, presented one by one with a set of stimuli, tries to rate each one on a scale having a number of categories—for example, the numbers 1 through 10; or, say, the adjectives very weak, weak, moderate, strong, very strong; or on a line labeled from very faint to extremely strong (a procedure sometimes dubbed "visual analog rating"). The most widely used ratio scaling procedure is *magnitude estimation.* Here the subject (in a typical experiment each of 10 or more) tries to assign numbers in direct proportion to the sensation magnitudes aroused by each of several levels of the stimulus magnitude. For example, to the first of a set of levels a subject might assign the number "10." The next level might receive the number "30," say, or "5," if the second seemed to be three times or one-half as strong as the first, and so on until all levels, presented in random order, have received a number from the subject. Implicit in this procedure is the understanding that the ratios among the numbers assigned should reflect the ratios among the sensation magnitudes experienced, so that it makes sense to speak of one sensation as being, say, "three times" or "one-half" times as large as another. Controversy perennially surrounds the issue whether people can truly do this, but the results of countless experiments (with several variations on the same theme) led S. S. Stevens (1975) to state a generalization that drew the attention of students of all of the senses, not just the thermal: Namely, that to a first approximation the estimated sensation magnitude is proportional to the stimulus magnitude raised to some power, or, in other words, that sensation magnitude grows as a *power function* of stimulus magnitude. Power functions are common stuff in science and have the simple equation:

$$y = kx^\beta \tag{1}$$

where y stands for sensation magnitude (usually the averaged magnitude estimates from a group of subjects) and x stands for stimulus intensity. The power β (exponent) reflects the rate of increase of sensation with respect to increase of stimulus; if β is smaller than 1.0, a given increase in stimulus magnitude, for example, doubling it, would produce less than double an increase in sensation magnitude; similarly if β is larger than 1.0 then doubling the stimulus magnitude would more than double the sensation magnitude. Whether β is less than 1.0 (a kind of law of diminishing returns), larger than 1.0 (a kind of law of expanding returns), or equal to 1.0 (a simple proportionality), depends on the sense modality (e.g., typically small for smelling, typically large for degree of color saturation; for a list of exponents, see S. S. Stevens, 1975). The exponent can vary also within a modality, depending on particular stimulus dimensions: as we shall see later, sensation of warmth depends jointly on stimulus magnitude and on stimulus area of stimulation in ways that can best be described in terms of values of β and k in Equation 1.

Equation 1 can be written in another form when the goal is to learn whether a given data set can be described by a power function and, if so, this form provides an estimate of the constants β and k. One simply takes the logarithm of both sides of Equation 1 so that it now becomes:

$$\log y = \log k + \beta.\log x \tag{2}$$

This equation describes a straight line whose *slope* is β. The test of conformity to the power law is now *linearity,* and the growth rate (power) is *slope.*

Equations 1 and 2 both may need refinement in order to cover sensations near absolute threshold. Then it has been useful to think of the stimulus magnitude as a distance above the threshold, or, mathematically as $(x - x_0)$, where x_0 approximates absolute threshold. This constant is critically important in the thermal domain (Stevens & Stevens, 1960).

In summary, category ratings provide simple and useful scales of sensory experience, but ratio scaling, especially magnitude estimation, has provided a psychophysical description that can deal with a broad scope of modalities, and of stimulus dimensions within a modality, in terms of the behavior of three constants: β, k, and x_0.

Simple Reaction Time

It usually happens throughout the sensory domain that the greater the sensation magnitude, the faster is the simple reaction time (for a review, see Woodworth & Schlosberg, 1954). Wright (1951) showed that reaction time to warmth varies inversely with stimulus intensity and areal extent, implying that intensity and area can be traded one for the other to determine any particular reaction time, or, in other words, that reaction time might substitute for thresholds and magnitude estimates to determine the rules of spatial summation. It was for Banks (1976) to work out these rules, not only for spatial summation but also for temporal summation (i.e., how magnitude and duration trade to preserve a constant reaction time) and to show that the rules of spatial and temporal summation are the same whether generated by response magnitude (e.g., by magnitude estimation) or by response latency.

PSYCHOPHYSICAL PROPERTIES OF THE THERMAL SENSES

Absolute Sensitivity

The ability to detect a thermal event, whether a minimal sensation of cold or warmth, depends not only on stimulus magnitude but also on factors listed earlier. These are touched on briefly here, but because of their predominant roles in thermal sensation, such subjects as spatial and temporal summation, regional distribution, and adaptation are also treated separately in later sections so as to take into account how they behave not only with respect to absolute sensitivity but also to sensory magnitude, hedonics, and reaction time.

Sensitivity clearly depends on the areal extent and locus of stimulation, but we start with the ability to detect whole-body (anterior or posterior) warming by infrared radiation (Hardy & Oppel, 1937). Although this quantity is small—about 1 milliwatt/cm² (or roughly a hundredth of the flux density cast by the sun normal to the body surface)—it is nevertheless some 15 billion times greater than the radiance necessary to cause a visual (threshold) impression. Nevertheless, this level of irradiation translates into an increase of skin temperature of only about 0.003°C. Thresholds for smaller parts of the body surface, such as the forehead, entire face, forearm plus hand, and face plus chest, have about the same magnitude as the threshold for the whole body, implying that there are limits on the area over which spatial summation can operate. Hardy and Oppel pointed out that even the fully clothed body is maximally sensitive to the thermal environment via the face or the arms and hands alone. A similar point could be made regarding animals whose integuments are protected by layers of fur, feathers, and scales.

Hardy and Oppel (1938) also examined cooling thresholds by radiation to a heat sink created by dry ice. Like warmth, cold shows spatial summation, but when the area of stimulation was large enough to encompass the head and chest (the closest they came to whole-body stimulation) the threshold turned out to be similar to that for warming—in both radiometric and temperature terms. Subsequent measurements of warm and cold thresholds for a part of the forearm suggest slightly greater sensitivity to cooling than to warming (Gray et al., 1982; Kenshalo, Holmes, & Wood, 1968; Kenshalo & Scott, 1966).

Heretofore in the discussion of absolute sensitivity, changes in radiation level of the body or changes of skin temperature have been considered as alternative measures of stimulus intensity. The tie between these alternatives was brought home best, perhaps, in a study by Kenshalo et al. (1967), which refuted earlier suggestions (Jenkins, 1951) that radiant and conducted thermal energy might act on different receptors or in different ways on the same receptors. This study made three important points, namely that thermal sensitivity depends on: (1) body site (forehead, forearm, and back) and (2) areal extent (spatial summation), but (3) not on whether the change in skin temperature at threshold was effected by radiation or conduction of heat to the skin.

Sensitivity would seem in the final analysis to be likewise independent of the spectrum of electromagnetic radiation of the stimulus, although it might appear otherwise simply because the skin absorbs some wavelengths (e.g., infrared) better than others (e.g., visible)—and black skin better than white skin—and at some depths better and faster than others (e.g., microwaves are strongly penetrating). Because the absorption of radiation depends on physical properties, investigators have deliberately varied those in order to get clues about how deep in the skin the receptors might lie (for a review, see Stevens, 1983). Although the exact depth(s) remains uncertain, it is clear, for example, that sensitivity to microwaves appears poorer than to infrared when surface skin temperature is arbitrarily (but customarily) taken as the measure of stimulus strength, simply because microwaves penetrate deeply into the body and thereby "bypass" thermal receptors nearer the surface. In conclusion, what would seem to matter is the change in temperature at the receptors.

Finally, there are doubtless personal differences in thermal sensitivity. Gross defects turn up infrequently, simply because sensitivity is necessary for personal survival. Smaller differences among people may exist but be difficult to prove. For example, no significant difference in warm and cold thresholds emerged from comparison, by a forced-choice procedure, of children and adults (Gray et al., 1982). Nor did any overall difference show up between young subjects (19–31 years old) and older ones (55–84) in detection of warm, cool, and pain thermally aroused, but in the same subjects and at the same dermal loci (hand and foot) aging brought deterioration of the detection of static and vibratory touch (Kenshalo, 1986). Similar deterioration characterizes vision, hearing, taste, and smell (for bibliographies on aging and the senses see Abramson & Lovas, 1988, and Corso, 1987).

Differential Sensitivity

As has been mentioned, scant attention has been paid to the capacity to detect changes or differences of thermal stimuli, apparently none at all for whole-body stimulation or as a function of virtually all of the variables shown to matter for absolute sensitivity (e.g., spatial and temporal configuration, adaptation, and spectral makeup of a radiant stimulus). Insufficient data exist to test rigorously Weber's law under any conditions of stimulation; however, what can be said is that with the hand a person can detect changes as small as $\Delta^0C = -0.025$ in cooling and $\Delta^0C = +0.01$ in warming (Johnson, Darian-Smith, & LaMotte, 1973). Whole-body changes should be no less detectable.

Temporal Factors and Thermal Perception

Adaptation and Recovery. We begin with *adaptation* and *recovery*, that is, the loss of responsiveness to thermal stimulation as a result of ongoing exposure to stimulation and its subsequent recovery during freedom from stimulation. The sensation of warmth aroused in a hand thrust into warm water gradually fades and may eventually vanish (complete adaptation), and water that hitherto felt thermally neutral may now feel cool; just the opposite occurs when the hand is initially thrust into cool water (facts already remarked in the 17th century by John Locke). By adaptation one can manipulate the temperature that feels neutral, called by the 19th-century physiologist Ewald Hering the *Nullpunkt,* or "physiological zero." Although all the senses exhibit adaptation, for thermal sensation, as for vision and smell, it ranks as one of two or so most salient features. Yet it has been charted sketchily at best and is only imperfectly understood, as compared, for example, with a second salient feature, spatial summation (details in a later section).

An issue of historical interest (see Kenshalo, 1978) concerns the limits of complete adaptation—in other words, the range of physiological zero, which a large number of studies going back to the turn of the century attempted to establish, but with egregious disagreement, presumably reflecting errors associated with different methods as well as the properties of adaptation specific to various body sites and areal extents. For example, sensations associated with small stimulus areas and low local sensitivity (and consequently weak subjective magnitude) seem to adapt faster and more completely, but we lack a quantitative model and a good physiological theory. Since adaptation depends on stimulus area, it would seem that central as well as peripheral (e.g., skin receptor) events must be involved, but we have little to go on.

To assess adaptation, a dynamic procedure came into use by Kenshalo and Scott (1966; see also Hensel, 1952), whose subjects adjusted the temperature of a heater–cooler device so as to maintain, in the face of continuous adaptation over time, a just-detectable warm or cool sensation in the forearm. Over some 40 min, skin temperature had to be increased (warm) and decreased (cool) to offset the effect of adaptation (Fig. 3.3). By this method and for this body site and area, the limits (asymptote) of adaptation ranged between only about 28^0 and 37.5^0C. Extension of this novel approach to representative sites and areas of the skin could greater broaden the picture and possibly clear away the ambiguities left by the earlier studies.

Even so, these and other studies narrow the attention to threshold sensations; in the long run we need to know also about how the "everyday" levels of suprathreshold sensation depend on adaptation level (as well as the locus and area) of the skin, in order to achieve a parametric and realistic schema of this basic thermal property.

Rate of Change.   Related to adaptation is rate of stimulus change. The same increment (or decrement) may prove detectable or undetectable, depending on whether gradual or abrupt. Thus, reflecting similarities in vision and hear-

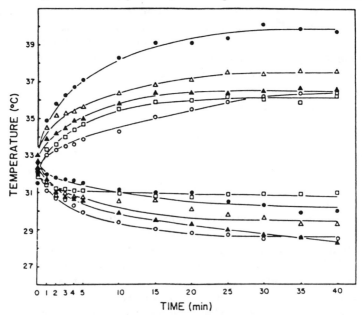

FIG. 3.3.   Showing the temperature selected by various subjects in order to maintain a just-perceptible sensation of warm (top curves) and cold (lower curves) over time. The asymptotes of these curves show the limits of complete thermal adaptation. Data from Kenshalo and Scott, 1966 and Kenshalo, 1970 (reprinted by permission of Academic Press).

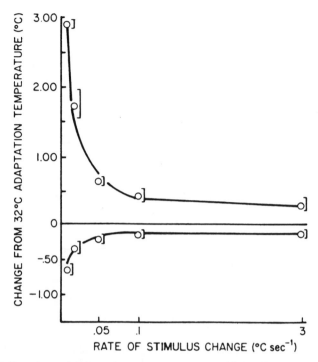

FIG. 3.4. Showing how absolute thresholds (ordinate) of cool (lower curve) and warm (upper curve), expressed as an increase or a decrease from adaptation level of 32°C, depend on the rate of stimulus change (abscissa) (reprinted from Kenshalo, 1970, by permission of Academic Press).

ing, detection might take an increment as large as 3⁰ or as small as 0.2⁰, depending on rate (see Fig. 3.4).

Temporal Summation. Another factor is duration. Often it happens that duration and intensity of a stimulus can trade one for the other to preserve a threshold or a suprathreshold sensation, a property called temporal summation. Stevens et al. (1973) showed that the warmth intensity threshold varied in nearly inverse proportion to the duration of infrared irradiation of a large part of the forehead. One second proved to be the critical duration, longer than which duration no longer matters (a much greater critical duration than the 0.1 to 0.2s found in vision and hearing) and shorter than which duration and thermal intensity trade, not quite, but almost, proportionally. This means, for example, that the intensity needed for detection is halved if the duration is approximately doubled—unless, of course, the duration is longer than a second. For suprathreshold warmth sensations, duration and intensity also trade, but the exact rules are more complex (see Marks & Stevens, 1973).

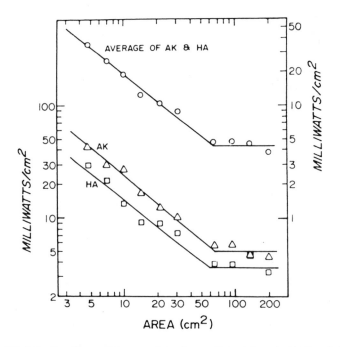

FIG. 3.5. Showing spatial summation of warmth for infrared radiation. Left ordinate applies to the individual results of two subjects; right ordinate to the average (geometrical mean) of the two subjects' results (reprinted from Stevens, Marks, & Simonson, 1974).

Spatial Factors and Thermal Perception

We deal here with the way warm and cold sensations depend on areal extent (spatial summation) and on local body site. Methods include thresholds, magnitude estimation, reaction time, and measures of spatial acuity.

Spatial summation means that intensity and areal extent can be traded to preserve threshold or any suprathreshold sensation from weak to strong or any reaction time from slow to fast. Trading varies from virtually complete reciprocity at threshold (e.g., doubling the area halves the threshold intensity) to no trading at all near the level of stimulation that feels just painful. Newcomers to this property often seem unimpressed that thermal sensations should grow greater with increasing skin area, but remember that vision, for example, behaves quite differently: Expanding the area of a light makes it look bigger in area, not brighter. In contrast, with pure thermal stimuli, one generally feels little or no gradation in apparent area, rather in apparent warmth or cold level! Of all characteristics of thermal sensibility none stands out more pervasively than spatial summation.

Several studies have measured absolute threshold at various body sites, such as the forehead, arm, chest, and back (among them, Hardy & Oppel, 1937; Kenshalo et al., 1967; Stevens, Marks, & Simonson, 1974). Fig. 3.5. shows results for the back. Here observe that area and irradiant flux trade in near proportionality; that means, for example, that when the area is doubled, the intensity (flux density) may be approximately halved and still preserve the threshold. However, this "reciprocity" breaks down abruptly at a critical area of about 60 cm². The horizontal segment beyond 60 cm² signifies total absence of summation; that is, increasing the area further leaves the threshold unchanged. Hardy and Oppel interpreted this area (undoubtedly different for different body sites) as corresponding to the stimulus threshold level of the most sensitive thermal receptors.

Figs. 3.6 and 3.7 illustrate how the rules for suprathreshold warmth summation on the back yielded to magnitude estimation (Stevens & Marks, 1971; Stevens et al., 1974); in these two studies the forehead, cheek, and calf all yielded the same basic picture as did the back. The subject estimated the apparent warmth of various combinations of area, from large to small, and intensity from weak to strong of infrared irradiation, each presented for 3s. The average estimate plots as a function of irradiation in the log–log coor-

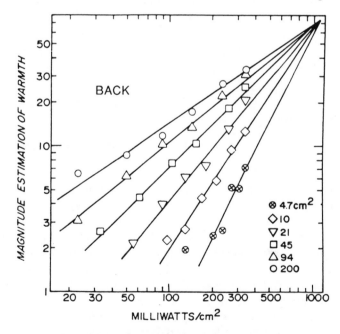

FIG. 3.6. Magnitude estimates of warmth averaged from 15 subjects (ordinate) plotted in log–log coordinates as a function of radiant intensity delivered to the back. The parameter is the areal extent of stimulation in square centimeters. Redrawn from Stevens, Marks, and Simonson, 1974.

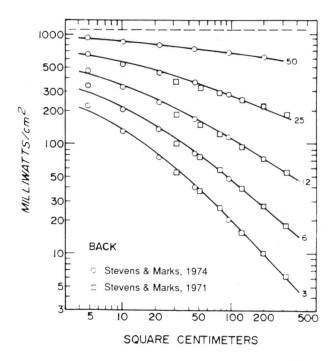

FIG. 3.7.   Equal-sensation contours for the back, showing how radiant intensity (ordinate) and areal extent (abscissa) trade to preserve several different levels of warmth from weak (3) to strong (50). The dotted line indicates the threshold
of thermally aroused pain, at which there is little or no spatial summation. The
circles were determined by Stevens, Marks, and Simonson (1974) from horizontal
cuts, at various levels of warmth, through the functions of Fig. 3.6. The squares
came from a similar study conducted by Stevens and Marks in 1971 at a different time of year and from another 14 subjects. Redrawn from Stevens, Marks,
and Simonson, 1974.

dinates of Fig. 3.6. Here one can note that (1) the functions plot as approximations to straight lines (obey S. S. Stevens's power law); (2) the slope (exponent) varied from about 0.7 ["diminishing returns"] for 200 cm² to about 2.0
["expanding returns"] for 4.7 cm²; (3) the functions converge at a high stimulus level, about 1000 milliwatt/cm², which approximates the thermal pain
threshold—at which, in accordance with independent assessments, little or
no spatial summation takes place (Green & Hardy, 1958); (4) a vertical cut
through the family of lines at any constant stimulus level (abscissa) reveals
that subjective warmth grows as a function of areal extent; and (5) a horizontal
cut at any constant warmth level (ordinate) serves to generate the various
combinations of area and intensity that arouse a constant level of apparent
warmth. The results of several such horizontal cuts at different warmth levels appear in the log–log coordinates of Fig. 3.7, showing suprathreshold trad-

ing functions analogous to the threshold trading function of Fig. 3.5. Note there the agreement between two data sets for studies done in 1971 and 1974 at different times of the year and on different subjects.

From these and other studies of other body sites emerges a general principle of thermal sensibility, namely that rich spatial summation always occurs near the threshold of warmth but declines gradually to zero summation at the threshold of pain. The warmth sense seems to furnish a compromise between two biological needs: (1) to register the heat over large stretches of the body, since from the point of view of body temperature regulation a low level integrated over area may amount to a very significant thermal load, and (2) the diminution of summation with increasing warmth frees the warmth sense for better acuity (localization) of stimuli that threaten to inflict local damage to the skin. In other words, summation and acuity tend to be mutually exclusive and level-dependent (see a later section).

It is one thing to note and to characterize psychophysically these two fundamental properties of the warmth sense, but quite another to explain them in terms of underlying anatomical and physiological principles. Stevens and Marks (1971) and Marks and Stevens (1973) have speculated that two populations of warmth receptors—(1) low-threshold units that converge on higher-order central integrators, and (2) nonsummating, high-threshold units—would explain the facts; physiological confirmation, however, is needed.

Finally, three experiments showed the operation of summation in novel functional ways. Marks and Gonzalez (1974) demonstrated that spatial summation operates along with internal body temperature (Cabanac, 1969), air temperature, and intensity, to codetermine the degree of pleasantness–unpleasantness of warming the skin; thus, the same thermal intensity can be judged pleasant or unpleasant depending on area. Likewise, in a series of painstaking measurements, Banks (1976) demonstrated that the trading rules for spatial and temporal summation of warmth are the same when constant reaction times are substituted for constant criterion warmth levels (the same for cold still needs to be demonstrated). And finally, Marks, Stevens, and Tepper (1976) demonstrated that spatial and temporal summation could operate to codetermine the warmth threshold for two infrared pulses delivered, with intervals between, to the sides of the forehead, proving that both temporal and spatial summation can take place interchangeably across the body midline (and therefore in the central nervous system).

In a study of spatial summation of cold (Stevens & Marks, 1979) subjects made magnitude estimations of the cold sensation aroused by touching briefly (2 to 8 s) copper disks having various areal extents and various temperatures, on three different occasions to the forearm, cheek, and back. The disks were embedded in Styrofoam surrounds that made the total area of skin contact a constant every time; under this condition the subjects were able to register no differences in area, only in cold sensation. The stimulus intensity was reckoned to be the change of skin temperature, Δt_{sk}, effected by application and measured with a thermocouple at the surface.

Average cold estimations appear in log–log coordinates, in Fig. 3.8 as a function of Δt_{sk} and in Fig. 3.9 as a function of areal extent. Straight lines approximate both families of functions, except for a tendency of the functions in Fig. 3.8 to approach a ceiling at high Δt_{sk} (definitively demonstrated in later experimentation; Stevens, 1979b). From Figs. 3.8 and 3.9 one can note that (1) Estimated cold approximates a power function of stimulus intensity (average exponent approximately constant at about 1.0) and of area A (average exponent constant at just a little less than 1.0); (2) The parallel lie of the functions argues that, unlike warmth summation, cold summation is level-independent. It follows from the fact that cold magnitude grows in near proportion to both intensity and area that these two variables are approximately equally important and can be traded for each other to produce any degree of cold sensation. This means, for example, that one can produce

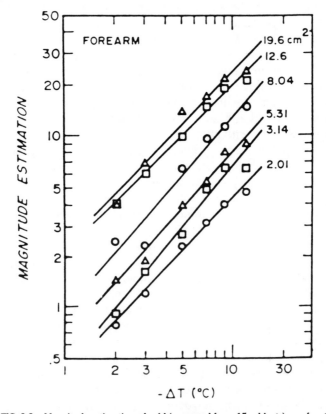

FIG. 3.8. Magnitude estimation of cold (averaged from 15 subjects) as a function in log–log coordinates of decrease of skin temperature from resting level. The parameter is areal extent on the forearm (reprinted from Stevens & Marks, 1979).

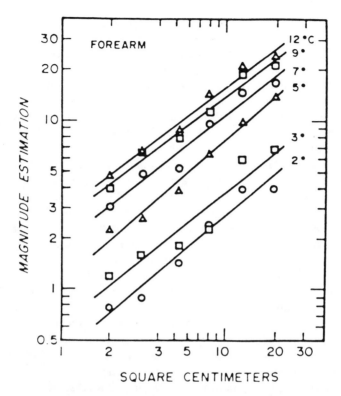

FIG. 3.9.   Same magnitude estimation of cold shown in Fig. 3.8, but here plotted in log–log coordinates as a function of areal extent. The parameter is the
decrease in skin temperature from resting level (reprinted from Stevens & Marks,
1979).

the same cold sensation by halving the intensity provided the area is doubled.

Why do the warmth and cold senses differ from each other with respect to level (in)dependence? The answer may relate to the relative urgency of high-level heating (burning), compared with cooling. It usually takes long to damage the skin by freezing so that localization may be less crucial (see a later section). Unfortunately, there appear to be no data on localization of cold like those relating localization to warmth magnitude.

Regional Skin Differences in Thermal Perception.   It has long been recognized that some body sites are more responsive than others to thermal stimulation, but until the utilization of suprathreshold scaling methods there were
only scattered "handbook" data, thresholds, and spot mappings, difficult to
generalize and interpret. Magnitude estimation has furnished a more functional and comprehensive picture. Graded sets of warm (Stevens, Marks, &
Simonson, 1974) and cold (Stevens, 1979b) stimuli were applied briefly one

by one to 10 body sites as shown in Fig. 3.10 and estimated on a common scale of sensation. A psychophysical function was thereby generated for each site. All 10 warmth functions approximated power functions, whose constants β and k characterized the particular site; so did the 10 cold functions, except that each approached a ceiling beyond which cold sensation grew no further with decrease of stimulus temperature.

By means of horizontal cuts through this family of 10 psychophysical functions for warmth, analogous to the cuts made through Fig. 3.6 to obtain the functions of Fig. 3.7 relating area and intensity for constant warmth (spatial summation), one can generate regional "profiles" of warmth sensitivity, shown in Fig. 3.11. The most prominent feature is the progressive diminution in slope of the profiles, from a low-level warmth level (a little above threshold) to a high one (near pain threshold). Thus, at the lowest level shown the calf requires four times stronger stimulation than the forehead, but near the pain threshold about the same level of stimulation. This finding reminds one of similar differences among different areal extents within a given body site: low-level sensitivity differences related both to areal extent and to body site give way to uniformity of sensitivity as the pain threshold and the peril of local burning approach.

The "ceiling" on the cold functions prevented construction of good profiles like those in Fig. 3.11; instead, the results are shown in Fig. 3.12 as the degree of cold estimation, for each of the 10 regions as a function of stimulus intensity. One sees, though, that the striking differences at low-level stimulation (30°C) give way to fairly uniform response at high-level stimulation (e.g., 9°C).

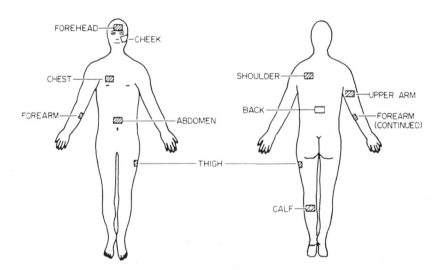

FIG. 3.10. The 10 body sites stimulated by warm (reprinted from Stevens, Marks, & Simonson, 1974) and by cold (Stevens & Marks, 1979).

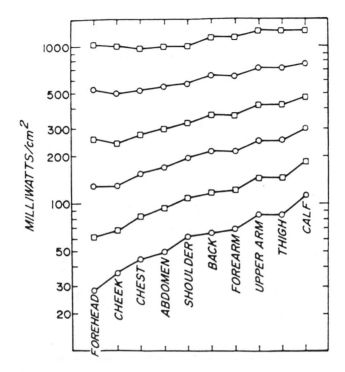

FIG. 3.11. Six equal-warmth profiles for the 10 regions shown in Fig. 3.10, here arranged in order of decreasing sensitivity. Each profile shows the stimulus level needed to arouse a given constant level of warmth from a little above the warmth threshold (lowest profile) to the threshold of pain (highest profile). Note the progressive flattening of the profiles (reprinted from Stevens, Marks, & Simonson, 1974).

Thus, for neither warmth nor cold does threshold sensation tell the whole story about regional responsiveness to thermal stimulation. Nevertheless, the regional differences in ability to detect low levels of stimulation are interesting, and strikingly different for warmth and cold. For warmth the body regions fall into three clusters: head, trunk, limbs, in that order of sensitivity; for cold into the same clusters: in the (*different*) order of sensitivity trunk, limbs, head. These differences can readily be observed when bathing in cool and tepid water.

Spatial Acuity. The measures here are thermal analogs of the two-point threshold and error of point localization in touch; that is, how well can a person distinguish two purely thermal fields from one? how well distinguish the locus of one field from another? For cold, no data seem to exist, but for warmth the answer to the first question is, *hardly at all* (Cain, 1973), because the two fields fuse to a single image, usually vaguely localized midway; to the sec-

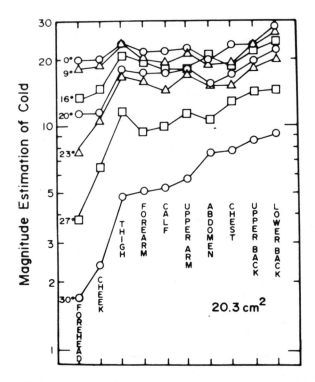

FIG. 3.12. Magnitude estimation of cold sensation (averaged from 15 subjects) in the 10 regions shown in Fig. 3.10, here arranged in order of increasing sensitivity to 30°C stimulation. The parameter here is temperature (°C) of a 20.3-cm² stimulator (reprinted from Stevens, 1979b).

ond question, *poorly,* but the warmer the stimulation, the better the localization (Nathan & Rice, 1966; Simmell & Shapiro, 1969; Taus, Stevens, & Marks, 1975). This level-dependence fits well the two-function model of the warmth sense (Stevens & Marks, 1971). Thermal localization can prove fickle; a person often confuses warmth, but never tactile, stimulation of the front and back of the body! (Cain, 1973)

THERMOTACTILE INTERACTIONS

For the last century warmth, cold, touch, and pain have generally been treated as separate modalities, but there are interactions among them. Some of these (1–3 of the following list) seem to involve thermal stimulation of touch receptors, others (4–7) genuine interactions among the outputs from thermal, tactile, and pain receptors.

    1. *Thermal adaptation of touch.* Prolonged cooling of the skin degrades

several kinds of tactile discrimination: (a) two-point and two-edge discrimination; (b) punctate pressure sensitivity (Stevens et al., 1977); (c) vibration thresholds (Green, 1977a); (d) static pressure sensation (Stevens & Hooper, 1982); (e) electrocutaneous sensitivity (Larkin & Reilly, 1986); (f) electrically aroused pain (Bini, Cruccu, Hagbarth, Schady, & Torebjörk, 1984); and (g) perceived roughness (Green, Lederman, & Stevens, 1979). Degradation could reflect cold block of neural activity or physical changes in the skin and its blood supply. Prolonged warming (short of painful) has little or no adverse effect and sometimes even enhances sensitivity (Green, 1977a; Green et al., 1979; Larkin & Reilly, 1986; Stevens & Hooper, 1982; Stevens et al., 1977).

2. *Thermal intensification.* In 1846, Weber noted that cold objects on the skin can feel heavier than warm ones. This phenomenon received little attention until the 1950s, when physiologists first noted that many neural fibers from the skin that respond primarily to mechanical indentation of the skin also respond secondarily to cooling. Further investigation (Stevens, 1979a; Stevens & Green, 1978b) confirmed and extended Weber's observation with the following generalizations (see Fig. 3.13): (a) compared with a neutral object, the colder an object, the heavier it feels, and to any site on the skin; (b) the warmer an object, the heavier it feels, but this (warm) intensification is smaller than cold intensification, though reliably measurable at some body sites; (c) weight (pressure) does not, in "reverse," intensify thermal sensation (Zimmermann & Stevens, 1982).

3. *Thermal sharpening.* The experiments on thermal intensification revealed that to a touch-sensitive site, such as the palm, the same weight feels

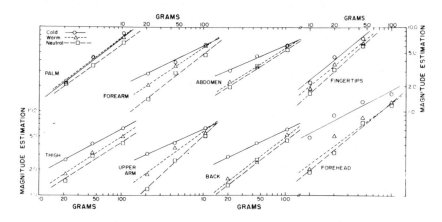

FIG. 3.13. Magnitude estimation (averaged from 20 subjects) of apparent heaviness of cold, warm, and neutral weights, plotted in log–log coordinates as a function of weight in grams. The six body regions shown to the left are replotted from Stevens (1979a); the results at the right for the forehead (20 subjects) are from Stevens and Green (1978) and, for the fingertips (20 subjects), previously unpublished.

heavier than to a less sensitive site, such as the back, and, furthermore, that weight-sensitive areas such as the palm typically also have greater spatial acuity as gauged by the two-point threshold and the error of point localization. This led to the prediction that in addition to intensifying tactile magnitude, temperature might also *sharpen* tactile acuity; and, indeed, measures of the two-point threshold at forehead, forearm, and palm showed that the colder and warmer the points are, the easier they are to discriminate (Stevens, 1982, 1989). This finding is provocative in view of the near-absence of two-field discrimination of pure thermal stimulation mentioned earlier. Thermal sharpening may reflect a steepening of the spatial gradient of mechanoreceptor activity in the vicinity of the contact points.

4. *Thermal referral.* It is well known that the pain from a heart attack is usually "referred" away from its origin to a remote site, such as the arm or chin. In similar but "normal" fashion a thermal sensation may be localized far from its site of stimulation. In general, touch sensations localize quite accurately and they tend to "draw" simultaneous thermal sensations to their apparent locus. Green (1977b, 1978) studied this and other interactions by simultaneously touching two or three heater-cooler stimulators in a line; when, for example, the two outer units are warm (cold) the inner unit also feels warm (cold); that this referral is no mere "suggestion" follows from the observation that no referral takes place from two fingers of the left hand to a finger of the right hand. In its simplest manifestation, a referral requires only two sites of stimulation, one touch, the other thermal; the thermal and touch sensations will, within limits (up to at least 16 cm on the arm), localize to the site of the touch. Thus, the thermal senses seem to "borrow" the superior localization capacity of the touch system, and that explains why we have the illusion that we can localize the source of heating or cooling with precision.

5. *Thermal enhancement.* When two simultaneous thermal stimuli have unequal intensities but the same quality, the stronger of the two enhances the strength of the weaker; stated another way, uneven thermal stimulation tends to result in a more unitary, "smoothed out," sensation. The thermal senses seem to "suppress" quantitative variegation.

6. *Thermal dominance.* When two simultaneous thermal stimuli have opposite qualities and different intensities the stronger quality may inhibit (dominate) the weaker quality so that only one is experienced; in other words the thermal senses tend to "suppress" qualitative as well as quantitative variegation.

7. *Synthetic heat.* Green confirmed that nearby simultaneous warm and cold stimulation may also arouse so-called "synthetic heat" (Alrutz, 1898), a surprisingly salient experience of "stinging," but not painful, heat. This phenomenon, usually studied with alternating hot and cold strips, and having a history of controversy, has frequently been invoked to explain "heat"

sensation as aroused normally by simultaneous firing of warm and of (paradoxically) cold receptors.

OVERVIEW

It may have struck the reader that the global response of the human organism to the thermal environment is relatively simple. This response is often categorical—either acceptance or avoidance, pleasure or discomfort, seeking or escaping—depending on whether the well-being of the organism (or one of its parts) is promoted or jeopardized by its circumstances. In contrast, the events that lead up to the simple response are anything but simple and demand no less than the integration of a vastly complex spatiotemporal pattern of stimulation of the body. It has been a goal of this chapter to enlarge the reader's appreciation of the variety of mechanisms by which this is achieved.

It may also have struck the reader that the study of the thermal senses has been a multidisciplinary affair involving the insights of the physicist, physiologist, and psychologist. Indeed, the study of the senses in general has benefited from a blending of their peculiar methods, history, objectives, and fads. At times these practitioners have proceeded as if the others did not exist, sometimes with the admitted vision that single-mindedness affords, at other times, though, with the blindness that provincial isolation inflicts. At still other times, but rarely, one individual is able to do the work of all three, as for example Helmholtz and others in the visual domain, von Békésy in the auditory, and J. D. Hardy in his lifetime career devoted to the study of human responses to the thermal environment (Hardy, Gagge, & Stolwijk, 1970; Stevens & Green, 1978a). The multidisciplinary spirit that Hardy and his many collaborators breathed in the middle half of our century, with its respect for the insights and tools of many, could well serve as inspiration for the future.

ACKNOWLEDGMENT

Preparation supported by Grant No. NS15419 from the National Institutes of Health.

REFERENCES

Abramson, M., & Lovas, P. M. (1988). *Aging and sensory change: An annotated bibliography.* Washington, DC: Gerontological Society of America.

Alrutz, S. (1898). On the temperature senses: II. The sensation "hot." *Mind, 7*(2), 140–144.

Banks, W. P. (1976). Areal and temporal summation in the thermal reaction time. *Sensory Processes*, *1*, 2–13.

Bini, G. G., Cruccu, J., Hagbarth, K. E., Schady, W. S., & Torebjörk, E. (1984). Analgesic effect of vibration and cooling on pain induced by intraneural electrical stimulation. *Pain, 18*, 239–248.

Blix, M. (1884). Experimentele Beiträge zur lösung der Frage über die spezifische Energie des Hautnerven. *Zeitschrift für Biologie, 20,* 141–156.

Boring, E. G. (1942). *Sensation and perception in the history of experimental psychology.* New York: Appleton-Century-Croft.

Cabanac, M. (1969). Plaisir ou déplaisir de la sensation thermique et homothermic. *Physiology and Behavior, 4,* 359–363.

Cain, W. S. (1973). Spatial discrimination of cutaneous warm. *American Journal of Psychology, 86,* 169–181.

Corso, J. F. (1987). Sensory–perceptual processes and aging. In K. W. Schaie, & C. Eisdorfer (Eds.), *Annual review of gerontology and geratrics* (Chap. 2, pp. 29–55). New York: Springer.

Dallenbach, K. (1927). The temperature spots and end-organs. *American Journal of Psychology, 39,* 402–427.

Darian-Smith, I. (1984a). Thermal sensibility. In J. M. Brookhart, V. B. Mountcastle, I. Darian-Smith, & S. R. Geiger (Eds.), *Handbook of physiology: The nervous system* (pp. 879–913). Bethesda, MD: American Physiological Society.

Darian-Smith, I. (1984b). The sense of touch: Performance and peripheral neural processes. In J. M. Brookhart, V. B. Mountcastle, I. Darian-Smith, & S. R. Geiger (Eds.), *Handbook of physiology: The nervous system* (pp. 739–788). Bethesda, MD: American Physiological Society.

Darian-Smith, I., Johnson, K. O., and Dykes, R. W. (1973). "Cold" fiber population innervating palmar and digital skin of the monkey: responses to cooling pulses. *Journal of Neurophysiology, 36,* 325–346.

Darian-Smith, I., Johnson, K. O., LaMotte, C., Kenins, P., Shigenaga, Y., and Ming, C. V. (1979). Coding of incremental changes in skin temperature by single warm fibers in the monkey. *Journal of Neurophysiology, 42,* 1316–1331.

Donaldson, H. H. (1885). On the temperature sense. *Mind, 10,* 399–416.

Duclaux, R., and Kenshalo, D. R. Sr. (1980). Response characteristics of cutaneous warm receptors in the monkey. *Journal of Neurophysiology, 43,* 1–15.

Fechner, G. (1860/1966). *Elements of psychophysics* (H. E. Adler, Trans.). (pp. 167–175). New York: Holt, Rinehart, & Winston.

Gagge, A. P., Stolwijk, A. J., & Hardy, J. D. (1967). Comfort and thermal sensations and associated physiological responses at various ambient temperatures. *Environmental Research, 1,* 1–20.

Gescheider, G. A. (1985). *Psychophysics: Method, theory, and application.* Hillsdale, NJ: Lawrence Erlbaum Associates.

Gisolfi, C. V., & Wenger, C. B. (1984). Temperature regulation during exercise: Old concepts, new ideas. In R. L. Terjung (Ed.), *Exercise and Sport Sciences Reviews, 12,* 339–372. Lexington, MA: Collamore Press.

Goldscheider, A. (1884). Die spezifische Energie der Temperaturnerven. *Monatshefte Praktische Dermatologie, 3,* (Pt. 1, 198–208; Pt. 2, 225–241).

Gray, G., Stevens, J. C., & Marks, L. E. (1982). Thermal stimulus thresholds: Sources of variability. *Physiology and Behavior, 29,* 355–360.

Green, B. G. (1977a). The effect of skin temperature on vibrotactile sensitivity. *Perception & Psychophysics, 21,* 243–248.

Green, B. G. (1977b). Localization of thermal sensation: An illusion and synthetic heat. *Perception & Psychophysics, 22,* 331–337.

Green, B. G. (1978). Referred thermal sensations: Warmth vs. cold. *Sensory Processes, 2,* 220–230.

Green, B. G., Lederman, S. J., & Stevens, J. C. (1979). The effect of skin temperature on the perception of roughness. *Sensory Processes, 3,* 327–333.

Green, L. C., & Hardy, J. D. (1958). Spatial summation of pain. *Journal of Applied Physiology, 13,* 457–464.

Hardy, J. D. (1961). Physiology of temperature regulation. *Physiological Review, 41,* 521–605.

Hardy, J. D., Gagge, A. P., & Stolwijk, J. A. J. (Eds.) (1970). *Physiological and Behavioral Temperature Regulation.* Springfield, Ill.: Charles C. Thomas.

Hardy, J. D., & Oppel, T. W. (1937). Studies in temperature sensation III. The sensitivity of the body to heat and the spatial summation of the end organ responses. *Journal of Clinical Investigation, 16,* 533–540.

Hardy, J. D., & Oppel, T. W. (1938). Studies in temperature sensation IV. The stimulation of cold sensation by radiation. *Journal of Clinical Investigation, 17,* 771–778.

Hardy, J. D., Wolff, H. G., & Goodell, H. (1952). *Pain sensations and reactions.* Baltimore: Williams & Wilkins.

Head, H. (1920). *Studies in neurology.* London: Oxford Medical Publications.

Hellon, R. F., & Mitchell, D. (1975). Convergence in a thermal afferent pathway in the rat. *Journal of Physiology, 248,* 359–376.

Hensel, H. (1952). Physiologie der Thermoreception, Ergebnisse der Physiologie. *Biolgischen Chemie und Experimentellen Pharmakologie, 47,* 166–368.

Hensel, H. (1982). *Thermal sensations and thermoreceptors in man.* Springfield, IL: Charles C. Thomas.

Jenkins, W. L. (1951). Somesthesis. In S. S. Stevens (Ed.), *Handbook of experimental psychology* (pp. 1172–1190). New York: Wiley.

Johnson, K. O., Darian-Smith, I., & LaMotte, C. (1973). Peripheral neural determinants of temperature discrimination in man: A correlative study of response to cooling skin. *Journal of Neurophysiology, 36,* 347–370.

Katz, D. (1925). *Der Aufbau der Tastwelt.* Leipzig, Germany: Barth. (For an English translation, see L. E. Krueger, Ed. [1989]. *The world of touch.* Hillsdale, NJ: Lawrence Erlbaum Associates)

Kenshalo, D. R. (1976). Correlations of temperature sensitivity in man and monkey, a first approximation. In F. Y. Zotterman (Ed.), *Sensory functions of the skin in primates* (pp. 305–329). New York: Pergamon Press.

Kenshalo, D. R., and Duclaux, R., (1977). Response characteristics of cutaneous cold receptors in the monkey. *Journal of Neurophysiology, 40,* 319–322.

Kenshalo, D. R. (1978). Biophysics and psychophysics of feeling. In E. C. Caterette, & M. P. Friedman (Eds.), *Handbook of perception. VI B* (Chap. 2, pp. 30–74). New York: Academic Press.

Kenshalo, D. R. (1986). Somesthetic sensitivity in young and elderly humans. *Journal of Gerontology, 41,* 732–742.

Kenshalo, D. R., Decker, T., & Hamilton, A. (1967). Spatial summation on the forehead, forearm, and back produced by radiant and conducted heat. *Journal of Comparative and Physiological Psychology, 63,* 510–515.

Kenshalo, D. R., Holmes, C. E., & Wood, P. B. (1968). Warm and cool thresholds as a function of rate of stimulus temperature change. *Perception & Psychophysics, 3,* 81–84.

Kenshalo, D. R., & Scott, H. A. J. (1966). Temporal course of thermal adaptation. *Science, 151,* 1095–1096.

Larkin, W. D., & Reilly, J. P. (1986). Electrocutaneous sensitivity: Effects of skin temperature. *Somatosensory Research, 3,* 261–271.

Marks, L. E. (1974). *Sensory processes: The new psychophysics.* New York: Academic Press.

Marks, L. E., & Gonzalez, R. R. (1974). Skin temperature modifies the pleasantness of thermal stimuli. *Nature, 247,* 473–475.

Marks, L. E., & Stevens, J. C. (1973). Spatial summation of warmth: Influence of duration and configuration of the stimulus. *American Journal of Psychology, 86,* 251–267.

Marks, L. E., Stevens, J. C., & Tepper, S. J. (1976). Interaction of spatial and temporal summation in the warmth sense. *Sensory Processes, 1,* 87–98.

Nathan, P. W., & Rice, R. (1966). The localization of warm stimuli. *Neurology, 16,* 533–540.

Perl, E. R. (1984). Pain and nociception. In J. M. Brookhart, V. B. Mountcastle, I. Darian-Smith, & S. R. Geiger (Eds.), *Handbook of physiology. Sec. 1: The nervous system* (Vol. 3, pp. 915–975). Bethesda, MD: American Physiological Society.

Rein, H. (1925). Über die Topographie der Warmempfindung. *Zeitschrift für Biologie, 82,* 513–535.

Simmell, M. L., & Shapiro, A. (1969). The localization of non-tactile thermal sensations. *Psychophysiology, 5,* 415–425.

Stevens, J. C. (1979a). Thermal intensification of touch sensation: Further extensions of the Weber phenomenon. *Sensory Processes, 3,* 240–248.

Stevens, J. C. (1979b). Variation of cold sensitivity over the body surface. *Sensory Processes, 3,* 317–326.

Stevens. J. C. (1982). Temperature can sharpen tactile acuity. *Perception & Psychophysics, 31,* 577–580.

Stevens, J. C. (1983). Thermal sensation: Infrared and microwaves. In E. R. Adair (Ed.), *Microwaves and thermoregulation.* New York: Academic Press, 191–201.

Stevens, J. C. (1989). Temperature and the two-point threshold. *Somatosensory and Motor Research, 6,* 275–284.

Stevens, J. C., & Green, B. G. (1978a). History of research on feeling. In E. C. Carterett & M. P. Friedman (Eds.), *Handbook of perception. 6B* (pp. 3–25). New York: Academic Press.

Stevens, J. C., & Green, B. G. (1978b). Temperature–touch interaction: Weber's phenomenon revisited. *Sensory Processes, 2,* 206–219.

Stevens, J. C., Green, B. G., & Krimsley, A. S. (1977). Punctate pressure sensitivity: Effects of skin temperature. *Sensory Processes, 1,* 238–243.

Stevens, J. C., & Hooper, J. E. (1982). How skin and object temperature influence touch sensation. *Perception & Psychophysics, 32,* 282–285.

Stevens, J. C., & Marks, L. E. (1971). Spatial summation and the dynamics of warmth sensation. *Perception & Psychophysics, 9,* 391–398.

Stevens, J. C, & Marks, L. E. (1979). Spatial summation of cold. *Physiology and Behavior, 22,* 541–547.

Stevens, J. C., Marks, L. E., & Simonson, D. C. (1974). Regional sensitivity and spatial summation in the warmth sense. *Physiology and Behavior, 13,* 825–836.

Stevens, J. C., Okulicz, W. C., & Marks, L. E. (1973). Temporal summation at the warmth threshold. *Perception & Psychophysics, 14,* 307–312.

Stevens, J. C., & Stevens, S. S. (1960). Warmth and cold: Dynamics of sensory intensity. *Journal of Experimental Psychology, 60,* 183–192.

Stevens, S. S. (1975). *Psychophysics: Introduction to its perceptual, neural, and social prospects.* New York: Wiley.

Strughold, H., & Porz, R. (1931). Die Dichte der Kaltpunkte auf der Haut des menschlichen Körpers. *Zeitschrift für Biologie, 91,* 563–571.

Swets, J. A. (Ed.). (1964). *Signal detection and recognition by human observers.* New York: Wiley.

Taus, R. H., Stevens, J. C., & Marks, L. E. (1975). Spatial localization of warmth. *Perception & Psychophysics, 17,* 194–196.

Weber, E. H. (1978). *The sense of touch.* The English translations of De Tactu (1834) and Der Tastsinn by H. E. Ross & D. J. Murap. London: Academic Press.

Woodworth, R. S., & Schlosberg, H. (1954). *Experimental psychology* (rev. ed., pp. 274–275). New York: Holt, Rinehart, & Winston.

Wright, G. H. (1951). The latency of sensations of warmth due to radiation. *Journal of Physiology, 112,* 344–358.

Zimmermann, R. J., & Stevens, J. C. (1982). Temperature–touch interactions: Is there a reverse Weber phenomenon? *Bulletin of the Psychonomic Society, 19,* 269–270.

4

PAIN RESPONSIVENESS

Gary B. Rollman
University of Western Ontario

Given the universal nature of pain, it is surprising how difficult its definition can be. A moment's reflection may, however, bring the difficulty to the fore. Can you define pain without invoking synonyms such as "hurt" or variants such as "painful?"

Further reflection may raise additional problems. Is pain a sensation, a perception, an emotion, or a thought? How should it be compared with the other sensory experiences described in this volume? Does it belong in a unique category or is it part of a continuum with pressure or heat or cold?

Individuals faced with the task of dealing with pain, whether as researchers or clinicians, need to consider these philosophical dilemmas, but they also need to get on with the task of quantifying pain, attempting to alleviate it, and addressing the efficacy of their treatments. Fascinating challenges confront them in each of these endeavors.

While there is no universally accepted definition of pain, there is, in fact, an "official" one, presented by the Subcommittee on Taxonomy of the International Association for the Study of Pain (Merskey, 1986a). Their definition states that pain is "an unpleasant sensory and emotional experience associated with actual or potential tissue damage, or described in terms of such damage."

Note, first, that the definition emphasizes two components of pain: the sensory and the emotional. While the two are often linked, evidence from laboratory and clinical studies suggests that they can be distinguished and, often, treated separately.

Note, also, that pain is not necessarily linked to tissue damage. In fact, pain can arise in the absence of any evident physical injury and, in other instances, can persist long after the healing of a wound.

The difficulty in evaluating pain is well summarized by the subcommittee's note that "pain is always subjective." While insurance companies, attorneys, or worker's compensation boards may understandably wish for a "pain thermometer" to distinguish between "real" pain and "unreal" pain motivated by compensation claims (Mendelson, 1984), such a device will never be developed. Individual pain experiences are inextricably linked to early life events, social and cultural conditioning, and the behaviors of role models (Craig, 1986). Pain judgments are often relative, not absolute (Rollman, 1979). As the subcommittee aptly stated, if individuals "regard their experience as pain, it should be accepted as pain."

THEORIES OF PAIN

The classical view of pain, best exemplified by the description offered by Descartes in the 17th century but carried over to more recent anatomical and physiological thinking, sees the pain system as involving a direct path from the skin to the brain. Injury at the periphery is signaled to a central pain monitor. In Descartes's model, the message is likened to a tug on a rope that rings a bell in a church steeple; the more contemporary version of this model speaks of barrages of neural impulses arising from the site of injury and conveyed directly through the central nervous system to a cortical pain center. Both approaches emphasize the notion of *specificity:* specific peripheral receptors, pathways, brain centers, and sensations. Such theories, while attractive, are clearly wrong in the light of present-day knowledge of anatomy, physiology, and clinical data.

An alternative view of the mechanisms underlying pain led to the development of pattern theory. In its extreme form (e.g., Nafe, 1929), it suggested that an individual fiber "could at one time contribute towards the experience of a sensation of touch, and at another towards the experience of pain, cold, or warmth" (Sinclair, 1955). The emphasis was on the temporal and spatial components of the peripheral neural activity—factors such as frequency of action potentials, duration of activity, and the number of responding fibers.

Both pattern theory and specificity theory were challenged by anatomical and physiological data. Specificity theory is shown to be wrong by the lack of receptors, nerve fibers, spinal tracts, or brain areas whose activity invariably gives rise to reports of pain and by the failure of neurosurgical or pharmacological interventions at any of these putative pain units to eliminate pain reliably. Pattern theory is an oversimplification. Nerve endings are not equally sensitive to all cutaneous modalities. As we'll see, evidence shows that there is a high degree of specialization within the peripheral somatosensory system, such that many nerve fibers respond only to very intense stimuli and are uninfluenced by light touch or moderate heat or cold.

An adequate pain theory needs to consider anatomical and physiological knowledge, clinical data on the causes and treatment of pain, and the influence of psychological factors on pain behaviors. Specificity theory and pattern theory dealt somewhat poorly with the first, very poorly with the second, and wholly ignored the third. A revolution in pain research and treatment was begun in 1965 by the publication of an article entitled "Pain Mechanisms: A New Theory," written by an experimental psychologist, Ronald Melzack, and a neurophysiologist, Patrick Wall. The two, who were then colleagues at the Massachusetts Institute of Technology, introduced an integrative theory, which, as we'll see, was far-reaching in its impact on pain research and management.

THE ANATOMY AND PHYSIOLOGY OF PAIN: ASCENDING SYSTEMS

Three regions require examination: the peripheral receptors and nerve fibers, the ascending tracts within the spinal cord, and the subcortical and cortical areas of the brain (see Fig. 4.1).

Little is known about receptor cells in the skin that might respond to noxious inputs (and thus would be called nociceptors). Von Frey (1895) had suggested that the free nerve endings serve this purpose, while the encapsulated endings such as Pacinian corpuscles, Ruffini cylinders, and Krause end bulbs mediate other somatosensory experiences such as pressure, warmth, and cold. Although von Frey's assignment of specific receptors to specific sensations is certainly wrong, the attention of physiological investigations of the periphery has largely been devoted to studying the afferent nerve fibers rather than the receptors.

Examination of these fibers reveals a wide range of diameters as well as the presence or absence of a myelin sheath. This discussion will emphasize those fibers that convey sensory information, but it should be noted that many of the fibers are sympathetic axons that regulate autonomic functions or motor axons that influence muscles.

The sensory fibers are divided into three distinct groups: the myelinated A-beta and A-delta fibers and the unmyelinated C-fibers. The A-beta fibers, with a diameter of 5 to 20 microns (a micron is one-thousandth of a millimeter, or about one-twenty-five-thousandth of an inch) are relatively large, rapidly conducting, and maximally responsive to weak mechanical stimulation. The A-delta fibers have an intermediate size (1–5 microns), a moderate conduction velocity, and respond best to intense pressure or heat, although some also respond to cold and irritating chemicals. Because of their high threshold

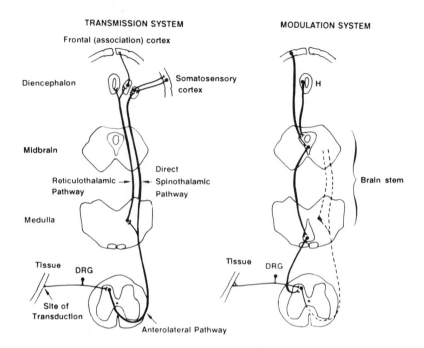

FIG. 4.1.   A schematic diagram of the major ascending and descending systems involved in the transmission and modulation of nociceptive information. DRG-dorsal root ganglion; H-hypothalamus (from M. Osterweis, A. Kleinman, & D. Mechanic (Eds.), *Pain and Disability. Clinical, Behavioral, and Public Policy Perspectives;* copyright, 1987, by the National Academy of Sciences, National Academy Press, Washington, DC; reprinted by permission).

and the finding that stimulation of the A-delta fibers often gives rise to a sharp, pricking pain, these afferents have been labeled "myelinated nociceptors."

The narrow diameter (.3 to 2 microns), unmyelinated C-fibers are very slowly conducting. They, too, respond best to noxious levels of stimulation in their rather small receptive fields. Interestingly, they are the most common fiber in most peripheral nerves and, generally, respond only to intense stimulation.

The nature of the stimulus is less important than its intensity: high levels of pressure, heat, cold, or chemicals (such as bradykinin or the prostaglandins that are released from damaged tissue) will induce bursts of activity in these fibers, causing them to be labeled "unmyelinated nociceptors" or "C polymodal nociceptors." Their action seems to be associated with delayed but prolonged experiences of dull or burning pain. In fact, observers presented with repetitive thermal or electrical pulses report two pains: The first is sharp and the second, which may occur as much as a second later, is described as burning or throbbing (Price, Hu, Dubner, & Gracely, 1977). The differential response time is in keeping with the idea that the first is subserved by the rapidly conducting A-delta fibers, while the second is due to activity in the slowly conducting C-fibers. So, too, is the finding that first pain can be abolished by a pressure block of the myelinated fibers (Price et al., 1977), while the second pain is eliminated by selective blocking of unmyelinated fibers using local anesthetics.

The pain transmission process only begins at the periphery. The capacity to stimulate large and small fibers selectively, to record their electrical activity in human subjects (Torebjörk & Hallin, 1973) and to correlate neural information with subjective reports of quality and intensity provides the opportunity for very elegant psychophysical investigations. Nonetheless, the more central spinal cord and brain mechanisms modulate the activity arising in the sensory fibers and provide the locus for psychological factors to interact with first-order physiological variables mediated by the primary afferents.

The second-order neural pathways are found in the spinal cord. Here, the simplicity of the peripheral coding mechanism gives way to a system of enormous complexity. The spinal cord receives inputs from both nociceptive and nonnociceptive afferents, receptive fields for spinal neurons are often much larger than for nerve fibers, and excitatory influences are balanced by inhibitory ones that arise from both afferent activity and descending influences from the brain stem and cortex (Fields, 1987).

The examination of spinal influences on nociception is focused on the dorsal horn at the rear of the cord. Examination of a cross-section of this gray matter reveals a series of 10 layers or laminae. The A-delta fibers project to laminae I and V, the C-fibers end principally in lamina II, while the larger A-beta fibers terminate in lamina III and deeper.

Nociceptive projection neurons that pass the message to higher brain centers are identified by their ability to respond maximally to noxious stimuli, by their projection to areas known to be involved in pain processing, by the generation of pain experiences when they are activated electrically, and by the reduction of pain when their activity is reduced (Fields, 1987). Such neurons are widely distributed within the spinal cord.

About a quarter of the spinal neurons respond only to noxious stimuli. These analogues of the peripheral nociceptors (which, in fact, project directly to them) are labeled "nociceptive-specific" neurons. They are outnumbered, however, by neurons that receive input from both low-threshold mechanoreceptors and high-threshold nociceptors. Such "wide dynamic range" neurons, which tend to have large receptive fields, respond weakly to brushing, pressure, and mild pinch but vigorously to strong pressure or pinch.

It may seem surprising to have two distinct classes of spinal cord neurons involved in relaying information about pain. It may also seem surprising that the second class, the wide dynamic range neurons, are activated by both noxious and innocuous stimuli. Consider, however, that pain can be produced by a wide variety of stimuli—intense heat or cold, strong pressure or pinch, electrical pulses, certain classes of chemicals. The resulting pain sensations are not identical—they differ in quality, intensity, location, and duration. A straight-through pain system that signaled simply the absence or presence of pain would not provide the coding mechanisms necessary for such a complex range of experiences.

Intense levels of heat or pressure applied to the same area of the skin will each excite wide dynamic range neurons and some common nociceptive-specific units. However, the heat will selectively excite some nociceptive-specific neurons while intense mechanical stimulation will excite others. As well, a pinch or prick will excite low-threshold mechanoreceptive neurons. Consequently, different patterns of stimulation, involving wide dynamic range neurons, two types of nociceptive-specific neurons, and low-threshold neurons can underlie the capacity to distinguish between different noxious inputs (Price, 1988). Furthermore, the nociceptive-specific neurons, with their small receptive fields, may play a particular role in conveying information about the site of stimulation, whereas the wide dynamic range neurons, particularly given their overlapping receptive fields, may better signal the intensity of the stimulus applied to the skin.

The neural processing of pain does not, of course, end at the spinal level. As we'll see shortly, the situation at the cord is even more complex than already mentioned, but it is necessary to note that spinal neurons project, via a number of ascending pathways, such as the spinothalamic and spinoreticular tracts, to a variety of sites in the brain stem (particularly the reticular formation of the medulla), the midbrain, and the medial and lateral thalamus (see Fig. 4.1).

Cells in the reticular formation may contribute in large part to aversive drive and resulting escape behaviors. Those in the midbrain seem to trigger emotional reactions such as fear, aversion, and other negative affects. The neurons in the lateral and medial thalamus receive input from the nociceptive specific and wide dynamic range neurons of the spinal dorsal horn and pass these messages, in turn, to the somatosensory cortex or the association areas of the frontal cortex. Many of the former appear to be involved in the localization of pain and discrimination of its sensory intensity. Neurons in the frontal lobes appear to subserve emotions brought on by the pain and motivations to escape or avoid it.

THE GATE CONTROL THEORY OF PAIN

Much of the physiological data mentioned in the preceding sections was unknown 25 years ago, when Melzack and Wall (1965) proposed their new theory of pain. Nonetheless, enough had been determined to provide the foundation for a radically different approach and Melzack and Wall were prescient in their ability to anticipate some major new developments.

In formulating their theory, Melzack and Wall considered the data on physiological specialization, clinical information about prolonged pain syndromes that far outlast tissue damage, the difficulty of treating pain with pharmacological or surgical procedures designed to interrupt afferent pathways, and the counterintuitive aspects of many successful pain treatments (Melzack & Wall, 1988). One example of the last is the manner in which we often deal with a cut or bruise: We rub the injured area, hold it under cold water, or apply a warm dressing. These tactile or thermal stimuli markedly increase the total afferent barrage, yet they reduce or eliminate pain rather than rendering it even more severe.

Melzack and Wall (1965) considered the psychology of pain as well as its physiology. They had to consider a host of anecdotal and clinical data: individuals severely injured in military battle, accidents, or athletic competition frequently fail to complain of pain until many hours later; initiation ceremonies, tribal rituals, and religious observances often involve trauma, but the individual appears to be in a state of ecstasy rather than discomfort; individuals of different cultural background often show widely divergent pain behaviors; early experience and the behavior of family role models appear to shape responses to noxious events; expected painful procedures (such as an inoculation) seem less aversive than unexpected ones; noninvasive therapies, such as hypnosis, often seem to ameliorate pain; pain is amplified by anxiety and attenuated by relaxation or distraction; personality, coping behaviors, and knowledge about the source of the pain markedly affect pain complaints; about one-third of patients report sizable decreases in their levels of discomfort after being given a placebo (Melzack & Wall, 1988).

Clearly, it was wrong to think of pain as simply a sensation arising from overstimulation of pain fibers and consequent stimulation of a cortical pain center. At the least, one had to invoke processes of perception, emotion, evaluation, and reaction. These affective and cognitive mechanisms didn't seem to exist as independent processes that followed pain as a sensory event; rather, they appeared to interact with sensory mechanisms from the inception of the transmission process.

Melzack and Wall's theory made much of this interaction, suggesting inhibitory relations at numerous levels of the nervous system. The initial version of the "gate control theory" is presented in Fig. 4.2. Briefly, it proposed that noxious stimuli activate small-diameter (S) A-delta and C-fibers that project to transmission cells (T) in the spinal cord and, from there, to an "action system" locally and in the brain. As noted earlier, the cord also receives input from large-diameter (L) myelinated A-beta fibers that are excited by low levels of mechanical stimulation.

These excitatory connections are muted by a complex interplay of inhibi-

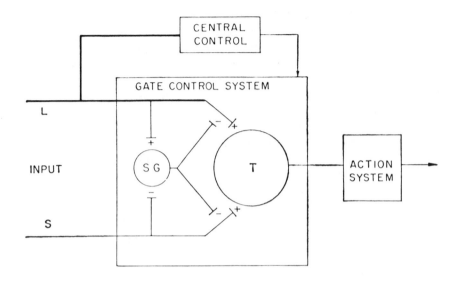

FIG. 4.2. A schematic representation of the original gate control model of pain.
L and S represent the large- and small-diameter fibers, respectively, which project
to transmission cells (T) in the spinal cord. The fibers also project to the substantia gelatinosa (SG) cells, modifying, by means of excitatory (+) and inhibitory (−) actions, its influence on the transmission cells. Further regulation from
central areas is also shown (from R. Melzack, and P. D. Wall (1965), "Pain
Mechanisms: A New Theory," *Science, 150*, 971–978; copyright, 1965, by the
American Association for the Advancement of Science; reprinted by permission).

tory influences mediated through the substantia gelatinosa (SG) (jelly-like substance), a region of interconnecting neurons in laminae I and II of the dorsal
horn. In the initial version of the theory, Melzack and Wall (1965) proposed
that the SG has an inhibitory influence on the T-cells and that it, in turn, was
subject to an excitatory influence from the L-fibers and an inhibitory one from
the S-fibers. Thus, noxious inputs would make a powerful contribution to T-
cell activity; small fiber activity would directly excite the T-cells and would
inhibit the inhibitory influence of the substantia gelatinosa (a process called
"disinhibition").

Activity in large fibers, however, brought on by lower levels of input, would
excite the substantia gelatinosa neurons and, consequently, exert a strong
inhibitory effect on the T-cell. This would account, at least in part, for the
pain-alleviating effects of massage, rubbing, acupuncture, and other forms
of peripheral stimulation, although a second mechanism will be described
shortly.

An important component of the gate control theory was the notion of
descending influences on T-cell activity in the spinal cord that arise at "central control" areas of the brain stem, midbrain, or cortex. This activity, which

is inhibitory, can diminish or block the transmission of pain information in the dorsal horn.

A rather dramatic notion was being proposed: the passage of information from the cells of the spinal cord could be likened to the passage of an object through a gate; an open gate allows the pain message to flow uninterrupted, whereas a gate that is partly or completely closed (due to inhibitory effects from large fiber activity from the periphery or descending influences from the central brain regions) moderates the spinal activity and reduces the afferent barrage (and the pain).

Subsequent anatomical and physiological knowledge about the substantia gelatinosa has led to a modification of the gate control theory, although the basic idea of inhibitory influences from both peripheral and central impulses remains. The revised model (Melzack & Wall, 1988), shown in Fig. 4.3, provides for multiple excitatory influences arising from small fiber input, showing both direct effects on T-cells and indirect ones from interneurons in the SG. The large fibers, as before, contribute directly to T-cell activity (combining with small fiber input to produce wide dynamic range cells, as opposed to nociceptive specific cells that receive input from only S-fibers). However, the L-fibers also inhibit the T-cells through the substantia gelatinosa.

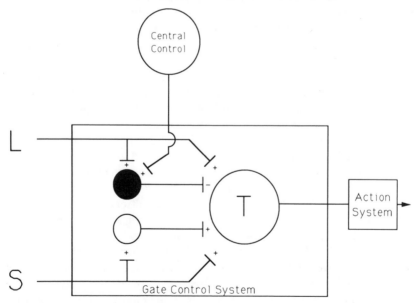

FIG. 4.3   A schematic representation of Melzack and Wall's (1988) revised gate control model, showing cells in the substantia gelatinosa, which exert inhibitory (solid circle) and excitatory (open circle) influences on dorsal horn transmission cells (T) after activation of large (L) and small (S) diameter afferents. The modulating influence of higher nervous system activity is depicted by the input from central control areas.

In a manner rather more complex than earlier thought, powerful inhibitory effects from the brain stem also act to inhibit T-cell activity, through their facilitation of inhibitory interneurons. These descending effects provide for both inhibition of pain by psychological factors and for a negative feedback loop in which some noxious inputs activate brain stem structures that exert an inhibitory effect on continued transmission through the spinal cord. The curious phenomenon of counterirritation, in which intense levels of heat, cold, pressure, or electrical stimulation can help reduce pain may be due to activity in fast-conducting afferent pathways influencing, in turn, activity in inhibitory efferent ones.

DESCENDING INHIBITORY SYSTEMS

In the late 1960s, experiments conducted in two laboratories (Mayer, Wolfe, Akil, Carder, & Liebeskind, 1971; Reynolds, 1969) demonstrated powerful analgesic effects produced by midbrain stimulation in the rat. Electrical pulses applied to the periaqueductal gray (PAG) area yielded analgesia that was long-lasting, applicable over a wide range of pain-inducing situations, and, ultimately, generalizable to humans (Meyerson, 1983; Young, 1989). This "stimulation-produced analgesia" appears to be mediated by a descending circuit that projects to the nucleus raphe magnus of the medulla and then to nociceptive neurons in various laminae of the dorsal horn of the spinal cord. Fig. 4.1 shows inputs from the frontal association cortex and the hypothalamus impinging upon cells in the midbrain which, in turn, send fibers to the medulla and then the cord. Inhibition of spinal pain-transmission cells by this system modifies the pain experience.

This descending system has been studied extensively in recent years because it has become clear that it is intimately linked to the neural substrates of opiate analgesia. The resulting emphasis on neurochemistry of pain modulation has produced an enormously fertile area for research on the interactions among structure, function, chemical transmitters, and behavior.

Stimulation produced analgesia (SPA) can be mimicked by microinjections of morphine into the periaqueductal gray (Bennett & Mayer, 1979). The PAG has a high density of opiate receptors. Tolerance effects observed with morphine occur as well with SPA. In fact, there is also a cross-tolerance effect, so that continued administration of morphine reduces the effectiveness of midbrain stimulation and vice versa. Naloxone, a morphine antagonist that binds to opiate sites and blocks the morphine molecule, also reduces the effectiveness of SPA (Watkins & Mayer, 1982).

The identification of opiate receptors raised a provocative question: Did Mother Nature provide such sites in the hope that someday individuals would harvest poppy plants, extract the milky fluid from the unripe seed pods, process it, and inject it into pain sufferers? That seemed highly unlikely. More likely was the thought that the presence of such receptors indicates that there are also endogenous opiates—morphine-like chemicals that naturally occur within the body. Verification of the existence of such neurochemicals occurred in the late 1970s and they were labeled endorphins ("endogenous morphine") and enkephalins ("within the brain"). Numerous variants of these polypeptides have been discovered: several types of enkephalins, larger molecules called dynorphins, and the complex beta-endorphins. A whole witch's caldron of other neurotransmitters is known to influence pain transmission (Yaksh & Aimone, 1989) and enormous efforts are under way to create synthetic molecules that provide the analgesic effects of the opiate drugs but not the major side-effects: nausea, constipation, respiratory depression, tolerance, and dependence.

The endogenous opiates play an important role in the pain experience. Nonetheless, it is clear that a separate pain suppression system exists as well. For example, certain forms of stress (e.g., intermittent foot shock or immobilization) produce a marked increase in pain tolerance in animals ("stress-induced analgesia") (Lewis, Cannon, & Liebeskind, 1980), which can be reversed with the morphine antagonist naloxone. Other forms of stress (brief continuous foot shock, centrifugal rotation, cold-water swims) also produce analgesia, but these effects are uninfluenced by naloxone, although they are attenuated by drugs which block other neurotransmitters such as serotonin (Coderre & Rollman, 1984).

In humans, certain forms of intense, low-frequency electrical stimulation applied through the skin to peripheral nerves (acupuncture-like transcutaneous electrical nerve stimulation—TENS) produce analgesic effects which are naloxone-reversible; other parameters (high frequency) of TENS also have analgesic effects, but naloxone does not interfere with these (Sjolund & Eriksson, 1979). Appropriately, only the low-frequency TENS produced an elevation of beta-endorphins measured in human cerebrospinal fluid (CSF).

Measurement of endogenous opiates in CSF and in blood plasma has become a fascinating, if controversial, area. Controversy focuses on a number of issues: the utility of such peripheral information, especially when obtained from blood fractions, and the ethics and risks of tapping into the spinal cord for CSF (Sternbach, 1979).

Subjects with high levels of endorphins showed greater tolerance to experimentally induced pain than those with low endorphin levels (von Knorring, Almay, Johansson, & Terenius, 1978). In a related study, surgical patients with low preoperative levels of endorphins required more opiate analgesia postoperatively to relieve their pain than did patients with higher endorphin levels (Tamsen, Sakurada, Wahlstrom, Terenius, & Hartvig, 1982). Finally, a small group of chronic-pain patients with clear neurological signs of organic lesions showed lower levels of endorphins than patients in which no nerve damage could be found (Almay, Johansson, von Knorring, Terenius, & Wahlstrom, 1978). This raises the intriguing question of whether these individuals developed a chronic syndrome because they had low levels of endorphins prior to the onset of their disorder, rendering them less able to recover, or because the nerve damage, and resulting pain, puts unusual demands on their endogenous opiates, reducing the capacity of the endorphin system. Some evidence for the latter view comes from the finding that there is a negative correlation between the endorphin levels and the duration of the pain syndrome.

There is an intriguing counterposition to the situation of chronic-pain patients with low endorphin levels. Some individuals are congenitally insensitive to pain; they do not feel it. Lest you consider them lucky, reflect on the ambivalent situation in which we are placed by pain; it is one of the scourges of humankind, yet it serves to warn us of mild damage so that we can withdraw or seek attention before it becomes more severe, it forces us to rest so that the body can recuperate, it helps us learn to avoid future dangers. Congenitally insensitive persons are unable to utilize the beneficial aspects of pain and often experience serious burns, cuts, and bruises as well as severe damage to the joints and bones that lead to tragically brief lives (Melzack & Wall, 1988). It's likely that several different mechanisms underlie this disorder, but consider two for the moment: The affected individuals may have a neurological deficit in which nociceptive transmission is attenuated in some manner or they may have an overabundance of endorphins, producing an effect something like a constant infusion of morphine.

Some recent findings support both of these concepts. One case study discovered an absence of A-delta fibers in the roots feeding the dorsal horn and a reduced size of the major ascending tract that carries small fiber afferents to the brain stem (Swanson, Buchan, & Alvord, 1965). A second study was conducted on the foreskin of a 4-year-old boy who showed no sensitivity to noxious or thermal stimuli and had many scars from self-damage, particularly on the tongue. It, too, revealed a marked deficit in the number of small myelinated fibers (Bischoff, 1979). As well, there was an almost total absence of C-fibers. Microscopic analysis of the tissue, however, revealed Pacinian corpuscles, Meissner's corpuscles, and large myelinated A-fibers. Not surprisingly, reaction to tactile stimuli was clearly present.

An alternative account of the factors underlying at least some cases of congenital pain insensitivity comes from the investigation of Dehen, Willer, and Cambier (1979). Their patient was a 34-year-old woman who was brought to their attention when she suffered a third-degree burn of the hand after placing it on a radiator. She showed "no behavioral reactions to pain," no matter how intense the noxious stimulus or where it was applied. She was, however, normal in her capacity to judge warm from cold, know the position of her joints or identify objects by touch. In her case, unlike the patients cited earlier, nerve biopsy was normal.

The investigators studied a nociceptive flexion reflex of the lower limb by placing electrodes over the sural nerve at the heel and measuring a long latency reflex at the thigh that involves narrow diameter fibers and typically arises at about the threshold for pain (Willer, 1977). The threshold for normal subjects was about 10 mA; that for their patient was 45 mA. However, after injection of naloxone, the opiate antagonist that blocks the sites at which the endorphins bind, her nociceptive reflex threshold fell to about 16 mA (whereas naloxone had no effect on the controls). Interestingly, the woman still did not describe the shock as "painful;" rather, she said it gave rise to a sensation of "warmth." Nonetheless, the data suggest that the patient had an endorphin system that was "permanently hyperactive" and produced a tonic inhibition via the descending system described earlier. Only when the naloxone temporarily blocked this inhibition was the woman able to demonstrate a normal nociceptive reflex and at least some sensation, albeit still far from painful, from the electrical pulse train applied to her foot.

CHARACTERISTICS OF PAIN

It won't be a revelation to note that not all pains are the same. Pain experiences differ in quality, intensity, location, extent, and duration. Some pains are cramping; others seem stabbing, burning, or pounding. Some are mild or moderate; others are excruciating. Pains due to burns are enormously different than those arising from headaches or back injuries or stomach aches. A pinprick is localized to a small spot on the finger, whereas the inflammation of the nerves produced by the virus herpes zoster (shingles) leaves some people with a postherpetic pain that not only covers large body parts, but creates an extensive area that is also exquisitely sensitive to mild tactile or thermal stimuli. This effect, called hyperesthesia, is accompanied by alterations of summation that are akin to the auditory phenomenon of recruitment: a warm stimulus applied to the skin may have no effect for a while, but then a sudden, intense pain, explosive in character, renders the stimulus unbearable (Noordenbos, 1959).

The duration of pain is of key importance in regard to both its experience and its psychological effect. Three particular categories deserve attention: transient, acute, and chronic pain.

Transient pain is usually sudden and brief—a pinprick, a jab from an elbow, a spill from a coffee cup. It is the closest that pain comes to being purely a sensation. A fleeting experience of discomfort leads to escape behavior and, if the individual is fortunate, the matter is over.

More severe injury causes greater tissue damage and, with that, the release of chemicals such as prostaglandins and bradykinin, which sensitize nearby nerve endings. The pain experience now is considerably prolonged, often variable in intensity, and likely to trigger a series of emotions and thoughts that accompany the sensory experience. Such pain is called acute.

Usually, the recovery process is straightforward and, as the injury heals, acute pain diminishes and then disappears. Nonetheless, even when the cause of the pain is quite evident, there is at least some concern about the duration and extent of limited activity. When the cause is not immediately evident, as is frequently the case for pain arising within the body, the concern is considerably greater. Does the pain signal a serious disease? Is it going to last a long time? Might it become increasingly severe? Anxiety, often of severe magnitude, accompanies the pain. Moreover, the anxiety may amplify the pain experience. Assurance from a physician that the cause of the problem is a minor matter often causes the anxiety to fade quickly—and with that, also the pain.

Regretfully, sometimes pain persists, often well past the time of tissue healing. Acute pain, when it lasts longer than 6 months, becomes chronic. More than simple duration distinguishes acute from chronic pain. Psychological factors become inextricably woven with organic ones, in regard to both the reaction to the discomfort and in its becoming a chronic problem in the first place. A key characteristic of the chronic-pain patients is depression (Merskey, 1986b). Not unexpectedly, the individual is deeply distressed by the many months the pain has lasted, by the inability of a series of physicians to provide a quick fix, by the ineffectiveness of many analgesic drugs to control the situation, and by the dramatic changes in the patient's life that are brought about by the pain. These effects are seen in restrictions on the patient's daily activities, changed relationship with family members and friends, reduced income, and increased medical expenses. As Sternbach (1989) notes, "whereas acute pain may promote survival, chronic pain is usually destructive physically, psychologically, and socially."

Psychological methods are often used to help in both the diagnosis and treatment of chronic pain. Psychological tests such as the Minnesota Multiphasic Personality Inventory (MMPI) are employed to identify personality disturbances that, depending on the view of the investigator, are predisposing factors in the onset of the chronic-pain disorder or consequences of it. That is, a personality disturbance may cause an individual to assume the role of a chronic-pain patient when faced with a disease or injury that would quickly heal in another individual. On the other hand, a "normal" personality may undergo major alterations as a consequence of prolonged and unremitting pain.

MMPI profiles of chronic pain patients often show elevations on three primary scales: depression, hysteria, and hypochondriasis. This "neurotic triad" or "conversion-V profile" (based upon a common pattern of response) is then assumed to represent a personality disturbance (before or after the pain, although the return toward normal levels after successful treatment suggests the latter is more likely).

Another account, however, seems even more plausible. The original MMPI was established as a test of psychopathology and its norms are based on psychiatric patients. Its use for medical patients is a common but irregular practice. If individuals taking the MMPI answer "True" to items such as "I feel weak all over much of the time" or "My sleep is fitful and disturbed" or "False" to the questions "I have few or no pains" or "I am about as able to work as I ever was," the scoring procedure adds points to all three scales: hypochondriasis, depression, and hysteria. Thus two problems emerge. First, common symptoms of pain disorders inevitably boost the scales that are used to diagnose a neurotic disorder. Second, because individual items contribute to the scores on several scales, the scales are not independent. As Smythe (1984) observed, "The MMPI is not an appropriate scale for use in patients with organic diseases causing pain or disability." While there may be a psychological component in chronic-pain disorders, personality tests with such built-in biases must be interpreted with extreme caution.

Chronic-pain disorders are often unresponsive to pharmacological, surgical, and other medical interventions. In recent years, such patients have been aided by a wide range of psychological treatments: cognitive–behavioral therapy (Turk, Meichenbaum, & Genest, 1983), behavioral therapy (Fordyce, 1976), hypnosis (Hilgard & Hilgard, 1975), relaxation and biofeedback (Jessup, 1989), psychotherapy (Merskey, 1986b), and family therapy (Roy, 1986). Not all patients are helped; those who fail with one may respond to another. The therapeutic approaches tend to share some common features, such as providing a rationale for the patient's pain, communicating a message of hope and optimism, tailoring the approach to the individual, and relying heavily on the patient's participation in his or her own treatment (Turk & Holzman, 1986). Nonetheless, they differ widely in both philosophy and technique. A major challenge to psychological research is to identify the individual factors that will optimize the patient–therapy link, so that customization rather than happenstance characterizes the treatment provided.

PAIN ASSESSMENT

The definition presented at the outset of this chapter indicated that pain is "an unpleasant sensory and emotional experience." Both intróspection and experimental data suggest that the two are quite different: Pain as a sensation involves concepts of intensity, quality, duration, location, and area, while pain as an emotional reaction involves considerations of unpleasantness, motivational drive toward escape, and cognitive interpretation of the situation in regard to previous experiences, knowledge about the current status, and concern about future outcomes.

Melzack and Casey noted that:

> To consider only the sensory features of pain and ignore its motivational and affective properties, is to look at only part of the problem, and not even the most important part of that. Even the concept of pain as a perception, with full recognition of past experience, attention, and other cognitive determinants of sensory quality and intensity, still neglects the crucial motivational dimension. (1968, p. 423)

While some earlier notions had differentiated between "pain sensation" and "reactions to pain," the latter was generally seen as a secondary consideration, which arose after the pain sensation had occurred. Clinical evidence challenged that conception. Beecher's (1959) report that soldiers badly wounded on the battlefield "entirely denied pain from their extensive wounds or had so little that they did not want any medication to relieve it" suggested that pain could be blocked by cognitive activities.

Patients given prefrontal lobotomies (Barber, 1959) as a last-ditch attempt to treat intractable pain, still describe a sensory component of their internal pain, but they don't show facial or bodily reactions, appear not to be anxious, and don't ask for medication. Sometimes they suggest the "little pain" is still there but the "big pain" is gone. Again, the data point to a complex interaction between motivational and emotional factors and sensory ones.

Melzack and Casey (1968) proposed a new conceptual model that had three highly interdependent components of the pain experience: (1) the sensory-discriminative system, (2) the motivational–affective system, and (3) the cognitive–evaluative system.

The proposed scope of activities mediated by these systems fits well with the known function of the principal neural loci reviewed earlier. The sensory-discriminative dimension seems particularly linked to activity projected via the neospinothalamic system from the spinal cord to the lateral thalamus and then to the somatosensory cortex. The motivational–affective dimension, underlying the unpleasant feelings and escape behaviors associated with noxious stimuli, activates neurons in the brain stem reticular formation, medial thalamus, limbic forebrain structures, and frontal cortex. The cognitive–evaluative dimension, subserving the interpretation of the pain experience, is tied to the frontal cortex and other association areas.

Although there are numerous points of interconnection between these systems, and consequent opportunity for interactions, critical questions still remain about the extent to which the systems should be considered part of a parallel processing network, as Melzack and Casey (1968) proposed, or a sequential processing network, in which pain sensations and arousal are activated in parallel but emotional responses and cognitive appraisals interact at higher levels to determine the pain expression (Price, 1988).

While there is disagreement about the particular role of the various ascending and descending pathways and about the precise nature of the spinal gating mechanism, it is clear that the gate control theory and the tridimensional conceptual model played an enormously important role in introducing psychology to a field that had earlier been almost exclusively the domain of neurology, physiology, and pharmacology. By emphasizing the complexity of the pain experience, the crucial role of emotion and thought, and the possibility of modulating the experience through manipulation of affect and cognition, Melzack and his colleagues established an enormously fruitful research area.

More importantly, they provided a rationale for the psychological treatments mentioned earlier. Melzack and Casey showed both sensitivity and foresight when they wrote,

> The therapeutic implications of the model should be obvious; but because of the historical emphasis on the sensory dimension of pain, they are not obvious at all. The surgical and pharmacological attack on pain might well profit by redirecting thinking toward the neglected . . . contributions of motivational and cognitive processes. Pain can be treated not only by trying to cut down the sensory input by anesthetic block, surgical intervention, and the like, but also by influencing the motivational–affective and cognitive factors as well. Relaxants, tranquilizers, sedatives, suggestion, placebos, and hypnosis are known to influence pain, but the historical emphasis on sensory mechanisms has made these forms of therapy suspect, seemingly fraudulent, almost a sideshow in the mainstream of pain treatment. Yet, if we can recover from historical accident, these methods deserve more attention than they have received. (1968, p. 435)

The foregoing makes it clear that the assessment of pain requires attention to three dimensions: sensory, affective, and cognitive. Interestingly, attention in both clinical and laboratory settings has focused almost entirely on the first two, although some recent studies have considered the nature of the interactions between multiple sources of pain. The adaptation level and hypervigilance models (Rollman, 1979, 1983; Scudds, Rollman, Harth, & McCain, 1987) focus on the modulation of judgments of experimentally induced pain induced by intense pain states elsewhere in the body; the functional model (Algom, Raphaeli, & Cohen-Raz, 1986) addresses the summation between more nearly equal pain states. Inhibition is frequently seen in the former condition; summation in the latter.

For approaches that emphasize the sensory and affective components, there is controversy about the relative emphasis that ought to be paid to each member of the pair and the philosophical and methodological orientation of the assessment process. Wall (1979), for example, distinguishes between two types of sensory experience: one, evoked by external events, such as seeing and hearing and a second, produced by internal events, such as hunger and thirst. Based on a number of criteria (e.g., ability to describe and localize the stimulus, effects of distraction and suggestion, association with emotional response and predictable behavior), he suggests that pain has more in common with the second class. Moreover, the imprecise link between tissue damage and pain intensity as well as the inability to utilize pain information as a warning, since damage has already occurred, suggests to Wall that pain signals a body state (as do hunger and thirst) that, in this instance, leads to escape, treatment, and recovery.

Wall claims that pain and its associated emotion are "two faces of the same coin" and that attempts to split the experience into two components is an artifact of training subjects. While claims that sensory and affective components of pain can be independently assessed are unwarranted, two approaches to the assessment process demonstrate that distinctions between sensation and affect are possible, even with naïve observers.

The first example comes from the clinical domain. Clinical pain assessment often involves simple questions: Is the pain mild, moderate or severe?" or "where would you rank the pain on a five-point scale?" Such approaches have the benefit of speed and simplicity, but they lack quantitative rigor (being, at best, ordinal scales) and they fail to capture the complexity of the pain experience.

Melzack and Torgerson (1971) reflected on the fact that patients generally talk about their pain using adjectives—a "splitting" headache, a "shooting" pain in the knee, a "cramping" stomach ache. After gathering more than 200 pain-related adjectives, they categorized the words into 3 major classes and 16 subclasses. Later, they added 4 supplementary subclasses. The words in the first class described sensory qualities of pain: temporal characteristics (flickering, pulsing, pounding), spatial characteristics (jumping, shooting), punctate pressure (pricking, drilling), thermal (hot, burning), and so on. The second class, which had 5 categories, compared with 10 in the first one, brought together affective terms relating to such emotions as tension (tiring, exhausting), fear (frightful, terrifying), or punishment (cruel, vicious). The third category, evaluative, had but a single subclass, containing words such as annoying, troublesome, miserable, and unbearable.

Melzack and Torgerson then asked various groups to rank order the words within a subclass in terms of severity. Quite reliably, individuals established a hierarchy, such that "stinging," for example, was more severe than "smarting," which was, in turn, more severe than "itchy" and "tingling." The fourth category had miscellaneous terms that were largely sensory in nature.

From this multidimensional scaling, Melzack (1975) established the McGill Pain Questionnaire (MPQ; Fig. 4.4), which has been widely adopted in pain clinics throughout the world. Patients are asked to examine each subclass, decide if one of the terms is descriptive of their pain, and, if so, to check the appropriate one.

Up to 20 words could be selected, although patients generally choose far fewer. Melzack devised a Pain Rating Index (PRI), based upon the summed

McGill Pain Questionnaire

Patient's Name _____ Date _____ Time_____am/pm

PRI S_____ A_____ E_____ M_____ PRI(T)_____ PPI_____
   (1-10)   (11-15)   (16)   (17-20)   (1-20)

1 FLICKERING	11 TIRING	BRIEF ___ RHYTHMIC ___ CONTINUOUS ___
QUIVERING	EXHAUSTING	MOMENTARY ___ PERIODIC ___ STEADY ___
PULSING	12 SICKENING	TRANSIENT ___ INTERMITTENT ___ CONSTANT ___
THROBBING	SUFFOCATING	
BEATING	13 FEARFUL	
POUNDING	FRIGHTFUL	
2 JUMPING	TERRIFYING	
FLASHING	14 PUNISHING	
SHOOTING	GRUELLING	
3 PRICKING	CRUEL	
BORING	VICIOUS	
DRILLING	KILLING	
STABBING	15 WRETCHED	
LANCINATING	BLINDING	
4 SHARP	16 ANNOYING	
CUTTING	TROUBLESOME	
LACERATING	MISERABLE	
5 PINCHING	INTENSE	
PRESSING	UNBEARABLE	
GNAWING	17 SPREADING	
CRAMPING	RADIATING	
CRUSHING	PENETRATING	E = EXTERNAL
6 TUGGING	PIERCING	I = INTERNAL
PULLING	18 TIGHT	
WRENCHING	NUMB	
7 HOT	DRAWING	
BURNING	SQUEEZING	
SCALDING	TEARING	
SEARING	19 COOL	
8 TINGLING	COLD	
ITCHY	FREEZING	
SMARTING	20 NAGGING	
STINGING	NAUSEATING	COMMENTS
9 DULL	AGONIZING	
SORE	DREADFUL	
HURTING	TORTURING	
ACHING	PPI	
HEAVY	0 NO PAIN	
10 TENDER	1 MILD	
TAUT	2 DISCOMFORTING	
RASPING	3 DISTRESSING	
SPLITTING	4 HORRIBLE	
	5 EXCRUCIATING	

FIG. 4.4 The McGill Pain Questionnaire. The verbal descriptors fall into four categories: 1–10 are sensory, 11–15 are affective, 16 is evaluative, and 17–20 are miscellaneous. The Pain Rating Index (PRI) is the sum of the rank values of the words selected in each category. The Present Pain Intensity (PPI) is based on a six-point category scale (from R. Melzack (1983), The McGill Pain Questionnaire; in R. Melzack (Ed.), *Pain Measurement and Assessment* (pp. 41–47); New York: Raven Press; reprinted by permission).

rank order of the words chosen; "pulsing" in category 1 provides three points, since it is ranked third, while "flickering" provides one point. The potential range, then, of the PRI is from 0 to 77.

There are problems with this scheme: There is a preponderance of sensory items, some subclasses have more words than others, the intervals between words are uneven. Furthermore, some patients lack the linguistic skills to complete the form. Nonetheless, the MPQ has proven to be a robust instrument for assessing a wide range of clinical syndromes. It has acceptable reliability and validity (Reading, 1983), it is moderately sensitive to analgesic procedures, its emphasis on three dimensions of pain is generally supported by factor-analytical studies (Prieto & Geisinger, 1983). A brief form has recently been published (Melzack, 1987). The high intercorrelations among the sensory, affective, and evaluative subscales have led to some concern about the discriminant validity of the MPQ (Melzack, 1985; Turk, Rudy, & Salovey, 1985). Although different pain syndromes tend to produce different profiles on the MPQ (higher in sensory scales for some, higher in affective for others), evidence is still sparse about the capacity of the MPQ to identify alterations in one component of pain after a specific therapeutic intervention (e.g., a reduction in the affective score) while leaving the other main component (in this case, the sensory) relatively unaffected.

Data suggestive of such selective modulation of pain have appeared in several studies involving other approaches which attempt to assess directly the sensory and affective components of pain. Price, McGrath, Rafii, and Buckingham (1983) had pain patients and healthy volunteers describe the intensity and affective magnitude of a series of noxious heat pulses applied to the forearm through a contact thermode. The responses were made on printed visual analog scales (VAS), which were 15-cm lines anchored by the terms "no sensation" and "the most intense sensation imaginable" in the case of the sensory judgment and "not bad at all" and "the most intense bad feeling possible for me" in the case of the description of emotion.

The two components did not increase at the same rate when the temperature was increased from 43^0 to 51^0C. The slope of the power function linking sensation intensity to temperature was 2.1, while the slope of the function between affective magnitude and temperature was nearly twice as large (3.8). These data suggest that the unpleasantness of a noxious stimulus increases much more rapidly than the intensity of the pain. Acupuncture treatment of chronic-back-pain patients gradually reduced both the sensory and affective ratings over a 4-month period; there is a suggestion that the affective component changed more than the sensory.

In a subsequent study, Price, von der Gruen, Miller, Rafii, and Price (1985) reported a reduction in affect but not intensity following low doses of morphine, but changes in both following higher doses. The synthetic narcotic fentanyl also reduced both components (Price, Harkins, Rafii, & Price, 1986).

However, when it was used to treat low-back pain, fentanyl caused a significantly larger decrease in VAS affective responses (dropping by 65%) than sensory ones (a decline of 51%).

These data don't show that the two components, sensory and affective, are independent. In fact, it would be difficult to imagine that the emotional component of the pain experience is unrelated to the sensory intensity of the pain. The findings do suggest, however, that analgesic treatments, whether they be pharmacological, surgical, or psychological, might alter sensation and affect differentially. A tranquilizer, for example, could reduce the emotional reaction to discomfort while leaving the intensity of the sensation unchanged (Gracely, McGrath, & Dubner, 1978). An assessment tool that focused only on intensity would mistakenly conclude that the patient's condition was unimproved.

As noted earlier, pain patients are faced with a disease or injury that has both sensory and emotional consequences. Price, Harkins, and Baker examined whether

> Affective VAS ratings of clinical pain will be higher in patients whose pain is likely to be associated with a serious threat to health or life in comparison to patients whose pain is likely to be less threatening . . . for comparable levels of pain sensation intensity. (1987)

Their results indicate that affective VAS ratings were, as expected, generally greater than sensory ratings for patients suffering from back pain, the burning causalgia pain that follows nerve injury, and cancer pain. Those suffering from the dental myofascial pain dysfunction (MPD) syndrome had no difference between the two ratings. Women undergoing labor, which is an acute pain with a very positive outcome, rated the emotional component as significantly *less* intense than the sensory. The steep increase in affective response to experimentally induced pain in volunteer subjects, compared with the sensory response, was not replicated.

Pain assessment is a complex but rewarding area of research. Rigorous psychophysical procedures (Chapman et al., 1985; Gracely, 1989; Rollman, 1989) can be utilized to assist in diagnosis and to evaluate treatment. The last 25 years have seen an explosive interest in pain research and treatment, in the establishment of international research societies and journals, in the proliferation of pain clinics, and in the understanding of the physiological and psychological factors that contribute to the experience of pain and to its alleviation. There is no cause for complacency about the status of pain control, but there is much cause for hope.

REFERENCES

Algom, D., Raphaeli, N., & Cohen-Raz, L. (1986). Integration of noxious stimulation across separate somatosensory communications systems: A functional theory of pain. *Journal of Experimental Psychology: Human Perception and Performance, 12,* 92–102.

Almay, B. G. L., Johansson, F., von Knorring, L., Terenius, L., & Wahlstrom, A. (1978). Endorphins in chronic pain. I. Differences in CSF endorphin levels between organic and psychogenic pain syndromes. *Pain, 5,* 153–162.

Barber, T. X. (1959). Toward a theory of pain: Relief of chronic pain by prefrontal leucotomy, opiates, placebos, and hypnosis. *Psychological Bulletin, 56,* 430–460.

Beecher, H. K. (1959). *Measurement of subjective responses.* New York: Oxford University Press.

Bennett, G. J., & Mayer, D. J. (1979). Inhibition of spinal cord interneurons by narcotic microinjection and focal electrical stimulation in the periaqueductal central gray matter. *Brain Research, 172,* 243–257.

Bischoff, A. (1979). Congenital insensitivity to pain with anhidrosis: A morphometric study of sural nerve and cutaneous receptors in the human prepuce. In J. J. Bonica, J. Liebeskind, & D. Albe-Fessard (Eds.), *Advances in pain research and therapy* (Vol. 3, pp. 53–65). New York: Raven Press.

Chapman, C. R., Casey, K. L., Dubner, R., Foley, K. M., Gracely, R. H., & Reading, A. E. (1985). Pain measurement: An overview. *Pain, 22,* 1–32.

Coderre, T. J., & Rollman, G. B. (1984). Stress analgesia: Effects of PCPA, yohimbine, and naloxone. *Pharmacology, Biochemistry, and Behavior, 21,* 681–686.

Craig, K. D. (1986). Social modeling influences: Pain in context. In R. A. Sternbach (Ed.), *The psychology of pain* (2nd ed., pp. 67–95). New York: Raven Press.

Dehen, H., Willer, J. C., & Cambier, J. (1979). Congenital indifference to pain and endogenous morphine-like system. In J. J. Bonica, J. C. Liebeskind, & D. Albe-Fessard (Eds.), *Advances in pain research and therapy* (Vol. 3, pp. 553–557). New York: Raven Press.

Fields, H. L. (1987). *Pain.* New York: McGraw-Hill.

Fordyce, W. E. (1976). Behavioral methods for chronic pain and illness. St. Louis: C. V. Mosby.

Frey, M., von (1895). Beitrage zur Sinnesphysiologie der Haut. *Ber. sachs. Ges. Wiss. math-phys. Cl., 47,* 166–184.

Gracely, R. H. (1989). Methods of testing pain mechanisms in normal man. In P. D. Wall & R. Melzack (Eds.), *Textbook of pain* (pp. 257–268). Edinburgh: Churchill Livingstone.

Gracely, R. H., McGrath, P., & Dubner, R. (1978). Validity and sensitivity of ratio scales of sensory and affective verbal pain descriptors: Manipulation of affect by diazepam. *Pain, 5,* 19–30.

Hilgard, E. R., & Hilgard, J. R. (1975). *Hypnosis in the relief of pain.* Los Altos, CA: William Kaufman.

Jessup, B. A. (1989). Relaxation and biofeedback. In P. D. Wall & R. Melzack (Eds.), *Textbook of pain* (pp. 989–1000). Edinburgh: Churchill Livingstone.

von Knorring, L., Almay, B. G. L., Johansson, F., & Terenius, L. (1978). Pain perception and endorphin levels in cerebrospinal fluid. *Pain, 5,* 359–365.

Lewis, J. W., Cannon, J. T., & Liebeskind, J. C. (1980). Opioid and non-opioid mechanisms of stress analgesia. *Science, 208,* 623–625.

Mayer, D. J., Wolfe, T. L., Akil, H., Carder, B., & Liebeskind, J. C. (1971). Analgesia from electrical stimulation in the brainstem of the rat. *Science, 174,* 1351–1354.

Melzack, R. (1975). The McGill Pain Questionnaire: Major properties and scoring methods. *Pain, 1,* 277–300.

Melzack, R. (1985). Re: Discriminative capacity of the McGill Pain Questionnaire. *Pain, 23,* 201–202.

Melzack, R. (1987). The short-form McGill Pain Questionnaire. *Pain, 30,* 191–198.

Melzack, R., & Casey, K. L. (1968). Sensory, motivational, and central control determinants of pain: A new conceptual model. In D. Kenshalo (Ed.), *The skin senses* (pp. 423–443). Springfield, IL: Thomas.

Melzack, R., & Torgerson, W. S. (1971). On the language of pain. *Anesthesiology, 34,* 50–59.

Melzack, R., & Wall, P. D. (1965). Pain mechanisms: A new theory. *Science, 150,* 971–979.

Melzack, R., & Wall, P. D. (1988). *The challenge of pain.* London: Penguin.

Mendelson, G. (1984). Compensation, pain complaints, and psychological disturbance. *Pain, 20,* 169–178.

Merskey, H. (1986a). Classification of chronic pain: Descriptions of chronic pain syndromes and definitions of pain terms. *Pain*, Suppl. 3, S1–S226.

Merskey, H. (1986b). Traditional individual psychotherapy and psychopharmacotherapy. In A. D. Holzman & D. C. Turk (Eds.), *Pain management. A handbook of psychological treatment approaches* (pp. 51–70). New York: Pergamon Press.

Meyerson, B. A. (1983). Electrostimulation procedures: Effects, presumed rationale, and possible mechanisms. In J. J. Bonica, U. Lindblom, & A. Iggo (Eds.), *Advances in pain research and therapy* (Vol. 5, pp. 495–534). New York: Raven Press.

Nafe, J. P. (1929). A quantitative theory of feeling. *Journal of General Psychology, 2,* 199–210.

Noordenbos, W. (1959). *Pain.* Amsterdam: Elsevier.

Price, D. D. (1988). *Psychological and neural mechanisms of pain.* New York: Raven Press.

Price, D. D., Harkins, S. W., Rafii, A., & Price, C. (1986). A simultaneous comparison of fentanyl's analgesic effects on experimental and clinical pain. *Pain, 24,* 197–204.

Price, D. D., Harkins, S. W., & Baker, C. (1987). Sensory–affective relationships among different types of clinical and experimental pain. *Pain, 28,* 297–308.

Price, D. D., Hu, J. W., Dubner, R., & Gracely, R. H. (1977). Peripheral suppression of first pain and central summation of second pain evoked by noxious heat pulses. *Pain, 3,* 57–68.

Price, D. D., McGrath, P. A., Rafii, A., & Buckingham, B. (1983). The validation of visual analogue scales as ratio scale measures for chronic and experimental pain. *Pain, 17,* 45–56.

Price, D. D., von der Gruen, A., Miller, J., Rafii, A., & Price, C. (1985). A psychophysical analysis of morphine analgesia. *Pain, 22,* 261–270.

Prieto, E. J., & Geisinger, K. F. (1983). Factor-analytic studies of the McGill Pain Questionnaire. In R. Melzack (Ed.), *Pain measurement and assessment* (pp. 63–70). New York: Raven Press.

Reading, A. E. (1983). The McGill Pain Questionnaire: An appraisal. In R. Melzack (Ed.), *Pain measurement and assessment* (pp. 55–62). New York: Raven Press.

Reynolds, D. V. (1969). Surgery in the rat during electrical analgesia induced by focal brain stimulation. *Science, 164,* 444–445.

Rollman, G. B. (1979). Signal detection theory pain measures: Empirical validation studies and adaptation-level effects. *Pain, 6,* 9–21.

Rollman, G. B. (1983). Measurement of experimental pain in chronic pain patients: Methodological and individual factors. In R. Melzack (Ed.), *Pain measurement and assessment* (pp. 251–258). New York: Raven Press.

Rollman, G. B. (1989). Measurement of pain in fibromyalgia in the clinic and laboratory. *Journal of Rheumatology, 16* (Suppl. 19), 113–119.

Roy, R. (1986). A problem-centered family systems approach in treating chronic pain. In A. D. Holzman & D. C. Turk (Eds.), *Pain management. A handbook of psychological treatment approaches* (pp. 113–130). New York: Pergamon Press.

Scudds, R. A., Rollman, G. B., Harth, M., & McCain, G. A. (1987). Pain perception and personality measures as discriminators in the classification of fibrositis. *Journal of Rheumatology, 14,* 563–569.

Sinclair, D. C. (1955). Cutaneous sensation and the doctrine of specific energy. *Brain, 78,* 584–614.

Sjolund, B. H., & Eriksson, M. B. E. (1979). Endorphins and analgesia produced by peripheral conditioning stimulation. In J. J. Bonica, J. C. Liebeskind, & D. Albe-Fessard (Eds.), *Advances in pain research and therapy* (Vol. 3, pp. 587–599). New York: Raven Press.

Smythe, H. A. (1984). Problems with the MMPI. *Journal of Rheumatology, 11,* 417–418.

Sternbach, R. A. (1979). Ethical problems in human pain research. In J. J. Bonica, J. C. Liebeskind, & D. Albe-Fessard (Eds.), *Advances in pain research and therapy* (Vol. 3, pp. 837–842). New York: Raven Press.

Sternbach, R. A. (1989). Acute versus chronic pain. In P. D. Wall & R. Melzack (Eds.), *Textbook of pain* (pp. 242–246). Edinburgh: Churchill Livingstone.

Swanson, A. G., Buchan, G. C., & Alvord, E. C., Jr. (1965). Anatomic changes in congenital insensitivity to pain. *Archives of Neurology, 12,* 12–18.

Tamsen, A., Sakurada, T., Wahlstrom, A., Terenius, L., & Hartvig, P. (1982). Postoperative demand for analgesics in relation to individual levels of endorphins and substance P in cerebrospinal fluid. *Pain, 13,* 171–184.

Torebjork, H. E., & Hallin, R. G. (1973). Perceptual changes accompanying controlled preferential blocking of A & C fibre responses in intact human skin nerves. *Experimental Brain Research, 16,* 321–332.

Turk, D. C., & Holzman, A. D. (1986). Commonalities among psychological approaches in the treatment of chronic pain: Specifying the meta-constructs. In A. D. Holzman & D. C. Turk (Eds.), *Pain management. A handbook of psychological treatment approaches* (pp. 257–267). New York: Pergamon Press.

Turk, D. C., Meichenbaum, D., & Genest, M. (1983). *Pain and behavioral medicine. A cognitive–behavioral perspective.* New York: Guilford Press.

Turk, D. C., Rudy, T. E., & Salovey, P. (1985). The McGill Pain Questionnaire reconsidered: Confirming the factor structure and examining appropriate uses. *Pain, 21,* 385–398.

Wall, P. D. (1979). On the relation of injury to pain. *Pain, 6,* 253–264.

Watkins, L. R., & Mayer, D. J. (1982). Organization of endogenous opiate and non-opiate pain control systems. *Science, 216,* 1185–1192.

Willer, J. C. (1977). Comparative study of perceived pain and nociceptive flexion reflex in man. *Pain, 3,* 69–80.

Yaksh, T. L., & Aimone, L. D. (1989). The central pharmacology of pain transmission. In P. D. Wall & R. Melzack (Eds.), *Textbook of pain* (pp. 181–205). Edinburgh: Churchill Livingstone.

Young, R. F. (1989). Brain stimulation. In P. D. Wall & R. Melzack (Eds.), *Textbook of pain* (pp. 925–931). Edinburgh: Churchill Livingstone.

II

DEVELOPMENT AND INTERMODAL RELATIONS

How should we understand the relationship between the senses of touch and vision? David Warren and Matt Rossano have argued that we need to understand the influence of vision on touch in order to gain a proper understanding of the sense of touch. The relationship between the senses turns out to be rather complicated, and changes over the course of development, as Bushnell and Boudreau point out.

Much of our knowledge about stimuli derives from input from more than one sense (see Heller, 1982). It is certainly possible to blindfold subjects (and mask sound with headphones or white noise) in a laboratory to study the sense of touch. This control methodology is clearly the dominant sort of research paradigm. However, sighted people often see the things they touch, and hear the sound of fingers in contact with objects. We visually monitor hand movements as we explore the environment. In addition, we can hear the sound of a fingernail or fingertip tapping on a surface. Contact with wood sounds different from contact with metal, and this auditory input can aid in the identification of surface characteristics, such as texture (e.g., Lederman, 1979).

There are a number of possible statements that might characterize the relations between the senses, and Warren and Rossano discuss these alternatives at length. Vision may dominate touch when discrepant information is presented to the two modalities. The most common method for inducing a discrepancy between the senses has involved manipulating vision of an object with a lens. This was the approach used by Rock and Victor (1964). They distorted vision of a square so that it appeared to be a rectangle, but subjects touched a square. Given this sort of intersensory conflict, most people believed they experienced a rectangle, and were fooled into making a perceptual error by the sense of vision.

Many researchers have assumed that intersensory dominance may depend on which sense is most appropriate for perceiving an attribute, say texture. This modality appropriateness issue is relevant to questions of intersensory dominance, since we may rely on the sense that is most likely to provide good information when the senses are confronted with a conflict (Freides, 1974; Welch & Warren, 1980). Of course, people may simply rely on a sense that is more attention demanding, or that operates more quickly.

It is possible, however, that the senses normally operate in a cooperative manner. They may sometimes provide redundant information about events. In addition, they may even engage in a division of labor, with vision often providing guidance of the hand, and with touch used to gain information about surface characteristics or substance qualities, such as texture, hardness or softness, or thermal properties (Heller, 1982). Warren and Rossano have emphasized this complex sort of interaction in adults. In addition, Bushnell and Boudreau point out that infants often rely on vision for guidance of the hand while examining objects.

Vision may be superior to touch for some types of spatial judgments, but there are cases in which touch may prove better than sight. Touch is "superior" to vision for some of the very smoothest textures (e.g., Heller, 1989). There are important textures we can see but not feel (e.g., the color of wood grain). Wood grain is not always readily tangible. Wood grain can be known via touch for a wood like fir, but not necessarily with a hardwood such as beech. We discover the grain when we use a tool such as a plane or chisel and the wood splits or splinters, because we have misjudged the grain. We also have textures we can feel, but not see "properly" (e.g., sharpness of a razor's edge). In addition, touch can sometimes prove better than sight for temporal judgments. One can feel and hear the vibration of the rods of an Optacon, but these same vibrations are invisible without a strobe light at the proper frequency. Similarly, M. Heller has observed that automobile mechanics often rely on touch to assess the vibration of a car, and prefer to use the hand (or the seat of the pants) rather than the sense of sight. Carl Sherrick has pointed out that people often prefer to test the smoothness of a shave with their hands rather than their eyes.

Researchers have wondered if visual dominance represents the normal relationship between the senses in adulthood and in infancy. It is entirely possible that the relationship between the senses is more complicated, and that intersensory dominance may depend on the particular attribute we are considering, and the status of the observer. For example, while vision appears dominant over touch for identification of two-dimensional forms, this may depend on the increased speed of processing form via sight. If we blur vision sufficiently, normal observers rely on touch (Heller, 1983). Moreover, visual dominance may break down under circumstances where vision is blurry, as in peripheral vision, or in people with low vision. One would further expect that dominance relationships might shift for people undergoing progressive loss of a sense, as with a person losing sight or hearing.

This raises the question of the "normal observer." Most discussions of intersensory relations assume a "normal" observer. We have methods for testing this in sight, and norms are readily available for acuity, contrast sensitivity, and so on. Unfortunately, we don't have this information for touch. We really don't know what normal touch might be, and this greatly complicates any discussion of intermodal relations. It seems likely that just as there are myopic individuals, and those with poor hearing, there are people with poor touch. This is obvious when a person has neuropathy owing to diabetes, or has peripheral nerve damage. However, we don't even have a name for this sort of defect in the sense of touch. Thus, it becomes difficult to answer questions about which sense is most appropriate for perception of a particular attribute, when we can't assess a "normal" observer, and screen out people with "low touch."

Intermodal relations and perceptual saliency are not constant over the course of development. Newborn animals may be more likely to depend on cutaneous input (Gottlieb, 1971). Furthermore, it is entirely possible that there is a shift in reliance on the mouth for exploration of objects to the hands in early infancy (see Turkewitz & Mellon, 1989). Bushnell and Boudreau have focused their discussion on the use of the hands for haptics, and perceptual saliency in early infancy.

REFERENCES

Freides, D. (1974). Human information processing and sensory modality: Cross-modal functions, information complexity, memory, and deficit. *Psychological Bulletin, 81,* 284–310.

Gottlieb, G. (1971). Ontogenesis of sensory function in birds and mammals. In E. Tobach, L. R. Aronson, & E. F. Shaw (Eds.), *The biopsychology of development* (pp. 67–128). New York: Academic Press.

Heller, M. A. (1982). Visual and tactual texture perception: Intersensory cooperation. *Perception & Psychophysics, 31,* 339–344.

Heller, M. A. (1983). Haptic dominance in form perception with blurred vision. *Perception, 12,* 607–613.

Heller, M. A. (1989). Texture perception in sighted and blind observers. *Perception & Psychophysics, 45,* 49–54.

Lederman, S. J. (1979). Auditory texture perception. *Perception, 8,* 93–103.

Rock, I., & Victor, J. (1964). Vision and touch: An experimentally created conflict between the two senses. *Science, 143,* 594–596.

Turkewitz, G., & Mellon, R. C. (1989). Dynamic organization of intersensory function. *Canadian Journal of Psychology, 43,* 286–301.

Welch, R. B., & Warren, D. H. (1980). Immediate perceptual response to intersensory discrepancy. *Psychological Bulletin, 88,* 638–667.

5

INTERMODALITY RELATIONS: VISION AND TOUCH

D. H. Warren
M. J. Rossano
University of California, Riverside

INTRODUCTION

The guiding premise of this chapter is that in order to understand the sense of touch, one must consider the possibility that tactual perception is not entirely independent of vision. Thus the question to which this chapter is addressed is the following: What must we know about the relationship between vision and touch in order to understand touch?

A priori, there are several possibilities for potential interactions. First, vision and touch may be capable of processing the same or similar events, but they may do so largely independently of one another, with little or no interaction. Second, for some events, vision may mediate better perception than touch, and may, when information is available to both modalities, supersede touch entirely. Third, the reverse may happen. Finally, vision and touch may be differentially suited for different events and may interact in various ways, depending on the nature of the perceptual performance that is involved. For example, vision may add substantially to the quality of localization of tactual targets but may contribute little to the tactual discrimination of texture. To skip to the "bottom line," this fourth possibility best describes the literature—the interactions are complex and interesting, and they do not submit to simple conclusions.

One does not have to search very far for instances of the interactions of touch with vision. For example, if for some reason the tactual and visual systems provide different information to the observer about the size of an object, judgments based on the tactual information are not independent of the visual information. Nor are tactual judgments about spatial location or orientation free of the influence of discrepant visual information. (Conversely, visual judgments sometimes are influenced by discrepant tactual information.)

Vision and touch do not only interact in competition, however. For example, Manyam (1986) found judgments of shape to be better when both vision and touch were involved than when just touch was used; similarly, Heller (1982) found that judgments of surface texture were more accurate when both visual and tactual information were available.

Our intention is not to provide an exhaustive review of the literature on visual–tactual interactions. Instead, we review key studies that are representative of larger sets of studies or that illustrate a particularly important point.

A note on terminology is appropriate at the outset. We use the terms "touch" and "tactual" to refer generically to the various ways in which the finger/hand/arm system and its various types of receptors receive information about the external environment. We opt for this shorthand usage while recognizing that there are legitimate and useful distinctions to be made among "proprioception," "kinesthesis," and "haptics." We often use the more specific terms in relation to specific research studies; in the more general case, we use the generic term and beg, in advance, the forebearance of the purist.

RESEARCH PARADIGMS AND EVIDENCE

In this section, our general approach is to consider several varieties of tactual perception, beginning with the perception of texture. In each instance, we consider the quality of tactual performance alone, then review the evidence about how this performance changes when vision is added. We then add to this, where appropriate, consideration of cross-modality transfer, and finally evidence from conflict paradigms.

Perception of Texture

In recent years Lederman and her colleagues have conducted a series of definitive experiments on the perception of texture by touch as well as by vision and audition, and they have addressed the question of visual–tactual interaction as well. Lederman and Abbott (1981) compared visual-only and tactual-only judgments of texture, and they found virtually identical discrimination functions for both accuracy and variability measures. Not surprisingly, these results may be experimentally altered, such as by degrading visual contrast and thereby causing a deterioration of visual performance (Brown, 1960).

Jones and O'Neil (1985) conducted several experiments in which visual and tactual judgments of texture were compared. Generally, tactual performance was about equal to visual performance, as was performance when a visual–tactual cross-modality judgment was required. However, visual judgments were performed more quickly. Jones and O'Neil suggested that in making tactual judgments, observers make a reasonable speed/accuracy tradeoff: "In the nature of things, it will take longer to run one's fingers over an object than it will to scan the same object visually" (p. 71).

In another condition, Lederman and Abbott (1981) allowed subjects both visual and tactual access to the stimuli; this condition showed the same accuracy and variability results as each of the single-modality conditions.

Lederman and Abbott (1981) also gave subjects conflicting information about stimulus texture. In this situation, the relative dominance of vision and touch was virtually identical: Each modality affected the responses to stimuli perceived by the other modality about equally. Furthermore, when the response was made tactually, the tactual texture information dominated, while the visual texture information dominated when the response was made visually. Thus, in this kind of performance, in which the two separate modalities are equally adept at perceiving texture, neither modality produces an improvement when added to the other, and neither is, on balance, dominant over the other in the outcome of a conflict condition.

Heller (1982) found that visual and tactual information, obtained separately, produced equivalent performance on a task involving judgment of smoothness. In this respect, the results confirmed those of Lederman and Abbott (1981). However, using the two modalities together produced a slight improvement over the vision-alone performance. In a subsequent experiment, Heller determined that it was not the availability of visible texture that led to improved performance in the bimodality condition (in fact, he concluded that the visible texture was relatively ignored), but rather the availability of visual guidance of the hand's activity in exploring the tactual texture. Thus Heller concluded that vision and touch are cooperative in the discrimination of texture, with vision performing a supportive role via guidance of hand movements.

Based on a series of experiments, Lederman, Thorne, and Jones (1986) provided an appropriate tentative conclusion about the relationship between vision and touch in the perception of texture, by demonstrating that texture is processed by vision and touch in different ways and for different purposes. Depending on the demand characteristics of the task, observers concentrated on different aspects of the information that was available about a stimulus. Lederman et al. concluded that texture is a multidimensional stimulus quality—the spatial distribution aspects of texture are accessed in order to segment the visual array, whereas tactually, texture is used to judge the surface properties of objects. While not identical to the argument of Heller (1982), the conclusion of Lederman et al. (1986) is similar in making it clear that different aspects of texture information are used differently by the visual and tactual systems.

Perception of Figure

In this section we consider the perception of aspects of figure and the role that vision may have in the tactual perception of figure. By the term "figure," we mean to include not only shape perception, but also other figural properties such as tilt, size, and curvature.

Tilt. Very little work has been done on the visual influence on the tactual perception of tilt. Over (1966) had subjects set a bar so that it felt horizontal; in the three conditions, subjects could either see, or feel, or simultaneously see and feel the bar. Performance was about equally good in the three conditions. When an optical discrepancy was introduced by means of a double Dove prism, orientation judgments corresponded to the visual information up to about 30^0 of discrepancy; beyond 30^0, intersubject variability increased dramatically, but as the discrepancy approached 90^0, judgments of felt orientation were made virtually independently of the visual information. Apparently, the discrepancy was so great that touch and vision were regarded as conveying information about entirely different events.

Klein (1966) used a similar procedure with a 40^0 discrepancy between vision and touch: for young adults, the visual influence on touch averaged about 40%, but there was extremely high intersubject variability. This result is consonant with that of Over (1966), since it was in the mid-range of discrepancy that intersubject variation reached a maximum.

Size and Length. With respect to magnitude estimation of length, touch and vision are generally comparable in providing accurate estimates (Abravanel, 1971; Teghtsoonian & Teghtsoonian, 1965), although relatively small lengths tend to be underestimated by touch in comparison to vision (Teghtsoonian & Teghtsoonian, 1970). Milewski and Iaccino (1982), using a different method, had subjects experience a stimulus length either visually or haptically and then match it, using the same or the other modality. Visual–visual matches were done more accurately than haptic–haptic matches. For cross-modality matching tasks, the quality of performance was generally intermediate but was clearly restricted by the quality of haptic perception.

When subjects are given conflicting visual and tactual information about stimulus length, judgments tend strongly to be based on the information of the visual system (Teghtsoonian & Teghtsoonian, 1970). Similarly, working with the natural magnifying effects of viewing through water, Kinney and Luria (1970) found a heavy reliance on the distorted visual information, even when the subject's own (magnified) hand was also visible for comparison and should have informed the subject that the optical situation was abnormal. In the same vein, Rock and Harris (1967) found virtually complete visual dominance using optical reduction of the visual image.

Thus with respect to the relatively simple properties of size and length, touch is certainly a capable modality in its own right, but it is often not as accurate as vision; when the two modalities convey conflicting information, subjects tend to rely on the visual information.

Shape. A study by Manyam (1986) illustrates a basic approach to the evaluation of shape. Subjects experienced a standard shape (a circle) and adjusted a variable ellipse to match the standard. The standard and variable stimuli were presented simultaneously, so that memory was not involved. The standard and variable were both available to only vision, or only kinesthesis (active movement of a stylus), or kinesthesis and vision together. Performance with visual stimuli was better than that with kinesthetic stimuli, and performance with vision and kinesthesis available was like performance based on vision alone. More generally, Jones (1981) provided a review of the literature on visual and haptic matching of shape and concluded without question that visual performance is better.

A cross-modality judgment paradigm was used by Lobb (1965), who had subjects experience a standard shape either visually or tactually, and then select one of a group of four comparison shapes to match the standard, again using either vision or touch. The stimuli were relative complex, irregular shapes. With a 15-s examination of the standard, visual–visual performance was virtually errorless, far better than tactual–tactual performance. With more difficult shapes and shorter examination time, visual–visual performance was still far better. Cross-modality performance (both VT and TV) was much like tactual–tactual performance. There was a tendency for task variations involving visual inspection of the standard to be performed better than those involving tactual inspection. It is likely that far more complete and therefore more effective visual than tactual inspection can be accomplished in an equal time period, and that the limitations on the quality of tactual–visual and tactual–tactual performance in particular were due to inadequate processing of the tactually experienced standard stimulus.

The classic study of visual–tactual conflict in perception of shape is that of Rock and Victor (1964), who arranged an optical compression of one axis of an object that the subject could simultaneously see and feel. Whether the subject made a response by vision, by touch, or by drawing, the conflict was resolved entirely in favor of the visual information. Rock and Victor concluded that "vision is so powerful in relation to touch that the very touch experience itself undergoes a change" (p. 595). The stimulus shape used by Rock and Victor was not cognitively known to the subject; Power (1981) found similar results for objects with known shape.

Heller (1983) used an ingenious method to place vision and touch into conflict with respect to the perception of shape: The quality of the visual information was degraded by the interposition of stained glass, to the extent that the accuracy of performance with vision alone was similar to that of performance with touch alone. Under these conditions, and with very large degrees of discrepancy between vision and touch, touch was found to dominate in the conflict situation. Thus the usual visual dominance is not immutable but is susceptible to experimental manipulation; presumably the dominance relationships are similarly sensitive to naturally occurring variations in environmental conditions.

It is clear from the result reviewed so far that (a) Tactual judgments of figural properties are generally not as accurate as visual judgments; (b) Adding visual information to tactual information facilitates performance, and (c) When vision and touch provide conflicting information, the visual information is heavily relied upon at the expense of the tactual. The question that remains is how and why these interactions occur.

It does not seem to be the case that tactual information is simply ignored. For example, Over (1966) found that with increasing discrepancy the tactual information was increasingly relied upon. Instead, tactual information may be processed in relation to visual attributes. Rock and Victor's (1964) conclusion, that the "touch experience itself undergoes a change," is not atypical, and it is generally supported by the literature on longer-term adaptation to conditions of visual–tactual conflict, in which proprioceptive information is considered to be reinterpreted in the context of the rearranged visual experience (cf. Welch, 1978, for a review). Lobb (1970) demonstrated a clear asymmetry in cross-modality training effects that supports this notion. When subjects were given practice at visual discrimination, their subsequent tactual discrimination performance was significantly better than without visual practice; however, there was no such improvement in visual discrimination performance following tactual discrimination training. The perception of tactual stimuli was changed as a result of visual experience: Tactual experience did not affect judgments of visual stimuli.

Easton and Falzett (1978) demonstrated a related visual influence on tactual judgments of curvature. Subjects traced a straight or curved rod with the forefinger, either with or without vision, and finger pressure was recorded as tracing occurred. While judgments about the shape of the rod were better when vision was available, the finger pressure patterns were similar whether the eyes were open or closed. In another condition, subjects traced a straight rod while viewing the rod through a curvature-inducing prism, or traced a rod that was actually curved to match the optically induced curvature while viewing through clear glass. The pressure profiles were not different for the two situations: Clearly the finger's tracing activity was not solely directed by tactual feedback, but was influenced by the visually based expectation of what the stimulus shape was.

Heller (1985) demonstrated a similar kind of visual influence on tactual judgments of Morse code and braille patterns. Stimuli were experienced tactually, but in some conditions subjects were able to view their hands through stained glass, which had the effect of preventing sight of the details of the stimuli but permitting the movements of the hand to be seen. Performance was better when visual monitoring was allowed. As in the case of the Easton and Falzett work (1978), the situation was not that of a direct choice between visually and tactually experienced information, but rather one in which vision effectively guided the hand's activity.

These studies show a visual influence on touch that is not of a direct nature, but more a matter of strategy or guidance. Lederman, Klatzky, Chataway, and Summers (1990) demonstrated a type of visual influence on haptic perception that is yet another level removed from direct visual perception of stimulus information. The task involved recognition of raised-line depictions of common objects. The objects' (visual) imageability ratings were positively related to both the speed and the accuracy of their recognition judgments. When raised-line depictions of three-dimensional objects were used, imageability was lower and speed and accuracy decreased. Apparently, aspects of visual representation (in this case imaging) allow the information supplied by the hand to be processed at some level in relation to a visual framework.

This pattern of results is of interest at a theoretical level, and it has potential practical consequences. For example, in designing conditions for tasks in which skilled manual dexterity is at a premium, it may prove advantageous to prevent visual access to the materials that are better felt than seen, while allowing visual monitoring of the larger activities of the hands, for example, intermanual coordination. The precise nature of the coordination between sight and touch in such situations is not known for any given situation, but the potential for facilitating their coordination is evident. Similarly for the visually impaired, it may be that encouraging monitoring of the hands' activities by means of any remaining visual capability can enhance the perception of such arrays as work surfaces or tactile maps.

Perception of Spatial Location

By spatial location, we refer to the observer's ability to perceive and discriminate locations in the spatial environment. The issue of basic sensitivity can be addressed through two different questions: How accurate is localization, and how reliable are localization judgments? Fisher (1960) compared the accuracy of tactual localization with that of visual localization by having observers reach to targets presented to either modality. Tactual acuity was less good than visual, although it was better than auditory acuity. Similarly, Smothergill (1973) had subjects point to visual or proprioceptive targets. Constant errors were greater for proprioceptive than for visual targets.

Smothergill also found variability scores higher for localization of proprioceptive than of visual targets. In our own work over the years, we have found this result consistently, as we suspect others have, but it is rare to find such basic data reported.

Smothergill (1973) assessed a third condition, in which subjects saw their hand as a target, in addition to feeling its location. Constant errors for this condition were more similar to those for visual targets alone than those for proprioceptive targets alone. Adding visual information to proprioceptive changed performance so that it was similar to that for vision alone. Furthermore, variability scores for the visual-plus-proprioceptive condition were more similar to those for vision alone, and smaller than those for proprioception alone.

Thus, when visual information is added to proprioceptive information about spatial location, performance is evidently based largely on the visual information. (A similar situation apparently exists for audition and vision: Schiff and Oldak [1990] found that judgments of arrival times of oncoming stimuli are more accurate when based on visual information than auditory, and that when both sources of information are available, performance is essentially like that with visual information alone.)

Warren and Platt (1975) assessed accuracy and variability of pointing with the unseen hand to a visual target and looking in the direction of the unseen hand. Both tasks were performed quite capably, with mean error and variability of 3.5^0 and 3.0^0, and 6.2^0 and 4.9^0, respectively. Clearly both cross-modality tasks are performed at far better than chance levels.

Perhaps the most telling evidence about the relationships between touch and vision in spatial localization comes from studies that have used the conflict paradigm, in which the observer is presented with a situation in which tactual information indicates one location and visual information indicates a different location.

Hay, Pick, and Ikeda (1965) had the subject view the forefinger through a 26-diopter wedge prism, which had the effect of displacing the optical image of the finger laterally by 14^0. Asked to point to the location of the forefinger with the other, unseen hand, the subject pointed to a location considerably farther toward its optical location than toward its actual, felt location. Hay et al. referred to this visual influence on proprioception as "visual capture," after the usage of Tastevin (1937). Their conclusion, indeed, suggested that the proprioceptive information was largely if not entirely ignored when competing visual information was available.

Considerable follow-up research ensued, in which the conditions under which such visual capture occurred were explored. In an early study, Pick, Warren, and Hay (1969) asked subjects in this conflict condition to do two things: indicate the location where the finger *feels,* and indicate the location where the finger *looks* to be. In the former condition, subjects again indicated a location more toward the optical location than the actual, but the mean response indicated significantly less than total "capture" of proprioception by vision, in contrast to the earlier result of Hay et al. Furthermore, when asked to respond to the seen location of the finger, subjects indicated a mean location that departed significantly from the optical location. Both results suggest that while vision is heavily relied upon in this situation, the nonvisual proprioceptive information does play a significant role and is certainly not completely lost.

In this study, subjects indicated, when asked, that they had not noted the discrepancy between the felt and seen locations, which was about 11^0 of azimuth angle. Warren and Cleaves (1971) reasoned that with larger amounts of imposed discrepancy, the difference might become apparent, leading to a diminution of the reciprocal effects. Indeed, discrepancies of 10^0 and 20^0 produced results that suggested that no discrepancy between felt and seen locations was experienced, but discrepancies of 40^0 and 60^0 were clearly experienced as such.

Warren (1979) demonstrated that the typical heavy reliance on visual information in conditions involving moderate amounts of discrepancy is extremely robust: When the observer's view of the target forefinger was impeded by a dramatic decrease in illumination, visual bias of proprioceptive location was not diminished.

Collectively, this body of conflict research indicates that when sources of visual and proprioceptive information about spatial location are both available, the proprioceptive information is not completely ignored, but that it does tend to be relatively neglected in favor of the visual location information. While the tactual sense can mediate perfectly capable spatial localization behavior when left on its own, it becomes a distinctly subordinate sensory modality when vision is also available.

One implication of this body of evidence is that even under very degraded visual conditions, there is considerable reliance on visual rather than proprioceptive–kinesthetic experience, and vision may serve to direct and facilitate motor activity of the hands and arms even in such extreme situations. In the case of skilled performance by sighted observers in which visual and tactual information about different spatial events must be processed and used, it is important to avoid any indication that the visual and tactual information may be in conflict, since in such situations the tendency is strong to interpret the two modalities as delivering information about just one event, with the consequential relative inattention to the tactual information. Finally, for activities involving the discrimination of spatial location and skilled performance with spatial arrays by visually impaired persons, the use of any residual visual function may be even more important than it is for tasks involving the discrimination of texture.

THEORETICAL APPROACHES

Throughout the history of the study of perception, theoretical alternatives have been offered to account for the relationships among the sensory modalities in general, and in particular about the relationship between touch and vision. Of these, some address visual–tactual relationships in the mature observer, whereas others address developmental issues as well. We touch briefly here on the major developmental views, then focus on theories about visual–tactual organization in the mature observer.

Among the developmental views, perhaps the most famous maxim is that that "touch teaches vision." According to the philosophical empiricist Berkeley, the array on the eye's retina does not have inherent meaning: The observer learns to attribute meaning to the visual array through the establishment of associations between patterns of visual stimulation and patterns of tactile and motor experience. Said another way, tactile/motor experience "calibrates" visual experience. For all of its historical durability and inherent appeal, this notion is not well supported by empirical evidence (cf. Pick, Pick, & Klein, 1967, for a critical review).

Bower (1974), following Hayek (1952), argued on logical grounds that the touch teaches vision formulation could not be valid, since both the visual and the hand systems undergo significant physical growth during infancy; furthermore, their unequal rates of growth would prevent either from serving effectively as a metric of calibration for the other. Instead, Bower argued that there is a "primitive unity" among the senses of the neonate: "Developmentally, visual tangibility precedes tactual tangibility, whereas undifferentiated visual–tactual concordance precedes both" (p. 117). Later, around 5 to 6 months of age, as differentiation proceeds and integration emerges, vision becomes controlling (dominant) of tactile experience.

A theoretical alternative for which there is substantial empirical support may be called a "developmental integration" view. Piaget (1953), for example, described the progression from manual and haptic behavior that is essentially reflexive in the neonate to that which is highly controlled by vision by midway through the first year. The activity of the hand is initially independent of vision but later comes firmly under visual control. Uzgiris (1967), among others, viewed this progression as part of the developing conceptual life of the infant: As the infant's separate visual and tactual experiences with objects become integrated, objects acquire identity as objects, rather than as sets of sensations that are experienced via one modality or another.

Regardless of how various theorists regard the events of the first several months, they tend to agree that by midway in the first year of life, vision and touch are well along toward being organized and integrated with one another, with vision generally playing the dominant role.

This "visual dominance" notion also has characterized much theory about visual–tactual relationships in adults. Both the early work on visual "capture" of touch (e.g., Hay et al., 1965; Rock & Victor, 1964) in situations of immediate response to experimentally imposed discrepancy, and the evidence from adaptation studies (cf. Welch, 1978), in which observers were exposed to a more prolonged experience, tends to show that vision is predominant both in being initially relied upon and in serving as the benchmark for adaptation. Indeed, the visual dominance theory about intermodality organization extends to audition as well on the basis of evidence from localization conflict studies dating back at least to Young (1928).

However, a simple visual dominance view is clearly too broad to cover all aspects of visual–tactual relationships, let alone audition as well. As an example, touch is at least as accurate as vision in the perception of texture under most circumstances, and it is not surprising that vision is not generally dominant (Lederman & Abbott, 1981). Similarly, audition is more effective than vision for the perception of temporally distributed events, and auditory information generally dominates visual in discrepancy situations involving temporal rate (e.g., Myers, Cotton, & Hilp, 1981). In the case of stimuli that rapidly approach the observer on some trajectory, both spatial and temporal information are involved; recent evidence (Schiff & Oldak, 1990) suggests that adding auditory to visual information does not improve the judgment of arrival time. The conflict paradigm has apparently not been applied to the question of spatial–temporal trajectories.

Freides (1974) suggested that the sensory modalities are specialized for different tasks and noted that specialization emerges more strongly as the complexity of the task increases. Along similar lines, Welch and Warren (1980) concluded that whereas visual dominance is indeed the general case for perception of events when the information is spatially distributed, other modalities may dominate in other instances. Welch and Warren proposed a general model of intermodality relationships in which they noted (a) the evidence that the sensory modalities are variously precise at, and thus appropriate for, perception of various kinds of events, and argued (b) that observers distribute their attention among the various available sources of information according to the relative appropriateness of the modalities for the task at hand; thus mediated by differential attention, (c) observers tend to rely on that modality that is more appropriate for the event in question (e.g., touch for texture, vision for spatial location, audition for temporal rate).

DISCUSSION

At a general level, the modality appropriateness formulation makes sense and accounts for a large body of evidence. However, at a more specific level, the formulation may be inadequate. It is well established that the perception of texture does not parallel the perception of shape or azimuth spatial location: Texture information is processed with about equivalent proficiency by either modality, and neither modality dominates the other in conflict situations. In contrast, shape and azimuth spatial location are generally more accurately perceived visually than tactually, and vision tends to predominate in situations of conflict. So, clearly, texture must be considered separately from shape and spatial location in formulating any general rule about the relationship between touch and vision.

Can the perception of shape and spatial location be accounted for by a single general rule? Certainly the evidence shows them to be more similar to one another than either is to texture, but in fact there are considerable points of difference between them as well.

The most compelling evidence for their difference comes from the conflict paradigm. When vision and touch receive conflicting information about the shape of an object, the dominance of vision is complete. As Rock and Victor (1964) noted, touch experience changes, and it changes to correspond to the visual experience, no matter what kind of response is used. In contrast, while resolution of a tactual–visual conflict about spatial location is typically resolved in favor of vision, the visual dominance has generally not been found to be complete. In contrast to the situation with shape, in which the visual information prevails completely, there is a compromise between the visual and the tactual information in the case of location. The compromise does indeed favor vision, but it also takes the tactual information significantly into account.

So it is apparently not possible to generalize across shape and spatial location tasks, let alone across texture, in describing the relationship between touch and vision.

We think that in any case a less categorical, more functional approach is required to evaluate these relationships, and we propose a framework for accomplishing this analysis.

Generally speaking it is important to consider the specific characteristics of any particular perceptual task in relation to the specific properties of the sensory modality (or modalities) that provides information for performance of the task. By the characteristics of a task, we refer to such things as the nature of the distribution of information (whether that information is distributed temporally, spatially, or both), the extent of the spatial and/or temporal distribution, the distinctiveness of the information (e.g., the amount of visual contrast), and the like. By the properties of a sensory modality, we refer to structural and functional properties and limitations, such as the manner of organization of the receptors, the motility of the receptor surface, the capability of the receptors to mediate temporal and spatial distinctions, and the like.

Translated into more practical terms, this principle involves the precise analysis of the visual and the tactual demands of the task. For example, what is the level of illumination, what is the discriminability of the visual information and the tactual information in relation to the limitations of those modalities, what is the timing of the visual and the tactual parts of the task, what are the memory requirements that might bear on the integration of information over time?

This approach suggests the following four general propositions:

(1) The success with which a given modality can mediate a given perception event can be accounted for by evaluating the relationship between the characteristics of the task and the properties of the modality. If the match is good, the quality of perception will be good;

(2) The relative success of two modalities in mediating perception of a given event can be accounted for by comparing those relationships. The modality whose properties provide the better match to task characteristics will mediate perception of a higher quality;

(3) If perception of some event is mediated by one modality (touch, in the case of the present chapter) and another modality (vision, in this case) is added, any change in perception can be accounted for by reference to the properties that the second modality adds to those of the first modality, in relation to the observer's distribution of attention and the characteristics of the task; and

(4) The relative contributions of two modalities when they deliver conflicting information about a perceptual event may be accounted for by evaluating the relationship between the characteristics of the task and the properties of the modalities, mediated by the distribution of the observer's attention to the information coming to the modalities.

Space does not allow complete analysis of these propositions, but we will illustrate how they might account for several of the major phenomena that have been reviewed.

Texture

Lederman (1982) has provided a detailed review of the variables that are involved in tactual texture perception. For our purposes, it is sufficient to note that the skin of the fingertip passes over texture elements with some rate of speed, and that the judgment of texture depends not only on the spatial distribution of the texture elements from moment to moment, but also on the rate of the finger's travel over the texture elements. (We do not suggest that discrimination of texture varies as a function of finger speed, only that it is necessary for the subject to assess the distribution of texture elements in relation to finger speed, and that without information about finger speed, or with incorrect information about finger speed, texture discrimination would suffer.)

The tactual system, with its cutaneous receptors and scanning capabilities, is as good at this as the visual system, with its retinal mosaic and scanning capabilities, is at discriminating optically distributed texture elements. It is not surprising that the two modalities contribute about equally in conflict situations.

What, though, of Heller's (1982) observation that allowing visual monitoring of the hand's activity, even without visible optical texture information, adds to the quality of tactual performance? To address this, we need to ask what specific functional properties of the visual system are being added, and how they might produce an improvement. Optical information about texture was *not* added, and thus the retina's capability for discriminating optical texture is not relevant. Visual monitoring of the hand's movement *was* added. We suggest that visual monitoring allows the subject a better evaluation of the rate of the finger's travel over the texture surface than is available without vision, when kinesthetic cues from the hand/arm system must suffice.

Spatial Location

What about tasks involving spatial location? Consider a task in which the subject runs the forefinger from the midline of the chest out along a radial track to a specified location, and then judges that location in relation to the midline, say by magnitude estimation. The information that is available for this performance is contained in the orientation of the radial and the end location point. The properties of the perceiving system that are involved are kinesthesis (as the hand/arm unit follows the radial), proprioception (of the hand/arm unit as it rests on the target location), and of course the subject's sense of the midline.

Now consider how the addition of vision of the hand's activity would change the task. Suppose that performance takes place in the dark, but with a point of light attached to the subject's fingertip. The added visual information specifies the direction of the radial and the target location. The property of the visual system that comes into play is oculomotor. To the extent that oculomotor cues about eye direction are better than proprioceptive–kinesthetic cues about the hand/arm system, we would expect performance to improve.

Now, though, suppose that performance takes place in a lighted environment against a visually textured background. Now, more information has been added in the form of visible texture, and an additional property of the visual system, its ability to experience simultaneously a spatial array of texture, comes into play. Because the capability of the visual system to use this information is far better than either the use of oculomotor cues about eye direction or proprioceptive–kinesthetic cues about the hand/arm system, we would expect a dramatic improvement in performance. The important difference is that a different kind of information has become available, a kind of information that the visual system is well equipped to use. The situation is analogous to the condition of Heller (1982) when visual monitoring information was added and facilitated the tactual discrimination of texture.

What about visual–tactual conflict in spatial location tasks? Let us consider the task used by Pick et al. (1969), in which the subject's forefinger was passively placed on the target. Without vision, all that is available to determine target location is the proprioceptive information of the hand/arm system. Then (spatially discrepant) visual information is added. In that study, the subject's finger rested on one of a circular array of pegs, so that there was considerable visual texture available in addition to the oculomotor cues about the eye direction necessary to foveate the target finger. Under this condition, with both oculomotor and textured visual information available, we should expect a high degree of reliance on visual information, and indeed visual bias scores ranged from 59% to 70%.

Warren and Cleaves (1971) evaluated visual bias in a situation that was similar but which differed in two very important ways. First, the subject found the target location by actively running the forefinger out along a radial. Thus tactual localization was mediated by kinesthetic information from the hand/arm system as well as proprioceptive information about the hand's position on the target. Second, in the condition in which (spatially discrepant) visual information was added, there was a minimum of visible texture: The subject's finger was seen against a background of cardboard. Thus while oculomotor cues about eye direction were available, as in the Pick et al. (1969) situation, visual texture was minimal. The fact that there was less visual information and more tactual information should produce a lower visual bias, and indeed the value reported by Warren and Cleaves was only 35%, well below the range of values found in other work.

Shape

When the fingers grasp an object (for example, a two-dimensional shape) passively, judgment of the object's shape requires spatial integration of information about the locations of the fingers relative to one another. If the fingers move actively on the contours of the object, then judgment again requires spatial integration of the relative locations of the fingers, but the relative locations change from moment to moment, so that temporal as well as spatial integration is required. If just the forefinger is used to explore the contours of the object, then spatial integration of the different fingers is not required, but spatial–temporal integration of the kinesthetic information from the forefinger/hand/arm system must occur. In each of these cases, there is a substantial demand placed on the perceiver to integrate information spatially and/or temporally. Furthermore, if the contour of the object is textured (for example, the dimpling of a golf ball), the high salience of texture information for the fingertips may detract from the attention that can be devoted to the necessary spatial and/or temporal integration.

Consider now the situation where vision is added, so that the subject may not only see the shape of the object, but may also see the actions of the hand in contacting the object. What additional information is available, and what properties of the visual system can come into play to facilitate performance?

The objects that have typically been used in such studies are relatively small: For example, the square used by Rock and Victor (1964) was 25 mm on a side. At the viewing distance of 40 cm, the visual angle subtended by the nonreduced dimension of the square was only about 3.5^0. The amount of eye scanning required to view an object of this size is minimal, and it is fair to say that the shape of such a stimulus may be seen "at a glance," without the need for temporal or spatial integration of its various parts. Thus quite different demands were placed on the visual and tactual systems in that experiment, different particularly in the need for spatial integration of elements of the shape.

Second, allowing a view of the hand's activities as it contacts the object may improve performance, not because of the additional optical information about shape, but because of the visual system's capability of providing for the necessary spatial and temporal integration of the hand's activities. The analogy to Heller's (1982) visual monitoring of the hand as it experiences texture is evident and intended.

Still another kind of visual function may occur when the object is imageable: Lederman et al. (1990) found more accurate recognition of the objects depicted in raised-line stimuli when those objects were highly visually imageable.

Thus comparatively speaking, shape perception is an awkward task for touch compared with vision, given the characteristics of the stimulus information and the properties of the two modalities, and it is clear how adding vision should facilitate tactual performance. Given this, it is not surprising that in conflict situations, there is overwhelming reliance on the visual information regarding outline shape, and relative neglect of the tactual.

CONCLUSION

In sum, we can account for the changes (or lack of changes) in tactual performance when vision is added to touch, but we cannot do so simply by invoking a global relationship between the two modalities. Furthermore, we cannot do so by referring to the task as generally involving shape, location, or texture information. We *can* do so by evaluating the kinds of information that are available in the various stimulus situations, and by evaluating the properties of the tactual and visual systems that engage the available stimulus information. This functional approach to human perception may hold promise for analysis of other situations of intermodality relations as well as that between vision and touch.

The similarity of this formulation to the analysis of complex tasks to be performed by robotic systems is evident. In analyzing the demands on a robotic system, it is necessary to specify the information sources with precision, to evaluate the capabilities of various components of the system in relation to those sources of information, and to evaluate the output capabilities of the performance end of the system. It is necessary for robotics engineers to use a flexible approach to the relationships among information, information sensors, and output characteristics. Similarly, perceptual psychologists must avoid categorical approaches to information sources, sensory modalities, and motor capabilities, and must instead consider the functional relationships among these elements in order to achieve a full understanding of the nature of the relationships among the sensory modalities within the larger context of adaptive perception.

REFERENCES

Abravanel, E. (1971). Active detection of solid shape information by touch and vision. *Perception & Psychophysics, 10*, 358–360.

Bower, T. G. R. (1974). *Development in infancy.* San Francisco: W. H. Freeman.

Brown, I. D. (1960). Visual and tactual judgments of surface roughness. *Ergonomics, 3*, 51–61.

Easton, R. D., & Falzett, M. (1978). Finger pressure during tracking of curved contours: Implications for a visual dominance phenomenon. *Perception & Psychophysics, 24*, 145–153.

Fisher, G. H. (1960). Intersensory localisation in three modalities. *Bulletin of the British Psychological Society, 41*, 24–25A.

Freides, D. (1974). Human information processing and sensory modality: Crossmodal functions, information complexity, memory, and deficit. *Psychological Bulletin, 81*, 284–310.

Hay, J. C., Pick, H. L., Jr., & Ikeda, K. (1965). Visual capture produced by prism spectacles. *Psychonomic Science, 2*, 215–216.

Hayek, F. A. (1952). *The sensory order.* Chicago: University of Chicago Press.

Heller, M. A. (1982). Visual and tactual texture perception: Intersensory cooperation. *Perception & Psychophysics, 31*, 339–344.

Heller, M. A. (1983). Haptic dominance in form perception with blurred vision. *Perception, 12*, 607–613.

Heller, M. A. (1985). Tactual perception of embossed Morse code and braille: The alliance of vision and touch. *Perception, 14*, 563–570.

Jones, B. (1981). The developmental significance of cross-modal matching. In R. D. Walk & H. L. Pick, Jr. (Eds.), *Intersensory perception and sensory integration.* New York: Plenum Press.

Jones, B., & O'Neil, S. (1985). Combining vision and touch in texture perception. *Perception & Psychophysics, 37*, 66–72.

Kinney, J. A. S., & Luria, S. M. (1970). Conflicting visual and tactual-kinesthetic stimulation. *Perception & Psychophysics, 8,* 189–192.

Klein, R. E. (1966). *A developmental study of perception under conditions of conflicting sensory cues.* Doctoral dissertation, University of Minnesota.

Lederman, S. J. (1982). The perception of texture by touch. In W. Schiff & E. Foulke (Eds.), *Tactual perception: A sourcebook* (pp. 130–167). Cambridge, England: Cambridge University Press.

Lederman, S. J., & Abbott, S. G. (1981). Texture perception: Studies of intersensory organization using a discrepancy paradigm and visual vs. tactual psychophysics. *Journal of Experimental Psychology: Human Perception and Performance, 7,* 902–915.

Lederman, S. J., Klatzky, R. L., Chataway, C., & Summers, C. D. (1990). Visual mediation and the haptic recognition of two-dimensional pictures of common objects. *Perception & Psychophysics, 47,* 54–64.

Lederman, S. J., Thorne, G., & Jones, B. (1986). Perception of texture by vision and touch: Multidimensionality and intersensory integration. *Journal of Experimental Psychology: Human Perception and Performance, 12,* 169–180.

Lobb, H. (1965). Vision versus touch in form discrimination. *Canadian Journal of Psychology, 19,* 175–187.

Lobb, H. (1970). Asymmetrical transfer of form discrimination across sensory modalities in human adults. *Journal of Experimental Psychology, 86,* 350–354.

Manyam, V. J. (1986). A psychophysical measure of visual and kinaesthetic spatial discriminative abilities of adults and children. *Perception, 15,* 313–324.

Milewski, A. E., & Iaccino, J. (1982). Strategies in cross-modality matching. *Perception & Psychophysics, 31,* 273–275.

Myers, A. K., Cotton, B., & Hilp, H. A. (1981). Matching the rate of concurrent tone bursts and light flashes as a function of flash surround luminance. *Perception & Psychophysics, 30,* 33–38.

Over, R. (1966). An experimentally induced conflict between vision and proprioception. *British Journal of Psychology, 57,* 335–341.

Piaget, J. (1953). *The origin of intelligence in the child.* London: Routledge & Kegan Paul.

Pick, H. L., Jr., Pick, A. D., & Klein, R. E. (1967). Perceptual integration in children. In L. E. Lipsett & C. G. Spiker (Eds.), *Advances in child development and behavior* (Vol. 3, pp. 192–220). New York: Academic Press.

Pick, H. L., Jr., Warren, D. H., & Hay, J. C. (1969). Sensory conflict in judgments of spatial direction. *Perception & Psychophysics, 6,* 203–205.

Power, R. (1981). The dominance of touch by vision: occurs with familiar objects. *Perception, 10,* 29–33.

Rock, I., & Harris, C. S. (1967). Vision and touch. *Scientific American, 216,* 94–104.

Rock, I., & Victor, J. (1964). Vision and touch: An experimentally created conflict between two senses. *Science, 143,* 594–596.

Schiff, W., & Oldak, R. (1990). Accuracy of judging time to arrival: Effects of modality, trajectory, and gender. *Journal of Experimental Psychology: Human Perception and Performance, 16,* 303–316.

Smothergill, D. W. (1973). Accuracy and variability in the localization of spatial targets at three age levels. *Developmental Psychology, 8,* 62–66.

Tastevin, J. (1937). En partant de l'experience d'Aristote. *L'Encephale, 1,* 57–84, 140–158.

Teghtsoonian, M., & Teghtsoonian, R. (1965). Seen and felt length. *Psychonomic Science, 3,* 465–466.

Teghtsoonian, R., & Teghtsoonian, M. (1970). Two varieties of perceived length. *Perception & Psychophysics, 8,* 389–392.

Uzgiris, I. C. (1967). Ordinality in the development of schemas. In J. Hellmuth (Ed.), *Exceptional infant* (Vol. 1, pp. 315–334). Seattle: Special Child Publications.

Warren, D. H. (1979). Spatial localization under conflict conditions: Is there a single explanation? *Perception, 8,* 323–337.

Warren, D. H., & Cleaves, W. T. (1971). Visual-proprioceptive interaction under large amounts of conflict. *Journal of Experimental Psychology, 90,* 206–214.

Warren, D. H., & Platt, B. B. (1975). Understanding prism adaptation: An individual differences approach. *Perception & Psychophysics, 17,* 337–345.

Welch, R. B. (1978). *Perceptual modification: Adapting to altered sensory environments.* New York: Academic Press.

Welch, R. B., & Warren, D. H. (1980). Immediate perceptual response to intersensory discrepancy. *Psychological Bulletin, 88,* 638–667.

Young, P. T. (1928). Auditory localization with acoustical transposition of the ears. *Journal of Experimental Psychology, 11,* 399–429.

6

THE DEVELOPMENT
OF HAPTIC PERCEPTION
DURING INFANCY

Emily W. Bushnell
J. Paul Boudreau
Tufts University

INTRODUCTION

The evolution of the forepaws into prehensile hands adapted to explore, maneuver, and exploit objects is recognized as a critical factor in the phylogeny of humans. Similarly, the development of the skillful use of the hands for these purposes is a significant aspect of human ontogeny. Parents and pediatricians alike chart children's "fine motor development," which encompasses a variety of intricate manual behaviors involved in self-feeding, self-dressing, tool use, and writing. In addition to achieving these well-known performatory milestones during the first years of life, children also gain considerable ability to use their hands as a means for acquiring information about objects and surfaces, for discriminating and identifying them. The early development of this *perceptual* function of the hands is the focus of this chapter. We will consider how the infant becomes able to use the hands to assess qualities of objects such as shape, texture, hardness, size, temperature, and weight.

Our discussion will not be exhaustive. For one thing, we will not incorporate infants' abilities to perceive object properties orally. Although mouthing is often considered a form of tactual exploration and is surely an important source of information for infants, its developmental course and its functioning with regard to various object properties are quite different from those of manual exploration (see Rochat, 1987; Ruff, 1989). Hence, we think it is appropriate to treat mouthing as essentially a different modality from per-

ception with the hands, at least during infancy. Indeed, in some places in
the chapter, we shall refer to the oral system as such. Also, our comments
and arguments pertain only to the perception of objects (or parts of objects)
of hand-holdable size. These are surely the stimuli to which the hands' functions are adapted; the haptic perception of either elephants or pinpoints may
involve more complex memory and analytical operations. Finally, developmental changes in the anatomy and physiology of the various skin and joint
receptors involved in haptic perception will not be examined. Instead, the
emphasis will be on "top–down," higher-order processes and on processes
from other domains that may constrain the development of object perception with the hands.

As a framework for the points we intend to make here, we will rely on
the work of Klatzky and Lederman and their colleagues regarding adults'
haptic perception (Klatzky, Lederman, & Metzger, 1985; Klatzky, Lederman,
& Reed, 1987; Lederman & Klatzky, 1987; in press). They argue convincing-
ly that haptics is an impressive and distinctive perceptual system, oriented
toward the encoding of object substance (i.e., what material the object is made
of) rather than object structure (i.e., how the material is arranged in space).
They have observed, for example, that subjects are remarkably good at recognizing real, everyday objects by touch alone, although they are notably poor
at haptically recognizing raised-contour "drawings" of objects that preserve
spatial information but do not retain temperature, texture, or hardness cues
(Klatzky et al., 1985). In support of the same point, Klatzky et al. (1987) found
that the dimensions of texture and hardness were relatively salient for blindfolded subjects asked to freely sort objects by similarity, whereas shape was
more salient for subjects able to see or instructed to visualize the objects.

Lederman and Klatzky (1987; in press) explain the special perceptual abilities of the hands by calling attention to particular hand movements that they
call *exploratory procedures* or "EPs." An EP is a stereotyped pattern of hand
movement that maximizes the sensory input corresponding to a certain object property. For example, rubbing the fingers back and forth across the
surface of an object produces changes in local skin pressure with relative
motion. This sort of sensory input varies according to an object's surface texture (roughness); thus, engaging in the "lateral motion" EP makes texture
easy to assess. In their empirical work, Lederman and Klatzky (1987; in press)
have documented strong linkages between hand movement profiles and the
perception of specific object properties. When the solution to an experimental task hinged on *texture*, subjects engaged in the "lateral motion" EP
described earlier; for *hardness*, they engaged in the "pressure" EP (squeezing or poking the object); for *temperature*, they engaged in either "static contact" or "enclosure" (enveloping as much of the object as possible with the
hands); for *volume* (three-dimensional size), they also engaged in "enclosure";
for *weight*, they engaged in "unsupported holding" (resting the object flat

in the hand and lifting it away from any supporting surface, often repeatedly); and for *exact shape,* they engaged in "contour following" (moving the fingers smoothly and nonrepetitively over the edges of the object).

Furthermore, by comparing performance across trials on which subjects were restricted to the use of single, prespecified EPs, Lederman and Klatzky (1987) were able to determine the relative efficiency (i.e., accuracy and speed) of the different EPs for extracting information about the various dimensions of objects. Some EPs, enclosure for example, proved to be broadly sufficient, permitting above chance but not always highly accurate performance for most object dimensions. Other EPs were more highly specialized, yielding the most accurate information about some one object dimension but little or no precise information about others. Lateral motion, for example, was primarily effective for assessing texture, and pressure was primarily effective for assessing hardness. Contour following was unique in that it was the *only* EP to yield above chance performance for exact shape; it also permitted above-chance but not the best performance on most of the other dimensions.

From their collected findings, Klatzky et al. (1987) concluded that the nature of haptic object perception is generally dictated by "ease of encoding" considerations involving EPs. The most salient object properties are those for which relative precise information may be extracted with hand movements that are relatively fast and simple to execute. Thus, an object's texture, temperature, and hardness are prominent with spontaneous haptic exploration because they become evident with just brief, repetitive hand movements applied over any limited part of the object. An object's shape, however, is not prominent with spontaneous handling because it becomes fully apparent only with contour following, a slow-to-execute EP that involves precise motor tracing (usually performed with both hands) around the entire object. In cases when instructions or other factors lead one to be interested in a specific object property, such a focus promotes the use of hand movements that are necessary or optimal to extract that information, at the expense of other EPs and thus at the expense of acquiring the information they optimally yield.

The foregoing discussion can be summarized by positing that the payoff (perceptually speaking) of any given haptic encounter with an object is a function of the perceiver's answers to two questions: "Is there anything special that I need or want to know about this object?" and "What is the most effective way I can move my hands to gather (that) information about it?" We think that the answers to these same two questions may delimit what an infant perceives about an object from an episode of handling it. If an infant has no awareness of or reason to attend to a particular object property, he or she would not be motivated to generate specialized hand movements that enhance sensitivity to it, and the baby would therefore be unlikely to perceive the property in question with any precision. And even if an infant is cognizant of a particular object property, if he or she is unable to motorically execute the EP that is optimal for it, again the baby would be unlikely to perceive the object property precisely. Conversely, if a particular EP is a motor behavior that an infant commonly engages in for some reason, such activity may lead the infant to become aware of the related object property, heretofore unknown. Thus, it seems that the developmental course of haptic perception may be constrained by the development of attention to object properties and by the development of the ability and inclination to execute various movements with the hands. This is the crux of our argument and will be elaborated and supported in the remainder of the chapter.

THE DEVELOPMENT OF HAPTIC PERCEPTION— EMPIRICAL FINDINGS

In order to ground our argument in fact, it is appropriate at this point to review what is presently known about haptic perception during infancy. We will organize this survey of the literature according to the various object properties that are haptically perceivable. This strategy will allow us to sketch a developmental timetable for haptic perception, specifying the sequence in which different sensitivities seem to emerge. This timetable will then be discussed in light of the constraints that have been identified.

Shape

Most studies of infants' haptic abilities have focused on the object property of shape. To illustrate how psychologists determine what shapes infants can perceive by touch, we will describe an early study by Rose, Gottfried, and Bridger (1981a). These researchers tested 12-month-old infants using an adaptation of the familiarization-recognition test procedure developed by Fantz (1956; Fantz & Nevis, 1967) to study infant visual perception. Each infant sat on a parent's lap in a totally dark room. A tray containing five identical small plastic shapes (e.g., stars) was placed in front of the baby, and he or she was encouraged to handle and play with the objects for a familiarization period of 1 min. Five replicas of a new shape (e.g., circles) were then added to the tray and the baby was allowed to handle and play with the 10 objects (5 familiar and 5 novel) for a test period of 2 min. The infant's behavior throughout the experiment was recorded with an infrared video system. Rose et al. found that during the test period, infants spent significantly more time handling the novel objects than handling the familiar ones. Such a systematic preference could only be possible if the infants recognized the one shape by touch and discriminated the other shape from it, also by touch. In other words, such a preference implies that the infants were able to haptically perceive the two shapes and the difference between them.

Using this method, Rose et al. (1981a) found that 12-month-old infants were able to haptically distinguish a star from a circle, an octagon from an hourglass shape, and a sphere with a protruding nipple from a sphere with a rectangular notch or missing segment. With a similar procedure, Soroka, Corter, and Abramovitch (1979) found that 10-month-olds haptically discriminated a ring from a cross. Likewise, Streri and Pecheux (1986) found that 5-month-olds distinguished a star from a lobed, flower-like object and a solid square from a square with a hole in the middle. Finally, Streri (1987) found that 2- to 3-month-olds haptically discriminated a solid disk from a disk with a hole in the middle (a ring).

Also pertinent to infants' haptic perception of shape are the results of studies on the development of cross-modal perception. The question of interest in these studies is whether infants can recognize the equivalence of a shape experienced haptically and the same shape experienced visually. Typically, infants are familiarized with a certain shape in one modality (e.g., haptically) and then are offered a test choice between that shape and a novel one both presented in the alternative modality (e.g., visually). A systematic preference for the novel test shape over the familiar one implies that the infant had perceived the shape in the one modality during the familiarization period and then transferred this knowledge to the other modality to recognize it and discriminate it from the novel object during the test period. Therefore, a positive result on this sort of task means that the infants are able to haptically (and visually as well) perceive and distinguish the two shapes involved. Null results are rather more ambiguous, because they might be due to a failure to distinguish the shapes either haptically or visually *or* to a failure to relate the information across vision and touch even though it was perceived within each modality. However, research with older children and adults indicates that haptic sensitivity is usually the limiting factor in cross-modal performance (Jones, 1981), so we will take the results of cross-modal studies with infants as indicative of their haptic perceptual abilities.

Accordingly, cross-modal research conducted by Gottfried, Rose, and Bridger (1977) and by Rose, Gottfried, and Bridger (1981b) provides evidence that 12-month-olds and 6-month-olds, respectively, can haptically distinguish a cross from an ellipsoid and also a cylinder from a cylindrical finial (a cylinder with multiple protrusions and indentations along the sides). Similarly, Ruff and Kohler (1978) found that 6-month-olds can discriminate a cube from a sphere by touch, and Streri and Spelke (1988) found that 4-month-olds can haptically discriminate two rings connected by a rigid bar from the same two rings not connected. The prototypical cross-modal study of Bryant, Jones, Claxton, and Perkins (1972) revealed that 6.5- to 11-month-olds can haptically distinguish an ellipsoid from an ellipsoid with a rectangular notch or missing segment.

However, Bryant et al. (1972) found that their subjects did *not* similarly distinguish a cube from a cube with a rectangular notch or missing segment. Bushnell (1978) and Bushnell and Weinberger (1987) also reported null results regarding certain shapes in a cross-modal task. They employed the "violation-of-expectancy" paradigm; infants were observed as they responded to "trick" trials (created via a mirror arrangement) on which what they felt in a certain place was discrepant from what they could see there. Bushnell (1978) observed that for certain discrepancies, 15-month-olds exhibited surprise and problem-solving behaviors such as manual search. However, the infants did not seem to detect a discrepancy between a cube and a cross-like solid. Bushnell and Weinberger (1987) reported that 11-month-olds likewise had difficulty discriminating the same two shapes. Finally, Brown and Gottfried (1986) studied the cross-modal abilities of 1-, 3-, and 5-month-olds. They tested each infant with four pairs of objects: a sphere vs. a sphere with nubs, a cylinder vs. a pyramid, a cylinder vs. a cross-like solid, and a cylinder with a notch or segment missing vs. a cube. They found no consistent evidence of cross-modal transfer for any of the age groups.

To summarize the results of work pertaining to infants' haptic perception of shape, the various studies can be sorted into three types, according to the nature of the stimuli employed. In some studies, the stimuli differed *topologically,* meaning that the differences between them would be preserved even under hypothetical bending and stretching, as with Streri's (1987) disk versus a disk with a hole in it and Streri and Spelke's (1988) connected versus not connected rings. In other studies, the stimuli differed *featurally;* one contained abrupt angles, edges, and protrusions while the other contained only smooth curves, as with Ruff and Kohler's (1978) cube versus a sphere, Rose et al.'s (1981a) octagon versus an hourglass, and Brown and Gottfried's (1986) cylinder versus a pyramid. In the third sort of studies, the stimuli differed *configurationally;* that is, both stimuli contained the same kind of features, such as angles and edges, but these were different in number or spatial arrangement for the two stimuli. This is the case, for example, with Bushnell's (1978; Bushnell & Weinberger, 1987) cube versus a cross-like solid and with Bryant et al.'s (1972) cube versus a notched cube. When the results of the shape studies are examined with this classification scheme in mind, it seems that infants as young as 2, 3, and 4 months old can haptically perceive topological shape differences. It also seems that from about 6 months on, but perhaps not at younger ages, infants can haptically perceive featural shape differences. Finally, it seems that even rather "old" infants (i.e., 6.5- to 11-month-olds, 15-month-olds) may have difficulty haptically perceiving configurational shape differences. Indeed, the youngest documented instance of configurational shape perception by touch is that reported by Landau (1990) involving 18-month-old blind children. This pattern of distinct results for the three types of shape differences will be important to our later interpretive discussion.

Texture

The evidence regarding infants' haptic sensitivity to the object property of texture is both less ample and less direct than that for shape. To our knowledge, there are no published studies involving the exclusively haptic presentation of stimuli differing in texture. The clearest data come from several studies designed to investigate the perception of texture across vision and touch, which of course entails the perception of texture by touch. Using the violation-of-expectancy paradigm described earlier, Bushnell (1982) found that both 9.5-month-olds and 11-month-olds detected a visual–tactual discrepancy between a fur-covered cylinder and a knobby object made of smooth plastic. Similarly, Bushnell and Weinberger (1987) found that under certain conditions, 11-month-olds detected a discrepancy between a fur-covered cube and a smooth wooden cube. In a third study, Bushnell, Weinberger, and Sasseville (1989) presented infants with wooden dowels to grip. Along the back of some of the dowels (where it could not be seen from the infant's initial position), there was a strip of fur, sandpaper, or bumps; other dowels were plain. Bushnell et al. found that 12-month-olds, and to a lesser extent 9-month-olds, were more likely to lean forward in order to look at the back of the dowel after gripping a textured dowel than after gripping a plain one. They reasoned that such exploratory behavior could only have been predicated on haptic sensitivity to the textures involved.

Preliminary observations from two ongoing studies in our lab further indicate that infants can haptically perceive texture during the second half-year of life. In one study, 8- to 10-month-old infants are given small cylinders to handle under "dim lighting" conditions intended to reduce the influence of vision. The cylinders are either smooth (wooden dowels covered with contact paper), furry (wooden dowels covered with soft fur material), rough (rigid, bristly hair curlers), or compressible (sponge hair curlers). The results from the 10 infants tested so far indicate that they moved their fingers over the objects for longer durations when they were rough or furry than when they were smooth. In a second study, 7- to 8-month-old infants sitting in the dark are presented with surfaces textured on one side (either covered with soft bristles, comprised of a small depth of water, or bearing several short cylinders) and plain on the other; their behavior is observed via infrared video recording. Infants invariably touch the textured side of the stimulus longer than they touch the plain side, indicating that they discriminate the two. Furthermore, it seems that the infants engage in different manual behaviors according to the nature of the particular texture presented, suggesting that they can haptically discriminate the various stimuli from one another.

Finally, a number of studies have focused on infants' responses to texture in "naturalistic" situations, in which the infants can simultaneously see the stimulus objects as they handle them. The results of such studies are difficult to interpret *vis-à-vis* haptic perception, since an object's texture is visible as well as palpable. Thus, any special responses on the infants' part to different textures might be motivated by visual discrimination rather than haptic discrimination. Nevertheless, the results of these studies also indicate that infants from 6 to 12 months of age are sensitive to texture with their hands. Ruff (1982) found that 12-month-olds fingered textured objects (generally "bumpy" ones) more than smooth objects, and Ruff (1984) reported the same finding for 6-, 9-, and 12-month-olds. Similarly, Lockman and McHale (1989) observed that 6-, 8-, and 10-month-olds fingered rough objects more than smooth ones, and Palmer (1989) found that 6-, 9-, and 12-month-olds picked up, released, scooted, and squeezed furry objects more than smooth plastic ones. Lastly, Steele and Pederson (1977) reported that 6-month-olds familiarized with either a furry ball or a smooth ball subsequently responded to the alternate stimulus with both increased looking and increased manual contact.

Somewhat surprisingly, there have been no studies designed to investigate the abilities of infants younger than 6 months to perceive texture, whether by touch alone or across modes or accompanied by vision. However, some of the studies that focus on shape perception may be relevant to texture perception and helpful in this regard. In particular, we think that featural shape differences may be akin to texture differences. An object with abrupt angles, edges, and protrusions may be considered "bumpy" in comparison with an object comprised of smooth curves. The hand as it grips the former sort of object or the fingers as they move over it make contact with the object discontinuously, whereas the gripping hand or moving fingers contact the latter sort of object more constantly. If haptic and cross-modal studies involving featural shape differences are included as studies of texture perception, their results are consistent with the conclusion that infants are haptically sensitive to texture by about 6 months of age (e.g., Rose et al., 1981b; Ruff & Kohler, 1978). They furthermore suggest that at younger ages, infants may not readily perceive texture (e.g., Brown & Gottfried, 1986).

Hardness

The evidence concerning infants' haptic perception of hardness is similar in quality to that regarding texture. Again the only available information derives from studies investigating cross-modal perception and from observations of infants' naturalistic play with objects. Gibson and Walker (1984) reported that 12-month-olds visually preferred either a rigid or a flexible cylinder, depending on which of these they had previously handled in the dark. They also observed that during the dark period, the infants typically squeezed and pressed on the flexible object, whereas they tended to strike the rigid object against the table. Lockman and Wright (1988) and Palmer (1989) both observed infants playing with objects in the light and likewise found that infants ranging in age from 6 to 12 months tended to squeeze spongy objects and bang hard ones. In the same vein, McCall (1974) found that infants 8, 10, and 11.5 months old exhibited more manipulation when playing with more flexible objects, and Pederson, Steele, and Klein (1980) similarly found that 6-month-olds exhibited more touching and pulling with more flexible toys. Finally, in the preliminary work we have conducted in "dim light," 8- to 10-month-old infants banged and rotated (waved) the wooden cylinders more than the compressible ones, and they fingered the compressible ones more than the hard ones. Thus it seems that from 6 or 7 months on, infants may haptically discriminate hard objects from flexible or compressible ones. Rochat (1987) reported similar abilities on the part of newborns, 2-month-olds, and 3-month-olds, but his dependent measures may have just reflected the grasp reflex. Thus, the haptic abilities of younger infants *vis-à-vis* the object property of hardness are not yet known.

Size (Volume)

Object size (or volume, as Lederman & Klatzky, 1987, call it) has been explicitly varied in only two studies with any relevance to infant haptic perception. Bushnell (1978) reported that 15-month-olds readily detected a visual–tactual discrepancy between a small cube and a large cube, and Palmer (1989) observed that 6-, 9-, and 12-month-olds picked up small objects, released them, switched them from hand to hand, and touched them with one hand rather than with two hands more frequently than large objects. Younger infants' sensitivity to object size has not been directly investigated, but here again the results of some studies that focus on shape may be helpful. In this case, we think that the shape differences we characterized as topological may reduce to size differences. An object with a hole in it (such as a ring) is usually gripped handle-style, with the fingers through the hole, provided the hole is large enough and the hands small enough. As such, the hand encloses something of much smaller dimensions than if it were to span the whole object, as it must when the object is solid. Meanwhile, to support an even larger object, both hands must cooperatively span the breadth of the object, whereas when holding two smaller objects, the two clenched hands can move independently. Thus Streri's (1987) results with a ring versus a disk and Streri and Spelke's (1988) results with the connected rings versus the not connected ones may reflect that very young infants can discriminate the different manual postures involved in holding small, medium, and large objects. At any rate, the admittedly very limited literature related to infants' haptic perception of object size has produced no null findings—as young as infants have been tested, they have appeared to haptically discriminate things of different sizes.

Temperature

A similar conclusion can be reached regarding infants' haptic perception of temperature. Only two studies have focused on this property; both involved 6-month-olds as subjects. Bushnell, Shaw, and Strauss (1985) and also Bushnell et al. (1989) familiarized infants with little cylinders that were either warm or cool to the touch and then observed their responses to a cylinder of the alternative temperature. Infants in both studies touched the cylinder of a new temperature longer than they touched a control stimulus of the familiar temperature, thus demonstrating haptic sensitivity to temperature at 6 months of age. No studies have examined sensitivity to temperature on the part of younger infants, although certainly very young infants withdraw their hands reflexively from stimuli that are painfully hot or cold.

Weight

Lastly, as with object size and temperature, infants' haptic perceptual abilities for object weight have received very little attention in the empirical literature. What little evidence there is suggests that haptic sensitivity to weight emerges somewhat later in development than seems to be the case for size and temperature and also for texture and hardness. Ruff (1984) found that neither 9- nor 12-month-old infants responded in any special way to an object heavier or lighter than one with which they had been familiarized, although they showed increased looking and increased manual exploration toward objects changed in shape or in texture. Palmer (1989) found that 9- and 12-month-olds waved light objects more than heavy ones; however, 6-month-olds did very little waving in general and did not wave the light and heavy objects differentially. Finally, in a tangentially related study concerning infants' ability to anticipate the weight of an object from its visual appearance, Mounoud and Bower (1974) found that 9.5-month-olds exhibited appropriate arm tension during manual retrieval of the object, but 6-, 7-, and 8-month-olds did not.

Summary of the Empirical Literature

From the evidence presented regarding infants' haptic sensitivity to individual object properties, it is immediately obvious that there are many gaps in the literature. Most of the work cited has been conducted with infants 6 months or older, and most of it has involved either cross-modal or bimodal (i.e., with vision available) stimulus presentations rather than strictly haptic ones. These limitations mean that the developmental course of haptic sensitivity to certain object properties can be outlined only rather imprecisely and with some attendant qualifications. In the case of hardness, for example, we know from Gibson and Walker's (1984) work that 12-month-olds can distinguish hard objects from compressible ones without vision. However, the behavior of 6- to 11-month-olds with hard and compressible objects has been observed only with vision available, and the behavior of infants younger than 6 months has not been properly examined under either circumstance. Thus, it could be that infants just 1 or 2 months old can perceive hardness with their hands without vision, or it could be that infants as old as 9 or 10 months can perceive hardness only when they can see the consequences of their manipulations; from the evidence currently available, either of these scenarios or anything in-between is possible. Similar ambiguities exist with respect to infants' perception of texture, size, and temperature. Clearly, further normative research on infants' haptic perception is called for.

Despite the lacunae duly noted, a general picture of the way in which haptic sensitivity unfolds does emerge from our survey of the various object properties. This picture is all the more clear and consistent if featural shape differences are included as texture differences and if topological shape differences are included as size differences, as has been discussed. It seems that infants are probably able to perceive size (volume) and temperature with the hands very early on, during the first months of life. They may also be able to perceive hardness haptically at very young ages; alternatively, sensitivity to hardness may emerge somewhat later, at about 6 months of age. Sensitivity to texture seems to be absent or minimal prior to about 5 or 6 months and then develops from there. Weight perception seems to be absent for an even longer part of the first year; it becomes evident at about 9 months at the earliest. Finally, haptic sensitivity to shape (i.e., to configurational shape), seems to emerge last of all, sometime after the first 12 or 15 months of life.

THE DEVELOPMENT OF HAPTIC PERCEPTION— EXPLANATIONS AND PREDICTIONS

We believe the developmental timetable just outlined is explainable and even predictable from a consideration of the constraints on haptic perception identified at the beginning of the chapter. Recall our conclusion from Klatzky and Lederman's work (Klatzky et al., 1985; Klatzky et al., 1987; Lederman & Klatzky, 1987; in press) that the developmental course of haptic perception must be constrained by both the development of attention to object properties and the development of the ability and inclination to execute various movements with the hands. In the remainder of the chapter, we will present relevant aspects of infant cognitive and motor development and show how they combine to determine the developmental timetable for haptic perception that emerged from our review of the literature.

Motor Prerequisites

The development of manual motor behavior during infancy will be discussed first, because its maturational sequence is relatively straightforward and well established. Generally speaking, infants' actions with objects in their hands progress through three phases during the first year. At birth and through about 3 months of age, infants given an object simply clutch it tightly in the fist; this behavior is mediated by the palmar grasp reflex, which is present even before birth (Erhardt, 1973; Twitchell, 1965). Thus clutched, the object is typically either simply held in the one hand, brought to the mouth (Rochat, Blass, & Hoffmeyer, 1988), or brought to midline and also clutched with the second hand (White, Castle, & Held, 1964). There is very little independent finger movement; if the fingers move at all, they open and close synergistically in a kitten-like "kneading" pattern.

Sometime during the third month or so, infants begin to develop visual control of the hand as well as more differentiated finger movements. They look at the hand as it moves through space and at the fingers as they open and close, sometimes synergistically and now sometimes sequentially also (Piaget, 1952; White et al., 1964). At first these activities are conducted in empty space ("visual hand regard") or with the other hand serving as the object which is touched and fondled ("midline finger play"). Later, once the infant has achieved visually guided reaching in the fourth or fifth month (see Bushnell, 1985), these activities are conducted toward objects held in the hands or sometimes in the mouth. The movements of the hands in this second phase of manual behavior are characterized by repetition. The infant engages in the same movement pattern over and over again, so much so that Thelen (1979, 1981) dubbed these activities "rhythmical stereotypies." She observed that manual rhythmical stereotypies peak in frequency at 6 or 7 months of age and include such behaviors as scratching objects, rubbing them, squeezing them, poking them, waving them, banging them, and passing them from hand to hand. When accompanied by looking, these activities are called "examining behavior" (Ruff, 1986; Uzgiris, 1967); such activities with and without looking comprise the predominant styles of play with objects between 6 and 9 months (Belsky & Most, 1981; Fenson, Kagan, Kearsley, & Zelazo, 1976). The repetitive hand movements are typically carried out with only one hand, while the other hand either stabilizes the object against a surface or against the infant's torso or counterbalances the infant in the newly achieved and therefore fragile sitting posture (Rochat & Senders, 1990).

By 9 or 10 months, infants have developed good postural control for sitting, so that this body position no longer demands that one hand be reserved for propping up or balancing the torso. At this point, infants enter the third phase of manual behavior with objects, characterized by "complementary bimanual" activities (Bruner, 1971; Ramsey, Campos, & Fenson, 1979; Ramsey & Weber, 1986). In these activities, one hand supports or operates on one part of an object while the other hand manipulates another part of the object. Furthermore, the infant's activities are no longer repetitive and stereotypical but begin to be functional and tailored to the particular object involved (Belsky & Most, 1981; Fenson et al., 1976). Thus, an infant approaching the first birthday may attempt to dial a telephone with one hand while holding it with the other, comb a doll's hair with one hand while holding it with the other, use a hammer or screwdriver with one hand while holding the nail or screw with the other, and so on.

The progression of manual behavior with objects from simple clutching to rhythmical stereotypies to complementary bimanual activity is a function of neurological development and motor practice, and it both impels and is impelled by cognitive development during infancy. Most important for our purposes, the progression also imposes strong constraints on the development of haptic perception during infancy. The hand behaviors typical of each phase approximate certain EPs identified by Lederman and Klatzky (1987) as linked to the perception of certain object properties. Accordingly, during each phase, infants might be able to haptically perceive those object properties that are related to the EPs their hand movements resemble; however, they would be unlikely to perceive properties of objects related to EPs more intricate than the hand movements they execute. Let us reconsider the progression of hand behaviors with objects during infancy in this light and see what it implies regarding the development of haptic perception.

During the first three or four months of life, infants mainly simply clutch objects with their hands. This clutching is akin to the static contact and enclosure EPs described by Lederman and Klatzky (1987). According to their results, static contact and enclosure are the most useful EPs for apprehending object temperature and size (volume). Enclosure is also moderately useful though not optimal for apprehending texture and hardness. Neither enclosure nor static contact is very useful for apprehending object weight or configurational shape. Thus, reasoning from their available hand movements, very young infants might be able to haptically perceive temperature and size rather well. Their abilities for perceiving texture and hardness might be somewhat more dubious, and one would not expect them to be able to perceive weight or configurational shape with any precision at all.

From the fourth or fifth month on through about 9 months of age, infants' manual activities with objects are stereotypical and repetitive; among other things, babies scratch objects, poke and squeeze them, and wave and bang them. These activities are similar to Lederman and Klatzky's (1987) lateral motion, pressure, and unsupported holding EPs, respectively. According to their results, lateral motion is the most effective EP for apprehending texture, pressure is the most effective EP for apprehending hardness, and unsupported holding is the most effective EP for apprehending weight. None of these EPs is especially effective for apprehending other object properties, though. Thus, when they are between about 5 and 9 months of age, one would expect from their hand movements that infants might be able to haptically perceive texture, hardness, and weight. Like younger infants, they would also be able to perceive temperature and size, since merely holding the object is sufficient for perceiving either of these. However, one would expect these infants to have difficulty haptically perceiving configurational shape, because neither holding an object nor repetitively acting on it in any simple way is sufficient for that purpose.

Finally, after 9 or 10 months of age, infants are capable of more precise, differentiated hand movements with objects. They can maneuver or position an object with one hand while acting upon it with the other. This sort of complementary bimanual activity is involved in the contour-tracing EP, the only EP that Lederman and Klatzky (1987) found to be effective for the apprehension of configurational shape. Thus one would expect infants to be proficient at haptically perceiving configurational shape only after the age of about 10 months, when they can manipulate objects in the complex way required for contour tracing.

The sequence of development for haptic perception that we have inferred from considering motor development is consistent with the timetable identified from the review of the literature in many respects. The ability to perceive temperature and size with the hands is present very early, the abilities to perceive texture and hardness become reliable at about 6 months and may be rudimentarily present before that, and the ability to perceive configurational shape emerges much later, after 10 months of age. The one notable exception to a good fit between our expectations based on motor development and our observations from the literature concerns the object property of weight. The waving and banging that infants frequently do with objects from about 6 months on is akin to the unsupported holding EP that Lederman and Klatzky (1987) identified as optimal for apprehending weight, yet the literature suggests that infants do not haptically perceive weight until at least 9 months of age.

Cognitive Considerations

To account for the relatively late onset of weight perception and to understand further the order in which other haptic sensitivities emerge, we must consider the other factor identified earlier as important to infants' haptic perception, namely, the development of attention to object properties. We believe that this factor acts in combination with motor development to determine haptic perception. Appropriate hand movements may be thought of as a necessary prerequisite for perceiving a certain object property. That is, in order to perceive a certain object property with any precision, an infant must be able to execute the sort of hand movements that are effective for the apprehension of that property. Merely doing so for spurious reasons may in fact lead the infant to discover or become aware of the corresponding variations amongst objects. However, some a priori knowledge of the object property or some reason to attend to it will increase the probability of its being perceived, given the requisite hand movements. Thus, to explain further the sequence in which different haptic sensitivities seem to emerge, it should be useful to examine factors which make different object properties more or less known and more or less important to infants of various ages.

The outline of infant cognitive development described by Piaget (1952) provides some indications regarding the relative importance of various aspects of objects at particular ages. Piaget observed that the behaviors of young infants are centered on what might be called the aesthetic consequences of the actions for themselves. His second (1 to 4 months) and third (4 to 8 months) stages of sensorimotor development are characterized by "primary" and "secondary circular reactions," respectively. In primary circular reactions, infants repeat activities involving their own bodies that provide interesting sensory feedback; they suck their fingers, babble, watch their hands as they move, and play with their toes. In secondary circular reactions, infants similarly seek to "make interesting sights (and other experiences) last," but in this case the activities involve external objects; babies shake rattles to hear their noise, bat at mobiles to watch them swing, stroke stuffed animals to feel their softness, and so on. Through these activities, infants presumably come to understand key features of how their bodies work and how they can affect objects. With this foundation, infants then move into the fourth sensorimotor stage (8–12 months), characterized by functional behaviors, that is, by actions using objects as means to ends. Now infants may use sticks to retrieve out-of-reach toys, use buckets as containers for other objects, roll balls to knock down towers of blocks, and so on. Through these activities, according to Piaget, infants consolidate knowledge about spatiotemporal and cause–effect relations.

If the several object properties under discussion are considered as they might relate to the infant behaviors described by Piaget, it seems that some properties are probably more relevant to interesting sensory feedback, whereas others may be more relevant to the functions for which an object may be used. In particular, an object's temperature, texture, and hardness may primarily relate to its aesthetic value. Skin contact with a warm or cool object can be soothing, uncomfortable, or painful, depending on the degree of warmth or coldness. Stroking a textured object often provides pleasant tactile feedback and sometimes also interesting visual consequences, as does squeezing or poking a compressible object. Indeed, we have seen that beginning at about 6 months of age, infants preferentially exhibit these behaviors toward textured and compressible objects. Variations in haptic weight or shape do not seem to be as intrinsically interesting. We do not enjoy aimlessly hoisting things of a given weight or tracing things of a given shape to the same extent that we derive pleasure from just stroking things of certain textures and squeezing things of certain compressibilities (witness the commercial success of the functionless Koosh ball). However, both weight and shape are extremely relevant to an object's utility. Only round things roll, only flat things can fit under the couch, only reasonably heavy things will knock down the aforementioned tower of blocks, only light things can be easily picked up, and so on. An object's temperature and even more so its texture and hardness may also constrain its utility, to be sure, but arguably not as much as its weight and shape do. Finally, the property of size is certainly as relevant to an object's utility as weight and shape are, but size may have an aesthetic relevance for infants as well, in that only smallish things can successfully be grasped and put in the mouth.

The aesthetic versus functional relevances of the different object properties may have implications for the emergence of haptic sensitivity to them, in light of Piaget's observations regarding the nature of infants' activities at different stages of development. Because younger infants are particularly focused on the pleasurable or interesting sensory feedback that results from their actions with objects, one would expect them to notice especially the more aesthetically relevant properties of objects, namely, temperature, texture, and hardness, and perhaps also size. One would not expect them to be so attentive to less aesthetically relevant properties, such as weight and shape. After 8 or 9 months of age, when their cognitive focus shifts toward an interest in how objects can be purposefully exploited, then weight and shape would become more salient to infants, on account of their high functional relevance. This cognitive constraint may help explain why haptic perception of weight seems to emerge somewhat later than haptic perception of texture and hardness, even though infants can execute the hand movements appropriate for weight as soon as they can those for texture and hardness.

Attentional considerations of another sort may also be important for the developmental timetable for haptic perception. Here our comments are based on the information-processing notion of attention as a limited commodity. From this notion we derive the premise that during a given interaction with an object, an infant may not be able to attend to each and every aspect of the situation. Both Bushnell (1985) and Ruff (1989) relied on this premise in addressing other issues of infant development. For our purposes, the limited-attention premise implies that as an infant handles an object, some of its properties will be granted attention and others will be overlooked. Accepting this, it then seems reasonable to suppose that object properties toward which the infant is somehow directed will have the advantage in getting attention and are more likely to be perceived than others.

One way in which an infant's attention may be "invited" or "called" to a particular object property rather than another is through its aesthetic or functional value, as has been discussed. A second way that an object property may gain the attentional advantage over others is by being multiply instantiated, that is, by being apparent or having consequences to more than one sensory modality. For example, an object's texture and its size are specified visually as well as tactually, whereas its color and its weight are specified only in one mode or the other. Similarly, an object's temperature, texture, and hardness are readily accessible to the mouth as well as to the hand, but again neither an object's color nor its weight is easily registered orally. Thus we might expect infants to perceive texture, temperature, and other "doubly available" attributes of objects more readily than they perceive color or weight. There is indeed some evidence to this effect. Several researchers have found that infants permitted to mouth, manipulate, and look at objects subsequently responded to changes in temperature, texture, or shape, but they did not respond to changes in color, weight, or surface pattern (Bushnell et al., 1985; Casey, 1979; Ruff, 1982, 1984; Zikman, 1983). These findings are all consistent with the idea that properties "compete" for attention during infants' play with objects and that properties represented in multiple ways are the winners. This consideration provides another reason for why haptic weight perception onsets later than haptic texture or hardness perception, despite the availability of appropriate hand movements. It may also contribute to a relative lack of attention to configurational shape prior to 10 or 12 months, because until infants can engage in the contour-tracing EP required to haptically apprehend configurational shape, it is effectively a unimodal (visual) property (at least for objects too large to fit in the mouth). In fact, several researchers have reported that infants younger than 12 months old seemed inattentive to an object's shape when they were allowed to touch as well as look at the stimulus, although results from control conditions showed that the infants could visually perceive the shapes involved (Gottfried, Rose, & Bridger, 1978; MacKay-Soroka, Trehub, Bull, & Corter, 1982; Rolfe & Day, 1981; Ruff, 1981). Presumably during touching, the infants were attending to multiply available aspects of the objects, such as texture or size.

A related matter of competition for limited attention may also work against the haptic perception of weight in particular. The infantile versions of the unsupported holding EP optimal for apprehending weight are the rhythmical stereotypies of waving and banging objects. Several researchers have noted that infants are most likely to engage in these behaviors with objects that produce noise upon being waved or banged (cf. Gibson & Walker, 1984; Lockman & McHale, 1989; Palmer, 1989). Thus when engaging in just the right hand movements ideal for perceiving weight, the infant may be preoccupied with the acoustic feedback from the activity and therefore relatively inattentive to the proprioceptive feedback specifying weight.

A final attentional consideration that should be mentioned concerns the behavior of other individuals who engage in object play along with infants. Their behavior may be an important factor in directing attention toward particular object properties, especially after infants have attained the cognitive maturity to respond to didactic devices such as pointing, demonstrating, and labeling. (These "symbolic functions" typically emerge near the end of the first year.) Lockman and McHale (1989) observed mothers playing with their 6-, 8-, and 10-month-old infants with special sets of textured, colored, and sound-producing objects. They found that the *mothers'* activities were contingent on the nature of the objects; they fingered the textured objects and touched them to their infants' skin, they pointed at and rotated the colored objects, and they shook the sound-producing objects. Mothers even took their infants' fingers and moved them over the textured objects, and they also held and shook the sound-producing objects jointly with their infants. These maternal behaviors seem uniquely designed to call the infant's attention to the distinctive attributes of the objects and to demonstrate how to handle them so as to produce interesting feedback. It would be interesting to see how mothers would behave with their infants with objects differing only in weight or in configurational shape. One might suppose that the attention-directing activities of adults are especially crucial for leading infants to become aware of these object properties, which do not inherently attract attention by being aesthetically relevant or multiply available.

A MODEL FOR THE DEVELOPMENT
OF HAPTIC PERCEPTION

The several attentional issues discussed all concur in suggesting that the object property of weight may be less salient to young infants than properties such as temperature, texture, and hardness. They also provide some indications that configurational shape is less salient as well. As such, these cognitive considerations may explain why haptic sensitivity to weight and to configurational shape emerge later in development than other sensitivities do and, at least in the case of weight, later in development than motor considerations would lead us to expect. Indeed, if we think of the motor constraints and the cognitive ones together, as a sort of double filter, the sequence in which haptic sensitivities would be predicted to emerge matches very nicely with the developmental timetable evident in the empirical literature. The idea here is that milestones in motor development set the lower bounds for when certain haptic sensitivities might possibly be present. Cognitive considerations then modulate whether infants perceive a particular attribute as soon as motor development permits or whether it takes some time for awareness to dawn regarding that attribute even in the context of the apropriate motor activity.

In accordance with this "double-filter model," object temperature and size are perceivable very early perhaps from birth, because they require only static contact or enclosure to be apprehended and because they command attention by being both aesthetically relevant and multiply available. Texture and hardness require simple, repetitive finger movements to be apprehended; because they, too, are aesthetically relevant and multiply available, they become perceivable immediately upon the emergence of these rhythmic stereotypies in motor development, at about 5 or 6 months of age. Object weight likewise requires only simple, repetitive movements to be apprehended. However, it is not typically aesthetically relevant nor multiply available, and so weight perception emerges rather slowly, becoming evident several months after the appearance of the requisite motor ability. Finally, configurational shape has about the same attentional status as weight, but it requires more complex and precise hand movements to be apprehended. Consequently, the haptic perception of configurational shape begins a slow emergence only after infants become capable of complementary bimanual activities at about 10 months. By way of summary, these motor and cognitive constraints on haptic perception and the developmental timetable they both predict and explain are illustrated in Fig. 6.1.

We think that our double-filter model for the development of haptic perception is important and interesting for several reasons. First of all, as we have argued in this last part of the chapter, the model accounts for what is currently known about the unfolding of haptic perception during infancy. Beyond that, it allows us to make predictions about aspects of haptic perception that have not been investigated. For example, the commentary about weight perception suggests that it might be more readily evidenced by blind infants or by sighted infants manipulating objects in the dark. In these instances, texture and other such attributes would not have the attentional advantage they normally have by virtue of being multiply available, and thus they might not lead the infant away from attending to weight. Similarly, we might suppose that weight perception would be facilitated in contexts where it *is* multiply available, for instance in play with a scale or in water play, where correlates of weight (i.e., the scale's balancing or not, objects floating or sinking) are visible. We can also refer to the model to make predictions regarding the perception of object attributes that have not been studied. One that comes to mind, for example, is the property of stickiness (as in cellophane tape or wet paint). We predict that infants would be able to discriminate sticky from nonsticky material at about 7 or 8 months of age, sometime after they haptically discriminate textures and sometime before they haptically discriminate weights. This prediction is based on the facts that a simple, repeti-

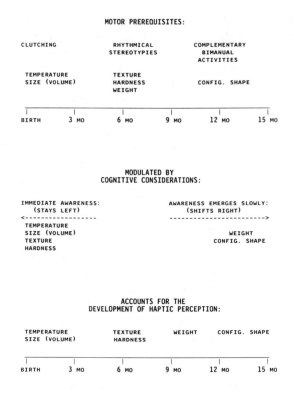

FIG. 6.1.   A summary representation of the "double-filter model" for the development of haptic perception.

tive hand movement analogous to the pressure EP is sufficient to apprehend stickiness and that stickiness is arguably less salient than texture (because it is not multiply available) but more salient than weight (because it does provide interesting feedback). Lastly, the double-filter model to explain the development of haptic perception is an appropriate one because it is a multifaceted model, as all developmental models should be. In humans, and probably in most organisms, the development of any one process or ability is multiply determined, constrained and impelled by developments on many other fronts. Accordingly, we have accounted for the development of haptic perception in terms of motor development and cognitive development. As we proposed at the outset, which qualities of objects infants can perceive by touch is a matter of the answers to the questions "how can infants move their hands?" and "what do infants want or need to know about objects?"

ACKNOWLEDGMENT

Some of the research conducted by the first author and described in this chapter was supported by NIH Research Grant No. R01 HD18093.

REFERENCES

Belsky, J., & Most, R. K. (1981). From exploration to play: A cross-sectional study of infant free play behavior. *Developmental Psychology, 17,* 630–639.

Brown, K. W., & Gottfried, A. W. (1986). Cross-modal transfer of shape in early infancy: Is there reliable evidence? In L. P. Lipsitt & C. Rovee-Collier (Eds.), *Advances in infancy research* (Vol. 4, pp. 163–170). Norwood, NJ: Ablex.

Bruner, J. S. (1971). The growth and structure of skill. In K. J. Connolly (Ed.), *Motor skills in infancy* (pp. 245–269). New York: Academic Press.

Bryant, P. E., Jones, P., Claxton, V., & Perkins, G. M. (1972). Recognition of shapes across modalities by infants. *Nature, 240,* 303–304.

Bushnell, E. W. (1978, August). *Cross-modal object recognition in infancy.* Paper presented at annual meeting of the American Psychological Association, Toronto.

Bushnell, E. W. (1982). Visual–tactual knowledge in 8-, 9½-, and 11-month-old infants. *Infant Behavior and Development, 5,* 63–75.

Bushnell, E. W. (1985). The decline of visually guided reaching during infancy. *Infant Behavior and Development, 8,* 139–155.

Bushnell, E. W., Shaw, L., & Strauss, D. (1985). Relationship between visual and tactual exploration by 6-month-olds. *Developmental Psychology, 21,* 591–600.

Bushnell, E. W., & Weinberger, N. (1987). Infants' detection of visual–tactual discrepancies: Asymmetries that indicate a directive role of visual information. *Journal of Experimental Psychology: Human Perception and Performance, 13,* 601–608.

Bushnell, E. W., Weinberger, N., & Sasseville, A. (1989, April). *Interactions between vision and touch during infancy: The development of cooperative relations and specializations.* Paper presented at the biennial meeting of the Society for Research in Child Development, Kansas City.

Casey, M. B. (1979). Color versus form discrimination learning in 1-year-old infants. *Developmental Psychology, 15,* 341–343.

Erhardt, R. P. (1973). Sequential levels in development of prehension. *American Journal of Occupational Therapy, 28,* 592–596.

Fantz, R. L. (1956). A method for studying early visual development. *Perceptual and Motor Skills, 6,* 13–15.

Fantz, R. L., & Nevis, S. (1967). Pattern preferences and perceptual–cognitive development in early infancy. *Merrill-Palmer Quarterly, 18,* 77–108.

Fenson, L., Kagan, J., Kearsley, R. B., & Zelazo, P. R. (1976). The developmental progression of manipulative play in the first two years. *Child Development, 47,* 232–236.

Gibson, E. J., & Walker, A. S. (1984). Development of knowledge of visual–tactual affordances of substance. *Child Development, 55,* 453–460.

Gottfried, A. W., Rose, S. A., & Bridger, W. H. (1977). Cross-modal transfer in human infants. *Child Development, 48,* 118–123.

Gottfried, A. W., Rose, S. A., & Bridger, W. H. (1978). Effects of visual, haptic, and manipulatory experiences on infants' visual recognition memory of objects. *Developmental Psychology, 14,* 305–312.

Jones, B. (1981). The developmental significance of cross-modal matching. In R. D. Walk & H. L. Pick, Jr. (Eds.), *Intersensory perception and sensory integration* (pp. 109–136). New York: Plenum Press.

Klatzky, R. L., Lederman, S. J., & Metzger, V. A. (1985). Identifying objects by touch: An "expert system." *Perception & Psychophysics, 37,* 299–302.

Klatzky, R. L., Lederman, S. J., & Reed, C. (1987). There's more to touch than meets the eye: The salience of object attributes for haptics with and without vision. *Journal of Experimental Psychology: General, 116,* 356–369.

Landau, B. (1990, April). *Spatial representation of objects in the young blind child.* Paper presented at the International Conference on Infant Studies, Montreal.

Lederman, S. J., & Klatzky, R. L. (1987). Hand movements: A window into haptic object recognition. *Cognitive Psychology, 19,* 342–368.

Lederman, S. J., & Klatzky, R. L. (in press). Haptic classification of common objects: Knowledge-driven exploration. *Cognitive Psychology.*

Lockman, J. J., & McHale, J. P. (1989). Object manipulation in infancy: Developmental and contextual determinants. In J. J. Lockman & N. L. Hazen (Eds.), *Action in social context: Perspectives on early development* (pp. 129–167). New York: Plenum Press.

Lockman, J. J., & Wright, M. H. (1988, April). *A longitudinal study of banging.* Paper presented at the International Conference on Infant Studies, Washington, DC.

MacKay-Soroka, S., Trehub, S. E., Bull, D. H., & Corter, C. M. (1982). Effects of encoding and retrieval conditions on infants' recognition memory. *Child Development, 53,* 815–818.

McCall, R. B. (1974). Exploratory manipulation and play in the human infant. *Monographs of the Society for Research in Child Development, 39* (Whole No. 155).

Mounoud, P., & Bower, T. G. R. (1974). Conservation of weight in infants. *Cognition, 3,* 29–40.

Palmer, C. F. (1989). The discriminating nature of infants' exploratory actions. *Developmental Psychology, 25,* 885–893.

Pederson, D. R., Steele, D., & Klein, G. (1980, April). *Stimulus characteristics that determine infant's exploratory play.* Paper presented at the International Conference on Infant Studies, New Haven, CT.

Piaget, J. (1952). *The origins of intelligence in children.* New York: Norton.

Ramsey, D. S., Campos, J. J., & Fenson, L. (1979). Onset of bimanual handedness in infants. *Infant Behavior and Development, 2,* 69–76.

Ramsey, D. S., & Weber, S. (1986). Infants' hand preference in a task involving complementary roles for the two hands. *Child Development, 57,* 300–307.

Rochat, P. (1987). Mouthing and grasping in neonates: Evidence for the early detection of what hard or soft substances afford for action. *Infant Behavior and Development, 10,* 435–449.

Rochat, P., Blass, E. M., & Hoffmeyer, L. B. (1988). Oropharyngeal control of hand–mouth coordination in newborn infants. *Developmental Psychology, 24,* 459–463.

Rochat, P., & Senders, S. J. (1990, April). *Sitting and reaching in infancy.* Paper presented at the International Conference on Infant Studies, Montreal.

Rolfe, S. A., & Day, R. H. (1981). Effects of the similarity and dissimilarity between familiarization and test objects on recognition memory in infants following unimodal and bimodal familiarization. *Child Development, 52,* 1308–1312.

Rose, S. A., Gottfried, A. W., & Bridger, W. H. (1981a). Cross-modal transfer and information-processing by the sense of touch in infancy. *Developmental Psychology, 17,* 90–98.

Rose, S. A., Gottfried, A. W., & Bridger, W. H. (1981b). Cross-modal transfer in 6-month-old infants. *Developmental Psychology, 17,* 661–669.

Ruff, H. A. (1981). Effect of context on infants' responses to novel objects. *Developmental Psychology, 17,* 87–89.

Ruff, H. A. (1982). Role of manipulation in infants' responses to invariant properties of objects. *Developmental Psychology, 18,* 682–691.

Ruff, H. A. (1984). Infants' manipulative exploration of objects: Effects of age and object characteristics. *Developmental Psychology, 20,* 9–20.

Ruff, H. A. (1986). Components of attention during infants' manipulative exploration. *Child Development, 57,* 105–114.

Ruff, H. A. (1989). The infant's use of visual and haptic information in the perception and recognition of objects. *Canadian Journal of Psychology, 43,* 302–319.

Ruff, H. A., & Kohler, C. J. (1978). Tactual–visual transfer in six-month-old infants. *Infant Behavior and Development, 1,* 259–264.

Soroka, S. M., Corter, C. M., & Abramovitch, R. (1979). Infants' tactual discrimination of novel and familiar tactual stimuli. *Child Development, 50,* 1251–1253.

Steele, D., & Pederson, D. R. (1977). Stimulus variables which affect the concordance of visual and manipulative exploration in six-month-old infants. *Child Development, 48,* 104–111.

Streri, A. (1987). Tactile discrimination of shape and intermodal transfer in 2- to 3-month-old infants. *British Journal of Developmental Psychology, 5,* 213–220.

Streri, A., & Pecheux, M. G. (1986). Tactual habituation and discrimination of form in infancy: A comparison with vision. *Child Development, 57,* 100–104.

Streri, A., & Spelke, E. S. (1988). Haptic perception of objects in infancy. *Cognitive Psychology, 20,* 1–23.

Thelen, E. (1979). Rhythmical stereotypies in normal human infants. *Animal Behaviour, 27,* 699–715.

Thelen, E. (1981). Rhythmical behavior in infancy: An ethological perspective. *Developmental Psychology, 17,* 237–257.

Twitchell, T. E. (1965). The automatic grasping responses of infants. *Neuropsychologia, 3,* 247–259.

Uzgiris, I. (1967). Ordinality in the development of schemas for relating to objects. In J. Hellmuth (Ed.), *Exceptional infant: Vol. 1. The normal infant* (pp. 316–334). Seattle: Special Child Publications.

White, B. L., Castle, P., & Held, R. (1964). Observations on the development of visually directed reaching. *Child Development, 35,* 349–364.

Zikman, S. R. (1983). *Bimodal perception of form, color, and substance in infancy.* Unpublished doctoral dissertation, Monash University, Clayton Victoria, Australia.

PART

III

TACTILE PATTERN
PERCEPTION

This part of the book is about tactile pattern perception. Most of us tend to think about the performatory role of the hands, that is, we focus on the use of the hands for action and manipulation of objects. However, all of us make use of the sense of touch to obtain information about the shapes of objects we manipulate, and for the detection of two-dimensional patterns. We use our hands while typing on a computer keyboard, and rely on our proprioceptive/spatial "knowledge" about the layout of the keys to permit typing. We can tell when we have hit a key through auditory and tactile feedback. It should be clear that we may know the position of the keys, even though we might not be able to provide oral directions for their location on the board. Nonetheless, we have no difficulty accurately typing while looking at the CRT screen with foveal vision. Very blurry peripheral vision of the keyboard remains, of course, but it is insufficient for identification of the key names. Thus, we often take haptic/tactual skills for granted, while the focus of our attention is directed toward visual matters.

The first chapter in this part, by Appelle, is concerned with pattern perception per se. Most of the research in this field has involved two-dimensional arrays. It is certainly hard to know how much of this information will generalize to three-dimensional configurations, as some researchers believe that the sense of touch is better suited for apprehension of solid, 3-D configurations. We will return to this issue in the concluding chapter of this volume, but we should point out that the study of tactile illusions leads to a general caution in this area. Touch and vision are affected rather differently by orienting two dimensional patterns in the vertical dimension (see chapter by Appelle; Day & Avery, 1970). For touch, movements toward the body are judged as longer than movements that don't converge on the body, and this may change how one tactually perceives embossed lines. It is difficult to know if these effects are changed by, or are a consequence of visual experience. It is also possible that these sorts of radial/tangential effects may be influenced by the amount and quality of an individual's haptic experience with two-dimensional arrays.

We can't rule out the possibility that when forms are perceived haptically, different principles are involved than when they are perceived visually. Touch is rather sensitive to spatial reference information (Heller, 1985, 1986, 1987a, 1989), as is demonstrated by the finding that it is very easy to lower identification performance if braille patterns are tilted. The critical factor here is that people may have difficulty understanding tactile input when they are denied sight of their hands touching a surface. Thus, their ability to interpret patterns depends on spatial understanding of the relationship and orientation of the finger and hand with respect to patterns that are touched. Tilt of the patterns lowers performance, as does tilt of the hand that touches them. It may be easier for naïve sighted subjects to manipulate visual images mentally than tactually derived "images." This finding is not limited to braille, as Heller has obtained an identical effect of orientation on embossed letters as on braille (Heller, unpublished research).

Considerable research has been directed toward an understanding of tactile pattern perception. The other chapters in this part by Foulke and Sherrick are devoted to research on touch that is concerned with theory, but also has clear application. Foulke discusses reading braille, and Sherrick has devoted much time to the study of vibrotactile stimulation for sensory aids for blind and/or deaf people.

A great many researchers have been interested in understanding braille, and this is the concern of Emerson Foulke's chapter. Reading braille is much slower than reading print, but is certainly a valuable skill. Unfortunately, far too many people who lose sight later on in life fail to become proficient readers of braille. Skilled braille readers engage in smooth, lateral movements of the index finger to track lines of braille characters. The skilled reader of braille rarely gets lost, and does not pause very much to retrace letters or words. This can be contrasted to the novice, or poor reader of braille. These unskilled individuals seem to spend considerable time tracing braille patterns, and engage in vertical scanning (scrubbing). They have difficulty identifying component braille characters, and seem to try to treat each braille character as an outline shape.

How is braille coded and represented through touch? One might assume that braille is stored in memory as an outline shape, as in visual letters (Nolan & Kederis, 1969). For example, the braille code for the letter "b" consists of two dots arrayed vertically, and one might suppose that individuals think of the shape as like a line, just as in visual letters. This, of course, is consistent with observations of naïve readers of braille who tend to try to trace out the braille patterns. Moreover, it is possible to make visual matches to tangible braille by watching people touch braille, even when the embossing can't be seen because of the blurring effect of stained glass (Heller, 1985). Heller's results are probably specific to sighted subjects, and a visual matching methodology. Visual matching may promote coding in terms of visual imagery.

However, there is a large body of research that suggests that both blind and sighted individuals are unlikely to code braille in the form of outline shapes. Millar has argued that blind readers do not normally code braille as outline shapes (e.g., see Millar, 1985, 1987b), since they find it easier to recognize the characters as dot patterns than outline shapes. Millar (1987b) has suggested that braille text is normally coded by fluent readers in terms of dot-gap density, rather than word shape. Furthermore, blind children were very poor at recognizing enlarged forms of letters, which they recognized easily in a smaller format (Millar, 1977). For these children, the problem with large letters was certainly not that of limited spatial acuity (or resolving power) of the skin, since larger letters are more discriminable than smaller ones. Rather, Millar concluded this meant the children were not using shape information to code braille configurations.

There are important differences, of course, between reading braille text and naming individual braille characters. Alternative physical behaviors are involved in reading text, as well as more sophisticated cognitive skills. Recently, there has been an increase in research activity in this area, with studies of laterality in braille reading (e.g., Harris, 1980; Millar, 1984; Mousty & Bertelson, 1985), the use of two hands for reading braille (e.g., Bertelson, Mousty, & D'Alimonte, 1985; Millar, 1987a), and an increase in the study of reading braille text (e.g., Millar, 1987b).

Sherrick provides an interesting account of research on vibrotactile pattern perception and sensory aids. Complex arrays of vibrators have been used to allow the skin to access pattern information. The Optacon, for example, consists of an array of 5 by 20 pins (in its latest version), which vibrate in the shape of patterns that are "seen" by a small, hand-held camera. Some blind people have learned to use the Optacon to read print. This sort of sensory aid allows blind people considerable independence, as they are able to read much material without the intervention of sighted persons. This is particularly important, of course, because a great deal of significant information is not translated into braille, in our society.

Some individuals become very proficient with devices such as the Optacon, reading at high rates of speed. However, it takes considerable time to learn to read with the Optacon. Simple pattern identification may require extensive training, as Sherrick and Cholewiak (1990) report that sighted subjects may only reach 50% correct in letter identification after hundreds of training trials. They find large individual differences in the facility with which people are able to perceive patterns with the Optacon, with some people failing at the task. It seems normal for researchers to reject some subjects in this area, since there are people who seem unable to use the Optacon and are "nonlearners" (see Craig, 1982).

Some possible difficulties for touch involve putative limitations in spatial and temporal resolution. If patterns are large enough, it is very easy to identify letters or numbers either drawn on the skin, or actively felt with the fingertips (Heller, 1986). Temporal limitations have been stressed by Heller (1980, 1986, 1987b) and Craig (1983) in rather different contexts (see discussion by Sherrick, this part). Masking can occur with the vibrotactile presentation of stimuli, whereby a prior pattern (forward masking) or an aftercoming pattern (backward masking) can lower recognition performance of target stimuli with the Optacon. Large masking effects occur within a brief time interval with vibrotactile stimulation ($<$ .5 s).

A number of researchers have been concerned with the possibility of modality differences in memory, and some have adopted modern paradigms for the study of tactile short-term memory (Gilson & Baddeley, 1969; Sullivan & Turvey, 1972; Watkins & Watkins, 1974). Aftersensations are persistent (about 3 s or more), when patterns are drawn on the skin, or the skin is poked or stroked (Melzack & Eisenberg, 1968). The time course of vibrotactile masking seems similar to that for vision, but results are very different for short-term memory tasks involving tapping or stroking the skin. Results with these alternative forms of tactile stimulation suggest more durable sensory storage for touch than vision.

REFERENCES

Bertelson, P., Mousty, P., & D'Alimonte, G. (1985). A study of braille reading: 2. Patterns of hand activity in one-handed and two-handed reading. *Quarterly Journal of Experimental Psychology, 37A,* 235–256.

Craig, J. C. (1982). Temporal integration of vibrotactile patterns. *Perception & Psychophysics, 32,* 219–229.

Craig, J. C. (1983). Some factors affecting tactile pattern recognition. *International Journal of Neuroscience, 19,* 47–58.

Day, R. H., & Avery, G. C. (1970). Absence of the horizontal–vertical illusion in haptic space. *Journal of Experimental Psychology, 83,* 172–173.

Gilson, E. Q., & Baddeley, A. D. (1969). Tactile short-term memory. *Quarterly Journal of Experimental Psychology, 21,* 180–184.

Harris, L. J. (1980). Which hand is the "eye" of the blind? A new look at an old question. In J. Herron (Ed.), *Neuropsychology of left-handedness.* New York: Academic Press.

Heller, M. A. (1980). Tactile retention: Reading with the skin. *Perception & Psychophysics, 27,* 125–130.

Heller, M. A. (1985). Tactual perception of embossed Morse code and Braille: The alliance of vision and touch. *Perception, 14,* 563–570.

Heller, M. A. (1986). Central and peripheral influences on tactual reading. *Perception & Psychophysics, 39,* 197–204.

Heller, M. A. (1987a). The effect of orientation on visual and tactual braille recognitions. *Perception, 16,* 291–298.

Heller, M. A. (1987b). Improving the passive tactile digit span. *Bulletin of the Psychonomic Society, 25,* 257–258.

Heller, M. A. (1989). Tactile memory in sighted and blind observers: The influence of orientation and rate of presentation. *Perception, 18,* 121–133.

Melzack, R., & Eisenberg, H. (1968). Skin sensory afterglows. *Science, 159,* 445.

Millar, S. (1977). Tactual and name matching by blind children. *British Journal of Psychology, 68,* 377–387.

Millar, S. (1984). Is there a "best hand" for braille? *Cortex, 20,* 75–87.

Millar, S. (1985). The perception of complex patterns by touch. *Perception, 14,* 293–303.

Millar, S. (1987a). The perceptual window in two-handed braille: Do the left and right hands process text simultaneously? *Cortex, 23,* 111–122.

Millar, S. (1987b). Perceptual and task factors in fluent braille. *Perception, 16,* 521–536.

Mousty, P., & Bertelson, P. (1985). A study of braille reading: 1. Reading speed as a function of hand usage and context. *Quarterly Journal of Experimental Psychology, 37A,* 217–233.

Nolan, C. Y., & Kederis, C. J. (1969). *Perceptual factors in Braille word recognition.* New York: American Foundation for the blind.

Sherrick, C. E., & Cholewiak, R. W. (1990). *Princeton Cutaneous Research Project* (Rep. No. 55, June, 1990), Princeton, NJ: Princeton University, Department of Psychology.

Sullivan, E. V., & Turvey, M. T. (1972). Short-term retention of tactile stimulation. *Quarterly Journal of Experimental Psychology, 24,* 253–261.

Watkins, M. J., & Watkins, O. C. (1974). A tactile suffix effect. *Memory & Cognition, 2,* 176–180.

7

HAPTIC PERCEPTION OF FORM: ACTIVITY AND STIMULUS ATTRIBUTES

Stuart Appelle
State University of New York,
College at Brockport

INTRODUCTION

According to a book containing the proceedings of an international symposium on "active touch" (Gordon, 1978), this expression and the concepts underlying it "have a long and honorable history." Yet, most of the book's own contents actually have little or nothing to do with tactual activity per se. Elsewhere, a chapter on haptics (Kennedy, 1978) defines its subject as "a conceptual enterprise" seeking to distinguish characteristics of "touch," "contact," and "exploration," and the editors of a volume on "tactual perception" (Schiff & Foulke, 1982) make distinctions among "tactile," "tactual," and "haptic." Still another review (Loomis & Lederman, 1986) classifies "tactual modes" into five separate categories of tactile, active and passive kinesthetic, and active and passive haptic events.

This proliferation of terms, and their various uses by different investigators, tells us something about our current understanding and our approaches to understanding how the manipulation of objects leads to object perception. Under normal conditions, this manipulation is neither exclusively active nor passive (the hand makes numerous starts and stops during object inspection) and is neither exclusively cutaneous (skin stimulation without muscle stimulation) nor kinesthetic (muscle stimulation without skin stimulation). These components of touch can be separated experimentally and experientially, but in the normal process of touching all are involved. If we are to understand the perception of objects by manipulation, we may examine contributions of each component separately, but we must examine them as they work together.

In this regard, my position is closest to that of James J. Gibson's (1966), which views haptics as a "perceptual system." Gibson argued that the manipulation of objects involves pressure, force, proprioception, vestibular stimulation, stimulation of the various receptors of the skin, and the activity of muscles, joints, and tendons. In short, he felt "active touch does not fulfill the supposed criteria for a single sense modality" (Gibson, 1962, p. 479). Instead, Gibson adopted the term "haptics" to refer to the functionally discrete system involved in the seeking and pickup of information by hand. This term, which comes from the Greek, meaning "able to lay hold of," was first introduced in 1931 by Revesz (cited in Revesz, 1950). For Gibson (1966) haptics covers the subsystems of "cutaneous touch" (stimulation of skin without movement of muscles or joints), "haptic touch" (stimulus of skin plus movement of the joints), "dynamic touch" (stimulation of the skin plus movement of the joints and the muscles), "touch-temperature," "painful touch," and "oriented touch" (skin stimulation plus vestibular stimulation). While this differentiation may seem a regression toward the reductionistic models that Gibson eschewed, his emphasis was on the emergent perceptual system and the information it obtains.

The first purpose of this chapter is to examine the dynamics of haptic activity in the perception of form. The second purpose is to examine the kinds of information that are obtained through haptic activity. While there is an extensive literature regarding form attributes in vision, the haptic literature is much less developed. Form, like haptics itself, is multidimensional. If we are to understand haptic perception of form, we must examine the dimensions of haptic activity, the dimensions of haptic form, and their interactions.

THE NATURE OF HAPTIC ACTIVITY: GENERAL DESCRIPTIONS AND THEORETICAL CONSTRUCTS

To understand haptic activity, a number of investigators have tried to develop a description based on the observed behaviors of subjects engaged in haptic exploration. Heller (cited in Revesz, 1950) was one of the first to develop such a schema and to distinguish between active and passive kinds of touch. Heller also distinguished between "synthetic" and "analytic" *functions,* which interacted with type of touch. Synthetic touch was directed by an attempt to obtain an overall (gestalt) impression of form and was carried out by the resting hand. Analytic touch was used by the moving hand to gain an exhaustive impression of an object's features.

Hippius (cited in Revesz, 1950) divided active touching into four categories. The first, "gliding" touch, involved short back-and-forth motions of the hand, a method Hippius felt was used primarily to obtain information regarding surface variations or texture (an observation consistent with that of Katz, 1925/1989). His second category of touch was the "sweep." This involved use of one or more fingers scanning across an object's surface to obtain information about contours, edges, and geometrical relationships of parts. The third category, "grasping," is like the glide or sweep but introduces use of the thumb so as to provide information about two or more surfaces simultaneously. Finally, "kinematic grasping" involved a comprehensive exploration of an object's features.

Revesz (1950), one of the pioneers in haptic perception, was influenced by Heller and Hippius, but preferred to emphasize the time element in haptic exploration. "Simultaneous touch" involved inspection of a form and its parts in a single act. "Successive touch" occurred whenever an object or its parts were touched in separate acts distributed over time. Revesz argued,

> It is impossible to gain anything approaching a correct idea either of the total form or of the relatively independent parts without making use of successive touch. . . . The process of successive touching represents the haptic process of recognition *par excellence*. (p. 61)

Nevertheless, after devoting most of his career to studying haptic perception, describing its dynamics, synthesizing the work of others, and contributing his own seminal work on the blind and haptic art, he was convinced that, unlike gestalt-form in vision, an object's "total appearance and the structure of the whole, cannot be grasped by our haptic sense, or at best only to a limited extent, after a complicated and tedious examination" (p. 132).

Rather than viewing the successive nature of touch as an obstacle to form perception, more recent theoretical perspectives have focused on just how the naturally executed motions of the hand can contribute to a unified perception of form. For example, Russian psychology has developed a motor-copy theory of haptic form perception in which the percept develops out of an image constructed from the movements of the hand. Zinchenko and Lomov (1960) have provided a detailed description of the development of such an image based on the filmed records of subjects engaged in haptic exploration. They interpret their observations as reflecting three separate functions. The "constructive function" is primarily involved in contour detection. The "function of measurement" involves use of the hand and its parts for calculations of extent, and the "function of checking and correction" is a more comprehensive use of the hands to develop an "adequate" and stable image of the explored form.

In all cases, the successive nature of exploration is the hallmark of the activity. They report that experiments eliminating the interrupted movements of the hand—requiring instead that the subjects explore in a continuous fashion without changing the way in which the fingers interact—results in a failure to develop an adequate image of form. The dynamics of the moving hand are seen as being "directly determined by the characteristics of the contour of the object in conjunction with the requirements of geometric construction" (p. 19). These movements, however, need not be in exact correspondence with the form, nor reproduce the object's contour. In fact, the hand movements observed were "only relatively isomorphous to the object" being explored.

Zinchenko and Lomov argue these deviations from the form's contour are neither accidental nor detrimental but are determined by the form, and help ensure the adequacy of the image. Moreover, pauses and regressions in movement are regarded with special importance. Pauses, they observe, occur mainly at points in the object's contours that specify its shape, corners, and intersections in particular. And regressions (movements over part of the form already explored) occur especially where complex aspects of the contour have been previously encountered. Except for Zinchenko and Lomov, the importance of pauses and regressions in haptic form perception has been almost completely ignored (however, the importance of these variables in braille reading has been pointed out; e.g., Davidson, Appelle, & Haber, in press).

Gibson (1962, 1966) rejected the notion that imagery is necessary to explain perception, but also viewed the successive motions of the hand as essential to perception of form. He felt "the purpose of the exploratory movements of the hand is to isolate and enhance the components of stimulation which specify the shape and other characteristics of the object being touched" (Gibson, 1962, p. 478). Thus, for Gibson the role of activity is critical to the pickup of information. In a seminal paper on active versus passive touch, Gibson (1962) reported a progressive increase in form recognition accuracy with an increase in the degree of movement allowed between object and perceiver. Using "cookie cutter" shapes, six different forms were presented to a subject's hand in various ways. When the form was pressed into the subject's palm by a mechanical device, accurate recognition was only 29%. When the forms were delivered by the manual action of experimenters, recognition rose to 49%. When the forms were pressed into the palm with deliberate rotation, recognition improved still further to 72%. Although these three conditions can all be considered "passive" presentations (in that subjects initiated no movements of their own) they approximate, to various degrees, the stimulation (if not the information) attained in active touch. By comparison, when allowed free ("active") exploration, form recognition was 95% correct. Similar results have been obtained in a number of replications (Cronin, 1977; Heller, 1984; Heller & Myers, 1983).

Landrigan and Forsyth (1974) sought to examine the components of "regulation of movement" (the course and direction of movement chosen by the subject) and "production of movement" (the self-initiated aspect of scanning) as variables underlying active touch. Both concepts were used by Gibson to differentiate the active from the passive condition. These aspects of touching were manipulated for subjects engaged in haptic matching judgments for a series of complex random polygon shapes. In the "self-regulation" condition, subjects picked the direction and course over which their scanning hand would move. In the "self-production" condition they moved their hand on their own volition. These conditions were compared with others in which the experimenter decided where the scanning hand would go or the experimenter moved the subject's "passive" arm by manipulating a mechanical device. Landrigan and Forsyth found that self-regulation was an important variable underlying the active–passive distinction but that self-production was not. They regard this finding as at variance with other studies showing a superiority for active over passive touch and with Gibson's argument about is importance.

It should be pointed out, however, that Landrigan and Forsyth required a very artificial method of scanning. For each successive scan, subjects were restricted to movement of their index finger along a given linear pathway. So even the self-regulated, self-produced condition was inconsistent with the more global process by which an observer usually goes about information pickup. Moreover, it is likely that such a search strategy would interfere with pickup of the *kind* of information Gibson felt was critical to haptic form perception.

Gibson (1962) argued that haptic exploratory movements "do not ever seem to be twice the same, but they are not aimless. . . . The purpose of the exploratory movements . . . is to isolate and enhance the component of stimulation which specifies the shape or other characteristics of the object being touched" (pp. 479–481). And what is the nature of this component?

> For the perception of objects it is the detection of distinctive features and the abstraction of general properties. This almost always involves the detection of invariants under changing stimulation. . . . The exploratory perceptual systems typically produce transformations so that the invariants can be isolated. (Gibson, 1966, pp. 270–271)

So, for Gibson, the solution to how ever-changing successive movements are converted into unified percepts lies in finding unchanging "invariant" characteristics to the exploratory *activity,* and invariant characteristics of the *information* obtained by such activity. From Gibson's point of view, only by identifying these invariants can haptic perception of form be understood.

Davidson (1972a, 1976) makes a similar argument in framing some of the important objectives for haptic research. He addresses the need "to tie accurate and inaccurate methods of scanning to the particular attributes they sample" (1972a, p. 21) and to determine what characteristics of the scanning process make one method effective for a particular attribute of form but not for some other attribute. His general suggestion is that "the major determinants of whether a strategy will be effective seem to be how well the strategy focuses on the relevant stimulus attribute and how well the attribute can be encoded" (1976, p. 198).

To identify some of the characteristics of haptic activity, Davidson, Abbott, and Gershenfeld (1974) studied the scanning strategies used by subjects making matching judgments to replicas of the three-dimensional free-form shapes developed by Gibson (1962) for his own studies of haptic form perception. Videotaped records of activity suggested four basic exploratory styles: "global search" (independent use of fingers to explore several stimulus aspects simultaneously), "detailed search" (coordinated use of fingers to focus on single aspects of the stimulus) "palmer search" (pressing the palm down onto the top of the stimulus), and "tracing" (moving fingertips along stimulus contours). Davidson et al., found a much greater use of "detailed" and especially the "global" strategy overall, with an increasing use of the other strategies as inspection time increased. This also resulted in greater recognition accuracy. The authors speculate that the use of effective or additional ways to gather information increases the pickup of information that best differentiates the stimulus properties. Unfortunately they did not specify what sources of information were obtained, or which scanning strategies were successful with which particular properties.

Another approach consistent with Gibson's ideas regarding haptic activity, and the objectives outlined by Davidson, has been used by Lederman and Klatzky (1987). They have been carrying out a series of experiments examining what they call "exploratory procedures" (EPs). An EP (a) is "a stereotyped pattern having certain characteristics that are invariant and others that are highly typical" (p. 344), (b) need not be represented by any particular motion, position of the hand, nor stimulated receptor array, but by a variety of characteristic activities maintaining the EP's invariant properties, and (c) is regarded as purposive, that is, is used to obtain information about a specific object property, and/or is elicited by that property.

On the basis of the performance of subjects spontaneously using an EP or restricted by instruction to using a particular EP, Lederman and Klatzky conclude that the EPs subjects chose to obtain property information are also the EPs that, under controlled conditions, yield "optimal" performance in obtaining such information. For example, they describe "pressure" (using the sense organ to exert force against the object) as the EP for hardness, "lateral motion"(sideways movement between skin and object) as the EP for texture, "enclosure" (simultaneous contact by the parts of the hand so as to mold the hand to the object's "envelope") for global shape, and "contour following" (smooth and repeated hand movement along a contour segment) for exact shape.

In related studies, the salience of (Klatzky, Lederman, & Reed, 1987) and ability to integrate (Klatzky, Lederman, & Reed, 1989) object properties was studied. Haptic shape was found to be relatively low in salience, a result attributed to the need for "contour following," a slow and deliberate EP for which encoding should not be intrinsically easy. The ability to integrate object properties was also found somewhat limited, a factor attributed to "motoric" or "regional" exploratory incompatibilities (motoric incompatibilities arise when the execution of a particular EP is nonoptimal for the two properties to be integrated; regional incompatibilities arise when the information to be integrated cannot be obtained from the same locations of exploration).

These findings contrast to those researchers' earlier conclusion (Klatzky, Lederman, & Metzger, 1985) that haptics is an "expert system" in regard to object identification, and the findings of other researchers who obtained excellent haptic perception of form or shape saliency, both with adults (Davidson et al., 1974; Kiphart, Auday, & Cross, 1988) and with young children (Abravanel, 1970). One common distinction between the studies finding excellent form perception and those that do not, is that the former use 3-D (solid) objects, whereas the latter use planar shapes for stimuli. Commenting on the discrepancy between his findings and previous work on object saliency with children, Abravanel (1970) argued that the haptic techniques of "grasping, holding, clutching, and palpating" are those that naturally "predominate in the haptic perception of young children," and that the children's attention to shape when using 3-D as opposed to planar forms "can be understood as a function of the compatibility between . . . preferred modes of perceptual exploration and the properties of the object" (p. 531).

Abravanel's conclusions may be applicable to adults as well. Lederman, Klatzky, Chataway, and Summers (1990) compared recognition for 2-D representations of common objects with recognition of their 3-D counterparts used earlier (Klatzky et al., 1985). They argue that the 2-D forms tax the natural abilities of the haptic system, requiring instead that haptic perception of 2-D shape be mediated by visual imagery. In contrast, 3-D objects allow the haptic system to "capitalize on its strengths" (p. 63) and directly apprehend object attributes. That is, tactual perception proceeds by either a direct perception or an image-mediated mechanism, depending on the stimulus characteristics.

ATTRIBUTES OF FORM AND HAPTIC EXPLORATORY STYLE

The theoretical development described in the previous section suggests that it is important to our understanding of haptic form perception to examine the attributes of form, the characteristics of haptic exploratory strategies, and attribute/strategy interactions. This next section reviews literature examining these variables. I have chosen to give at most passing mention to those studies whose focus on special populations (e.g., animals, infants and children, gender groups, etc.) perceptual and cognitive impairment (blindness; retardation), or cross-modal equivalency, tell us little about haptic perception of form per se. Much of this research can be found elsewhere.

Tangible objects have many properties (hardness, temperature, weight, texture, etc.). Our concern is with the property of shape, or form, that is, the spatial layout of an object. It is widely acknowledged that this can be specified largely in terms of contours or edges (see Zusne, 1970, for a useful discussion of this in regard to visual perception of form), especially at points of change (an object's borders, vertices, curves, corners, protuberances, etc.). An isolated contour can be described in regard to its extent and its position (or orientation). Contour interactions, or pattern, can be described in regard to contour number (form complexity), angle, relative extent (proportion) or unique configuration ("distinctive features"). Most of these attributes have received at least some attention in the experimental literature.

Extent

A review of the literature reveals more than 100 articles on the tactual perception of extent. However, most of these studies have looked at cutaneous sensitivity (passive pressure against the skin), or the accuracy of touch relative to vision. Only a small number of investigations have looked specifically at judgments of extent as a function of haptic activity. Nevertheless, one of the earliest studies in experimental psychology did just that. Jastrow (1886) had subjects judge distances by several methods of touch. They either held blocks between thumb and forefinger, guided a pencil over a given distance, or had their arms transported by an experimenter through a predetermined extent. Jastrow found that the impression of extent was influenced by the type of movement involved. For example, a distance between thumb and forefinger appeared to be equal to an objectively shorter (by 68%) distance covered by the moving arm (similar results were later reported by Hohmuth, Phillips, & Van Romer, 1976; but this result has not always been obtained, e.g., Cutsforth, 1933).

Stanley (1966) recorded estimates of length for stimulus rods either held at their ends between the index finger of each hand (which he called the "haptic" condition) or for similar extents judged by the outstretched arms, with fingers not in actual contact with the stimulus (the "kinesthetic" condition). Across a range of extents, judged size for the haptic condition was longer than for the kinesthetic condition. This effect, however, disappeared, for the longest stimulus used (33 in.).

Roeckelein (1968) also obtained tactual estimations of length. In doing so, he made an interesting observation, later confirmed by his subjects' own introspective reports. Many used their fingers "in the manner of a ruler" to measure off the extents. The effect of a measuring strategy was studied directly by Appelle, Gravetter, and Davidson (1980). They had subjects make same/different judgments of length to pairs of stimulus rods explored under three haptic conditions. An "unrestricted" condition allowed subjects to feel the stimuli any way they chose. A "no-measuring" conditioned allowed free exploration except for a specific injunction against use of their hand or fingers as a measuring device to "lay off" the extent directly. In a third condition, subjects were told to restrict their scanning activity so as to try deliberately to measure the extents (they were not given any instructions as to how to do this). The results indicated that overall accuracy increases with increasing stimulus length, and that the "measuring" group was significantly more accurate than either of the other two haptic conditions (more will be said on "measuring" as a haptic strategy in regard to the attribute of "proportion").

A number of studies have shown that perception of extent depends on the direction in which the exploring hand moves. Brown, Knauft, and Rosenbaum (1948) had subjects reproduce, by moving a pointer in the dark, distances specified by a previously presented visual marker. They found that the reproduction of extent through movements away from the body was more accurate than with movements toward the body. Compared with movements toward the body, movements away produced judgments that were more variable for long (10–40 cm) distances and less variable for short (.6–2.5 cm) distances. The finding that judged extent varies with scanning direction has been shown to be a "radial-tangential" effect. Davidon and Cheng (1964) had blindfolded observers feel an extent between two pointers and then adjust a variable extent to a subjectively equal distance. They found that "radial" movements (movements along any radius intersecting with the observer at the center) were consistently overestimated relative to "tangential" movements (movements at a tangent to any arc formed by the observer at the center). This finding has persisted across numerous replications (e.g., Cheng, 1968; Day & Wong, 1971; Deregowski & Ellis, 1972; Marchetti & Lederman, 1983) in spite of a variety of stimulus and task conditions.

Another interaction between the perception of extent and haptic activity occurs in what are usually called kinesthetic aftereffects. These generally are produced by alternate inspection of a long and short standard, followed by inspection of a comparison stimulus intermediate in extent. Typically the aftereffect is one of contrast, for example, after feeling a relatively long standard, a shorter comparison feels even shorter than it would if felt prior to inspecting the standard. The result has been obtained under a variety of experimental conditions (Hilgard, Morgan, & Prytulak, 1968; Walker & Shea, 1974; Walker, 1977, 1978) and is similar to an effect found by Appelle (1971) in which continuous inspection of two extents forming the arms of an angle that is progressively increasing in size (becoming less acute) produces the perception of a larger angle than a stationary standard.

Finally, a number of geometrical illusions of extent are subject to the kind of haptic inspection used. Fry (1975) presented haptic versions of the Müller-Lyer, concentric squares, and diamond-square illusions. Overall, active touch produced illusory effects that were almost twice as large as those for passive touch (pressing the embossed illusory figures into the subject's palm). The direction of the illusion, however, was not always what would be predicted from visual perception. Revesz (1950), who also demonstrated a wide range of tactual geometrical illusions, cautioned against assuming visual factors can account for haptic illusions just because there is perceptual similarity between them. The findings of Fry, as well as the radial–tangential interpretation of the haptic horizontal–vertical illusion (Cheng, 1968, Davidon & Cheng, 1964; Day & Wong, 1971) also suggest such a caution.

Orientation

Much of the literature on the haptic perception of orientation focuses on the relative salience of orientation for children. But one aspect of the literature focuses on haptic movement and orientation perception. As just discussed, the direction of haptic inspection affects perception of stimulus extent (the radial–tangential effect). A similar interaction may be involved in perception of stimulus orientation, specifically the haptic "oblique effect." The oblique effect (Appelle, 1972) refers to the widely obtained finding in vision that perception, discrimination, and sensitivity are poorer for obliquely oriented stimuli than for horizontally or vertically oriented stimuli.

Lechelt, Eliuk, and Tanne (1976) reported that a similar result obtains in regard to haptic perception. Their subjects were required to set a comparison rod felt with one hand to the orientation of a standard felt with the other hand. Consistent with the visual oblique effect, subjects were significantly more accurate in matching horizontal and vertical standards, whether by simultaneously scanning the two rods (one with each hand) or by setting a stimulus rod to an orientation verbally specified by the experimenter. In a follow-up study, Lechelt and Verenka (1980) extended this finding to a successive matching condition. Lechelt et al. (1976) suggest that the haptic oblique effect may arise from "the detection of limb position or orientation . . . based on differential neurological sensitivity to patterns of haptic input varying in tactile–proprioceptive composition . . . resulting from haptic exploration of stimuli in different orientations" (p. 467).

Appelle and Gravetter (1985) replicated these results but questioned whether the haptic oblique effect is due to factors intrinsic to the haptic system. Rather, they showed that the effect is probably mediated by well-established visual experience and imagery. In a follow-up study (Appelle & Countryman, 1986) this hypothesis was further tested by eliminating any prior knowledge of the standard orientations to be used (in all previous studies, subjects were shown or told what standards were to be reproduced). Controlling for this significantly reduced the haptic oblique effect but did not eliminate it, a finding suggesting some residual effect indeed intrinsic to haptics. The authors speculated that the nature of the matching task itself (rather than the oblique effect) could be responsible. In bilateral exploration of two stimulus rods, different scanning movements by the two hands is required for positioning obliques, but not for positioning rods to a horizontal or vertical position.

> Specifically, the hand contralateral to the slant of an oblique stimulus (e.g., the left hand scanning a right-leaning oblique) must move inward with respect to the midline of the body while the ipsilateral arm (e.g., the right hand scanning a right-leaning oblique) must move out from the body. Movement at the elbow and shoulder joints must also differ during bilateral matching of obliques. Horizontal and vertical placements allow homologous motions of the two arms. (p. 326)

When Appelle and Countryman controlled for these "bilaterally incongruent scanning patterns" by substituting a unilateral task (where, in addition, subjects had no prior knowledge of what orientations they would be asked to produce), the haptic oblique effect was eliminated.

These results are not consistent with the interpretation of differential haptic "sensitivity" to different stimulus orientations. They do emphasize the influence of haptic exploratory movements on perception of an attribute of form (of related interest, Nilsson & Geffen, 1987, report faster and more accurate ratings of similarity for pairs of planar shapes bilaterally explored in a "congruent" (parallel) than incongruent (mirror-image) direction.)

Curvature

Gibson (1933) was the first to recognize an interaction between haptic activity and the perception of a curved edge. Blindfolded subjects moved their fingers back and forth along a 30-cm-long convex curve (end points bending away from the subject). After 3 minutes of exploration the edge lost some of its subjective convexity and an objectively straight edge felt concave. Gibson reported this as a kinesthetic aftereffect.

Others have looked at phenomenal curvature as a product of haptic scanning. Rubin (1936) had subjects feel a bent ruler with one or two fingertips, either with forearm movements alone (from the elbow) or with the outstretched arm (from the shoulder). Subjects reported that a concave edge (ends bending toward the observer) felt straight, an "illusion" that was even greater with the forearm method of scanning. Although Rubin was unable to specify just how the variation in haptic method produced this result, he speculated that it was "to some extent dependent on the variations of pressure on the fingertips," characterizing the typical method of touch as involving "the fingers . . . stretched or bent in such a way that the edge passes through a (nearly) fixed trail in the fingertips" (p. 376). He also concluded that knowledge about which curvature standards would be used, and the resulting opportunity to resort to visual imagery, have a strong effect on phenomenal curvature. This conclusion is very similar to the one reached by Appelle and Countryman (1986) in regard to the influence of visual imagery and experience on the haptic oblique effect.

In an attempt to clarify some of the conditions that might be responsible for the subjective straightness of an objectively curved edge, Goodnow, Baum, and Davidson (1971) had blindfolded subjects indicate where the "high point," or center, of various curves appeared to be. The observers were required to scan the stimuli with either one or two fingers, and with either a left-to-right or right-to-left scanning motion. Also, the positioning of the stimulus was varied in relation to the arm's sweep. The results indicated that perceptions were highly skewed (subjective high points were shifted) in the direction of the moving hand (i.e., the apparent center of a curve was displaced to the right during left-to-right sweeping motions), an effect that was even more pronounced when two fingers were used to scan. Goodnow et al. speculate that in haptics "subjects may confuse a property of the exploratory activity with a property of the stimulus" (p. 256).

Hunter (1954) extended Rubin's experiment by replicating it (as did Blumenfeld, 1937; Crewdson & Zangwill, 1940) with persons who were blind. Compared with blindfolded sighted subjects, the judgment of blind observers was more objectively correct and less variable. Davidson (1972b) examined this finding by analyzing the varieties of haptic exploratory styles used by blind and sighted subjects. Based on videotape records, five scanning styles were identified: (1) "gripping"—curling three or four fingers over the front edge of the curve and scanning back and forth; (2) "pinching"—scanning back and forth while holding the edge in a pincer-like grasp between thumb and forefinger; (3) "fingertip sweeping"—subdivided into (a) a "top sweep," in which straight fingers scan the top of the edge and (b) "front sweep," in which the extended fingers scan across the edge's front surface; (4) "spanning"—fingers spread out across the edge's top, and (5) "tracing"—fingers held perpendicular to the top (pointing downward) while scanning the top edge. Davidson found that the blind, who were much more accurate than the sighted, used "gripping" 60% of the time, compared with 25% for the sighted subjects. However, when blindfolded subjects were instructed in use of the preferred method of the blind, their performance was just as good.

Davidson attributes the apparent straightness of an object's concave edge to the correspondence between the natural sweep of the arm (a concave path) and the concave arc of the stimulus. He speculates that gripping is the best method for veridical perception of curved contours because

> [I]t focused attention on the front edge of the stimulus, an arc in a different plane than sweeping arm movement. . . . In contrast, exploring only the top edge of the curve . . . seems to maximize the correspondence between stimulus arc and arm arc. (p. 54)

Moreover he argues that the distinguishing feature of a curve is its ends-to-middle relationship, information that the gripping might most effectively obtain by allowing kinesthetic triangulation of this relationship (Gordon & Morison, 1982, suggest that the "gradient of curvature," a measure that also takes the length of the edge into consideration, is the effective stimulus for curvature). In a later study (Davidson & Whitson, 1974) showing that recognition memory for curves also may be enhanced by gripping, it is suggested that strategies permitting simultaneous prehension of object attributes are better able to extract, integrate, and encode information than more successive strategies such as "sweep" or "trace."

The notion that exploratory activity may be confused with the property being explored (also raised by Goodnow et al., 1971) receives support from Easton (Easton, 1976; Easton & Falzett, 1978). A pressure transducer was used to determine the force applied to a curved edge while haptically scanning that edge. The basic finding was that haptic tracking of curvature results in a pressure profile opposite to that of the contour itself (greatest pressure is applied at the curve's center and least at its ends). This same relationship exists for experienced curvature as well (the phenomenal experience of a curved edge when feeling an objectively straight contour). That is, the perceived curvature of an edge does correspond to a characteristic (i.e., the pressure profile) of the scanning activity. Unfortunately, Easton only used a scanning method comparable with Davidson's (1972b) "fingertip sweeping," a haptic style found to contribute to the nonveridical percept of curvature. It would be interesting to see if the pressure profiles for gripping are more in correspondence with the actual curvature of the stimulus.

Proportion

Stimulus extent, orientation, and curvature are properties of isolated contours. However, stimulus properties involving higher-order relational information may be more meaningfully related to perception. Gibson (1966) has argued that relational variables, those involving the integration of information from different form components, are critical to all perceptual systems. Proportion has been of interest to haptic researchers because it is this kind of variable. Moreover, because a proportion can be transposed across objects of different absolute size, it is an invariant property, the kind

Gibson believed was particularly important to perceptual systems.

The earliest study of haptic perception of proportion was carried out by Cutsforth (1933). Subjects felt a rectangular block of wood, then reproduced the object by visually setting a pair of pointers. Haptic activity involved either placing the hand and fingers upon the object ("passive touch"), tracing the edges with the index finger, or free exploration (no restrictions). Among Cutsforth's many observations are that if an object's size is convenient for manual exploration this lends itself to more accurate perception; that the active method of touch, by emphasizing the discreteness of height and width, favors a more analytical perception of form; and that the passive method leads to perception of the form as a whole.

Blomhert's (1935) subjects were asked to feel a rectangle, then pick another of the same proportion (height-to-width ratio) from a comparison array. Blomhert observed the spontaneous use of three basic exploratory styles: each end of the rectangle being grasped between the thumb and forefinger of each hand; from this initial position, the fingers sliding down the rectangle's length and brought together at its ends; the index finger tracing the rectangle's outline. The performance of subjects was very accurate but Blomhert found that they labored over their judgments and all subjects spontaneously used a finger or part of the hand to measure the rectangle's extents. Indeed, this led him to impose a measuring prohibition on their otherwise spontaneous activity.

Drawing upon Blomhert's observations, Appelle and Goodnow (1970) examined the role of haptic exploratory style more closely. Blindfolded subjects were required to make same–different judgments to proportions (rectangles), using one of the spontaneous scanning styles described by Blomhert ("unrestricted," "pincer," "pincer-slide," or "trace"). The basic finding was that accuracy increased as the method of touch involved an increasing amount of activity (unrestricted was best; pincer worst). Appelle et al. (1980) extended this study by taking a closer look at the measuring function described by Blomhert, and at how information regarding extent (length and width) is integrated into a relational judgment of proportion. Subjects were assigned to three haptic scanning groups: "unrestricted" (subjects were given no special scanning strategies to use), "measuring" (subjects were required to try to measure the rectangle's extents), and "no-measuring" (subjects were prohibited from trying to measure directly).

In regard to the variable of length integration, accuracy in judging absolute extent was not related to judgment of proportion, but ability to judge the ratio between two extents covaried closely with the ability to judge proportion. This finding was not obtained, however, for the no-measuring condition. In regard to the direct effect of measuring on proportion judgments, the results suggested a strong role for measuring as a strategy. Subjects' spontaneous tendency to use measuring was very apparent. Fifty-three percent of the subjects in the unrestricted group were observed using obvious techniques of direct measurement. Post hoc subjective reports indicated that 80% of the subjects in the no-measuring condition would have tried to measure had they not been instructed to refrain. And pincer-slide, the method spontaneously chosen by 60% of the subjects in the measuring and the unrestricted conditions, was also used by 30% of subjects in the no-measuring condition. Many subjects in this latter group indicated they used this method to time their movements covertly, that is, they actually used pincer-slide for temporal measurement. Appelle et al., (1980) conclude that measuring is used extensively in all methods of judging proportion and that under normal conditions "proportion is neither a directly nor a spontaneously perceived attribute of form" (p. 161).

Other Higher-Order Attributes of Form

Surprisingly, other than proportion, higher-order attributes of form have not been a major focus of haptic investigations. Of the few studies of this kind that have been done, contour numerosity (form complexity) contour symmetry, and distinctive features of form have received some attention.

Just what constitutes a "distinctive feature" (Gibson & Gibson, 1955) in haptic form has not been determined, but Lobb and Friend (1967) observed that subjects asked to discriminate random-shape heptagons exhibited repeated scanning centered around the shapes' vertices. The authors speculate that subjects were primarily learning angular differences as distinctive features. Shaffer and Howard (1974) required subjects to learn to sort punctiform shapes into categories based on invariant features of change (relative position of dots comprising each stimulus). Subjects were able to identify stimuli based on their specific features but were unable to use schematic information (information about characteristics common to a stimulus class) to classify new stimuli varying in the same manner as those presented during training. Garbin and Bernstein (1984) found that subjects notice distinctive features of haptic form (projections, ridges, etc.) but classify stimuli primarily in terms of metric attributes (size, symmetry, complexity, etc.). These studies only provide a hint of what role invariants and distinctive features might play in the haptic perception of form.

In regard to complexity, Foulke and Warm (1967) obtained speed and accuracy measures for recognition judgments to punctiform metric figures. They found that both speed and accuracy decreased as stimulus complexity (dot numerosity) increased. Brumaghim and Brown (1968) had subjects rate form complexity when touching planar random polygons. Judged complexity increased with number of sides, as did the latency in making the judgment (i.e., exploration times). The authors attribute this to a linear increase in information gathering with an increase in complexity.

An experiment by Locher and Simmons (1978) looked at both complexity and symmetry. Subjects were presented with planar shapes that were either symmetrical or asymmetrical relative to their vertical axis, and varied in number of sides (12-30). The task was to either make a judgment regarding symmetry, or to identify a learned form from a stimulus array. The exploratory style of the subject was recorded on videotape and classified into three scanning methods: "simultaneous apprehension" (smooth and continuous movements involving more than one finger across both sides of the form at the same time), "trace" (finger(s) sliding over one edge of the shape), or "mixed" (use of both simultaneous and trace methods while scanning). Two scanning "processes" ("complete scan"—full sweep of form; "partial scan"—less than one full sweep of the form) were also classified. In addition to finding that reaction time increased with complexity, Locher and Simmons found that detection of asymmetry was faster than detection of symmetry, but learning (encoding) and recognition (identification accuracy) of shape was faster for symmetrical objects (however, Walk, 1965, found better learning and recognition for asymmetrical shapes). Scanning style did not vary with stimulus complexity, but it did vary with stimulus symmetry, and with the haptic task involved. For judgment of symmetry, the simultaneous styles and complete scans predominated when exploring symmetrical shapes. Trace and partial scans were used the most with asymmetrical stimuli. For recognition judgments, trace was used almost exclusively with asymmetrical shapes and predominantly for symmetrical shapes.

Locher and Simmons conclude that "there is an interactive effect of stimulus properties and task requirements upon haptic scanning processes" and that "much additional investigation of the psychophysics of form for the haptic mode . . . is needed" (p. 116). These are certainly conclusions we can agree with.

SUMMARY AND CONCLUSIONS

From its inception research on the haptic perception of form has shown interactions between the attributes of form, haptic exploratory activity, and the pickup of stimulus information. Although an occasional study fails to find active touch superior to passive in all situations (e.g., Heller, 1986; Magee & Kennedy, 1980; Schwartz, Perey, & Azulay, 1975) the bulk of the literature supports the superiority of active modes of exploration. The literature also suggests that global styles of touch (i.e., those involving greater activity and more simultaneous prehension of form) are superior to more restricted strategies. Beyond these generalizations, there appear to be specific compatibilities between particular attributes of form and exploratory style. These conclusions, however, need to be confirmed for a much wider range of both stimulus and activity variables. Three-dimensional solid form, stimulus objects most commonly manipulated by the hand in normal experience, have scarcely been studied in the laboratory. Distinctive features and relational (higher-order or invariant) properties, those attributes of form that are probably most important to perception, have been largely ignored. And Gestalt principles of organization, which have been worked out in detail for vision, have also not been studied in regard to form perception by touch. We also need to know more about what the hand *can* do as opposed to what it *does* do. A number of studies have demonstrated significant improvement in haptic performance with experience (Davidson, 1972b, Davidson, Appelle, & Pezzmenti, 1981; Simmons & Locher, 1979). Finally, although there is much descriptive work on haptic exploration strategies, little is actually known about how patterns of haptic movement allow for information pickup or emergent percepts of form. More detailed analysis of the macro- and micromovements of the exploring hand and fingers may provide the clues to this process.

REFERENCES

Abravanel, E. (1970). Choice for shape vs texture matching by young children. *Perceptual and Motor Skills, 31*, 527–533.

Appelle, S. (1971). Visual and haptic angle perception in the matching task. *American Journal of Psychology, 84*, 487–499.

Appelle, S. (1972). Perception and discrimination as a function of stimulus orientation: The "oblique effect" in man and animals. *Psychological Bulletin, 78*, 266–278.

Appelle, S., & Countryman, M. (1986). Eliminating the haptic oblique effect: Influence of scanning incongruity and prior knowledge of the standards. *Perception, 15*, 325–329.

Appelle, S., & Goodnow, J. J. (1970). Haptic and visual perception of proportion. *Journal of Experimental Psychology, 84*, 47–52.

Appelle, S., & Gravetter, F. J. (1985). Effect of modality-specific experience on visual and haptic judgment of orientation. *Perception, 14*, 763–773.

Appelle, S., Gravetter, F. J., & Davidson, P. W. (1980). Proportion judgments in haptic and visual form perception. *Canadian Journal of Psychology, 34*, 161–174.

Blomhert, G. (1935). Contribution to the study of the haptic perception of proportions. *Koninklijke Academie Von Wetenschappen, 38*, 931–942.

Blumenfeld, W. (1937). The relationship between the optical and haptic construction of space. *Acta Psychologica, 2*, 125–174.

Brown, J. S., Knauft, E. B., & Rosenbaum, G. (1948). The accuracy of positioning reactions as a function of their direction and extent. *American Journal of Psychology, 61*, 167–182.

Brumaghim, S. H., & Brown, D. R. (1968). Perceptual equivalence between visual and tactual pattern perception: an anchoring study. *Perception & Psychophysics, 4*, 175–179.

Cheng, M. F. (1968). Tactile–kinesthetic perception of length. *American Journal of Psychology, 81*, 74–82.

Crewdson, J., & Zangwill, O. L. (1940). A note on tactual perception in a blind subject. *British Journal of Psychology, 30*, 224–229.

Cronin, V. (1977). Active and passive touch at four age levels. *Developmental Psychology, 13,* 253-256.

Cutsforth, T.D. (1933). An analysis of the relationship between tactual and visual perception. *Psychological Monographs, 44,* 125-152.

Davidon, R. S., & Cheng, M. F. (1964). Apparent distance in a horizontal plane with tactile–kinesthetic stimuli. *Quarterly Journal of Experimental Psychology, 16,* 277–281.

Davidson, P. W. (1972a). The role of exploratory activity in haptic perception: Some issues, data, and hypotheses. *American Foundation for the Blind Research Bulletin, 24,* 21–27.

Davidson, P. W. (1972b). Haptic judgments of curvature by blind and sighted humans. *Journal of Experimental Psychology, 93,* 43–55.

Davidson, P. W. (1976). Some functions of active handling: studies with blinded humans. *New Outlook for the Blind, 70,* 198–202.

Davidson, P. W., Abbott, S., & Gershenfeld, J. (1974). Influence of exploration time on haptic and visual matching of complex shape. *Perception & Psychophysics, 15,* 539–543.

Davidson, P. W., Appelle, S., & Haber, R. (in press). Haptic scanning of braille cells by low- and high-proficiency blind readers. *Research in Developmental Disabilities.*

Davidson, P. W., Appelle, S., & Pezzmenti, F. (1981). Haptic equivalence matching of curvature by nonretarded and mentally retarded blind and sighted person. *American Journal of Mental Deficiency, 86,* 295–299.

Davidson, P. W., & Whitson, T. T. (1974). Haptic equivalence matching of curvature by blind and sighted humans. *Journal of Experimental Psychology, 102,* 687–690.

Day, R. H., & Wong, T. S. (1971). Radial and tangential movement directions as determinants of the haptic illusion in an L figure. *Journal of Experimental Psychology, 87,* 19–22.

Deregowski, J., & Ellis, H. D. (1972). Effect of stimulus orientation upon haptic perception of the horizontal–vertical illusion. *Journal of Experimental Psychology, 95,* 14–19.

Easton, R. D. (1976). Prismatically induced curvature and finger-tracking pressure changes in a visual capture phenomenon. *Perception & Psychophysics, 19,* 201–205.

Easton, R. D., & Falzett, M. (1978). Finger pressure during curved contours: Implication for a visual dominance phenomenon. *Perception & Psychophysics, 24,* 145–153.

Foulke, E., & Warm, J. S. (1967). Effects of complexity and redundancy on the tactual recognition of metric figures. *Perceptual and Motor Skills, 25,* 177–187.

Fry, C. L. (1975). Tactual illusions. *Perceptual and Motor Skills, 40,* 955–960.

Garbin, C. P., & Bernstein, I. H. (1984). Visual and haptic perception of three-dimensional solid forms. *Perception & Psychophysics, 36,* 104–110.

Gibson, J. J. (1933). Adaptation, after-effect and contrast in the perception of curved lines. *Journal of Experimental Psychology, 16,* 1–31.

Gibson, J. J. (1962). Observations on active touch. *Psychological Review, 69,* 477–491.

Gibson, J. J. (1966). *The senses considered as perceptual systems.* Boston: Houghton Mifflin.

Gibson, J. J., & Gibson, E. J. (1955). Perceptual learning: Differentiation or enrichment. *Psychological Review, 62,* 32–41.

Goodnow, J. J., Baum, B., & Davidson, P. (1971). A haptic error: Skew in a symmetrical curve. *Perception & Psychophysics, 10,* 253–256.

Gordon, G. (Ed.). (1978). *Active touch.* New York: Pergamon Press.

Gordon, I. E., & Morison, V. (1982). The haptic perception of curvature. *Perception & Psychophysics, 31,* 446–450.

Heller, M. A. (1984). Active and passive touch: The influence of exploration time on form recognition. *Journal of General Psychology, 110,* 243–249.

Heller, M. A. (1986). Central and peripheral influences on tactual reading. *Perception & Psychophysics, 39,* 197–204.

Heller, M. A., & Myers, D. S. (1983). Active and passive tactual recognition of form. *Journal of General Psychology, 108,* 225–229.

Hilgard, E. R., Morgan, A. H., & Prytulak, S. (1968). The psychophysics of the kinesthetic aftereffect in the petrie block experiment. *Perception & Psychophysics, 4,* 129–132.

Hohmuth, A., Phillips, W. D., & Van Romer, H. (1976). A discrepancy between two modes of haptic length perception. *Journal of Psychology, 92,* 79–87.

Hunter, I. M. (1954). Tactile–kinesthetic perception of straightness in blind and sighted humans. *Quarterly Journal of Experimental Psychology, 6,* 149–154.

Jastrow, J. (1886). The perception of space by disparate senses. *Mind, 11,* 539–554.

Katz, D. (1925/1989). *The world of touch* (L. E. Krueger, Trans.). Hillsdale, NJ: Lawrence Erlbaum Associates.

Kennedy, J. M. (1978). Haptics. In E. C. Carterette & M. P. Friedman (Eds.), *Handbook of perception, Vol 8: Perceptual coding,* New York: Academic Press.

Kiphart, M. J., Auday, B. C., & Cross, H. A. (1988). Short-term haptic memory for three-dimensional objects. *Perceptual and Motor Skills, 66,* 79–91.

Klatzky, R. L., Lederman, S. J., & Metzger, V. A. (1985). Identifying objects by touch: An "expert system." *Perception & Psychophysics, 37,* 299–302.

Klatzky, R. L., Lederman, S., & Reed, C. (1987). There's more to touch than meets the eye: The salience of object attributes for haptics with and without vision. *Journal of Experimental Psychology: General, 116,* 356–369.

Klatzky, R. L., Lederman, S., & Reed, C. (1989). Haptic integration of object properties: Texture, hardness, and planar contour. *Journal of Experimental Psychology: Human Perception and Performance, 15,* 45–57.

Landrigan, D. T., & Forsyth, G. A. (1974). Regulation and production of movement effects in exploration–recognition performance. *Journal of Experimental Psychology, 103,* 1124–1130.

Lechelt, E. C., Eliuk, J., & Tanne, G. (1976). Perceptual orientation asymmetries: A comparison of visual and haptic space. *Perception & Psychophysics, 20,* 463–469.

Lechelt, E. C., & Verenka, A. (1980). Spatial anisotropy in intramodal and cross-modal judgments of stimulus orientation: The stability of the oblique effect. *Perception, 9,* 581–587.

Lederman, S. J., & Klatzky, R. L. (1987). Hand movements: A window into haptic object recognition. *Cognitive Psychology, 19,* 342–368.

Lederman, S. J., Klatzky, R. L., Chataway, C., & Summers, C. D. (1990). Visual mediation and the haptic recognition of two-dimensional pictures of common objects. *Perception & Psychophysics, 47,* 54–64.

Lobb, H., & Friend, R. (1967). Tactual form discrimination with varying size and duration of exposure. *Psychonomic Science, 7,* 415–416.

Locher, P. J., & Simmons, R. W. (1978). Influence of stimulus symmetry and complexity upon haptic scanning strategies during detection, learning, and recognition tasks. *Perception & Psychophysics, 23,* 110–116.

Loomis, J. M., & Lederman, S. J. (1986). Tactual Perception. In K. R. Boff, L. Kaufman, & J. Thomas (Eds.), *Handbook of perception and human performance. Vol. 2: Cognitive processes and performance.* New York: Wiley.

Magee, L. E., & Kennedy, J. M. (1980). Exploring pictures tactually. *Nature, 283,* 287–288.

Marchetti, F. M., & Lederman, S. J. (1983). The haptic radial–tangential effect: Two tests of Wong's "moments of inertia" hypothesis. *Bulletin of the Psychonomic Society, 21,* 43–46.

Nilsson, J., & Geffen, G. (1987). Perception of similarity and laterality effects in tactile shape recognition. *Cortex, 23,* 599–614.

Revesz, G. (1950). *Psychology and art of the blind.* New York: Longmans, Green.

Roeckelein, J. E. (1968). Tactual size perception with the method of magnitude estimation. *Psychonomic Science, 13,* 295–296.

Rubin, E. (1936). Haptische Untersulchungen. *Acta Psychologica, 1,* 285–380.

Schiff, W., & Foulke, E. (Eds.). (1982). *Tactual perception: A sourcebook.* New York: Cambridge University Press.

Schwartz, A. S., Perey, A. J., & Azulay, A. (1975). Further analysis of active and passive touch in pattern discrimination. *Bulletin of the Psychonomic Society, 6,* 7–9.

Shaffer, R. W., & Howard, J. (1974). The transfer of information across sensory modalities, *Perception & Psychophysics, 15,* 344–348.

Simmons, R. W., & Locher, P. J. (1979). Role of extended perceptual experience upon haptic perception of nonrepresentational shapes. *Perceptual and Motor Skills, 48,* 987–991.

Stanley, G. (1966). Haptic and kinesthetic estimates of length. *Psychonomic Science, 5,* 377–378.

Walk, R. D. (1965). Tactual and visual learning of forms differing in degree of symmetry. *Psychonomic Science, 2,* 93–94.

Walker, J. T. (1977). Orientation-contingent tactual size aftereffects. *Perception & Psychophysics, 22,* 563–570.

Walker, J. T. (1978). Simple and contingent aftereffects in the kinesthetic perception of length. *Journal of Experimental Psychology: Human Perception & Performance, 4,* 294–301.

Walker, J. T., & Shea, K. S. (1974). A tactual size aftereffect contingent on hand position. *Journal of Experimental Psychology, 4,* 668–674.

Zinchenko, V. P., & Lomov, B. F. (1960). The functions of hand and eye movements in the process of perception. *Voprosy Psikhologi, 1,* 12–26.

Zusne, L. (1970). *Visual perception of form.* New York: Academic Press.

8

VIBROTACTILE PATTERN PERCEPTION: SOME FINDINGS AND APPLICATIONS

Carl Sherrick
Princeton University

INTRODUCTION

When psychologists speak of "the stimulus," the impression all too often gained by their audiences is of a kind of punctate experience in space and time, more or less in keeping with the original Latin definition of the word, which was "a goad." In fact, metaphorical extension of the term lets it comprise a great range of physical events of varying extent, duration, and complexity. In speaking of the tactile stimulus, therefore, we may be describing something as simple as a transient skin displacement, such as a puff of air on the cheek, or as complex as the traveling waves of displacement generated over the entire body when one sits in the chapel listening to a musical passage at full organ from a 32-foot bombard! For this reason it may be better to subsume such events under the general term "stimulus pattern," a phrase that connotes a more or less extended, durative display to the perceptual system, and more realistically represents the psychophysical catenary of events that precede the subject's report.

Definition of Vibrotactile Patterns. Patterns of vibration are not limited to those conditions involving the appearance of long-lasting, periodically varying displacements of the tissues; any transient or sustained disturbance can be analyzed as a distribution of energies over the entire spectrum of vibration frequencies (Bracewell, 1978; Loomis & Lederman, 1986). The patterns of displacement of the skin produced by braille characters, or by active palpation of two- or three-dimensional objects during attempts at haptic recognition, are the subjects of other chapters (see Appelle and Foulke, this volume), and will not be dwelt upon at length in the present discussion.

Vibratory patterns can be defined either as a continuous waveform of skin displacement in both space and time, or transient pressures, or as spatiotemporal textures generated by the relative motion between the skin and objects in the environment. This is, of course, a strictly physical point of view. We could argue that what is wanted is a definition of vibrotactile patterns, and that this must include the sensory organs of touch and their limits of arousal. It is clear that displacements having frequencies below 1 Hz or above 3 kHz will not, except under extraordinary conditions, affect most of the touch receptors (see Cholewiak & Collins, this volume), so a definition that does not specify the conditions of receptor excitation is hardly adequate. A similar argument could be made for a psychophysical criterion, in which the report of the person stimulated is one of the necessary conditions for defining the stimulus pattern.

History of Vibratory Pattern Generation and Perception.

With the exception of the use of the tactile sense by teachers to provide deaf or blind persons with some appreciation of the environment (see, e.g., Bentzen, 1980, p. 323ff.; Davis & Silverman, 1978), evidence of the range of human capacities for skilled perception of natural patterns is not in great supply. There are, however, persons with highly developed skills in tactual pattern perception. Geldard (1972, p. 313) describes the abilities of "cloth feelers" in grading textiles and other fabrics for use in clothing, and Harper (1952) has reported the discriminative skills used by persons in the dairy industry to determine the stage of cure of cheeses. Norton et al. (1977) and Reed et al. (1985) report the amazing abilities of certain deaf-blind individuals in comprehending continuous speech by use of what is called the Tadoma method. This involves integrating a number of separate patterns of touch generated on the "listener's" hand when it contacts the face of the talker.

In general such skills as those mentioned are rarely encountered, and the persons exhibiting them are commonly regarded as virtuosi. The concern among students of vibratory pattern perception has been to discover a set of tactile patterns that, like speech sounds or letters of the alphabet, are clearly discriminated, rapidly processed, and easily learned by persons with average cognitive skills. The "haptemes" thus generated could then be used in encoding environmental stimuli that are presently inaccessible for display to the subject.

Following the development of electronic amplification and electromechanical transducers, a number of systems were designed to recode environmental stimuli for use in sensory aids for disabled persons (Bliss, 1970; Craig & Sherrick, 1982; Kirman, 1973), or to reduce sensory overload in the performance of industrial or military tasks with supplementary tactual input (Geldard, 1974). Thus, optical patterns (Bliss, Katcher, Rogers, & Shepard, 1970) or sound patterns (Kirman, 1973; Sherrick, 1984) could be converted to vibrotactile space-time patterns in reading aids for blind persons or speech-analyzing aids for deaf persons. Similarly, a mechanical transducer attached to the control yoke of an aircraft has been used to provide attitude information to the pilot (Gilson & Fenton, 1974; Hirsch, 1974). In the latter cases, the information was redundant with that from cockpit visual displays as well as that from outside the cockpit, but it has been shown to be of use to novice pilots as well as to experienced ones in stressful conditions.

GENERATION AND PERCEPTION OF VIBRATORY PATTERNS

Single and Multiple-Driver-Distributed Arrays. In a very early attempt to provide a sensory substitute for hearing in deaf children, Gault (1924) experimented with an acoustical transmission system that produced vibrations on the hands of the deaf child. The original device was essentially a speaking tube that transmitted the voice of the talker as air column vibrations, converted at the end of the tube to skin vibrations when the palm was held against it. The child was taught to distinguish speech sounds thus produced, and progress was sufficient to encourage Gault to develop an electronic system, which he dubbed the Teletactor, to convey the spoken sounds from a microphone to a vibration transducer, then to the child's hand or fingers. Later, Gault (1927) improved this single vibrator system by introducing filters to subdivide the speech frequencies into five bands, each of which was sent to separate vibrators on the fingers and thumb of one hand. Insofar as the design represented the frequency of sound as a place of vibratory displacement on the skin, this device was probably one of the first systems constructed to model a sensory process for use in an aid. Because the frequencies that were sent to the vibrators were unmodified, however, and the skin requires enormous energies to respond to frequencies above about 1 kHz, the full range of pattern variations over the fingers was not perceived. What was being presented to the person receiving the speech stream was the play of vibrations across the fingers and thumb, varying in time in both frequency (redundantly with place of stimulation) and intensity as the talker intoned the message. As has been noted, because the upper formants of speech fall above 1 kHz, much of the speech energy that would be apprehended by a hearing person would fail to stimulate the skin using this device. Moreover, with the simultaneous presentation of vibrations to different fingers, the possibility of mutual masking of the vibratory sensations was great. The program of research was discontinued, but was taken up in other laboratories, as we shall see in the discussion of applications.

Another approach to the problem of transmitting information to the skin is typified by the design of the braille code (see Foulke, this volume). In this tradition, and to demonstrate the capacity of the skin for rapid information processing, Geldard and his students (Geldard, 1957) conducted a series of psychophysical studies that culminated in the design of a vibrotactile language, called "Vibratese." This was a relatively simple system that generated a code for the letters of the alphabet by assigning to each letter one of five skin locations, three durations, and three loudnesses (see Fig. 8.1). The spatial separation of the vibrators on the chest and the choices of durations and loudnesses were based on earlier studies made by Geldard and his students and colleagues. A small number of subjects were taught the code, and one skilled person was able to receive an extended message at the rate of 38 words per minute. This should be compared with the (auditory) rate of reception of Morse code, which at best seldom exceeds 30 wpm (for the tactual equivalent, see Foulke & Brodbeck, 1968). What is to be noted in the present system is the intention to provide a very spare alphanumerical code having little redundancy, a relatively small demand on parallel processing capability, and little or no opportunity for the occurrence of simultaneous masking effects. The

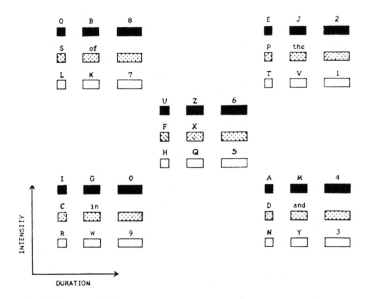

FIG. 8.1. The Vibratese code. The five clusters represent the five positions on the chest of the subject. Within a particular position, any one of the symbols represents a letter, number, or short word as shown. Thus, a short, weak burst of vibration at the lower left vibrator will mean an "R." A long, intense burst of vibration at the center vibrator will mean a "6." See text for other details (after Geldard, 1957). Copyright 1957 by the American Psychological Association. Adapted by permission.

limitation on rapidity of processing was owing in part to the fact that the dimension of duration, which was one of the major code elements, set the upper rate of presentation at 70 wpm. Interestingly, this figure is near that calculated as the lower acceptable limit for rate in continuous discourse tracking in speech testing of aids for hearing-impaired persons (see, e.g., Cholewiak & Sherrick, 1986; Levitt, Waltzman, Shapiro, & Cohen, 1986). The Vibratese code had a more serious shortcoming, however; subjects were confused by the interaction of the dimensions of loudness and duration. Subsequent research has shown the intimate relation of the two as a result of temporal summation (Gescheider & Joelson, 1983).

In later research, Geldard and Sherrick (1965) examined the subject's ability to discriminate a more complex array of patterns distributed over the body, in part as a first step in the generation of a new tactile code involving patterns of vibration across the entire body. Subjects were required to make discriminations between successively presented patterns, which could vary in number and position on the body. A total of 10 vibrator positions were studied, as shown in Fig. 8.2. The subjects performed a two-alternative, forced-choice task, responding "same" or "different" after two successive patterns were presented. Analysis of the errors produced yielded an attribute described as "communality," which was expressed as the number of vibrators shared between the two token patterns in the pair to be discriminated. When communality was factored out of the overall results, the effect of total number of vibrators, which was originally thought to be contributing to discrimination difficulty, was completely eliminated. With the same array slightly modified, Geldard and his students experimented with a device called the Optophone, developed by the Battelle Institute to permit blind persons to read ink print by converting the letters to complex auditory patterns. The photocell pickup of the device was employed to detect the letters on the page by scanning it as in the original device, but instead of controlling separate audio oscillators, each of the nine photocells was channeled separately to nine vibrators distributed over the body of the subject (Geldard, 1966). Fig. 8.2 illustrates the distribution of vibrators for the original series of studies. When individual letters of the alphabet were scanned by the pickup, the patterns of vibration generated over the body proved so difficult to discriminate that it was decided to use some of the unique symbols from the IBM type library to represent the letters of the alphabet (see Geldard, 1966). Here again, the design was based not on an available set of optical patterns such as letters of the alphabet, but rather on a set that experimentation showed could be readily discriminated from each other. Fig. 8.3 shows the patterns selected for representation of the alphabet.

Unlike the Vibratese code, in which a single vibrator was on at a time, the patterns of vibration for the Optohapt were distributed in time and space in a way that allowed several vibrators to be active at once. The great physi-

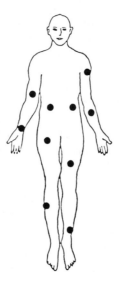

FIG. 8.2. Sites on the body used for the study of pattern discrimination. In a subsequent study, all but the site on the right side of the abdomen were employed to test the Optohapt system of coding. The nine positions correspond to the nine photocells of the Optohapt, such that as the ink-print pattern was scanned across the head, the appropriate vibrators were excited (after Geldard and Sherrick, *Journal of the Acoustical Society of America*, 1965).

cal separation of vibrators was intended to ensure that no interference among them could occur, but even with the isolation thus achieved, the patterns produced were perceived as integral wholes by the subject. In the process of combining these to form words and phrases, however, subjects often reported feeling unable to recall the initial letters in the word, almost as though they were aphasic. Whether this is owing to the poor short-term memory storage for touch patterns, and therefore their diffusion in time (see Murray, Ward, & Hockley, 1975; Keidel, 1968, p. 72), or to their diffusion over body space, or both, is not known. Gilson (1969) found that spatial differences between sites of vibratory maskers and targets could be compensated by onset time adjustments between them to alter the magnitude of masking effects. This finding, along with experiments analyzing the phantom of lateralization (Alles, 1970; Békésy, 1967), synthetic movement (Kirman, 1974b, 1974c, 1975; Sherrick & Rogers, 1966), the saltatory illusion (Geldard & Sherrick, 1972; 1983), and the Tau effect (Helson & King, 1931; Lechelt & Borchert, 1977), indicates that the trading relationship between space and time in tactile perception is very extensive, as we shall soon see. The reciprocity of these dimensions may yet prove to be a master key in the generation of graphic or linguistic codes for use in tactile monitoring of the environment.

Patterns Generated by Single Vibrators. As we have noted, all vibratory patterns may be viewed as distributions of energy in space and time; those produced by single driving points are generally somewhat less interesting to cognitive psychologists than patterns from multiple-point stimulators. It is nevertheless true that physical differences among single-point patterns are evident; moreover, some of them are perceptible, either directly as phenomenal changes, or indirectly as threshold, loudness, or location changes. There has been, for example, considerable study of the general disposition of energy propagated from a single point (Békésy, 1939; Franke, 1951; Geldard, 1975, p. 67ff.; Keidel, 1956, pp. 16–46; Moore, 1970; Sherrick, 1953). For the most part, these investigations have been limited to the propagation of energy along the surface of the skin, and to the mechanical impedance presented to the vibrating contactor (but see Keidel, 1956; Oestreicher, 1950). When the location, frequency, or amplitude of vibration is changed, observers can report noticeable differences in the "feel" of the pattern, for exam-

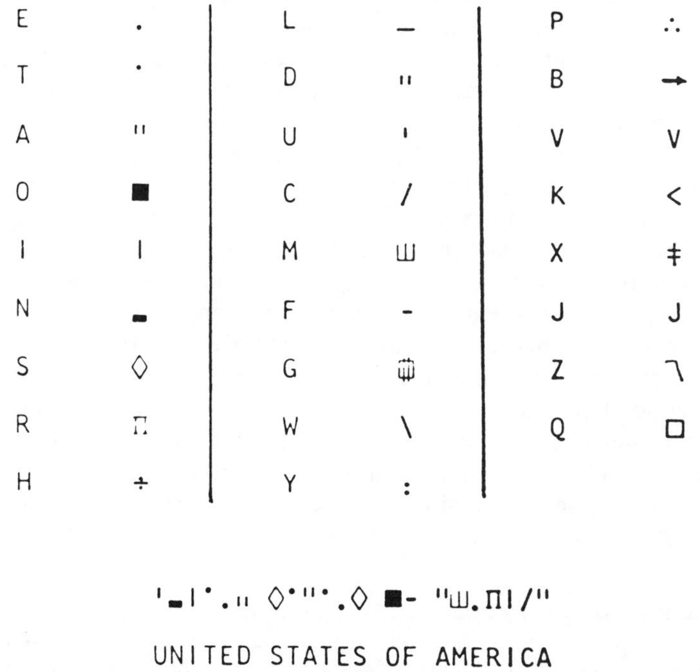

E	.	L	—	P	∴
T	·	D	‖	B	→
A	‖	U	၊	V	V
O	■	C	/	K	<
I	I	M	�咖	X	‡
N	▬	F	-	J	J
S	◇	G	丗	Z	⌐
R	⊓	W	\	Q	□
H	÷	Y	:		

' ▬ I · . ‖ ◇ · ‖ · . ◇ ■ - "Ш. ⊓ I / ‖

UNITED STATES OF AMERICA

FIG. 8.3. The alphabet of patterns used to code letters for the Optohapt system. The use of letters themselves yielded patterns of vibration that were too difficult to discriminate, and the ones shown were selected after subjects were tested with a much larger set. At the bottom is encoded the phrase "United States of America" (after Geldard, 1966). From *Perception & Psychophysics*, Vol. 1, 377–381, reprinted by permission of Psychonomic Society, Inc.

ple, changes in rate are discriminable (as vibratory "pitch" shifts) from frequencies of a few Hz up to 400 Hz (Rothenberg, Verrillo, Zahorian, Brachman, & Bolanowski, 1977; Sherrick, 1985). In some cases, the frequency change induces a shift in the feeling of density or of location of the pattern (Békésy, 1960, p. 594). In addition, for a given frequency of sinusoid, a change in amplitude may produce a shift in vibratory pitch (Békésy, 1960, p. 593), such that a higher amplitude feels like a lower rate. Rothenberg et al. noted that changing the width of a unidirectional mechanical pulse was perceived by the observers as a change in timbre (1977, p. 1006), and suggested that this dimension could be usefully encoded in a speech-analyzing aid. Owing to the demands on vibrator performance made by this parameter, no current devices use it in encoding speech. In an interesting study of frequency discrimination, Kirman (1986) found that this ability could be interfered with by both forward and backward masking, that is, the presence of unwanted signals either preceding or following the target. He hypothesized that as many as three factors may be operating to reduce discriminative capacity: a time-limited factor dependent on target/mask intensity ratios; one dependent on masker duration that operates only in backward masking over a long period; and one dependent mainly on target-masker similarity (communality?), operating over a 500-ms interval in both forward and backward directions.

When a static surround is added to a vibrating contactor, there has been no reported shift in the quality of vibration. Measurements of threshold for vibration show a distinct change, however. Verrillo was the first to examine systematically the effects of the presence of a surround (1963, 1966, 1979), and showed that the amplitude required for threshold was shifted in a manner that depended on frequency: At higher frequencies, thresholds rose in the presence of a surround, whereas at lower frequencies, they fell. This was attributed to the change in activity of the underlying receptor populations as a function of changes in certain physical properties of the stimulus patterns. In a similar manner, absolute thresholds and suprathreshold sensory magnitudes can be changed by altering the size of the contactor, its static force, and of course the location of the stimulator (Craig & Sherrick, 1969; Keidel, 1956; Lamoré & Keemink, 1988; Sherrick, 1960; Verrillo, 1974).

Patterns Generated by Multiple Distributed Arrays. When as few as two vibrators are placed on the skin and excited together, a large variety of perceptual phenomena can be elicited. For example, presenting sinusoidal bursts, or clicks, or other stimuli close in time to two different skin sites will result in a mutual masking effect, perceptible as either a change in absolute threshold or a change in suprathreshold sensory magnitude at the test site (Sherrick, 1964, p. 44).

If durative sinusoids of the same frequency are presented at two sites on the arm that are within 5 cm of one another, and their sensory magnitudes are equated, then a continuous variation of phase between them will be perceived as a vibratory sensation that commutes between the two locations at the rate of the phase shift (Békésy, 1967, p. 95). With this same arrangement, if the two sinusoids are presented in bursts that are about 100 ms long, and separated by about 60 ms, a sensation of movement occurs between sites very much like that which, visually experienced, is usually called "phi" movement (Kirman, 1974a, 1974b; 1975; Sherrick & Rogers, 1966).

Change the stimulus once again to a series of five pulses (at a rate of 20 pps) at one vibrator followed immediately by five at the second, thus producing a tapping sensation, and the experience is now one of a discrete "hopping" of the taps between the sites (Geldard & Sherrick, 1972). Change it for a fourth time to a single tap at each site, and keep the time interval between taps below 2 ms, and a single phantom will be perceived between the sites, located near the site first tapped. With exactly simultaneous taps, the phantom will appear near the middle ground. This phenomenon is called lateralization (Alles, 1970; Békésy, 1960, p. 571; Gescheider, 1965). Variation of the amplitude ratios of the two taps with the delay constant at zero will produce a spatial displacement of the phantom. Indeed, Alles applied the phenomenon to the generation of a proprioceptive cue, using the amplitude code to great advantage (1970, p. 86).

If the time between taps is extended to 20 ms and more, and if now the pair follows a tap at the first site by 1 s, a phantom is perceived once again between the sites. In this case as well, the position is determined by the time interval (Geldard, 1975; Geldard & Sherrick, 1983). This effect is thought to be related to the hopping phenomenon described in the previous paragraph (see Sherrick, 1982, pp. 18f).

The common thread in all these phenomena is the perception of a change in the location of all or part of the stimulus pattern when the time relations between the stimuli are manipulated. What is peculiar about the perception is the emergence of an object or objects for which there is no simple physical correlate, which is, of course, why it is dubbed a phantom. In the case of simple masking, it is assumed that the increased activity at one location dominates in the sensory inflow, and it is the disappearance of the (suprathreshold) target, not the appearance of a phantom, that is paradoxical. When magnitudes are equal and time is the dimension that differentiates the stimuli, the current excitation usually predominates, and the localization is assigned to it. This will explain the ultimate positions of the stimuli in the cutaneous phi phenomenon and the lateralization effect, but it does not explain the intermediate spatial positions taken.

One explanation made by Anstis (1986, p. 16-16ff.) for visual phi movement suggests that the eye is acting as a spatiotemporal filter, and when the apparent movement stimuli are presented, they are really square waves of displacement in space-time. The visual filtering system does not process the higher-frequency components that would allow analysis of the displacement as successive, but admits the lower-frequency information, which is encoded as a smooth transition between sites. Conceiving of the skin as a low-pass spatial filter, as Loomis has done (1990), one may arrive at a similar explanation for apparent cutaneous movement.

For the phantom of lateralization, the explanation given by Békésy (1967, pp. 92, 129; 1971) was based on a model of neural inhibition: Any delay between two neural signals gives priority to the first by forward inhibition, favoring assignment of its location by the CNS to the complex (this assumes that location on the skin is coded neurally as a quality of the stimulus). At the same time, the presence of the second will produce a backward inhibition effect, such that the second stimulus alters the information from the first. The result is a compound excitation that mixes localization information like colors or tones, to yield a single location that is an alloy of the two. The location of the perceived site will naturally depend on the timing, which provides the weighting values for encoding positions.

This explanation will not do for the saltation effect, since in this phenomenon the phantom is initially located near the second site when the time interval is shortest (Sherrick, 1982, p. 18). If the phantom were like that of lateralization, it should appear nearer the leading locus. Let the explanation be based on the perception of distance, however, and the saltation effect can be interpreted. The first or locator tap, being about a second before the critical pair and therefore not interfered with by either, defines the location of the first site. The third tap, at the second site, defines the location of the second site, since nothing follows it to distort its position. With these two locations established, the veridical distance between taps is defined (see, e.g., Sherrick & Cholewiak, 1986, pp. 12–26). The second tap, which occurs at the first site, and is followed at a variable time by the third tap, will then establish a second distance, with the third tap as the fixed position or benchmark for it. The result of the shorter time between taps two and three is, of course, a shorter apparent distance owing to the Tau effect (Helson & King, 1931), which is the perception of decreasing separation of two sites as the time between their stimulation decreases. Within the spatiotemporal framework of taps one and three, the cutaneous system interprets this second distance impression not as such, but rather as a phantom location of the second tap, and the gestalt is one of a succession of three taps at three locations (see Sherrick & Cholewiak, 1986, pp. 12–26). As the time between taps two and three gets longer, the apparent distance between them increases, and the location of the phantom tap returns to the veridical point.

Dense Arrays. In the 1960s and 1970s there were developed in several laboratories designs for multiple-contactor arrays that were confined to a single anatomical region. Bach-y-Rita and his colleagues (Bach-y-Rita, Collins, Saunders, White, & Scadden, 1969; Collins, 1970) reported the development of the Tactile–visual Substitution System (TVSS), which converted a television scene to a tactual image represented by 400 individual vibrators stimulating the back of a blindfolded observer. When allowed to manipulate the camera during attempts to identify objects placed in the field of view, observers noted that recognition was both more accurate and rapid, in this novel form of "active touch." In addition, observers often reported that the stimulus patterns took on an attribute of object quality, in that they were not perceived as vibratory patterns on the back, but were projected to the plane of the object in the camera field. Indeed, when the camera zoom lens was used to enlarge the image of an object very rapidly, as in looming, one observer moved to avoid it! (White, 1970). More recent attempts to ascertain the conditions under which the distal attribution effect occurs have been only partly successful (Epstein, Hughes, Schneider, & Bach-y-Rita, 1986). In subsequent studies with the TVSS system, Loomis and Apkarian-Stielau (Apkarian-Stielau & Loomis, 1975; Loomis, 1974; Loomis & Apkarian-Stielau, 1976) examined the acuity of the skin for letters under a variety of conditions of image elaboration, and in comparison with performance of the visual system under conditions of blurring.

In the same period Kirman was developing a 15 × 15 vibrator matrix for generating tactile patterns to display correlates of the speech stream (see Kirman, 1973). The locus of stimulation was the palm of the hand, and in addition to his studies of a system for encoding some of the formants of speech (Kirman, 1974a), this investigator undertook a number of basic studies of perceptual phenomena, in particular apparent motion (Kirman, 1974b, 1974c, 1975) and recognition masking (1984).

Craig (1974) studied letter-shape perception with the aid of what he dubbed a "Kinotact," a 10 × 10 matrix of vibrators placed against the observer's back. The encoding system was a 10 × 10 matrix of photocells, wired one-to-one with the vibrators. Subjects were given a block letter on a wand, with which they cast its shadow over the photocells, and caused the tactual image of the letter to appear on their back. With this method of presentation, Craig's subjects learned to identify the "pictorial mode" letter patterns to an average criterion of 80%–90% correct in 300 trials. When the photocell-vibrator wiring was rearranged by exchanging columns in the matrix so that the shape of the letters was no longer veridical ("abstract mode" presentations), subjects performed at the same level within 50 trials.

Craig's explanation for the results, which suggest that the image has little importance in cutaneous processing of contour information, emphasized the strategy used by his subjects in moving the letter over the photocell display. The search was for distinctive features at the edges of the display, similar to the manner of search of subjects using the TVSS system, as described by White (1970), and responses were not made to whole letter patterns, as Craig

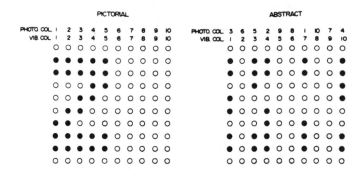

FIG. 8.4.   The Kinotact displays studied by Craig. On the left is the Pictorial
mode, which presents a one–to–one graphic image to the subject as shown.
On the right is the Abstract mode, produced by scrambling the wiring between
the photocells and the vibrators. In this case only the columns were scrambled. It is clear that the resulting visual image looks very complex (after Craig
1974). From *Cutaneous Communication Systems and Devices*, pp. 78–83, reprinted by permission of Psychonomic Society, Inc.

pointed out. Moreover, subjects all were familiar with the visual images of
the five target letters, and the only change in the tactual patterns from pictorial to abstract was in the relative positions of the vibrating contactors for
a given letter, as Fig. 8.4 shows. When the change from pictorial to abstract
was made, therefore, and the feature search was performed by the subject,
the appearance and disappearance of portions of the tactual field (read: features) occurred in concert with the movements of the letter at the edge of
the photocell array. Because we as readers view the static patterns of the
display as whole images, we perceive a much more radical shift in the patterns when moving from pictorial to abstract mode, and so are puzzled by
the subjects' seeming immunity to such distortion.

In an early attempt to devise a small matrix of vibrators under computer
control, Cholewiak and Sherrick (1981; Sherrick, 1982) were able to drive
an 8 × 8 matrix of piezoceramic Bimorphs with a DEC PDP–8 computer.
One of their initial findings involved the detection of the orientation of a line.
Subjects were asked to report whether a line was vertical, horizontal, or right
or left oblique. A number of different modes of image elaboration were
presented, including a tachistoscopic or static mode, exposing all parts of the
image at once, for a 300-ms period. Other modes were the so-called "Times
Square" mode, in which the image marches across the matrix, as in the famous electronic banner display in New York, and a slit-scan mode in which
the image is stationary behind a slit that moves across the field. A mode that
involved the saltation effect discussed previously was used to draw a cursive
pattern of the image on the skin. All modes required about the same time
for complete exposure of the image—300 ms.

When the various modes of elaboration were compared with and without the presence of a tactual "noise" background, it was found that the slit-scan and static modes were superior to those of saltation and Times Square in quiet conditions. When noise was present, the static mode emerged as best. If we compare this finding with Craig's analysis of the Kinotact results, we find a paradox: Craig's subjects were exploring featurewise for an uncontrolled length of time (maximum of 40 s) to identify their letters, and showed no evidence of identification by means of the whole-image exposure, whereas Sherrick and Cholewiak's subjects, with the brief whole-image exposure, seemed to capture a single gestalt, albeit a simpler one. We shall return to this problem shortly.

A development that emerged from several years of intensive basic and applied research at the Stanford University laboratories was an ink-print reading machine for blind persons. Named the Optacon for *Opt*ical to *Tac*tile *Con*verter, this device has been used by blind persons for two decades, and enjoys continued popularity around the world as an effective means for reading ordinary text using a variety of printed materials and lighting conditions (see Bliss, 1974; Bliss et al., 1970). With the aid of a small camera containing a lens that focuses the image on a bank of 6×24 photocells, the device converts the image electronically to a tactual display on an addressable 6×24 matrix of piezoceramic benders that covers the index fingerpad of the "reader." More recent models are equipped with a slightly smaller display, amounting to a 5×20 matrix, with no (as yet) reported loss of channel capacity. The benders vibrate at a frequency of 230 Hz, and form a spatial pattern that duplicates the symbol being imaged by the Optacon camera. As the reader moves across the page of text, the images pass from right to left under the reader's finger as if slowly moving across a small window, just as in the Times Square mode described previously.

Some Optacon users have achieved speeds of up to 60 or more wpm, but this is probably not the average value (see, e.g., Goldish & Taylor, 1974). Craig (1977) reported that two persons could read continuous text at rates of 100 wpm. When he studied the performance of these individuals, whom he described as extraordinary observers, with a variety of perceptual tasks, Craig found no differences between them and ordinary subjects except in two respects: The extraordinary observers showed no dependence on exposure duration in relation to their performance in identifying the letters, and they exhibited much less susceptibility to backward masking than their cohorts. Fig. 8.5 is adapted from the masking and exposure duration curves found by Craig in his investigation. If we are to take the information from such data literally, we might infer that the lack of dependence of discrimination on stimulus duration allows such persons to form an image in a much shorter time, thus allowing it to be passed to the lexical or some other categorical encoding process sooner. In addition, the resistance of these subjects

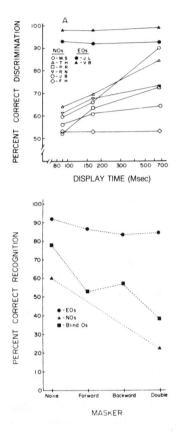

FIG. 8.5. Comparative performances of normal, extraordinary, and blind observers in identifying letter patterns with the Optacon, an ink-print reading machine for blind persons. At the top is shown discrimination performance, that is, percentage of correct responses when pairs of three-letter sequences were presented, requiring the subjects to detect whether "same" or "different" pairs appeared. Display time, that is, time of exposure of the letter across the tactile array, was varied as shown. At the bottom is plotted the variation of correct recognition of single letters as masking conditions are changed. Note the position of experienced blind Optacon users in this plot (after Craig 1977), from *Science*, Vol. 196, pp. 450–452. Copyright 1977 by the AAAS.

to backward masking must extend the available processing time even further, permitting an almost error-free combination of encoded elements in the lexical stream. The question for code designers must be, Are these properties of superior discrimination and resistance to masking intrinsic to the subject (e.g., does this person have a more intimate link between the somatosensory and associative areas than normal), or are they the result of some interaction between the subject and the patterns selected by the experimenter? If the latter is the case, one may speculate that there may be some ideal pattern set (or sets) that would enable more individuals to process the tactual information faster.

THE PERCEPTION OF CONTOUR AND SHAPE BY THE SKIN

Psychophysical Evidence for Contour and Shape Processing. In the search for means to replace the sense of hearing or of vision with that of touch, the question arises: How much is the skin like the eye or the ear in its processing of stimulus patterns? Usually the quest for an answer has been postponed in the interest of getting the applied work done, but there have been attempts to explain the results of applied studies (e.g., Bliss, 1974; Millar, 1981; Nolan & Kederis, 1969). In his analysis of the processing of letter patterns by various modes of image elaboration on the TVSS system, Loomis (1974) concluded that the most effective mode for his seven subjects, three of whom were blind, was a scanning mode in which successive parts of the letter were revealed as the preceding ones were occluded. His explanation for these results, which also demonstrated that whole-letter exposure was the least accurately processed, was that not only did the inferior spatial resolution of the skin limit the perception of high spatial-frequency components of the letters, but also the presence of active adjoining columns of vibrators further interfered with the detection of the necessary features when whole-letter exposure occurred. When successive features were exposed in the scanning modes, however, the effect of adjoining activity across columns of vibrators was eliminated, and spatial resolution was improved with temporal separation of these activities. In later papers (Apkarian-Stielau & Loomis, 1975; Loomis & Apkarian-Stielau, 1976) the original results of Loomis were repeated and extended, and the model of the skin as a low-spatial-frequency filter was compared with the visual system working under conditions of blur. Partial support for this analogy was adduced (see also Loomis, 1990; note that Loomis points out in this article that his theory of tactile pattern recognition does not include time as a variable).

The results from other form-recognition experiments that bear directly on the question of image elaboration have not always agreed with those of Loomis. Craig, for example, found in a series of studies with the Optacon that whole-letter exposure in a tachistoscopic mode (often called a "static" mode) was superior to scanning or cursive exposure modes, particularly at the shorter exposure durations, that is, 20 to 100 ms, that would be essential for a rapid communications system (Craig, 1980, 1981, 1983). When Loomis (1980) examined the scanning and static modes with the Optacon, using two sizes of letter and durations of 1500 ms, he found, in agreement with Craig, that the static mode was at least equivalent to the scanning mode for the larger-sized print, but the reverse was true for the smaller print. Loomis interpreted these results to mean that his hypothesis of the limited spatial acuity of the skin was still confirmed, for the reason that conditions of presentation of the Optacon display at the fingertip were such that spatial acuity was not limiting until smaller letter sizes were used.

Craig (1981) pursued this problem further in a study that varied the duration of exposure in the various modes of pattern elaboration. In his analysis of results, Craig pointed out that at the shortest exposure durations the performance levels for static and scanning modes are equal, and the correlations across letters are high, suggesting that similar processing mechanisms are at work between modes. As durations lengthen, however, performance levels for the static mode improve over those for the scanning mode, and the correlations decrease in value. Craig interpreted these results as evidence that the manner of processing at short durations is the same across modes, and that with increasing duration the manner or strategies diverge. One hypothesis was that a process of temporal integration at very short durations allowed the subject to piece together the separate scanned features of a letter to arrive at the whole image, with the result that the scanning and static modes yielded equivalent representations, with some possibility of parallel processing. Later research by Craig (1982a) demonstrated that the effects of temporal integration are dependent on the onset relations of the parts of the stimulus pattern, not its duration. Moreover, full integration may decline after about 10 ms stimulus onset asynchrony (SOA), and cease altogether after about 50 to 100 ms whether the stimulus pattern persists or not. At longer durations, therefore, only partial integration will occur at best, and some other strategy, such as that of successive feature analysis, must be substituted, as Loomis has suggested (1974).

When the entire letter shape is exposed, as in the static mode of presentation, subjects may perceive it just as they would if visually presented, or they may perceive a mixture of features, including two or three spatial features, an intensive impression limited to "soft" or "loud," and a textural impression relating to the compactness or dispersedness (spatial roughness or smoothness?) of the letter. Whether all of these aspects may be simultaneously received and processed, or must stand in line at the sensory-perceptual gate awaiting their turn, is not clear.

Physiological Evidence for Contour and Shape Processing.   In an ingenious study of peripheral processing of tactual spatial information in the monkey, Johnson and Lamb (1981) analyzed the response of single units of the first-order neuron in the monkey's hand when various numbers of embossed dots were presented to the receptive field of the unit (see Cholewiak & Collins, this volume, for details of these methods). The method of presentation was unique, in that the figure was carefully scanned across the receptive field in a kind of "relative active touch" mode, while at the same time a corresponding spatial plot of the neural activity of the unit was made. The result was that a more or less rough outline of the figure could be seen in the variation of density of neural activity in the resulting plot. For slowly adapting receptors, the outline was a good representation of the figure, whereas for the fast-adapting receptors it was not; Fig. 8.6 shows a sample of the response outlines generated by the method. An intricate analytical scheme was devised by the authors, but the information of interest for the present discussion is that, in the opinion of Johnson and Lamb, the neural shadow projected to the brain is sharpest for the slowly adapting receptors, somewhat less so for the fast adapting receptors, and probably inadequate for imaging for the Pacinian receptors. Furthermore, they consider that the limitation on spatial acuity lies in the density of distribution of the slowly adapting receptors. The crit-

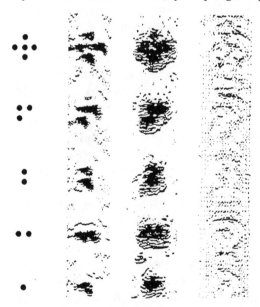

FIG. 8.6. The images of neural activity (spatial event recordings) produced by certain receptor classes when braille-like dot patterns, shown at the left, are traced across the skin of the monkey finger while recording from single units in the peripheral nerve. The dots are 1.2 mm diameter, and 2.0 mm between centers. Speed of motion of the pattern was 4.0 cm/sec, and the force on the skin was 60 gm for the SA receptors and 20 gm for the RA receptors. The images are produced by three different receptor classes. From the left, the first column is produced by slowly adapting (SA) afferent receptors, probably Merkel disks; the second column is produced by rapidly adapting (RA) receptors, probably Meissner corpuscles; the third column is produced by rapidly adapting (PC) receptors, probably Pacini or Golgi-Mazzoni corpuscles (adapted from Johnson & Lamb 1981), *Journal of Physiology*, Vol. 310, pp. 117–144. Copyright 1981 The Physiological Society.

ical dimension is about 1 mm on the skin of the fingertip. Any feature of a tactual contour that is below this dimension will not be processed as such. Features above the critical dimension will not be readily perceived when the skin is stationary, because then the slowly adapting receptors simply do not respond to them.

When the authors considered the neural events following active scanning of a tactile contour, including the successive neural images produced when nerve conduction velocities and scanning rates are calculated, the picture that emerged was of a succession of partial images at the first synapse something like what one experiences when figures move rapidly across a stage under stroboscopic illumination. As the authors point out, one might consider the available receptor array as analogous to a screen (the skin) with holes (the receptors) in it. When the screen is stationary, the image almost disappears; when the screen is moved, the image behind it emerges as a result of the process of spatiotemporal integration.

Evidence for both peripheral and central neural responses to vibratory stimulus patterns has been adduced by Gardner and her colleagues (see, e.g., Gardner, Hamalainen, Palmer, & Warren, 1989). This investigator has reported the results of studies in which the Optacon was applied to the monkey's hand, and recordings were made from both first-order and SI cortical neurons. An important finding is that the spatially acute SA receptors described by Johnson and Lamb (1981) do not seem to respond to the Optacon stimulus, which has a frequency of 230 Hz. Instead, the RA receptors, also densely distributed in the superficial layers of the skin (see Cholewiak and Collins, this volume), respond best, with the PC receptors showing activity as well. When the behavior of cortical neurons was examined, it appeared that the receptive field, so precisely outlined in peripheral nerve recordings, loses its sharpness at higher levels. For example, whereas the peripheral field responded to only two or three rows of the Optacon stimulator, the cortical cells in area SI responded to activity in the entire array. Gardner et al. think that, because the cortical cells show a more diffuse spatial response in addition to a filtering of high temporal frequencies, they provide the conditions for the perception of apparent movement (1989, p. 58). This brings to mind the spatiotemporal filtering explanation of Anstis for apparent movement, described earlier.

Cognitive Evidence for Contour and Shape Processing.   Millar conducted a succession of studies of the behavior of blind children in processing braille and other tactual shapes (for a review, see Millar, 1981, pp. 288–297). This author was able to show by a variety of experiments and deductions from other research that the rapid processing and identification of tactual forms is not based on a single mechanism. Rather, this ability may evolve from an entire family of sensory capabilities and learned skills. As an example, Millar was able to show that braille characters having similar-sounding names will show interference in recall when successively memorized in the same list. This suggests that coding is phonological; however, she also demonstrated that characters having similar shapes seemed to interfere as well, suggesting that physical features are coded. The conclusion must be that both strategies are available and are used in learning to recognize tactual patterns. Millar suggests that naming and feature detection not be thought of as steps in a processing hierarchy, but rather as alternative ways of coding forms. Further experiments indicated that when tactual features are processed, two kinds of coding may occur, namely, as spatial or shape features, or as textural features.

In later studies of young blind children showing retarded reading skills, Millar (1984) was able to show that the processing strategies available to these children were the same as for children reading at grade level. A possible reason for their poorer performance was that the children failed to choose those strategies that led to more rapid and accurate reading. Although one may think that the spatial strategies are superior, Millar (1985) has shown that the use of shape coding as such does not predict better reading performance in children.

A brief word should be said about the question whether braille or Optacon processing reveals an advantage of words over letters in reading, an effect that is well known in visual research (see, e.g., Tzeng & Singer, 1981). Krueger (1982) has shown a word superiority effect in braille reading that is comparable with that found in print reading, that is, he can show that target letters imbedded in words are significantly more rapidly detected than when they are imbedded in nonwords. The implication is that the letters in words are processed more rapidly than in nonwords, and Krueger's subjects told him that they could anticipate the target letters when searching the words, presumably owing to the redundancy effect (Krueger, 1982, p. 351). Krueger's subjects also made more errors with nonwords than with words. A report by Shetzer (1978) suggested that a similar effect of reduced processing time appeared in his studies of Optacon reading. Craig (1980a), testing instead for error rates only in identification of two-letter sets, found no improvement in correct identifications of letter pairs over performance predicted from individual letter identifications. Craig concluded that perception of Optacon words as integral units did not occur with his subjects.

The Masking of Vibrotactile Patterns. The phenomenon of masking is well known in sensory psychology, and is generally taken to mean detection masking, that is, the failure to detect a tactual stimulus when another is presented closely in time or space to the target (Cholewiak & Collins, this volume). Discrimination masking is also possible; the presence of a masker can interfere with the ability to detect changes in intensity, frequency, location, or another attribute of a target (see, e.g., Craig, 1989; Kirman, 1986). In pattern recognition studies, the form that this phenomenon takes is that of identity masking, that is, the reduction in recognition or identification performance as a result of the presence of a masking stimulus. Although others have examined this effect (e.g., Kirman, 1984; Loomis & Apkarian-Stielau, 1976), Craig and his colleagues have contributed most extensively to this area of study.

The importance of identity masking can be understood when we consider the problem of reading with a device such as the Optacon, or of processing speech with one of the available tactual aids for profoundly hearing-impaired persons. The successive patterns produced by transducing the letter shapes or speech correlates must be registered by the tactile sense, then encoded for storage and processing. As one pattern is accepted at the tactual window, another comes quickly behind it for incorporation in the lexical stream. The more rapid the movement of patterns through the window, the closer in time the patterns follow one another and the greater the possibility of mutual masking by successive patterns. This "traffic jam" of patterns works directly against the desirable attribute of speed of processing, just as in visual reading or speech perception, so an understanding of the nature of the identity masking process is clearly a primary goal of both basic and applied research.

In his first studies of masking, Craig (1976, 1977) was restricted to the standard Optacon Times Square mode of image elaboration, that is, scanning the image across the tactual window. Under these conditions, he was able to show that backward masking (masker follows target) was more effective than forward (masker precedes target) for Stimulus Onset Asynchrony (SOAs) less than 200 ms, and that the action of forward and backward maskers together (i.e., double masking) was most effective. In addition, letter maskers were no more effective than a wash stimulus, which Craig labeled an "energy" masker, consisting of all matrix points excited at once.

Craig's (1977) studies of extraordinary observers (EOs) has already been mentioned, but the main findings should be reiterated here, namely, the subjects who were fast readers did not differ from the ordinary subjects except in two respects. First, the two EOs showed no change in percentage of correct recognition as a function of duration of the stimulus, suggesting that whatever strategy they used in identification must be deployed at or soon after the onset of the signal. Secondly, the EOs showed no great decrement in percentage of recognition scores with masking stimuli, whether forward, backward, or double. This suggests, following the analysis by Millar that was discussed earlier, that some higher-order encoding strategy may have been adopted to move the pattern quickly to a buffer and protect it from its successors.

In later studies, Craig gained computer control of the Optacon display, and was able to present a variety of modes of image elaboration to his subjects. In one study, in which he compared the Times Square and static modes, Craig (1980b) was able to replicate some earlier findings, namely, that forward masking was less effective than backward at short time intervals, but longer lasting in its action. In addition, asymmetrical letters in which the right side yields more information than the left, such as R, B, P, K, are more readily masked than symmetrical letters such as S, M, and O when the Times Square presentation is made. Craig was able to show that this occurs because the scanning mode permits the masker, which is also scanned, to follow more closely in time the right-hand edge of the target letter. A plot of the masking effects is shown in Fig. 8.7. Craig has suggested that the overall difference of about 10% between the two modes is not necessarily significant, owing to the use of different groups to establish the various conditions.

When he compared energy with pattern maskers, Craig (1982a) found that pattern maskers, which were composed of letter segments, were far more effective than the feature-poor energy masker, which was produced by turning on all vibrators at once. This was true even though the pattern maskers were judged as having smaller sensory magnitudes than the energy masker. Moreover, the possibility that the sameness of the energy masker from trial to trial was reducing its effectiveness was tested by using the same

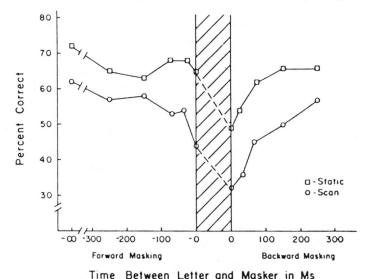

FIG. 8.7. Letter recognition performance on the Optacon in the presence of forward and backward masking by vibrotactile noise. Both letter and masker were presented for about 100 ms in the two modes of display shown. The masker was produced by turning on all available pins of the display for the desired duration. The difference between the two modes of display is not thought to be significant, but rather owing to the use of different groups of subjects for the tasks (after Craig 1980b). Copyright 1980 by the American Psychological Association. Adapted by permission.

pattern masker in several test trials. The pattern masker was still the more effective. Craig concluded that what was being masked was information, so that the pattern masker was imposing a limit on signal processing as well as on signal state (see Garner, 1974, p. 153ff.). Craig concluded that a two-factor theory of masking would explain his results: First, the presence of any additional noise in the system owing to the masker, whether of the "pattern" or "noise" type, would reduce contrast, and possibly introduce a state limitation. Secondly, the pattern masker in addition will add interfering features to the image, thereby distorting the information relevant to identification, and introducing a process limitation. In a very clever experiment that involved presenting a pattern masker and its complement in succession, Craig (1982b) was able to show increasing amounts of masking as the SOA of the masker–complement pair increased, thus evolving from an "energy" masker to a pair of "pattern" maskers. The two masking factors hypothesized by Craig should be compared with the three factors of Kirman (1986), described earlier.

The results of more recent studies (Craig & Evans, 1987; Evans & Craig, 1986) have suggested that the integration/interruption model of masking can be replaced by an integration/integration model. The integration of the masker with the target can be at the state level, in which the overall signal/noise ratio is reduced, and at the process level, in which the features in the masker are added to the features of the target to confuse its identity, thus to camouflage rather than mask the target. Curiously, in one investigation involving forward masking (Craig & Evans, 1987), it was found that when the target was also the masker pattern, neither significant improvement nor decrement in performance was found at SOAs at or above 300 ms. Because decrements occurred when different patterns were the masker at these SOAs, it is clear that the masker had an effect, and measures to detect whether masker information was integrated with the target showed that it was. One may then wonder why, since the unmasked performance was only at 78% correct for these patterns, some improvement in performance did not occur as a result of redundancy? Perhaps the instructions to ignore the masker are more readily followed when no change in features is detected during this type of trial. This train of thought further suggests that a means of determining exactly what a feature change is, might involve using this same paradigm to alter the pattern until a significant amount of masking occurs.

APPLICATIONS OF PATTERN PERCEPTION TO TACTILE AIDS

Visual Aids: Reading Devices. The device that currently has the most prominence in the reading of ink print must be the Optacon, which as we have just seen, is a prominent research tool as well. The number of Optacons now in use must be in the several thousands, and even though not all users can claim to be rapid readers, the independence conferred by having a device that recognizes print and silently conveys its message, is alone a priceless gain. The description by Goldish and Taylor (1974) is a useful summary of the Optacon's properties and utility.

Visual Aids: Electronic Travel Aids (ETAs). Given the number of alternative means for blind persons to take in written information, including braille, recordings, the Optacon, live readers, and the Kurzweil reader, which converts print to synthetic speech, one might conclude that further additions to the available technology might be unnecessary, although some refinements would be welcome. An area where need exists is that of mobility, the second (or perhaps the first) gateway to experience. Mobility in blind persons is in some ways analogous to speech perception by deaf persons, since rapid and accurate serial processing of information is needed, with little chance for retracing or review. To this is added the element of apprehension in the mobility task, when a misunderstood or lost cue may result in embarrassment or even injury.

The mobility task can be analyzed into at least two subtasks, namely, that of obstacle detection, and that of spatial localization and orientation. The latter problem boils down to the problem of where one is in the space from beginning of a trip to its end, and whether one is on trajectory; the former is the immediate problem of what hazard lies within the next few paces, whether a step, a barrier, a moving object, or a head-high obstacle such as a tree limb or street sign (see, e.g., Wardell, 1980). Mobility strategies using only the long cane and natural hearing cues are taught at a number of training centers, and other training using guide dogs can be obtained at a few places (see Blasch & Welsh, 1980; Whitstock, 1980). ETAs that provide information to the hearing sense have been developed and tested over a number of years, but the common complaint with these has been their interference with the use of hearing in interpreting ambient sounds for orientational and positional information (Working Group on Mobility Aids, 1986).

Nearly all ETAs that provide a tactual output are obstacle-detecting devices. The possibility of providing mobile users with a graphic tactual display of the environment was the motivation for design of the Smith-Kettlewell TVSS (see Collins, 1970; White, 1970). The Optacon was adapted as a scene-imaging system (Bliss et al., 1970, pp. 63–64) but with no signal success, and no such device is presently under test, to this writer's knowledge. There has been talk of embedding wires in pavement to provide signals for blind travelers equipped with simple receivers, but no large-scale tests of such devices are known (see Working Group on Mobility Aids, 1986, p. 71). It appears that expert opinion in this area finds consensus in the recommendation that the solution to the problem of mobility would be greatly advanced by more complete understanding of the cognitive aspects of such an open skill as orientation and mobility in everyday environments. Shingledecker and Foulke (1978) have suggested that a theory of mobility would advance progress in experimental analyses of performance on mobility tasks tremendously.

Auditory Aids: Sound and Speech-Analyzing Aids. In contrast to the paucity of available devices to reduce or alleviate the effects of the loss of sight, biomedical devices to replace the hearing function have increased in number in recent years. Primary among these is the cochlear implant, which can stimulate the eighth nerve with small electrical signals that are derived from a microprocessor that has been implanted beneath the skin of the patient's head. An external microphone picks up the acoustic signal, and an inductive device transmits this to the implanted processor. There are several varieties of this device, but the type with which the best results have been obtained is a multi-electrode system, which is designed to lay out, frequencywise, the energies of the speech signal over the component fibers of the acoustic nerve. There are now on record instances in which previously profoundly deaf persons (who lost their hearing after they learned to speak) equipped with these implants can carry on telephone conversations, that is, they need no supplementary lip-reading input (see Christman & Albert, in press).

For those instances in which cochlear implants are contraindicated, there remains the possibility of either a visual or a tactual aid, with the expectation that these may be supplemented by lipreading. It is assumed that the hearing-impaired individual desires to understand speech as well as to produce it; this is not always the case, of course. There are a number of deaf persons in the world who depend exclusively on sign language for communication, and feel a strong identification with this mode of communication. Even these persons, however, may want to have available a device that will alert them to ambient sounds that give vital information or warn of hazards.

Whereas visual aids for perception of acoustic events were of considerable interest a decade or more ago (see Pickett, 1968, 1977), tactual aids have in recent years seen a revival, owing in part to the development of cochlear implants and the resultant need for alternative rehabilitative strategies, as well as to the availability of more compact and efficient mechanical vibrators and microprocessors (see Kirman, 1973; Sherrick, 1984, in press). Although there are a number of tactual aids presently on the market, their worth relative to that of the cochlear implant or the hearing aid is only beginning to be established through comparative studies of performance under realistic testing conditions (Sherrick, in press). At present it appears that the most effective systems are multiple-vibrator devices that lay out the speech signal or its correlates as a spatial pattern representing frequency or voice formant relations. This of course corresponds to the experience with the cochlear implant design, as we have seen. In general, because the skin is much less sensitive to frequency than to spatial differences (Cholewiak & Collins, this volume), the translation to space is readily accepted by users, and the frequency of vibration can be kept at the value of maximum dynamic range of the system. A number of researchers feel that better representation by the aid of other dimensions of speech, for example, voicing, voice onset time, manner, place, and so on, will produce improved performance by users.

In general, the problem in designing a better tactual speech aid, as well as a better cochlear implant, lies in part in clarification of the models of hearing and speech perception. It was mentioned previously that speech perception by deaf persons and mobility of blind persons have some analogous characteristics. Perhaps the lack of a complete description of the processes involved in these two complex perceptual–motor skills remains the impediment to further refinement of the technology for rehabilitation.

REFERENCES

Alles, D. S. (1970). Information transmission by phantom sensations. *IEEE Transactions on Man-Machine Systems, MMS-11*, 85–91.

Anstis, S. (1986). Motion perception in the frontal plane. In K. Boff, L. Kaufman, & J. P. Thomas (Eds.), *Handbook of perception and human performance*. New York: Wiley, pp. 16/1–16/24.

Apkarian-Stielau, P., & Loomis, J. M. (1975). A comparison of tactile and blurred visual form perception. *Perception & Psychophysics, 18*, 362–368.

Bach-y-Rita, P., Collins, C. C., Saunders, F., White, B., & Scadden, L. (1969). Vision substitution by tactile image projection. *Nature, 221*, 963–964.

Békésy, G., von (1939). Über die Vibrationsempfindung. *Akustische Zeitschrift, 4*, 316–334.

Békésy, G., von (1960). *Experiments in hearing*. New York: McGraw-Hill.

Békésy, G., von (1967). *Sensory inhibition*. Princeton, NJ: Princeton University Press.

Békésy, G., von (1971). Auditory backward inhibition in concert halls. *Science, 171*, 529–536.

Bentzen, B. L. (1980). Orientation aids. In R. L. Walsh & B. B. Blasch (Eds.), *Foundations of orientation and mobility*. New York: American Foundation for the Blind, pp. 291–355.

Blasch, B. B., & Welsh, R. L. (1980). Training for persons with functional mobility limitations. In R. L. Welsh & B. B. Blasch (Eds.), *Foundations of orientation and mobility*. New York: American Foundation for the Blind, pp. 461–476.

Bliss, J. C. (Ed.). (1970). Tactile displays conference. *IEEE Transactions on Man-Machine Systems, MMS-11*, 1–122.

Bliss, J. C. (1974). Summary of three Optacon-related cutaneous experiments. In F. A. Geldard (Ed.), *Cutaneous communication systems and devices*. Austin, TX: Psychonomic Society, pp. 84–94.

Bliss, J. C., Katcher, M. H., Rogers, C. H., & Shepard, R. P. (1970). Optical-to-tactile image conversion for the blind. *IEEE Transactions on Man-Machine Systems MMS-11*, 58–64.

Bracewell, R. N. (1978), *The Fourier transform and its applications*. New York: McGraw-Hill.

Cholewiak, R. W., & Sherrick, C. E. (1981). A computer-controlled matrix system for presentation to the skin of complex spatiotemporal patterns. *Behavioral Research Methods and Instrumentation, 13*, 667–673.

Cholewiak, R. W., & Sherrick, C. E. (1986). Tracking skill of a deaf person with long-term tactile aid experience. *Journal of Rehabilitation Research and Development, 23*, 20–26.

Christman, C. L., & Albert, E. N. (Eds.) (in press). *Cochlear implants: A model for the regulation of emerging medical technologies.* Norwell, MA: Kluwer Academic Publishers.

Collins, C. C. (1970). Tactile television—mechanical and electrical image projection. *IEEE Transactions on Man-Machine Systems, MMS–11,* 65–71.

Craig, J. C. (1974). Pictorial and abstract cutaneous displays. In F. A. Geldard (Ed.), *Cutaneous communication systems and devices.* Austin, TX: Psychonomic Society, pp. 78–83.

Craig, J. C. (1976). Vibrotactile letter recognition: The effects of a masking stimulus. *Perception & Psychophysics, 20,* 317–326.

Craig, J. C. (1977). Vibrotactile pattern perception: Extraordinary observers. *Science, 196,* 450–452.

Craig, J. C. (1980a). *Vibrotactile letter recognition: The size of perceptual units.* Unpublished manuscript.

Craig, J. C. (1980b). Modes of vibrotactile pattern generation. *Journal of Experimental Psychology: Human Perception and Performance, 6,* 151–166.

Craig, J. C. (1981). Tactile letter perception: Pattern duration and modes of pattern generation. *Perception & Psychophysics, 30,* 540–546.

Craig, J. C. (1982a). Vibrotactile masking: A comparison of energy and pattern maskers. *Perception & Psychophysics, 31,* 523–529.

Craig, J. C. (1982b). Temporal integration of vibrotactile patterns. *Perception & Psychophysics, 32,* 219–229.

Craig, J. C. (1983). Some factors affecting tactile pattern recognition. *International Journal of Neuroscience, 19,* 47–58.

Craig, J. C. (1989). Interference in localizing tactile stimuli. *Perception & Psychophysics, 45,* 343–355.

Craig, J. C., & Evans, P. M. (1987). Vibrotactile masking and the persistence of tactual features. *Perception & Psychophysics, 42,* 309–317.

Craig, J. C., & Sherrick, C. E. (1969). The role of skin coupling in the determination of vibrotactile spatial summation. *Perception & Psychophysics, 6,* 97–101.

Craig, J. C., & Sherrick, C. E. (1982). Dynamic tactile displays. In W. Schiff & E. Foulke (Eds.), *Tactual perception: A sourcebook.* New York: Cambridge University Press.

Davis, H., & Silverman, S. R. (1978). *Hearing and deafness* (4th ed.). New York: Holt, Rinehart, & Winston.

Epstein, W., Hughes, B., Schneider, S., & Bach-y-Rita, P. (1986). Is there anything out there?: A study of distal attribution. *Perception, 15,* 275–284.

Evans, P. M., & Craig, J. C. (1986). Temporal integration and vibrotactile masking. *Journal of Experimental Psychology: Human Perception and Performance, 12,* 160–168.

Foulke, E., & Brodbeck, A. A., Jr. (1968). Transmission of morse code by electrocutaneous stimulation. *Psychological Record, 18,* 617–622.

Franke, E. K. (1951). *Mechanical impedance measurements of the human body surface.* (Rep. No. 6469). Dayton, OH: USAF, WADC.

Gardner, E. P., Hamalainen, H. A., Palmer, C. I., & Warren, S. (1989). Touching the outside world: Representation of motion and direction within primary somatosensory cortext. In J. S. Lund (Ed.), *Sensory processing in the mammalian brain: Neural substrates and experimental strategies.* New York: Oxford University Press, pp. 49–66.

Garner, W. R. (1974). *The processing of information and structure.* Hillsdale, NJ: Lawrence Erlbaum Associates.

Gault, R. H. (1924). Progress in experiments on tactual interpretation of oral speech. *Journal of Abnormal and Social Psychology, 14,* 155–159.

Gault, R. H. (1927). Hearing through the sense organs of touch and vibration. *Journal of the Franklin Institute, 204,* 329–358.

Geldard, F. A. (1957). Adventures in tactile literacy. *American Psychologist, 12,* 115–124.

Geldard, F. A. (1966). Cutaneous coding of optical signals: The optohapt. *Perception & Psychophysics, 1,* 337–381.

Geldard, F. A. (1972). *The human senses* (2nd ed.). New York: Wiley.

Geldard, F. A. (Ed.). (1974). *Cutaneous communication systems and devices.* Austin, TX: Psychonomic Society, pp. 1–112.

Geldard, F. A. (1975). *Sensory saltation: Metastability in the perceptual world.* Hillsdale, NJ: Lawrence Erlbaum Associates.

Geldard, F. A., & Sherrick, C. E. (1965). Multiple cutaneous stimulation: The discrimination of vibratory patterns. *Journal of the Acoustical Society of America, 37,* 797–801.

Geldard, F. A., & Sherrick, C. E. (1972). The cutaneous rabbit: A perceptual illusion. *Science, 178,* 178–179.

Geldard, F. A., & Sherrick, C. E. (1983). The cutaneous saltatory area and its presumed neural basis. *Perception & Psychophysics, 33,* 299–304.

Gescheider, G. A. (1965). Cutaneous sound localization. *Journal of Experimental Psychology, 70,* 617–625.

Gescheider, G. A., & Joelson, J. M. (1983). Vibrotactile temporal summation for threshold and suprathreshold levels of stimulation. *Perception & Psychophysics, 33,* 156–162.

Gilson, R. D. (1969). Vibrotactile masking: Some spatial and temporal aspects. *Perception & Psychophysics, 5,* 176–180.

Gilson, R. D., & Fenton, R. E. (1974). Kinesthetic–tactual information presentations—inflight studies. *IEEE Transactions on Systems, Man, and Cybernetics, SMC-4,* 531–535.

Goldish, L. H., & Taylor, H. E. (1974). The Optacon: A valuable device for blind persons. *New Outlook for the Blind, 68,* 49–56.

Harper, R. (1952). Psychological and physiological studies of craftsmanship in dairying. *British Journal of Psychology Monograph* (Suppl. 28).

Helson, H., & King, S. M. (1931). The Tau effect: An example of psychological relativity. *Journal of Experimental Psychology, 14,* 202–217.

Hirsch, J. (1974). Rate control in man-machine systems. In F. A. Geldard (Ed.), *Cutaneous communication systems and devices.* Austin, TX: Psychonomic Society, pp. 65–72.

Johnson, K. O., & Lamb, G. D. (1981). Neural mechanisms of spatial tactile discrimination: Neural patterns evoked by braille-like dot patterns in the monkey. *Journal of Physiology, 310,* 117–144.

Keidel, W. D. (1956). *Vibrationsreception: Der Erschütterungssinn des Menschen.* (Erlanger Forschungen, Reihe B, Band 2). Erlangen, Germany: Universitätsbund.

Keidel, W. D. (1968). Electrophysiology of vibratory perception. In W. D. Neff (Ed.), *Contributions to sensory physiology* (Vol. 3). New York: Academic Press, pp. 1–74.

Kirman, J. H. (1973). Tactile communication of speech: A review and an analysis. *Psychological Bulletin, 80,* 54–74.

Kirman, J. H. (1974a). Tactile perception of computer-derived formant patterns from voiced speech. *Journal of the Acoustical Society of America, 55,* 163–169.

Kirman, J. H. (1974b). Tactile apparent movement: The effects of interstimulus onset interval and stimulus duration. *Perception & Psychophysics, 15,* 1–6.

Kirman, J. H. (1974c). Tactile apparent movement: The effects of number of stimulators. *Journal of Experimental Psychology, 103,* 1175–1180.

Kirman, J. H. (1975). The effect of number of stimulators on the optimal interstimulus onset interval in tactile apparent movement. *Perception & Psychophysics, 17,* 263–267.

Kirman, J. H. (1984). Forward and backward tactile recognition masking. *Journal of General Psychology, 111,* 83–99.

Kirman, J. H. (1986). Vibrotactile frequency recognition: Forward and backward masking effects. *Journal of General Psychology, 113,* 147–158.

Krueger, L. E. (1982). A word superiority effect with print and braille characters. *Perception & Psychophysics, 31,* 345–352.

Lamoré, P. J. J., & Keemink, C. J. (1988). Evidence for different types of mechanoreceptors from measurements of the psychophysical threshold for vibrations under different stimulation conditions. *Journal of the Acoustical Society of America, 83,* 2339–2351.

Lechelt, E. C., & Borchert, R. (1977). The interdependence of time and space in somesthesis: The Tau effect reexamined. *Bulletin of the Psychonomic Society, 10,* 191–193.

Levitt, H., Waltzman, S. B., Shapiro, W. H., & Cohen, N. L. (1986). Evaluation of a cochlear prosthesis using connected discourse tracking. *Journal of Rehabilitation Research and Development, 23,* 147–155.

Loomis, J. M. (1974). Tactile letter recognition under various modes of stimulus presentation. *Perception & Psychophysics, 16,* 401–408.

Loomis, J. M. (1980). Interaction of display mode and character size in vibrotactile letter recognition. *Bulletin of the Psychonomic Society, 16,* 385–387.

Loomis, J. M. (1990). A model of character recognition and legibility. *Journal of Experimental Psychology: Human Perception and Performance, 16,* 106–120.

Loomis, J. M., & Apkarian-Stielau, P. (1976). A lateral masking effect in tactile and blurred visual letter recognition. *Perception & Psychophysics, 20,* 221–226.

Loomis, J. M., & Lederman, S. J. (1986). Tactual perception. In K. Boff, L. Kaufman, & J. P. Thomas (Eds.), *Handbook of perception and human performance: Vol. 2. Cognitive processes and performance* (pp. 31/1–31/41). New York: Wiley.

Millar, S. (1981). Cross-modal and intersensory perception and the blind. In R. D. Walk & H. L. Pick, Jr. (Eds.), *Intersensory perception and sensory integration.* New York: Plenum press, pp. 281–314.

Millar, S. (1984). Strategy choices by young braille readers. *Perception, 13,* 567–579.

Millar, S. (1985). The perception of complex patterns by touch. *Perception, 14,* 293–303.

Moore, T. J. (1970). A survey of the mechanical characteristics of skin and tissue in response to vibratory stimulation. *IEEE Transactions on Man-Machine Systems, MMS–11,* 79–84.

Murray, D. J., Ward, R., & Hockley, W. E. (1975). Tactile short-term memory in relation to the two-point threshold. *Quarterly Journal of Experimental Psychology, 27,* 303–312.

Nolan, C. Y., & Kederis, C. J. (1969). *Perceptual factors in braille word recognition.* American Foundation for the Blind Research Series, No. 20. New York: American Foundation for the Blind.

Norton, S. J., Schultz, M. C., Reed, C. M., Braida, L. D., Durlach, N. I., Rabinowitz, W. M., & Chomsky, C. (1977). Analytic study of the Tadoma method: Background and preliminary results. *Journal of Speech and Hearing Research, 20,* 574–595.

Oestreicher, H. L. (1950). *On the theory of propagation of mechanical vibrations in human and animal tissues.* USAF Air Materiel Command: USAF Technical Report No. 6244, November.

Pickett, J. M. (Ed.). (1968). Proceedings of the conference on speech analyzing aids for the deaf. *American Annals of the Deaf, 113,* 116–330.

Pickett, J. M. (Ed.). (1977). *Papers from the research conference on speech-processing aids for the deaf.* Washington, DC: Gallaudet Research Institute.

Reed, C. M., Rabinowitz, W. M., Durlach, N. I., Braida, L. D., Conway-Fithian, S., & Schultz, M. C. (1985). Research on the Tadoma method of speech communication. *Journal of the Acoustical Society of America, 77,* 247–257.

Rothenberg, M., Verrillo, R. T., Zahorian, S. A., Brachman, M. L., & Bolanowski, S. J., Jr. (1977). Vibrotactile frequency for encoding a speech parameter. *Journal of the Acoustical Society of America, 62,* 1003–1012.

Sherrick, C. E. (1953). Variables affecting sensitivity of the human skin to mechanical vibration. *Journal of Experimental Psychology, 45,* 273–282.

Sherrick, C. E. (1960). Observations relating to some common psychophysical functions as applied to the skin. In G. R. Hawkes (Ed.), *Symposium on cutaneous sensitivity* (Rep. No. 424). Fort Knox, KY: USAMRL, pp. 147–158.

Sherrick, C. E. (1964). Effects of multiple simultaneous stimulation of the skin. *American Journal of Psychology, 77,* 42–53.

Sherrick, C. E. (1982). Cutaneous communication. In W. D. Neff (Ed.), *Contributions to sensory physiology* (Vol. 6). New York: Academic Press, pp. 1–43.

Sherrick, C. E. (1984). Basic and applied research on tactile aids for deaf people: Progress and prospects. *Journal of the Acoustical Society of America, 75,* 1325–1342.

Sherrick, C. E. (1985). A scale for rate of tactual vibration. *Journal of the Acoustical Society of America, 78,* 78–83.

Sherrick, C. E. (in press). Tactual sound- and speech-analyzing aids for deaf persons. In C. L. Christman & A. N. Albert (Eds.), *Cochlear implants: A model for the regulation of emerging medical technologies.* Norwell, MA: Kluwer Academic Publishers.

Sherrick, C. E., & Cholewiak, R. W. (1986). Cutaneous sensitivity. In K. Boff, L. Kaufman, & J. L. Thomas (Eds.), *Handbook of perception and human performance* (pp. 12/1–12/58). New York: Wiley.

Sherrick, C. E., & Rogers, R. (1966). Apparent haptic movement. *Perception & Psychophysics, 1,* 175–180.

Shetzer, L. I. (1978). *The unit of recognition in the identification of tactually presented letter strings.* Unpublished master's thesis, University of Western Ontario. London: Canada.

Shingledecker, C. A., & Foulke, E. (1978). A human factors approach to the assessment of the mobility of blind pedestrians. *Human Factors, 20,* 273–286.

Tzeng, O. J. L., & Singer, H. (Eds.). (1981). *Perception of print: Reading research in experimental psychology.* Hillsdale, NJ: Lawrence Erlbaum Associates.

Verrillo, R. T. (1963). Effect of contactor area on the vibrotactile threshold. *Journal of the Acoustical Society of America, 35,* 1962–1966.

Verrillo, R. T. (1966). Specificity of a cutaneous receptor. *Perception & Psychophysics, 1,* 149–153.

Verrillo, R. T. (1974). Vibrotactile intensity scaling at several body sites. In F. A. Geldard (Ed.), *Cutaneous communication systems and devices.* Austin, TX: Psychonomic Society, pp. 9–14.

Verrillo, R. T. (1979). The effects of surface gradients on vibrotactile thresholds. *Sensory Processes, 3,* 27–36.

Wardell, K. T. (1980). Environmental modifications. In R. L. Welsh & B. B. Blasch (Eds.), *Foundations of orientation and mobility.* New York: American Foundation for the Blind, pp. 477–525.

White, B. W. (1970). Perceptual findings with the vision-substitution system. *IEEE Transactions on Man-Machine Systems, MMS-11,* 54–57.

Whitstock, R. H. (1980). Dog guides. In R. L. Welsh & B. B. Blasch (Eds.), *Foundations of orientation and mobility.* New York: American Foundation for the Blind, pp. 565–580.

Working Group on Mobility Aids for the Visually Impaired and Blind. (1986). *Electronic travel aids: New directions for research.* Washington, DC: National Academy Press.

9

BRAILLE

Emerson Foulke
University of Louisville

INTRODUCTION

Since early times, there have been numerous efforts to make print tangible so that blind persons could read. A thorough review of the disappointing experience with raised-print letters is provided by Farrell (1956). It was not until Louis Braille introduced his code in 1829 that a really useful means of reading by touch became available.

The acceptance of braille was delayed by a prolonged and often acrimonious dispute concerning the relative merits of several codes with dot patterns as characters, and several codes with different styles of print characters formed by raised lines (for an excellent review of the struggle that preceded the acceptance of a uniform Braille code, see Irwin, 1955). At the time this debate over the kind of letter best observed by touch took place, it was not customary to resolve such issues by experiment. However, the results of recent research are congruent with the experience of those blind persons who were using Braille's code.

Millar (1985) compared braille characters with tactile stimuli, which, though formed by continuous raised lines instead of dots, had the same outline shapes as the braille characters, and found braille characters to be more discriminable. Loomis (1981) hypothesized that the superior tangibility of punctiform patterns in comparison with patterns formed by raised lines is a consequence of the low spatial frequency that characterizes tactual observation. To test this hypothesis, he matched the spatial frequency of the visual system to the spatial frequency of the tactual system by using low-pass filtering to reduce the spatial frequency of print letters observed visually until they were no more legible than analogous raised letters observed tactually. By comparing the legibility of these letters with the legibility of braille letters observed visually, and with the legibility of braille letters observed tactually, he showed that braille letters were more legible than print letters, whether they were observed visually or tactually.

Ultimately, the differences of opinion concerning the utility of various punctiform codes were resolved in favor of a code that is fairly similar to the code proposed by Braille, and in 1932, the United States and Great Britain found that they could adopt standard braille codes so nearly the same that the differences between them do not seriously inconvenience braille readers. These codes are in use today throughout the English-speaking world.

The Braille Code

The symbols in the braille code are created by assigning meanings to the patterns of dots that can be formed in a matrix with six positions at which dots can appear. These positions are arranged in three rows and two columns. In the parlance of the community of braille readers and writers, the matrix in which dot patterns are formed is called a "cell." In a cell with six positions, 2^6 or 64 combinations are possible. In one of these combinations, no dot is present, and the empty space created by the use of this dotless cell indicates, as it does in print, the boundaries between words. The remaining 63 combinations of dots constitute the characters in the braille code (see Fig. 9.1.)

According to the braille production standards met by the American Printing House for the Blind, published by the Library of Congress, the centers of laterally and vertically adjacent dots within a cell are separated by 2.28 mm (0.09 in.). The centers of the dots in corresponding positions of laterally adjacent cells are separated by 6.35 mm (0.25 in.). The centers of dots in corresponding positions of vertically adjacent cells are separated by 10.16 mm (0.4 in.). In consequence of the limited control over the paper medium in which braille dots are embossed, their heights are allowed to vary between 0.381 mm (0.015 in.) and 0.508 mm (0.020 in.) (Zickel & Hooper, 1957).

The braille code has two levels of complexity. In Grade I braille, 26 of

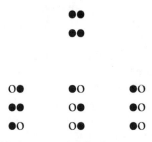

FIG. 9.1.   Four braille dot patterns.

●O ●● ●● ●O ●O O● O● ●O ●● ●● O● ●● ●●
OO O● O● O● ●● ●O ●● OO O● O● ●O O● ●●
●● ●O OO OO ●O ●O ●O OO ●O OO OO ●O OO
u n d e r s t a n d i n g

OO ●O O● ●● O●
O● OO OO ●O OO
OO ●● ●O ●● ●●
(under)(st)(and)(ing)

FIG. 9.2. The word *understanding* written without and with contraction.

the 63 available dot patterns stand for letters of the alphabet. Other dot patterns are used for punctuation marks. These assignments do not exhaust the supply of dot patterns, but meanings are not assigned to the remaining dot patterns. In Grade II braille, the remaining dot patterns stand for groups of letters that occur with high frequency in English language usage, and are called contractions (see Fig. 9.2.)

In addition to these contractions, Grade II braille includes a number of abbreviations, called short-form words (see Fig. 9.3).

The average braille reading rate for senior high school students is between 80 and 90 words per minute (Meyers, Ethington, & Ashcroft, 1958; Nolan & Kederis, 1969). This rate can be placed in perspective by comparing it with the silent visual reading rate. The average silent visual reading rate for high school students is between 250 wpm and 300 wpm (A.M. Harris, 1947; Taylor,

PEOPLE WHO LIKE KNOWLEDGE
WOULD RATHER RECEIVE MORE
HELP FROM FRIENDS, BUT, LIKE
IT OR NOT, THEY CAN DO IT AS
IT IS.

P (WH)O L K WD R RCV M HELP F
FRS, B L X OR N, (THE)Y C D X Z
X IS.

(Note: This sentence could have been shortened further by replacing the letters enclosed by parentheses with contractions.)

FIG. 9.3. A sentence written first without and then with short-form words.

1966), and is thus between 2.5 and 3 times as fast as the average braille reading rate. Of course, the reading rates found in studies of the sort just cited are usually means or medians, and both considerably faster and considerably slower individual reading rates are common. Grunwald (1966) and Umstead (1970) have both reported the measurement of braille reading rates in excess of 200 wpm.

The slow rate at which braille is normally read limits its usefulness for reading text that is primarily literal and not difficult to comprehend; but for text that requires slow and careful reading because it is conceptually difficult, text that includes mathematical expressions, or text in which layout is essential to its comprehension (for instance, tables), braille's slow reading rate is not a serious problem. However, reading rate is only one of several factors to be considered in evaluating the effectiveness of braille.

Printed information is spatially distributed, and can therefore be arranged in the space defined by a page in a manner that gives the reader of print the opportunity to read selectively by taking advantage of the excellent spatial ability of the visual system. This ability makes possible such operations as retracing in order to read missed words more carefully, and skipping ahead in order to pass over words that can be predicted with certainty. Paragraph indentations, skipped lines between paragraphs, centered headings, and so forth, make the logic of a composition more evident, and serve as cues that guide the search for desired information.

Text written in braille exhibits the same kind of spatial organization as text written in print, and the operations made possible by the spatial distribution of information on the printed page are also available to the braille reader, although in lesser degree. Some of the ability of the visual system to take advantage of spatial organization is lost because the haptic system cannot observe as much at one time as the visual system. Consequently, the spatial organization of the braille page must be discovered by serial examination. Serial examination requires more time, and makes the perception of spatial organization more difficult.

Because braille characters are displayed spatially, the braille reader, like the print reader, can adjust reading rate continually to meet the changing demands of momentary variations in reading difficulty. However, as a consequence of the slow braille reading rate, the range within which reading rate can be varied is restricted.

Like the print reader, the braille reader can save reading time by passing over upcoming text when letters, words, or phrases are predictable; retrace in order to re-examine ambiguous text; and use format cues such as indented paragraphs, chapter headings, and page numbers to aid in the search for desired information. However, the braille reader performs these operations more slowly than the print reader because reading fingers cannot be moved from one place on the page to another as rapidly as reading eyes.

AN OVERVIEW OF RESEARCH

Experiments conducted expressly for the purpose of investigating the reading of braille, and experiments whose results have implications for the reading of braille fall into several categories. The results of physiological investigations of the sensory and neural mechanisms involved in tactile and haptic perception have obvious implications. There are psychophysical experiments that complement physiological investigations, and provide data that can be related to aspects of braille reading performance. Other experiments are designed to afford opportunities for behavioral observations from which inferences can be drawn concerning the perceptual and cognitive processes on which the reading of braille depends, or behavioral observations that may disclose the most effective reading strategies.

In some experiments the characteristics of the braille display are varied. The purpose of these experiments is usually to learn how to optimize the display of braille, or to evaluate the effectiveness of the display that can be provided by some embodiment of technology, such as the VersaBraille.[1] However, in some of these experiments, it is the display of print that is altered. The purpose, in this case, is to require print readers to read under conditions resembling the conditions under which braille is read (for instance, the serial encounter of characters) in an effort to account for differences in the performance of braille and print readers (Foulke & Smith, 1973; Troxel, 1967).

The research of several investigators has had the practical objective of making the learning of braille more efficient. Their strategy is to identify variables that affect its learning, and to determine optimal values for those variables (e.g., Hall & Newman, 1987; Heller & Mitchell, 1985; Newman & Hall, 1987).

Finally, there is a group of opportunistic experiments, conducted by researchers who are not interested in the reading of braille per se but who have taken advantage of the availability of braille and braille readers to investigate other issues. For example, Hermelin and O'Connor (1971), Rudel, Denckla, and Spalten (1974), L.J. Harris (1980), and Millar (1984) have used braille readers as subjects and braille characters as stimuli in order to pursue their interest in the differential involvement of the cerebral hemispheres in the tactual perception of forms with which linguistic meanings have been associated. To take another example, in an experiment in which naïve sighted subjects observed embossed Morse code and braille characters by touch, Heller (1985) demonstrated the contribution that vision makes to the performance of perceptual–motor tasks in which the perceptual component is haptic, by providing a visual frame of reference for hand movements, and by discerning kinesthetic patterns of movement.

---

[1]The VersaBraille is sold by TeleSensory/VTEK, P.O. Box 7455, Mountain View, CA 94039–7455.

A thorough consideration of all of these experiments is an undertaking that would demand the scope of a book. The review that follows is concerned only with the reading behavior of braille readers, and the perceptual processes and strategies that can be inferred from their behavior. Even with this restriction, I have not been able to present a comprehensive review. The experiments I have cited are only examples of the various approaches that have been taken in the investigation of braille reading. Many other experiments would have been equally illustrative, and the choice of experiments to cite has often been arbitrary.

READING BEHAVIOR

Active vs. Passive Touch

It is customary to draw a distinction between active touch and passive touch (Gibson, 1962; Heller, 1986). Active touch occurs when some object or surface is explored by touch in order to acquire information about it. Passive touch occurs when a tactile stimulus is applied to the skin. Braille readers who move their reading fingers across the page in order to acquire the information written on it are engaging in active touch. When they read in this manner, they read much more effectively than they would if braille dot patterns were pressed, one after the other, against the distal pad of a reading finger. The experience of braille readers has consistently supported the superiority of active touch, and its superiority has recently been demonstrated experimentally by Heller (1985), and by Heller, Scrofano, and Nesbitt (1989), whose sighted subjects matched visually observed analogues of braille characters and words to passively or actively observed braille characters and words. They found a consistent advantage for active touch. The superiority of active touch is explained, in part, by the characteristics of mechanoreceptors (Iggo, 1982). Also, each dot of a braille character that moves across the distal pad of a reading finger stimulates many receptors, thereby increasing the supply of neural data delivered to the brain.

However, the explanation of the superiority of active touch involves more than the excitation of mechanoreceptors. The contraction of muscles, the stretching of tendons, and the movement of joints that take place when hands and fingers pass over lines of braille characters excite the receptors of the kinesthetic system, and this added excitation probably contributes to the superiority of active touch. Even more importantly, the movement of arms, hands, and fingers that characterizes active braille reading is ultimately controlled by the higher mental processes that guide the search for the information encoded in braille. It is at this point that intelligence begins to make its contribution to the perception of braille.

Letters as Perceptual Units

The slow braille reading rate that is typically observed is the rate to be expected if, because the "tactile scene" can be no larger than the surface of the distal pad of the finger with which it makes contact, braille characters must be observed serially. If letters are perceived serially, then it must be necessary to hold them in memory until enough of them have been perceived to permit the identification of a word.

To investigate this possibility, Nolan and Kederis (1969, Study II) used a device analogous to a tachistoscope that they called the Tachistotactometer. With this instrument, they determined the minimum exposure times needed by a large and representative group of braille readers in grade school and high school to identify the letters of the alphabet. Next, they determined the minimum exposure times needed by the same subjects to identify a large number of short, familiar words. They found that, for a majority of these words, the time needed to identify a word exceeded the sum of the identification times for the letters of which the word was composed. They proposed that this additional time was spent in integrating the individually perceived and remembered letters in order to achieve the identification of a word.

These data also suggested one of the factors involved in the explanation of individual differences in the braille reading rate. When they compared their subjects' letter identification times with their reading rates, they found that those subjects who were slow braille readers needed more time to identify letters than the fast readers.

The Role of Linguistic Knowledge. By taking advantage of linguistic cues, braille readers should occasionally be able to predict letters, syllables, and words, and by so doing, to save the time that would otherwise be spent in perceiving them. Such an ability would account for those instances in which the time needed by their subjects for the identification of a word did not exceed the sum of the times needed for the perception of its letters. That these subjects did, in fact, take advantage of linguistic cues is strongly implied by the finding that 10% of the words they presented were identified before all of the letters in those words had been touched.

The contribution of linguistic variables has been further clarified by several experiments whose results also extended the explanation of individual differences in the braille reading rate. The results of these experiments indicate that familiar context (Nolan & Kederis, 1969, Studies V, VI), syntactical regularity (Mousty & Bertelson, 1985), short words (Nolan & Kederis, 1969, Study II), frequently occurring words (Krueger, 1982; Nolan & Kederis, 1969, Study II), and frequently occurring braille contractions (Umstead, 1970) have a generally positive effect on the braille reading rate, and that this effect is stronger for fast readers than for slow readers.

The finding that fast braille readers are helped more by linguistic knowledge than slow braille readers is inconsistent with the compensatory hypothesis. This hypothesis proposes that slow braille readers overcome their handicap to some extent by taking fuller advantage than fast braille readers of linguistic knowledge in order to obviate the reading of some words and characters by predicting them, thus saving the time that would have been spent reading them. This hypothesis was given specific attention by Mousty and Bertelson (1985), who required both slow and fast braille readers to read scrambled words, seventh-order approximations of prose passages, and prose passages. If slow braille readers take fuller advantage of linguistic knowledge than fast braille readers, as slow readers progress from scrambled words to seventh-order approximations to prose passages, their reading rates should increase more than the reading rates of fast readers. This was, however, not the case. As the meaningfulness of reading passages was increased, both groups showed an increase in reading rate, but the slow readers did not achieve larger gains than the fast readers.

Braille-Reading Strategies

Although the reading of braille is not yet fully understood, the results of experiments and experience are sufficient to provide a fairly detailed picture of the braille-reading process. Many of the physiological, perceptual, cognitive, and display variables that affect the reading of braille have been identified and their effects determined. However, the reading rate realized by any given braille reader depends on the extent to which perceptual and cognitive aptitudes are developed, and on the way in which perceptual and cognitive abilities are employed. The manner of employment of perceptual and cognitive abilities is a reflection of the reading strategy adopted by the reader, and the consequences of various reading strategies have been studied by a number of investigators.

Larger Perceptual Units. The limitations on observation imposed by the perceptual system employed for reading braille, together with the perceptual processes proposed by Nolan and Kederis (1969) certainly seem to offer a reasonable explanation of the braille reading rate typically observed. However, other explanations are possible, and the explanation proposed by Nolan and Kederis has been disputed.

The position taken by Grunwald (1966) is a case in point. He did not dispute the braille reading rates reported by Nolan and Kederis, but he maintained that braille reading rates are typically slow and variable because most braille readers have not received the right kind of instruction. They have been taught to identify characters one at a time, or at least they have not been taught to do otherwise. If they were taught a different perceptual strategy, one that a few fortunate braille readers have discovered on their own, they would, in the general case, be able to read very much faster.

His observations of braille readers convinced him that when they employ a more efficient perceptual strategy than the one generally taught, they can read at over 200 wpm. The use of a different perceptual strategy by fast braille readers was implied by the results of an experiment Grunwald (1966) conducted in which he found that when the distal pads of reading fingers moved across lines of braille characters at the speed required for a reading rate in the neighborhood of 200 wpm, braille readers cannot discriminate between test stimuli with two dots and test stimuli with only one dot. It follows that fast braille readers must not be identifying many of the individual braille characters that move across the pads of their reading fingers, and cannot, therefore, be employing the perceptual process described by Nolan and Kederis.

As an alternative explanation, Grunwald proposed that fast braille readers perceive rhythmic patterns, disclosed by the passage of time. I have not found in his published reports a more detailed statement of this explanation, but as it stands, it seems to suggest a perceptual process of the sort indicated in the following description.

As fast braille readers pass rapidly over lines of braille characters, the stream of dots that flows beneath their reading fingers varies in spatial extension as a function of time. These variations form memorable patterns with which syllables, words, and even phrases can be associated. If this hypothesis is correct, a necessary condition for the emergence of such patterns is movement of the reading finger or fingers across lines of characters at a fast and constant speed. If movement is too slow, only individual characters will be perceived. If the speed of finger movement is allowed to vary, the necessary condition for the emergence of temporally extended patterns will not be realized, and the patterns will not be available for perception.

An analogy will help to make this point clear. Initially, students of Morse code learn to identify individual characters, but as they gain experience, they begin to identify entire words. A given sequence of dots and dashes no longer sounds like the letters D, O, and G, but like the word DOG. The relative temporal values of dots and dashes, and of the intervals between dots and dashes, within and between characters, are critical to the perception of the patterns expressed by individual characters and by sequences of characters. If these temporal values were allowed to vary at random, the legibility of the code would be destroyed. An explanation of the performance of fast braille readers that appears to be compatible with the preceding description has been suggested by Millar (1978). She proposes that the flow of dot patterns across the pads of reading fingers is encoded in terms of texture or dot density, which varies over time. Of course, reading fingers would have to move at a fairly constant rate for this variation to be interpretable.

The hypothesis implied by Grunwald's suggestion has some support. The observations of reading behavior made by Bürklen (1932), Eatman (1942), Kusajima (1974), Davidson et al. (1980), and Bertelson, Mousty, and D'Alimonte (1985) indicate that fast braille readers do exhibit the reading behavior required by the hypothesis. Their reading fingers pass over lines of braille characters at a fast and constant speed. Slow braille readers also exhibit the reading behavior required by the hypothesis. Their reading fingers pass over lines of characters at a slow and variable speed, leaving them no recourse but to identify characters one at a time. However, although these observations are consistent with the hypothesis, they are not decisive.

One test of the hypothesis would be to give braille readers practice in reading text written in a continuous line on tape that is transported across a display surface from right to left, beneath stationary reading fingers. When braille text is displayed in this manner, the emergence of the temporally extended patterns that specify words and phrases should be assured, because the speed with which braille characters move across the distal pads of reading fingers, and the constancy of that speed are controlled by the tape transport, and do not depend on the skill of the reader. With enough practice, a reader might discover the temporally extended patterns that specify much more than single letters can. The guidance provided by this knowledge should make it possible to learn the reading behavior required for the emergence of such patterns when braille is written in the conventional manner on sheets of paper.

Several experiments have been reported in which braille readers were given practice in reading braille written on tape that moved beneath their reading fingers (Ashcroft, 1959; Flanigan 1966; Flanigan & Joslin, 1969; Kederis, Nolan, & Morris, 1967; Nolan & Kederis, 1969, Study I; Stockton, 1965), but results have been disappointing. The increases in reading speed that were obtained were no greater than the increases in reading speed that are easily achieved by motivating instructions. In these experiments, readers were only given simple practice. It may be that the discovery of temporally extended patterns requires more practice than they received, or more sophisticated training procedures, which assure the correct sequence of appropriate experiences. However, as will shortly be seen, the evidence now available suggests that increases in reading speed are more likely to be realized, not by teaching braille readers to identify emergent patterns, but rather by teaching them to make more efficient use of reading hands and fingers.

Reading Fingers.   The way in which braille characters are examined by reading fingers has been studied by many investigators.The detailed observations made by Bürklen (1917/1932), by Eatman (1933), and by Kusajima (1974) are not always in agreement, but taken together, they provide a thorough description of the use of reading fingers by both good and poor readers.

There have been hypotheses concerning components of the process of perceiving braille that might be carried out by fingers other than index fingers (Hocheisen and Mell, cited in Bürklen, 1917/1932, p. 14 and p. 15, respectively) and speculations concerning the possibility of enlisting the perceptual ability of normally unused fingers (Funchess, 1934; Gigerl, cited in Bürklen, 1917/1932, p. 14; Lappin & Foulke, 1973). However, proceeding from the index finger to the little finger on either hand, there is a steep gradient of declining ability to identify braille characters (Foulke, 1964; Heller, cited in Bürklen, 1917/1932, p. 15) and observations of braille reading consistently indicate that, with rare exceptions, braille is read with either one or two index fingers (Bürklen, 1917/1932; Eatman, 1942).

The reading fingers of good readers move across lines of characters with a light touch, and at a relatively fast and fairly constant speed, and retracing to re-examine missed characters or words occurs infrequently. The reading fingers of slow braille readers move across lines of braille characters at a speed that is slow and variable. They use more finger pressure than fast braille readers, and retrace more frequently. When they examine characters, their reading fingers often make circular motions or up-and-down motions and they frequently stray from the line of characters they are reading (Bürklen, 1917/1932; Kusajima, 1974).

The reading behavior of poor braille readers suggests that they are having a problem with character legibility. It may be that the distal pads of their reading fingers are less sensitive than the distal pads of the reading fingers of good readers, and the relationship between finger sensitivity and character legibility should be studied more carefully.

It may also be that they need specific training to improve their speed and accuracy in identifying characters. Braille contractions occur less frequently, and are identified more slowly and inaccurately than letters by braille readers, in general. Umstead (1970) has shown that practice in the identification of contractions produces a significant increase in the silent reading rate. If poor braille readers were given practice in the identification of all of the characters in the braille code, the practice effect might be even larger.

Reading with 1 Hand. Investigators consistently find that those who use only one hand for reading braille read more slowly than those who use both hands. In these studies, data have usually been obtained from two-handed readers who have been asked to read with only one hand. It is not uncommon to find two-handed readers who use one of their hands only for nonreading functions, such as marking the beginning of the next line, but braille readers who use one hand exclusively are rare. Among the braille readers observed by Eatman (1942), it was found that very few used only one hand. In this group, the poorest readers were those who used only the left hand.

Reading with 2 Hands. The relationship between the manner of employment of two reading hands and the performance of the braille reader has been studied in detail by Bürklen (1917/1932), Kusajima (1974), Eatman (1942), Davidson et al. (1980), Millar (1987), and Bertelson et al. (1985). Although comparison of their findings discloses occasional disagreements, especially when reading is done with only one hand, they agree, in the main, concerning the effects associated with different ways of using both hands.

In conducting their research, Bertelson and Mousty were able to take advantage of instrumentation not available to earlier investigators, and their instrumentation enabled more detailed observation and more accurate measurement. Their investigation of hand usage by two-handed readers was thorough, and in order to avoid redundancy, I have based the following account primarily on the research reported in two of their articles (Bertelson et al., 1985; Mousty & Bertelson, 1985). However, for those who want a more complete understanding of the relationship between hand usage and braille reading performance, the reports of the experiments conducted by Bürklen, Eatman, Kusajima, Millar, and Davidson et al. also deserve careful study.

Among two-handed readers, the difference between the reading abilities of the two hands varies over a wide range. At one end of this range are readers who use one of their hands only for nonreading functions. At the other are readers who can read as well with one hand as with the other. There is a significant, negative correlation between the braille reading rate and the size of the difference between the reading abilities of the two hands; that is, the more nearly equal the two hands are in reading ability, the faster the reading rate. The reason for this is that when both hands can read, a more efficient reading strategy can be employed.

Many two-handed readers keep the index fingers of their two hands together as they read, and when they reach the end of a line, they move both index fingers to the beginning of the next line. Of course, no reading occurs while they are finding the beginning of the next line, and the cumulative effect of these unproductive intervals is a substantial reduction of reading rate.

For other two-handed readers, reading time is shared by the two index fingers. Both index fingers begin reading together, but before the end of the line is reached, the left index finger departs, and while the right finger finishes reading the line, the left finger finds the beginning of the next line. When the right finger reaches the end of its line, the left finger begins reading the new line, and is joined on this line by the right finger, at the place the left finger has reached by the time the right finger arrives. The two fingers move together until the end of the line is near, the right index finger finishes the current line, while the left index finger finds the beginning of the new line, and so on. During the time that elapses while one hand is moving to the next line, the other hand is reading, and thus, the interval during which no reading occurs is shortened or eliminated altogether.

When braille is read in this fashion, each line that is read can be divided into three segments, the segment at the left end of the line that is read by the left index finger alone, the middle segment of the line that is read by both index fingers, and the segment at the right end of the line that is read by the right finger alone. The length of the middle segment varies from reader to reader, and its length is negatively correlated with reading rate. It is read at a faster rate than the other two segments because reading rate is increased by the use of two index fingers, but as the fraction of the line occupied by the middle segment decreases in length, reading rate increases. The reason is that increasing the fractions of the line occupied by the left segment and the right segment decreases the time during which no reading occurs, and the resulting increase in reading rate exceeds the reduction in reading rate caused by the use of only one reading finger.

A few braille readers of the type just described start reading the beginning of the new line with the left index finger shortly before the right index finger has come to the end of its line. Thus, for a brief interval, the two index fingers are reading different characters at the same time. This rather surprising perceptual ability was also observed by Kusajima (1974).

CONCLUSION

Print owes many of its advantages as a reading system to the spatial arrangement of characters on the printed page. The spatial arrangement of text on the page makes specific information easy to find, and its location easy to remember. Braille text is spatially arranged in much the same way as printed text, and thus, braille retains many of the advantages of print. Its principal disadvantage is the slow rate at which it is read by the typical braille reader. This slow reading rate is the result of limitations imposed by the perceptual system used for reading braille.

Nevertheless, within the limits defined by the structure and functions of this perceptual system, the results of a number of experiments suggest the possibility of bringing about a worthwhile increase in reading rate by appropriate training. Psychophysical experiments with better control of the variation of physical properties of braille characters may suggest ways of improving the legibility of braille characters. Properly designed practice may improve the ability of readers, and especially poor readers, to identify the characters in the braille code. By training, it may be possible to provide the nonpreferred index finger with the same reading ability as the preferred reading index finger, and it may be possible to teach those who profit from such training to make the reading of braille more efficient by sharing reading time between the two index fingers.

REFERENCES

Ashcroft, S. (1959). *The IBM braille reader field test*. Unpublished progress report, George Peabody College for Teachers, Vanderbilt University, Nashville, TN.

Bertelson, P., Mousty, P., & D'Alimonte, G. (1985). A study of braille reading: 2. Patterns of hand activity in one-handed and two-handed reading. *Quarterly Journal of Experimental Psychology, 37A*, 235–256.

Bürklen, K. (1917/1932). *Touch reading of the blind* (F.K. Merry, Trans.). New York: American Foundation for the Blind. (Original work published 1917)

Davidson, P.W., Valenti, D., Reuter, S., Wiles-Ketteman, M., Haber, R.N., & Appelle, S. (1980). Relationships between hand movements, reading competence and passage difficulty in braille reading. *Neuropsychologica, 18*, 629–635.

Eatman, P.F. (1942). *An analytic study of braille reading*. Unpublished doctoral dissertation, University of Texas, Austin.

Farrell, G. (1956). *The story of blindness*. Cambridge, MA: Harvard University Press.

Flanigan, P.J. (1966). Automated training and braille reading. *New Outlook for the Blind, 60*, 141–146.

Flanigan, P.J., & Joslin, M.S. (1969). Patterns of response in the perception of braille configurations. *New Outlook for the Blind, 63*, 232–244.

Foulke, E. (1964). Transfer of a complex perceptual skill. *Perceptual and Motor Skills, 18*, 733–740.

Foulke, E., & Smith, T. (1973). Reading print a letter at a time. In E. Foulke (Ed.), *The development of an expanded reading code for the blind* (Pt. 2). (Final Rep., Project 7–1185, pp. 82–87) Washington, D.C.: U.S. Bureau of Education for the Handicapped.

Funchess, L.V. (1934). *The psychology of reading braille with eight fingers*. Unpublished master's thesis, Louisiana State University, Baton Rouge.

Gibson, J.J. (1962). Observations on active touch. *Psychological Review, 69*, 477–491.

Grunwald, A.P. (1966). A braille-reading machine. *Science, 154*, 144–146.

Hall, A.D., & Newman, S.E. (1987). Braille learning: Relative importance of seven variables. *Applied Cognitive Psychology, 1*, 133–141.

Harris, A.M. (1947). *How to increase reading ability*. New York: Longmans, Green.

Harris, L.J. (1980). Which hand is the "eye" of the blind: A new look at an old question. In J. Herron (Ed.), *Neuropsychology of left-handedness* (pp. 303–329). New York: Academic Press.

Heller, M.A. (1985). Tactual perception of embossed Morse code and braille: The alliance of vision and touch. *Perception, 14*, 563–570.

Heller, M.A. (1986). Active and passive tactile braille recognition. *Bulletin of the Psychonomic Society, 24*, 201–202.

Heller, M.A., & Mitchell, B.Y. (1985). Helping new braille readers: Effects of spacing, finger locus, and gloves. *Perceptual and Motor Skills, 61*, 363–369.

Heller, M.A., Scrofano, D.K., & Nesbitt, K.D. (1989). Effect of tactual scanning mode of braille and shape recognition. *Bulletin of the Psychonomic Society, 27*, 131–132.

Hermelin, B., & O'Connor, N. (1971). Functional asymmetry in the reading of braille. *Neuropsychologica, 9*, 431–435.

Iggo, A.A. (1982). Cutaneous sensory mechanisms. In H.B. Barlow & J.D. Mollon (Eds.), *The senses* (pp. 369–408). Cambridge, England: Cambridge University Press.

Irwin, R.B. (1955). *The war of the dots*. New York: American Foundation for the Blind.

Kederis, C.J., Nolan, C.Y., & Morris, J.E. (1967). The use of controlled exposure devices to increase braille reading rates. *International Journal for the Education of the Blind, 16*, 97–105.

Krueger, L. (1982). A word-superiority effect with print and braille characters. *Perception & Psychophysics, 31*, 345–352.

Kusajima, T. (1974). *Visual reading and braille reading: An experimental investigation of the physiology and psychology of visual and tactual reading*. New York: American Foundation for the Blind.

Lappin, J., & Foulke, E. (1973). Expanding the tactual field of view. *Perception & Psychophysics, 14*, 237–241.

Loomis, J.M. (1981). On the tangibility of letters and braille. *Perception & Psychophysics, 29*, 37–46.

Meyers, E., Ethington, D., & Ashcroft, S.C. (1958). Readability of braille as a function of three spacing variables. *Applied Psychology, 42*, 163–165.

Millar, S. (1978). Aspects of information from touch and movement. In G. Gordon (Ed.), *Active touch*. Oxford, England: Pergamon Press.

Millar, S. (1984). Is there a "best hand" for braille? *Cortex, 20*, 75–87.

Millar, S. (1985). The perception of complex patterns by touch. *Perception, 14*, 293–303.

Millar, S. (1987). The perceptual "window" in two-handed braille: Do the left and right hands process text simultaneously? *Cortex, 23*, 111–122.

Mousty, P., & Bertelson, P. (1985) A study of braille reading: 1. Reading speed as a function of hand usage and context. *Quarterly Journal of Experimental Psychology, 37A*, 217–233.

Newman, S.E., & Hall, A.D. (1987). Perceiving, learning and remembering braille. *British Journal of Visual Impairment, 2*, 43–44.

Nolan, C.Y., & Kederis, C.J. (1969). *Perceptual factors in braille word recognition* (AFB Research Series No. 20). New York: American Foundation for the Blind.

Rudel, R., Denckla, M.B., & Spalten, E. (1974). The functional asymmetry of braille letter learning in normal, sighted children. *Neurology, 24*, 733–738.

Stockton, G. H. (1965). *Effectiveness of programmed learning in braille: Instruction for the adult blind*. Unpublished doctoral dissertation, University of Wisconsin, Madison.

Taylor, E.A. (1966). *The fundamental reading skill, as related to eye movement photography and visual anomalies*. Springfield, IL: Charles C. Thomas.

Troxel, E.A. (1967). Experiments in tactile and visual reading. *IEEE Transactions on Human Factors in Electronics, HFE–8*, 261–263.

Umstead, R.G. (1970). *Improvement of braille reading through code recognition training*. Unpublished doctoral dissertation, George Peabody College for Teachers, Vanderbilt University, Nashville, TN.

Zickel, V.E., & Hooper, M.S. (1957). The program of braille research: A progress report. *International Journal for the Education of the Blind, 6*, 79–86.

IV

TACTILE PERCEPTION IN THE VISUALLY IMPAIRED

This part of the book is about blindness and perception. While the number of totally blind people is relatively small, the number of visually impaired individuals is much larger. If we include all of those people with a visual defect, the number is tremendous. Visual problems increase with aging. If we are lucky enough to reach old age (> 65), about 95% of us will wear corrective lenses (Morse, Silberman, & Trief, 1987). Many of these individuals will have low vision when they remove their eyeglasses. Those fortunate few with "normal" vision still have poor visual acuity under conditions of very low light or peripheral vision.

The aim of researchers in this area is to understand tactual and spatial perception in the blind person. Some researchers have been interested in the study of perception in blind people primarily because of a concern with understanding blindness. Many others have focused their research on what these experiments tell us about perception per se. Various research strategies are in use, but the most common has involved comparisons of the sighted with congenitally blind and late blind persons. The congenitally blind individual has never seen and must develop an understanding of space via the sense of touch. Late blind people have benefited from visual experience. Consequently, their use of haptics will be "colored" by visual imagery and early visual experience. Most researchers have assumed that we can learn a great deal about the sense of touch by comparing the haptic performance of sighted and congenitally blind people.

It is far too easy to confuse the issues of the ability of blind subjects versus

the capabilities of touch. There are a number of possible causes of low performance in any sample of blind subjects, and these may not relate to any
putative spatial limitations in touch. We need to recall that there are vast
differences between potential and performance, and this may alter experimental outcomes.

Warren (1978) has issued a methodological caution in research involving
blind subjects. He believes that there are a large number of methodological
problems inherent in work with blind persons. One doesn't select blind subjects randomly, since the number available is typically so small. Thus, any
given sample may not be representative of the blind population as a whole.
The blind population is so heterogeneous that it is very hard to know what
a representative sample might be.

Additional problems are involved in studies comparing sighted and blind
people. Warren argues that there are other differences between sighted and
blind subjects in addition to visual status and the presence or absence of visual
imagery. Blind people may have different educational backgrounds, they have
very different social environments (they may have been overprotected), and
some have been raised in institutional settings. We should also remember
that the sighted person may function abnormally when initially deprived of
sight—this can be disorienting. Also, there may be problems with the tasks
we use that have little to do with blindness, per se. Blind people may not
be as familiar as the sighted with some objects. For example, the totally blind
person may have little use for pencils. Similarly, the sighted individual may
be relatively unfamiliar with objects that are highly familiar to blind people
(e.g., a talking calculator or watch). We should bear these differences in mind
in designing any research in this area.

Warren (1978) has stated, "research that compares blind and blindfolded
sighted subjects is generally unsatisfying. . .the perceptual performance of
sighted subjects is not typically an appropriate yardstick against which to
evaluate the abilities of the blind." Warren's caution here is about the *comparison* of sighted and blind subjects. All researchers in the area believe that much
can be learned by studying tactual perception in blind people. This sort of
research will probably not tell us about deficiencies in the blind, as Warren
has warned, but may tell us something valuable about tactual perception.

The first chapter in this part summarizes a large body of work on tactual
perception and spatial cognition in blind people. The evidence seems to suggest that visual experience is hardly necessary for tactual perception. This
is especially likely for detection of substance-related qualities, such as texture. In addition, blind people may make more efficient use of the sense of
touch, especially when patterns are small (smaller than the hand or fingertip), or braille-like, or highly familiar to them. Mobility and perception of very
large-scale space may pose very different problems for the blind pedestrian.
The lack of early vision may delay the development of spatial reference

schemes. The evidence suggests that spatial reference information may be more important for the understanding of blindness and touch than the variable of visual imagery (Heller, 1989).

Raised-line drawings are used by blind people for acquiring information of the sort displayed by maps, graphs, and so on. Relatively few blind people actually make pictures. Their use for pictures has proven highly controversial, and is discussed in all three chapters. Revesz (see Introduction, this volume) believed that the sense of touch is directed toward the examination of solid, three-dimensional forms. He thought that 2-D configurations were problematical for touch. More recently, we find other researchers somewhat skeptical about the suitability of tangible drawings because of the difficulty some naïve subjects may show in recognizing selected raised-line pictures. Certainly, raised-line pictures are not color photographs, nor do they convey as much information as black-and-white photographs. Still photographs (or line drawings), however, are certainly lacking in dynamic information when compared with motion pictures or videotapes. Nonetheless, this does not diminish the usefulness of still photographs. Moreover, we should remember that we all need to learn how to use maps, whether we are sighted or visually impaired. Thus, the observation that some naïve persons may find tangible maps or pictures difficult does not mean that people can't learn their use. Heller reports that some tangible pictures are much easier than others to recognize, by both congenitally and late blind people. Furthermore, naïve, congenitally blind people were able to make recognizable drawings of simple geometrical shapes such as triangles and squares. Some blind individuals produce good illustrations of animals, people, chairs, and other complex objects.

Kennedy and his colleagues argue that raised-lines have inherent meaning: Tangible lines represent edges in pictures. Kennedy believes that pictures are universals. Consequently, blind persons are readily able to produce pictures with raised-line drawing kits. While much of Kennedy's work has concerned drawing in blind children, Kennedy, Gabias, and Nicholls have emphasized drawing in adults in their chapter. Of course, adults are far better than children at drawing, even without a history of exposure to this task. One might expect, furthermore, that specific instruction in drawing would lead to improvement.

Millar has drawn together a large body of literature and reports a study on drawing in blind children. She has noted that the production of drawings is often superior to their recognition (see Millar, 1988). Children may produce recognizable drawings of the human figure, yet may not recognize a tangible drawing of a person. This report is consistent with the observations in the chapters by Heller and Kennedy. Millar explains this discrepancy between the recognition and production of drawings in terms of a motor program specifying contours. It is easy to imagine, say, the movements that describe the contour of a side view of a person's nose. Thus, it can be relatively easy to draw this contour using a raised-like drawing kit. It may be quite different and more difficult, however, to feel a raised line on a surface and ascertain what the line represents. Millar proposes that recognition of tactual representations is indirect, and depends upon the nature of haptic representation. That is, for Millar, haptic representation is based on action plans and recognition is a function of retrieval cues.

Action often serves perception in touch, and Millar has cleverly stressed a way this could aid representation. There are numerous theoretical precedents for the idea that we code patterns in terms of representations of movement patterns. Piaget and Inhelder (1956) have argued that "haptic images" depend upon movement schemas. Thus, the image one constructs of a triangle depends on the movements used to explore that shape. Also, we have the observation of the aphasic with alexia that is unable to read a simple word (see Heller, 1985; Hulme, 1979). This individual recognized the word after tracing its outline with his finger. This is an additional indication of motoric coding of form. Millar's chapter ties together a lot of loose threads in the haptic literature.

REFERENCES

Heller, M. A. (1985). Tactual perception of embossed Morse code and braille: The alliance of vision and touch. *Perception, 14*, 563–570.

Heller, M. A. (1989). Tactile memory in sighted and blind observers: The influence of orientation and rate of presentation. *Perception, 18*, 121–133.

Hulme, C. (1979). The interaction of visual and motor memory for graphic forms following tracing. *Quarterly Journal of Experimental Psychology, 31*, 249–261.

Millar, S. (1988). Models of sensory deprivation: The nature/nurture dichotomy and spatial representation in the blind. *International Journal of Behavioral Development, 11*, 69–87.

Morse, A. R., Silberman, R., & Trief, E. (1987). Aging and visual impairment. *Journal of Visual Impairment and Blindness, 81*, 308–312.

Piaget, J., & Inhelder, B. (1956). *The child's conception of space.* London: Routledge & Kegan Paul.

Warren, D. H. (1978). Perception by the blind. In E. C. Carterette & M. P. Friedman (Eds.), *Handbook of perception.* New York: Academic Press.

10

HAPTIC PERCEPTION
IN BLIND PEOPLE

Morton A. Heller
Winston-Salem State University

Many researchers have been interested in tactile perception in blind people, because it is there that we are able to study the sense of touch without the intervention of visual experience or visual imagery. Some blind persons have never seen. These individuals must base their understanding of space on the senses of touch, proprioception, audition, and perhaps, olfaction. Do blind persons imagine objects as we do? Do they understand space in the same ways that the rest of us do? Do blind persons have images? These questions and many more will be addressed in this chapter.

Some of the research in this area has been influenced by the introspection of the sighted when deprived of vision. For example, imagine you are visiting a friend's house, and in rather unfamiliar surroundings. It is the middle of the night, there is no electrical power, and you need to get out of bed and go to another room in *total darkness*. Many of us have had a difficult time under these circumstances; a number of us may have walked repeatedly into obstacles. Some sighted persons may panic when suddenly denied visual support. It would be easy to assume erroneously that this accurately reflects the situation of the blind individual, but there are many differences between these circumstances and the perceptual and spatial tasks facing blind persons. Furthermore, problems in large-scale space may differ in some ways from tactile perception involving smaller configurations. It is a mistake to try to generalize from the introspection of the sighted to the psychological reality of blindness. Sighted persons have developed a reliance on vision. In addition, they have failed to learn some types of spatial skill based on tactile and auditory input. We would be far better off trying to answer theoretical issues with research and data.

CAUSES OF BLINDNESS

It is useful to include a brief discussion of some of the more common causes of blindness, prior to any consideration of theory. Sight may be absent at birth, or very soon thereafter. Persons born without sight are described as *congenitally blind.* These individuals may lack sight because of cataracts, a clouding of the lens that is very common in older individuals. This disorder is now treatable via surgery. In rare instances, persons are born without sight because of glaucoma, in which increased pressure within the eye damages the retina. Glaucoma can occur at any age in association with other visual disorders (Morse, Silberman, & Trief, 1987). The most common causes of congenital blindness probably involve disorders of the visual pathway (e.g., optic nerve) and the retina. Many individuals have lost sight rather early in life because of retrolental fibroplasia (RLF). More recently, this disorder has come to be called retinopathy of prematurity (ROP). In ROP, excessive oxygen administered to premature infants can lead to damage of the retina. In addition, people can be born without vision because of a number of congenital developmental disorders, when parts of the visual system, for example, the optic nerve, have not developed properly. Many persons have been blinded at birth owing to multiple causes, such as glaucoma *and* cataracts.

The congenitally, totally blind are small in number. Perhaps 10% of the individuals registered with American and Canadian services for the blind are totally blind (data from Canadian National Institute for the Blind), and very few are congenitally blind. Only about 3% of people registered with the CNIB in a recent year were 0–5 years of age. It was estimated that the annual incidence of congenital blindness in the United States is 14.9 per 100,000 live births (Dunlea, 1989). A number of these individuals are not diagnosed until the infants are 4 to 5 months old.

Many more individuals lose sight later in life and are described as late blind, or *adventitiously blind.* Some lose sight because of trauma to the eyes or other parts of the visual/neural system. Many people have been blinded by explosions or gunshot. A large number of older persons lose sight because of diabetes. Some of the disorders that can cause blindness at birth or in early childhood affect people later on in life (glaucoma and cataracts). The most common causes of blindness in individuals over 65 include diabetic retinopathy, cataracts, glaucoma (data from CNIB), and macular degeneration (Morse et al., 1987). Almost 10% of people between 65 and 75 show visual loss due to cataracts, and the frequency increases to about 34% for those over 75. It has been estimated that as many as 30% of those over 65 have some macular degeneration. There are a few individuals who have no sight in early child-hood because of retinitis pigmentosa, though this disorder probably damages vision in more persons later in life. The late blind have seen, and they may retain the benefits of visual experience throughout much of their lives.

We should bear in mind that there are many more visually impaired persons than those that are completely blind, or have only minimal light perception. Low vision, or very blurred vision, is far more common than complete blindness. Furthermore, there is great variability in the extent of visual loss. The legally blind person is limited to vision that can't be corrected beyond 20/200. However, people with low vision may see light, form, and have considerable useful vision. Even the ability to see in terms of "shadows" can provide immeasurable aid to mobility. The interested reader is referred to Hollins (1989) for a more detailed discussion of the causes of blindness.

HISTORY AND PHILOSOPHICAL BACKGROUND

Philosophical Roots

Philosophers have been interested in perception in congenitally blind people for a long time. Much of the present work in the field has been influenced by philosophical theorizing. The interest of philosophers centered about the question of the necessity of sensory experience for knowledge and one's mental life. John Locke, the British empiricist, devoted considerable time to what has become known as Molyneux's question (Morgan, 1977). Molyneux, a friend of Locke, asked if a person born blind would know simple geometrical shapes by sight if vision were suddenly restored. Presumably, the congenitally blind individual would be familiar with common geometrical shapes such as a cube and sphere. The problem concerned the person's ability to interpret visual sensations and *name* the shapes, that were previously known only to the sense of touch. To name the shapes correctly, the blind person would have to be able to relate visual impressions to previously acquired information through another sense. Locke argued that one needed prior sensory experience to be able to interpret visual input. Therefore, he answered Molyneux's question in the negative.

There have been a number of cases of the restoration of sight after surgical correction of congenital cataracts in adults. It is unfortunate that the many studies of the restoration of sight do not provide unequivocal answers to Molyneux's question. There is no doubt that people have visual sensations upon the restoration of vision. However, vision is not normal soon after cataract surgery because of an abnormal state of the eye. This makes it very difficult to generalize from the results of studies of the restoration of vision.

The number of such cases is limited, and surgeons generally attempt correction early in life. It can be difficult for psychologists or philosophers to gain access to these individuals immediately upon removal of bandages (the interested reader is referred to Gregory & Wallace, 1963, and Senden, 1932/1960).

Berkeley provided a radical answer to Molyneux's question. In his *New Theory of Vision*, Berkeley claimed (see Morgan, 1977, pp. 59–62) that the blind man could not possibly name a shape upon restoration of sight. Vision and touch hold nothing in common, according to Berkeley. Furthermore, Berkeley made the extraordinary claim that vision does not provide direct access to depth information. Senden (1932/1960) made the completely opposite, extreme assertion that touch can never allow an individual an adequate understanding of space.

An important component of the issue here is that vision and touch yield very different sensations. We have visual color experiences, but things feel hot, cold, sharp, hard, or rough. The seemingly different sensations produced by the senses can lead one to believe that the two senses give us very different information about the world. Thomas Reid and Gibson (Gibson, 1962, 1966), tried to resolve this problem by asserting that while sensations differ, percepts can be amodal and can transcend sensory input. Thus, in 1817, Reid suggested that the blind person can know perspective, geometry, and other aspects of space (Morgan, 1977, p. 113).

Where does this leave the blind individual, who is limited to the sense of touch? If we assume that vision and touch yield very different information about the world, we might doubt the ability of blind people to understand space. This conclusion is likely if we are skeptical about the ability of touch to provide information about spatial layout. This sort of attitude toward the sense of touch may reflect an argument from introspection. The sighted often notice that they generate visual images when touching objects in the dark. It is then a short step to the assumption that the generation of visual images is necessary for adequate form perception (see Katz, 1989; Revesz, 1950). After all, visual images can aid memory in the sighted, and have been tied to spatial cognition in general. We will return to this issue once again in a later section in this chapter.

RECENT HISTORY

Many contemporary thinkers have been influenced by Revesz (1950), who believed that both vision and touch can give us information about spatial relationships. He asserted, however, that touch was rather limited in its ability to provide detailed spatial features, and tends to focus on the gross structure of objects. Furthermore, Revesz believed that the sighted normally tend to translate tactile impressions into visual images when feeling shapes. He called this process "optification." While Revesz believed that congenitally blind people can know space, he had to believe they were diminished in spatial skills when compared with the sighted. Moreover, Revesz was extremely skeptical about the spatial and aesthetic ability of congenitally blind persons. He claimed, for example, that bas-relief sculpture is meaningless for the congenitally blind, since haptics requires sculpture in the round. In addition (p. 186), "the blind subject . . . is unable to perceive, still less execute, the overlappings or the subtle transitions from one plane to another, activities which are entirely dependent on a visual check." This did not prevent some congenitally blind individuals from engaging in remarkable creative activity. Revesz's book includes illustrations of a number of interesting sculptures produced by blind people (pp. 218–222, 226).

A rather influential study on the blind was reported by Worchel (1951). Worchel's experiments are frequently cited, and warrant discussion despite some flaws in research design. Worchel tried to compare the sighted and blind in form identification, pattern perception, and spatial cognition. The aim of the study was the examination of the role of visual experience and visual imagery. Worchel used subjects who varied in age from 8 to 21, with a mean age of under 15. He blindfolded all of his subjects, and first exposed them to simple shapes. He asked them to name the shapes and draw them with paper and pencil. Subsequently, subjects were exposed to a haptic recognition test. Finally, subjects were walked through two legs of a triangular path, and were asked to find their way back to the origin via the third leg, that is, they couldn't retrace their steps. An additional experiment involved giving subjects two parts of a form, and required them to imagine the complete configuration. Briefly put, the congenitally blind participants were poor at drawing or naming shapes, were inferior to the sighted and late blind subjects in the form construction problems, but did as well as the other subjects in the recognition task. The congenitally blind subjects also did not do as well as the other subjects in the mobility task. Worchel concluded that visual imagery is valuable for the solution of difficult spatial problems.

These experiments have had the unfortunate effect of leading psychologists to underestimate the spatial abilities of blind people. There are alternative explanations to the visual imagery notion advanced by Worchel. Many of his congenitally blind subjects were rather young, and there may be a lag in haptic apprehension of space (Piaget & Inhelder, 1956). Thus, the congenitally blind child may eventually reach the same level of spatial reasoning as the sighted child, but may simply take longer. It is also hard to generalize about defects in spatial cognition from the results of experiments involving drawing with a paper and pencil, since blind children are rarely taught to draw. Furthermore, the education of the blind individual may not be identical to that of the sighted child, especially since Worchel's subjects were raised in an institutional environment. It will be interesting to see what experimental data emerge after years of educational mainstreaming.

CURRENT ISSUES

Theoretical controversy still lingers in the realm of research on perception in blind people. Many of these issues are similar to those that confront researchers in vision. In the context of the study of tactile perception of the blind individual, however, the data have had clear implications for the status and education of blind persons.

Visual Imagery and Representation in the Blind

Do blind persons perceive objects and spatial relations in a deficient manner because they may lack visual imagery? What is the nature of their imagery? Are visual images necessary for some types of spatial understanding? A number of researchers have wondered about the impact of visual experience on tactual perception.

Spatial Frames of Reference and Blind People

Some researchers have argued that visual experience may aid sighted and late blind people because it helps them develop an appreciation for spatial frames of reference. Warren believes that visual experience is critical while children learn to walk (Warren, 1974). Thus, sight may help one understand the horizontal and vertical, which can impact upon tactual perception and spatial cognition. This is an alternative to the visual imagery position.

Developmental Issues

Some of these concerns are covered at greater length in other chapters in the present book (see Bushnell & Boudreau; Millar). However, touch may lag behind sight in the development of sighted children. Therefore, it may be a mistake to assume that the congenitally blind individual never reaches a "proper" understanding of space because some blind children do not perform as well as sighted ones. Studies show a 3-year lag in academic performance between the blind and sighted child (Hatwell, 1985). We shouldn't underestimate the spatial skills of the blind adult based on data from children. This has been a methodological problem because some studies have included data from children in order to obtain a larger sample (e.g., Worchel, 1951).

Intersensory Equivalence and Spatial Relations

Researchers have wondered if tactual knowledge of shape and spatial relations is identical to information acquired via the visual modality. How does one accomplish a translation across the modalities, namely acquire a visual understanding of something that has been touched? This issue is relevant to blind individuals, since they must develop an understanding of space through touch. If movement is an essential link between the senses in the sighted, one might expect that movement may be an important cue to spatial reasoning in blind people.

Jones (1975) has argued that a history of movement deprivation in blind individuals may limit their understanding of space. This is especially likely if, as commonly occurs, blind children are overprotected by their parents. Because sight often warns the individual of impending danger, the blind person suffers greater risk of injury, and may have lived in a more restrictive environment. This occurs with great frequency in institutional settings. On this view, spatial cognition in the blind individual could develop under appropriate circumstances. Any individual deficiencies may have accrued from limited experiences that were imposed on the person by society, that is, by parents or caregivers. An overprotective environment can therefore lead the blind person to develop feelings of inadequacy. Moreover, if overly restricted, the blind child may not develop certain skills that are needed in life. The obvious question: How does one learn to get around, if not permitted freedom to explore the environment? This question is sometimes ignored by those who determine the living conditions of blind individuals.

CURRENT EXPERIMENTAL EVIDENCE

There is a large body of research that has compared performance of congenitally blind subjects with sighted and later blind individuals. Congenitally blind persons have never seen, and an examination of tactual perception in these individuals will allow an evaluation of the impact of visual imagery and visual experience on tactual perception. Researchers have generally supposed that perception in later blind people has been influenced by visual experience, and that they retain visual imagery. Furthermore, one can examine the nature of tactual perception in a "pure" form in the congenitally blind person. These studies have been concerned with tactual perception of texture, form, complex spatial relations, memory, and pictures. The following discussion is not intended to be comprehensive, but will summarize some of the major findings.

Texture

Both vision and touch are highly accurate in making judgments of the roughness or smoothness of surfaces (Heller, 1982, 1989a; Lederman & Abbott, 1981).
Furthermore, congenitally blind subjects performed as well as the sighted
and late blind subjects in making judgments about the smoothness of surfaces (Heller, 1989a). These experiments suggested that visual imagery and
visual experience are not necessary for tactual texture judgments.

It is entirely possible that there are circumstances in which touch may provide more reliable information about texture than vision. It is therefore unlikely that people will code visually, if touch were sufficient, or even superi-
or to sight in judging relative smoothness. This is clearly the case for the car-
penter who feels a tool edge to determine whether it is sharp enough. A very
dull edge will reflect light. However, the visual sense is not adequate to discriminate a razor-sharp edge from one that is just not dull. Moreover, one
is often unable to make judgments about the smoothness of a wooden or metal surface through sight, but the sense of touch can provide this information.
Experimental verification of the superiority of touch for making judgments
about exceptionally smooth surfaces was reported by the present author
(Heller, 1989a). Separate groups of subjects had to examine pairs of Japanese
sharpening stones with the sense of touch or with sight. Performance was
superior for touch, but only for the smoothest surfaces where vision functioned at a chance level.

The superiority of touch for texture judgments suggests that blind people
need not suffer in this regard. They can know surface texture at least as well
as the sighted. There are some forms of texture that they are unfamiliar with,
namely optical textures determined by color or brightness variation. Blind
people, however, are well able to perceive textures that result from variation in surface characteristics.

Form and Pattern Perception

A large body of research has been concerned with the influence of visual
imagery and visual experience on form perception. Implicit in this work is
the assumption by some researchers that touch is inadequate for detection
of some types of configurations. Touch has a smaller "field of view" than
sight. Furthermore, tactile input is often spread out over time. In most cases,
vision will allow us to comprehend form in a much shorter time span. Thus,
one might think that it would be difficult for touch to gain an appreciation
of a large pattern (Lederman, Klatzky, Chataway, & Summers, 1990). As Juurmaa (1973) has pointed out, vision is often required to scan a scene sequentially, especially when the scene is large. This is the case, for example, when

one is close to a large building and attempts to get an idea of its overall form. We can therefore think of at least some of the difference between vision and touch as more quantitative than qualitative. Since blind people depend very heavily on the sense of touch, this problem about the sequential nature of input is important for the generation of expectations about their abilities. An important consequence of the sequential nature of tactile input is that some patterns can place a large burden upon memory.

Small patterns are no problem for early or late blind people, and they perform more efficiently than the sighted when restricted to the sense of touch (Heller, 1989a, 1989b; Heller & Kennedy, 1990). When shapes are smaller than the fingertip, the sighted are no more accurate than congenitally blind subjects (Heller, 1989a, 1989b), and may be substantially slower than blind individuals. Furthermore, congenitally blind subjects may be better than the sighted at making judgments of curvature (Davidson, 1972). It is likely that when forms are unfamiliar to the sighted, visual imagery may be largely irrelevant. Visual imagery effects in earlier research have often been linked to increased familiarity with patterns. We should remember that some shapes are more frequently encountered by the sighted than the totally blind person. For example, an individual without light perception is unlikely to spend much time feeling a flag. The shape of a flag is constantly changing as it flaps in the wind, and the colored patterns on the surface of the flag are not tangible.

Pictures, Maps, and the Blind

Can blind people make sense out of pictures and maps? There is little doubt that they can, and that visual imagery is not *necessary* for the understanding or production of pictures (Kennedy, 1982, 1983). This topic will be covered at greater length in later chapters, and so I will touch on the topic of pictures only briefly.

An alternative view is that vision and touch are not equally suitable for two-dimensional pattern recognition. Lederman and Klatzky (1987; Klatzky, Lederman, & Metzger, 1985) have claimed that touch is expert at object recognition given "normal," three-dimensional objects (see Revesz, 1950). They found that sighted, blindfolded observers are highly accurate when asked to identify common, familiar objects by touch alone. A deficiency in this skill is often used by neurologists to diagnose parietal damage, since it may be lost in the case of damage to one side of the brain. The affected individual may show normal tactual skills in the hand on the same side as the damaged cortex, because of contralateral projection (Critchley, 1971). Lederman et al. claimed that touch is only at a disadvantage when people are asked to try to interpret two-dimensional configurations such as tactile pictures with the sense of touch. They are good with solid, familiar objects because those objects vary in substance related qualities, namely thermal attributes, texture, and hardness or softness. Most people are highly skilled at the use of the sense of touch for judgments of texture (Heller, 1982, 1989a) and other substance-related properties of objects (Lederman & Klatzky, 1987). Thus, the argument boils down to the notion that substance-related properties (hardness, texture, thermal characteristics) are ecologically valid for touch, but pictures are not.

Tangible pictures may be difficult, according to Lederman, in part because of the differential spatial acuity of the finger and eye (e.g., see Loomis, 1990). Lederman and Klatzky (Lederman, 1990, personal communication) do not argue that it is impossible for people to make sense out of tactile pictures, only that the process is likely to suffer in comparison with vision. Moreover, structural information (as in contour) will be extracted slowly and sequentially by touch, and will then show the effects of memory constraints. Lederman suggests that it might be possible to improve tangible displays via the addition of textural information, variation in the third dimension, and with instruction.

I recently completed a study of picture perception in the blind that emphasizes the importance of cognitive processes for perception and identification of tangible pictures. This study (Heller, 1989b) compared sighted controls, early, and late blind subjects in identification of raised-line drawings. The raised-line drawings were produced with a Swedish kit on textured plastic material. A raised line is produced when a ballpoint pen is pressed and drawn over the surface. The pictures were simple line drawings of common objects, such as an umbrella, hanger, person, smiling face, battery, cane, and so on. No information was given about the size of the depicted objects, or their categorical status. After subjects attempted identification without feedback, they were told the set of names of the objects (but the names were never paired with the pictures). They then attempted to identify the pictures a second time. No time limits were imposed, and observers were encouraged to guess if uncertain. The sighted and early blind performed at a very similar level. The late blind subjects were much better than the other subjects, with more than 80% correct after the set of names was provided. It was significant that the congenitally blind subjects showed dramatic improvement after the set of labels was given. Some of the pictures were initially easy for all groups of subjects, and some were very difficult.

This study indicates that blind people are certainly capable of making sense out of pictures (also see Millar, 1975). Clearly, this conclusion is inconsistent with the theoretical viewpoint expressed by Lederman and Klatzky. How are we to understand the superiority of the late blind participants? It seems unlikely that their advantage derived solely from visual imagery, since the sighted did not do any better than the congenitally blind subjects. A more likely explanation is that the late blind subjects had better tactile skills than the sighted, and far greater familiarity with the rules governing the production of pictures than the early blind subjects. Such an explanation is likely, given the superior speed of blind subjects in pattern identification.

A number of the subjects were asked to produce drawings after completion of the picture naming task. Figs. 10.1 and 10.2 show spontaneous raised-line drawings generated by blind subjects in their first attempts at making tactile pictures. Fig. 10.3 shows raised-line copies of simple forms by congenitally blind subjects. It is probable that practice will lead to improvement in drawing skill. Furthermore, it should be pointed out that a number of congenitally blind subjects demonstrated the ability to copy their initials with the raised-line drawing kit upon the first try. This was noteworthy, since these older blind persons had never previously learned to write print or script letters; their education was limited to braille.

It should be remembered that the blind subjects in this study were unfamiliar with picture perception or production. They were raised in an environment lacking in pictures, because of the assumption of their teachers (and book publishers) that pictures are simply not suitable for the sense of touch. We should keep in mind that sighted children are exposed to pictures in infancy, and this may well alter how they think about things. It is possible that early familiarity with a modality may alter later performance. Blind persons are often very good with braille. Some blind persons read braille at high rates of speed, and the braille code consists of two-dimensional patterns (see Foulke, this volume). It is not unusual to find reports of braille reading speeds of more than 150 wpm for better readers (Foulke, this volume).

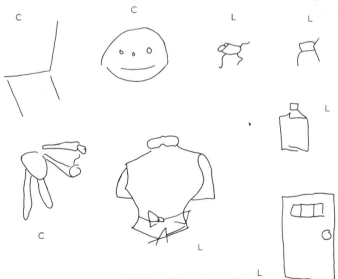

FIG. 10.1.   Raised-line drawings produced by congenitally blind (C) and late blind (L) subjects. The bottom, left drawing is a dog, as is the animal in the top line.

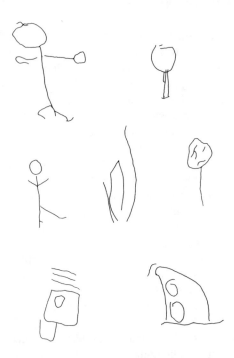

FIG. 10.2.   Raised-line drawings by congenitally blind subjects. The top-right drawing is a key. The middle row shows a stick figure, an abstract representation, and a flower. The bottom row shows a "boxing ring" and a "cloud with raindrops."

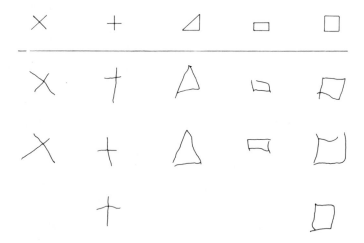

FIG. 10.3.   The top row shows models, while the bottom illustrates raised-line drawings, all by congenitally blind subjects.

Spatial Relations and Mobility

Can blind people understand complex spatial relationships? There is no simple answer to this question. Millar (1981) has suggested that blind children will tend to code egocentrically, and use a body-centered frame of reference. Thus, one might wonder if the congenitally blind adult could adopt the point of view of another person in a tactile analogue of the Piagetian three-mountain task. Piaget asked children to view three mountains and then imagine how the scene looks to people in different positions. Young children are egocentric and fail to take the point of view of the other person, when tested with photographs. Heller and Kennedy wondered if the blind person, especially the congenitally blind individual, could go beyond egocentrism and take a number of perspectives (Heller & Kennedy, 1990). Our response measure involved the use of raised-line drawings. One might think the three-mountain task would be a problem if space can only be known visually. For example, this seems implicit in Piaget's description of the child's understanding of a straight line, the demonstration of which is dependent on the use of a method of sighting (Piaget & Inhelder, 1956).

Sighted controls, early and late blind subjects were exposed to a simple, three-dimensional array (see Fig. 10.4). The sighted subjects were blindfolded, of course. Subjects were first asked to name the shapes (cube, sphere, and cone) after feeling them. Many subjects, both sighted and blind, did not name some of them correctly. The subjects were then asked to draw top and side views of each shape with the same Swedish Raised-line Drawing Kit that was described in the section on tactile pictures (see Figs. 10.5 and 10.6 for some examples). Subsequently, the subjects were asked to feel front and side view raised-line drawings and asked to identify them. Then, subjects were asked to draw a bird's eye view, and a frontal-side view of the array (Fig. 10.7). The subjects were then asked to anticipate side views, as the array would appear to someone sitting on their right, opposite them (Fig. 10.8), and on their left. Finally, subjects were shown the five drawings and asked to identify the point of view of the perceiver (i.e., the person who drew the picture).

The sighted subjects did not appear to have any advantage when denied vision. The congenitally blind subjects showed good performance both in the identification task and in drawing. In fact, a couple of subjects found drawing easier (and had better scores) than when interpreting someone else's drawings. Thus, the experimental evidence indicates the utility of drawing to assess spatial cognition in blind people.

Congenitally blind people are certainly capable of very sophisticated spatial judgments. If they run into difficulty in spatial mobility tasks, that may occur if heavy loads are placed on memory, or a task is speeded. Rieser, Guth, and Hill (1986), for example, reported that congenitally blind persons may

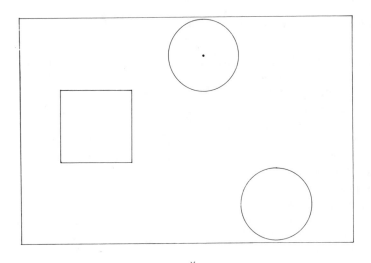

X

FIG. 10.4. The top view of the three shapes in the perspective task.

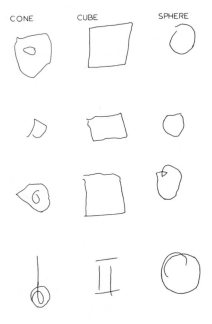

CONE   CUBE   SPHERE

FIG. 10.5. Raised-line drawings of the three solid geometrical shapes by congenitally blind subjects.

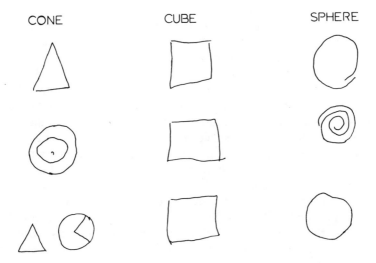

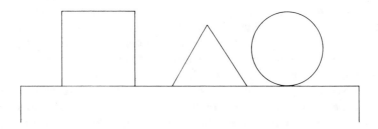

FIG. 10.6. Raised-line drawings of the solid geometrical shapes by late blind individuals.

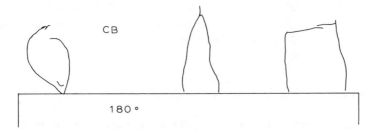

FIG. 10.7. Frontal-side view of the array of three shapes.

CB

180°

FIG. 10.8. Raised-line drawing of the array of three shapes, side view, 180 degrees, by a congenitally blind subject.

have difficulty in spatial perspective taking. It should be pointed out that Rieser loaded memory by requiring his sample of congenitally blind subjects to recall the locations of a large number of objects in a large (room-sized) space. Therefore, differences between the sighted and blind people in spatial reasoning may be quantitative and memory-dependent, rather than qualitative. The congenitally blind subjects in the Heller and Kennedy perspective task took twice as long as the sighted and late blind participants. It appears that the congenitally blind individual may be capable of the same type of reasoning (as reflected in perspective taking) as the sighted, but may simply function more slowly. It is not known, however, how much improvement could be expected with practice and training. It is reasonable to expect that practice in the representation of space with drawings would improve the efficiency of early blind people. Merry and Merry (1933) found that blind subjects showed great improvement in drawing skills with instruction. More recently, Craig (1988) has reported substantial improvement in pattern identification and gap detection through practice with the Optacon.

In small-scale (tabletop) space, the blind individual may perform as well as the sighted under some circumstances (Hollins & Kelley, 1988). These authors told subjects to examine objects from one location, walk to a new location, and then indicate the position of the objects from the new location. The blind subjects did well when replacement was used as an index of spatial knowledge, but they showed lower performance with pointing. Furthermore, blind individuals may be more accurate than blindfolded sighted persons in judgments of the vertical and horizontal when the body is tilted (Bitterman & Worchel, 1953). Other researchers have shown that spatial performance of the blind child may suffer when it depends on orientation to a reference point (Dodds & Carter, 1983). Most recently, Klatzky, Loomis, Golledge, Fujita, and Pellegrino (1990) studied navigation tasks similar to Worchel's (1951), but failed to find any differences between sighted, congenitally blind, and late blind subjects. These results suggest that task demands can alter the experimental outcome. It is clearly premature to try to draw sweeping generalizations about deficiencies in blind people and the necessity of visual experience from these data.

Skilled Performance and Art in the Blind

We should not forget that the educated blind person is capable of fine perceptual performance with the sense of touch. There are a number of detailed accounts of skilled perception in blind people (see Diderot, in Morgan, 1977; Keller, 1905; Villey, 1930).

A number of blind people are interested in art and study at museums. For example, blind individuals study art history at the Whitney Museum in New York. An organization called "Art Education for the Blind" is dedicated to the development of methods for the communication of art history to blind people. Elisabeth Salzhauer-Axel and a number of dedicated colleagues have developed two- and three-dimensional models, and raised-line drawings, for the illustration of artistic and architectural principles. They try to translate paintings into bas-relief format, and use textural variation to indicate color. Many blind people are interested in understanding and making art. They are able to make good use of the sense of touch for feedback while engaged in production of raised-line drawings, sculpture, and mixed media (see Kenney, 1983; Revesz, 1950). Paul Re (1983) has shown his raised-line drawings throughout the country, and currently has a traveling art exhibition.

REPRESENTATION: IMAGERY AND MEMORY

A fundamental theoretical problem for philosophy and all fields of psychology concerns the nature of representation. Do we think about the world in terms of images? Does the modality through which we obtain this information matter? This is a problem for memory researchers as well as those interested in spatial representation. Visual images may help one remember lists of concrete nouns (Paivio, 1971). In addition, it can be important to imagine objects interacting. Research on blind subjects permits the researcher to examine the nature of coding without the opportunity for vision.

Memory

Early blind people can learn to identify numerals printed on their palms (Heller, 1989c). This is hardly surprising, since the deaf-blind are taught, with varying success, to read words printed on the palm. However, the early blind participants had difficulty identifying numbers when they were tilted, or when they were drawn rather rapidly in sequences. While one might be tempted to conclude that this deficiency was the result of a lack of visual imagery, there are other possible explanations. Early blind subjects were simply less familiar with numbers, and may have had difficulty generating any sort of "image." Juurmaa (1967, 1973) found that when unfamiliar forms were used, early blind subjects did as well as the sighted and late blind subjects.

If one loads memory sufficiently, it is sometimes possible to demonstrate lower performance by early blind people. De Beni and Cornoldi (1988) found that early blind subjects were inferior only in the retention of multiple, interactive images. That is, recall of blind subjects suffered when they were required to recall pairs or triplets of nouns. A rather interesting finding emerged in the aforementioned study: Namely, all subjects showed improvement when high imagery nouns were used. Also, imagery instructions have been shown to aid congenitally blind people by other researchers (Jonides, Kahn, & Rozin, 1975). This suggests that imagery effects need not depend on vision (Zimler & Keenan, 1983).

Other researchers, however, have demonstrated superior retention of shape information by blind subjects, compared with the sighted under conditions of high memory demand (Davidson, Barnes, & Mullen, 1974). Again, it is inappropriate to argue that the sighted are superior to congenitally blind people in memory tasks, since they may not be. Davidson et al. suggested that blind people may perform better than the sighted when a task depends on skilled haptic performance. Whether sighted or blind subjects perform better in a retention task may depend on differential prior experience, memory demands, and familiarity.

Mental Rotation and Imagery

How does one verify the existence of an image and its importance for cognition? Images may exist, but do they necessarily have an impact on memory or perception? It is not enough just to ask people to introspect, since they may not describe their psychological states accurately. Do blind people have images? Are their images like those of the sighted? What are the implications of a lack of visual experience for imagery?

In vision research, one can try to verify the impact of imagery by asking subjects to engage in a timed task. The effect of imagery is inferred if it takes longer to engage in pattern recognition if stimuli are tilted, and if the magnitude of tilt determines the amount of time they require for their judgments. Several researchers have demonstrated mental rotation effects in congenitally blind subjects (Dodds, 1983; Hollins, 1986; Marmor & Zaback, 1976). These studies indicate that mental rotation does not depend on visual imagery. Furthermore, congenitally blind and sighted people show mirror reversals when the letters "p" and "q" are drawn on the forehead (Shimojo, Sasaki, Parsons, & Torii, 1989). Thus, if one does not identify the point of view that should be adopted, people all tend to adopt an egocentric perspective, and name a "q" when a "p" is drawn. It is almost "as if they are looking out" from the center of their heads. This occurs in both sighted and congenitally blind subjects, and is therefore not visually determined. There appears to be a normal tendency, especially under ambiguous circumstances, to adopt this body-centered frame of reference (see Millar, 1981).

If sighted persons make use of images, so do blind people (Kerr, 1983; Zimler & Keenan, 1983). Frankly, we have no greater justification for questioning the imagery of blind persons than the sighted. It is often difficult, however, to know how to interpret comments made by blind people, because they tend to use "visual" words. This tendency to use a visual language makes it hard to know how to interpret a blind person's assertion that he can imagine, for example, a chair. We can't readily know how visual images differ from other sorts of images, or even if they do. One would expect that there are some characteristics of visual imagery that may not occur in tactile images, such as color or perhaps shadow. Furthermore, we should remember that visual images can contain tactile and kinesthetic components.

"SUBJECT" PROBLEMS IN RESEARCH
WITH BLIND PEOPLE

Individual Differences

There are large individual differences among blind individuals, just as there are among the sighted. As with the sighted, some visually impaired persons have lower levels of skill in specific areas. After all, that is why we have different scales in intelligence tests. According to Villey (1930), there are some blind individuals who have very poor spatial skills because of educational deficiencies. These people are not typical of blind people, since according to Villey, they:

> [D]o not know how to use their limbs. They are frequently incapable of getting any exact ideas after feeling the various objects given to them. Their movements are not guided by any aim or object. Their fingers seem almost lifeless. Qualities of roughness or smoothness seem to interest them sometimes. The form of the object does not interest them. (p. 228)

The presence of tremendous variability in samples of blind individuals imposes a severe problem for researchers in this area. There are few congenitally blind people, and those with no additional medical burden are rare. This makes it difficult to conduct normal "experiments" that depend on random sampling. In addition, there are many articles published with extremely small samples. It is very hard to know if these subjects are truly representative of congenitally blind people. Lower average performance in a group of congenitally blind participants may simply mean that some subjects failed at a task, while the others did well. We should be extremely cautious about making any generalizations about the necessity of visual imagery or visual experience given the heterogeneity of blind subjects. For example, some RLF (retinal damage due to prematurity) subjects have good spatial skills, while some do not (see Hatwell, 1985; Heller, 1989a, 1989b, 1989c). It would be a real mistake to generalize about all RLF individuals based on the performance of a very few. Researchers in this area should always provide detailed subject information because of subject variability (see Warren, 1984).

SIGHTED AND BLIND PEOPLE DIFFER IN EDUCATION
AND FAMILIARITY WITH THE USE OF THE SKIN
FOR PATTERN PERCEPTION

Blind and sighted people have been educated very differently. Early blind individuals are far more experienced in the use of the skin for pattern perception. They are likely to be skilled braille readers. It is not surprising that late blind people have often performed better than the sighted in a number of tasks. They have the advantage of increased tactile skills (in small-scale space, as on a tabletop) that they hold in common with early blind people. In addition, they have the advantage of visual experience.

Society too often holds distorted expectations about blind people. Thus, the blind

> [W]ere often credited with supernatural powers. Even in present-day England most people interpret the techniques of the blind in terms of some mysterious sixth sense. . . .It is a strange perversity that people that credit the blind in general with these miraculous powers often treat the blind individually as the most pathetically helpless of mortals. (Wilson, 1948, p. 218)

Unfortunately, we have been too slow to overcome these unreasonable attitudes.

Some blind people have been limited by excessively low expectations by society. Prior to my conducting any of my experiments, I have often had occasion to speak to blind people about the research. Some of these individuals had preconceived notions about how my research would turn out. For example, it was not unusual to hear someone say, "I can tell you what will happen. The early blind will not do well. . ." This sort of bias has, unfortunately, been communicated by too many people to blind children. Communication of lower expectations has the unpleasant consequence of depressing the education and performance of the blind individual, whether adult or child. Psychologists and educators in this area need to be careful not to communicate their research predictions to their subjects, or their expectations will become a "self-fulfilling prophecy." The most careful researcher needs to be mindful that subjects may bring negative (or positive) expectations to their studies, and this may alter the outcome of experiments.

CONCLUSIONS

What should we conclude about the tactual and spatial capability of blind people? To begin with, we should be especially careful to distinguish tactual from general spatial skills. Clearly, many blind people are very skilled in the use of the sense of touch. They are able to outperform the sighted when stimuli are equally familiar, and the task entails skilled tactual performance.

Furthermore, when we ask about the potential of blind persons, we still do not have all of the answers. Potential needs to be distinguished from performance (Kimble, 1990; Millar, 1988). Blind people vary in their spatial and tactual skills. Some blind people do have difficulty with mobility, where a lack of visual experience may sometimes slow down the development of complex spatial coordinate systems. However, these are empirical questions (see Millar, 1988), and shouldn't be decided without sufficient evidence. In many ways, it makes a lot more sense to ask what blind people can do with the sense of touch, rather than wonder about what they can't do.

Touch can certainly provide precise spatial information, but operates far more slowly than sight. This may sometimes burden memory when the individual explores his or her environment. Smaller spatial arrays, however, can be comprehended very well via touch. Congenitally blind persons are capable of engaging in perspective taking, and this may require a high level of spatial understanding. This suggests that congenitally blind people may have the same spatial potential as the sighted. The size of the spatial configuration may matter, with much larger arrays placing increasing burdens upon memory (Barber & Lederman, 1988). These tasks can be a special problem when time constraints are placed on performance. However, the sense of touch need not depend on visual experience, and blind individuals are often highly skilled in its use.

REFERENCES

Barber, P. O., & Lederman, S. J. (1988). Encoding direction in manipulatory space. *Journal of Visual Impairment and Blindness, 82*, 99–106.

Bitterman, M. E., & Worchel, P. (1953). The phenomenal vertical and horizontal in blind and sighted subjects. *American Journal of Psychology, 66*, 598–602.

Craig, J. C. (1988). The role of experience in tactual pattern perception: A preliminary report. *International Journal of Rehabilitation Research, 11*, 167–183.

Critchley, M. (1971). *The parietal lobes.* New York: Hafner.

Davidson, P. W. (1972). The role of exploratory activity in haptic perception: some issues, data, and hypotheses. *Research Bulletin of the American Foundation for the Blind, 24*, 21–27.

Davidson, P. W., Barnes, J. K., & Mullen, G. (1974). Differential effects of task memory demand on haptic matching of shape by blind and sighted humans. *Neuropsychologia, 12*, 395–397.

De Beni, R., & Cornoldi, C. (1988). Imagery limitations in totally congenitally blind subjects. *Journal of Experimental Psychology: Learning, Memory, & Cognition, 14*, 650–655.

Dodds, A. G. (1983). Mental rotation and visual imagery. *Journal of Visual Impairment and Blindness, 77*, 16–18.

Dodds, A. G., & Carter, D. D. C. (1983). Memory for movement in blind children: The role of previous visual experience. *Journal of Motor Behavior, 15*, 343–352.

Dunlea, A. (1989). *Vision and the emergence of meaning.* Cambridge, England: Cambridge University Press.

Gibson, J. J. (1962). Observations on active touch. *Psychological Review, 69,* 477–490.

Gibson, J. J. (1966). *The senses considered as perceptual systems.* Boston: Houghton Mifflin.

Gregory, R. L., & Wallace, J. G. (1963). *Recovery from early blindness: A case study.* (Experimental Society Monograph No. 2). Cambridge, England: Heffer.

Hatwell, Y. (1985). *Piagetian reasoning and the blind.* New York: American Foundation for the Blind.

Heller, M. A. (1982). Visual and tactual texture perception: Intersensory cooperation. *Perception & Psychophysics, 31,* 339–344.

Heller, M. A. (1989a). Texture perception in sighted and blind observers. *Perception & Psychophysics, 45,* 49–54.

Heller, M. A. (1989b). Picture and pattern perception in the sighted and blind: The advantage of the late blind. *Perception, 18,* 379–389.

Heller, M.A. (1989c). Tactile memory in sighted and blind observers: The influence of orientation and rate of presentation. *Perception, 18,* 121–133.

Heller, M. A., & Kennedy, J. M. (1990). Perspective taking, pictures and the blind. *Perception & Psychophysics, 48,* 459–466.

Hollins, M. (1986). Haptic mental rotation: More consistent in blind subjects? *Journal of Visual Impairment and Blindness, 80,* 950–952.

Hollins, M. (1989). *Understanding blindness.* Hillsdale, NJ: Lawrence Erlbaum Associates.

Hollins, M., & Kelley, E. K. (1988). Spatial updating in blind and sighted people. *Perception & Psychophysics, 43,* 380–388.

Jones, B. (1975). Spatial perception in the blind. *British Journal of Psychology, 66,* 461–472.

Jonides, J., Kahn, R., & Rozin, P. (1975). Imagery instructions improve memory in blind subjects. *Bulletin of the Psychonomic Society, 5,* 424–426.

Juurmaa, J. (1967). *Ability structure and loss of vision.* New York: American Foundation for the Blind.

Juurmaa, J. (1973). Transposition in mental spatial manipulation: A theoretical analysis. *American Foundation for the Blind Research Bulletin, 26,* 87–134.

Katz, D. (1989). *The world of touch.* (L. E. Krueger, Trans.). Hillsdale, NJ: Lawrence Erlbaum Associates.

Keller, H. (1905). *The story of my life.* (J. A. Macy, Ed.). New York: Grosset & Dunlap.

Kennedy, J. M. (1982). Haptic pictures. In W. Schiff & E. Foulke (Eds.), *Tactual perception.* New York: Cambridge University Press.

Kennedy, J. M. (1983). What can we learn about pictures from the blind? *American Scientist, 71,* 19–26.

Kenney, A. P. (1983). A range of vision: Museum accommodations for visually impaired people. *Journal of Visual Impairment and Blindness, 77,* 325–329.

Kerr, N. H. (1983). The role of vision in "visual imagery" experiments: Evidence from the congenitally blind. *Journal of Experimental Psychology: General, 112,* 265–277.

Kimble, G. A. (1990). Mother nature's bag of tricks is small. *Psychological Science, 1,* 36–41.

Klatzky, R. L., & Lederman, S. J., & Metzger, V. A. (1985). Identifying objects by touch: An expert system. *Perception & Psychophysics, 37,* 299–302.

Klatzky, R. L., Loomis, J., Golledge, R., Fujita, N., & Pellegrino, J. (1990). Navigation without vision by blind and sighted. Paper presented at the meetings of the Psychonomic Society, New Orleans, L.A., Nov. 16.

Lederman, S. J., & Abbott, S. G. (1981). Texture perception: Studies of intersensory organization using a discrepancy paradigm and visual vs. tactual psychophysics. *Journal of Experimental Psychology: Human Perception and Performance, 7,* 902–915.

Lederman, S. J., & Klatzky, R. L. (1987). Hand movements: A window into haptic object recognition. *Cognitive Psychology, 19,* 342–368.

Lederman, S. J., Klatzky, R. L., Chataway, C., & Summers, C. D. (1990). Visual mediation and the haptic recognition of two-dimensional pictures of common objects. *Perception & Psychophysics, 47*, 54–64.

Loomis, J. M. (1990). A model of character recognition and legibility. *Journal of Experimental Psychology: Human Perception and Performance, 16*, 106–120.

Marmor, G. S., & Zaback, L. A. (1976). Mental rotation by the blind: Does mental rotation depend on visual imagery? *Journal of Experimental Psychology: Human Perception and Performance, 2*, 515–521.

Merry, R. V., & Merry, F. K. (1933). The tactual recognition of embossed pictures by blind children. *Journal of Applied Psychology, 17*, 148–163.

Millar, S. (1975). Visual experience or translation rules? Drawing the human figure by blind and sighted children. *Perception, 4*, 363–371.

Millar, S. (1981). Self-referent and movement cues in coding spatial location by blind and sighted children. *Perception, 10*, 255–264.

Millar, S. (1988). Models of sensory deprivation: the nature/nurture dichotomy and spatial representation in the blind. *International Journal of Behavioral Development, 11*, 69–87.

Morgan, M. J. (1977). *Molyneux's question. Vision, touch and the philosophy of perception.* New York: Cambridge University Press.

Morse, A. R., Silberman, R., & Trief, E. (1987). Aging and visual impairment. *Journal of Visual Impairment and Blindness, 81*, 308–312.

Paivio, A. (1971). *Imagery and verbal processes.* New York: Holt, Rinehart, & Winston.

Piaget, J., & Inhelder, B. (1956). *The child's conception of space.* London: Routledge & Kegan Paul.

Re, P. (1983). On raised line basic shape embossings: Art for blind persons. *Journal of Visual Impairment and Blindness, 77*, 119–121.

Revesz, G. (1950). *The psychology and art of the blind.* London: Longmans Green.

Rieser, J. J., Guth, M. A., & Hill, E. W. (1986). Sensitivity to perspective structure while walking without vision. *Perception, 15*, 173–188.

Senden, M., von. (1932/1960). *Space and sight* (P. Heath, Trans.). Glencoe, IL: Free Press. (Originally published 1932)

Shimojo, S., Sasaki, M., Parsons, L. M., & Torii, S. (1989). Mirror reversal by blind subjects in cutaneous perception and motor production of letters and numbers. *Perception & Psychophysics, 45*, 145–152.

Villey, P. (1930). *The world of the blind.* New York: Macmillan.

Warren, D. H. (1974). Early vs. late vision: The role of early vision in spatial reference systems. *New Outlook for the Blind*, April, 157–162.

Warren, D. H. (1984). *Blindness and early childhood development.* New York: American Foundation for the Blind.

Wilson, J. F. (1948). Adjustments to blindness. *British Journal of Psychology, 38*, 218–226.

Worchel, P. (1951). Space perception and orientation in the blind. *Psychological Monographs, 65*, 1–28.

Zimler, J., & Keenan, J. M. (1983). Imagery in the congenitally blind: How visual are visual images? *Journal of Experimental Psychology: Learning, Memory, and Cognition, 9*, 269–282.

11

TACTILE PICTURES

John M. Kennedy
University of Toronto
Scarborough, Ontario

Paul Gabias
Okanagan College
Kelowna, British Columbia

Andrea Nicholls
McMaster University
Hamilton, Ontario

INTRODUCTION

Could a picture make sense to someone who has never seen, someone who has never had visual experience with pictures or with objects that are shown in the pictures? To appreciate how depiction might be intelligible to touch, we need to consider theory of depiction and theory of touch. Most of the psychological research on tactile pictures uses outline drawings, so special attention needs to be paid to the processes outline can evoke.

The claims we will entertain are as follows: Pictures are universals. They are available to vision and touch. Outline drawing in particular relies on perceptual affinities between line and abrupt change in relief, rather than purely visual matters such as shadows or color patches on a surface. Some line junctions may act in touch as they do in vision. Rules governing configurations of relief features are identical in principle in vision and touch, since both senses garner information across time about the same layout of surfaces. Differences between vision and touch in relief perception are more a matter of degree than of kind, each sense having its advantages and disadvantages. Communication of motion via pictures can include violation of configuration rules producing apt pictorial metaphors that make sense to both the blind and the sighted without training.

A convenient device for making tactile pictures is an inexpensive kit consisting of a board and plastic sheets, available for example from the Swedish organization for the blind (RPH–SYN, Tomtebodevagan 11, S–171 64, Solna, Sweden). The board has a face coated with rubber. When the user puts a plastic sheet on the board and writes on the sheet with a ballpoint pen, the result is a raised line. The line is raised on the side from which pressure is applied by the stylus. This means a blind person can write on the sheet and feel the drawing as it is being made.

Consider some drawings made by a blind person. Tracy had visual problems as an infant and has been totally blind since c.24 months as a result of an operation for retinal blastomas. She is now in her 20s. She has used a raised-line drawing kit on many occasions, out of self-interest. No one taught her to draw, she reports. The response that she obtained for her initiatives was largely from her parents. It was nondirective, and took the form of praise for any efforts she made. She reports making drawings, checking them against the referent she intended to draw, and then redrawing the object, making changes she devised until she was finished, so far as she was concerned.

In interviews with Kennedy, she made some drawings with referents he requested, and volunteered some drawings herself. Among the drawings she volunteered were ones of a horse, dog, and bird. Drawings requested by Kennedy included a man standing and a man lying down. The depictions are recognizable at a glance (Fig. 11.1).

FIG. 11.1. Drawings of a horse, dog and bird, man standing and man lying down. By Tracy, a totally blind woman, aged 28, blind since 24 months as a result of an operation required by cancers of the retina. The drawings were made with a raised-line drawing kit. The other drawings in this chapter made for or by blind persons were also made with a raised-line drawing kit.

FIG. 11.2. Tracy's drawing of a card folded in half. The wider rectangle represents the part of the card facing the observer. The thinner rectangle represents the part receding from the observer. Tracy said the "big part is [the] one in front." The smaller rectangle "is the slanted side because its further away from you. The horizontal lines are shorter, that's all. Otherwise it's supposed to be the same as this side."

Another referent she was asked to draw was a card folded in half, and set on end. This presents a rectangle, facing the observer, and a rectangle receding in depth. Tracy drew this as a thick rectangle for the part facing towards her, and a thin rectangle for the receding part (Fig. 11.2).

Another referent she was asked to draw was a cubic box and an L-shaped block in three arrangements. In one, the box was alongside the L, and both were at the near edge of a table in front of Tracy. In the second, the box was halfway across the table. In the third, the box was at the far side of the table. Tracy drew the L-shaped block the same size in each of her three pictures. The box she drew as a square, with three different sizes, getting smaller the farther away (see Fig. 11.3).

Kennedy (1974, 1980, 1982a, 1982b, 1983, 1985a, 1985b) has reported studies on blind children and adults in Canada, the United States, and Haiti drawing and interpreting raised-line pictures. Tracy is exceptionally proficient at drawing. Many sighted adults cannot draw as well. But she is not alone (Fig. 11.4). In every country in which blind people have been tested, rudiments of pictorial abilities in blind people have been uncovered. Millar (1975) reported blind children in the United Kingdom could draw human figures. Fukarai (1974) reports blind schoolchildren in Japan drawing schematic but understandable forms, often including more than one figure and postures indicating actions such as a person releasing a bird.

However, the abilities underlying picture comprehension are highly controversial. Are they spontaneous, as Tracy's account indicates? Is tuition necessary? If so, tactual depiction would become a matter of learning by rote rules that only truly belong in vision. Fig. 11.5 is a depiction of two surfaces, one hard and one soft, indicated by a texture of undulating lines and a texture of zigzag lines. The blind and the sighted concur that the wavy lines mean a soft surface and the zigzags indicate a hard surface (Gabias & Kennedy, 1986). Are texture, temperature, and compressibility the natural domain of touch, and are lines showing the relief layout of extended surfaces actually unsuitable for tactile perception? What aspects of pictures should transfer readily to depiction? Can a flat surface depict depth for touch?

Tracy's striking abilities raise profound questions. These questions have been given a great deal of discussion since the last handbook on touch (Schiff

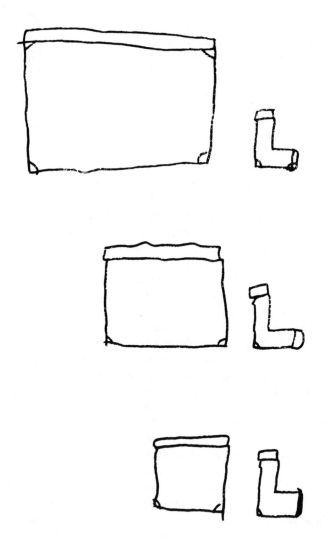

FIG. 11.3. An L-shaped object and a box, by Tracy. The large square represents the box close to the observer. The square gets smaller to represent an increase in its distance from the observer. Tracy said "I've drawn the box smaller because it's further away."

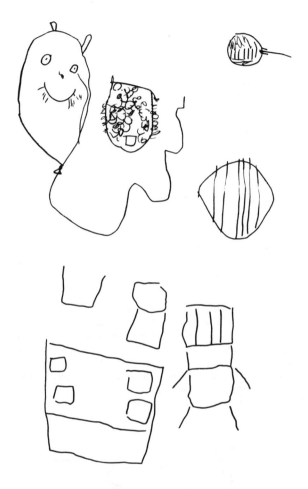

FIG. 11.4a. Drawings by blind people. The drawings include: A balloon with a cat face, on a long string (by a woman who has been totally blind since age 2). A glass of cold apple juice, with frosting around the outside, and an ice cube inside (by a girl of 13, congenitally totally blind). Two drawings of curved objects (by a man who has been totally blind since age 2). One is a balloon on a string. The convex curved front of the balloon is indicated by lines of different orientations. The other is a bowl, from above. Its concavity is indicated by lines becoming thinner to indicate parts that are farther away. Four drawings by a woman, congenitally totally blind. Two are drawings of a glass. One is a chair. The fourth is a chest of drawers.

FIG. 11.4b. Two drawings by a boy of 14, now totally blind, who had some form perception at birth, estimated at 2% of the vision in his best eye being intact. One drawing shows a man walking, indicated by the posture of the legs, shown pointing in the same direction. The second shows a tree on a windy day, leaves and twigs blowing in the wind, with clouds in the sky. Two more drawings by the man who has been totally blind since age 2 are a car, with exhaust smoke and an aerial, and a dog. The final picture is people standing in a circle (by a man, congenitally blind, with sensitivity to light but no form perception).

FIG. 11.5. Hard and soft. Blind and sighted adults find that the jagged texture indicates the hard substance, and the undulating texture indicates the soft substance.

& Foulke, 1982). We will review the debate here (for a short history of the scanty literature on haptic pictures prior to 1981, see Kennedy, 1982b).

The debate on the merits of tactile pictures has implications for many matters. For the first time, haptic pictures are now being advocated for use in education of the blind, including art education (Salzhauer-Axel, 1989). They also speak to matters in the philosophy of representation. They reflect on widespread assumptions about the role of vision in depiction. They provide new ways to investigate the development of drawing, and the child's mastery of systems of spatial projection.

We have much to cover. We shall begin with pictures per se. What kind of a thing is a picture, that Tracy could produce one?

PICTURES ARE UNIVERSALS

There are two principal theories of pictures: (1) Depiction is entirely conventional (Goodman, 1969; Steinberg, 1953; Wartofsky, 1984). (2) Depictions can be effective without any training in a convention (Kennedy, 1974; Gibson, 1979).

Certainly many aspects of pictures are conventional, for example, art styles, pragmatics of specific uses such as labels, and formats such as commemorative portraits of the last Duchess. But the extreme theory that pictures are as conventional as words is discomfited by evidence that novices, including people in nonpictorial cultures, recognize pictures. (Deregowski, 1989; Kennedy, 1989a; Kennedy & Ross, 1975). A child of 18 months untutored with pictures identified line drawings and photographs (Hochberg & Brooks, 1962). Kennedy and Silver (1974) found cave art in sites throughout the globe included recognizable outline drawings in every site. Infants of 5 to 7 months react appropriately to static pictorial cues to depth (Yonas & Owsley, 1987). Higher primates recognize objects in pictures (Cabe, 1980), as do pigeons (Cook, Wright, & Kendrick, 1987; Kendrick & Hardison, 1988).

Although pictures are universals, they may not be recognized instantly. Initially a picture may appear, as does the Shroud of Turin on first inspection, to be merely flat patches. In the case of an ambiguous picture, only one of the referents may be seen. However, the observer does not need to be taught to make sense of it, or to see the alternatives. Continued inspection alone is often sufficient for the picture to fall into place, or for the alternative referent to appear.

While pictures are universals, it is important to note that they are artificial universals. There are no reliable sources of outline drawings in nature. Pictures are not found in some zones in the world, providing a niche that humans evolved, over eons, learning to exploit. There is no evolutionary history whatsoever to picture use. Rather picture perception is a spin-off from an activity evolved to fit some other purpose. Picture perception is like Tang (an orange drink crystal), an offshoot from the Space Program, in being a by-product. Cave artists discovered that picture making and interpreting was a capacity in our brains, ready to be used. While it is true that picture making and recognition since the cave artists' discovery has been thought to be inherently visual, in our century we are in a position to show that vision is only one of the possible routes to picture comprehension. We still have to discover what psychological functions underlie pictures, and the crucial faculties may not be exclusive to vision. Furthermore, there is reason to suspect that purely visual matters, such as shadow patterns, cannot be depicted in outline.

VISUAL OUTLINE SHOWS WHAT IS TANGIBLE, NOT WHAT IS PURELY VISIBLE

One striking finding by Kennedy and Ross (1975) reporting on the Songe, a non-pictorial people living in Papua-New Guinea, asked to identify outline drawings of common objects, is that lines that the Songe failed to recognize reliably were ones that were surrogates for boundaries of color markings on surfaces. Likewise, cave art concentrates on lines showing boundaries of surfaces, not color markings on surfaces (Kennedy, 1983). This is all very odd to anyone who conjectures that what outline shows is the shapes of visible divisions, mimicking anything giving rise to the intensity changes at the eye and their geometrical distribution and organization (Hayes, 1988; Ratliff, 1971; cf. Marr, 1982, p. 37). Such divisions include color markings on surfaces, for example, half-moons on fingernails, hide-markings on zebras, black caps on chickadees. Many of these divisions are perfectly familiar to observers and quite specific to their objects. But outlines following their form do not allow observers to see the color divisions, while outlines following silhouette edges in depth allow novices like the Songe to perceive the depicted relief.

What relief features can outlines depict? Lines create impressions of change in slant or depth at borders of surfaces (Fig. 11.6). The change in slant is a corner (convex or concave). The change in depth is an occlusion (an occluding edge of a flat surface or an occluding boundary of a rounded surface). Occluding foreground surfaces depicted by lines or contours were called "figures" by Rubin (1915), with the change in depth to the background being to "ground" in Rubin's terms. Foreground and background are better labels since they indicate which surfaces are nearer to the vantage point of the observer. The line itself can depict a thin foreground surface, with background on either side of the line, like a wire suspended in front of a wall. The line can also have the appearance of a crack between two foreground surfaces.

The arrangements of foreground and background surfaces depicted by lines

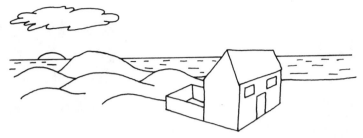

FIG. 11.6. Outline drawing showing relief features, that is, corners, occlusions, wires, and cracks.

are perfectly tangible. The issue that is suggested is this: Can lines act as surrogates for these arrangements in touch as well as vision?

Color change on a surface is not the only example of an inherently visual division. Other examples are shadow and highlights caused by illumination varying on the surface. We could say the "shading" in a black-and-white photograph mimics the reflectance and illumination variations on the surface. This shading can be called chiaroscuro, using Da Vinci's term. The chiaroscuro pattern in a picture can of course be copied in outline, but the evidence from the Songe suggests the outline will not evoke the same percepts of a scene. However, the Songe and cave art evidence is based on color change: Will the same failure of depiction be evident for illumination change? Consider black-and-white patchwork pictures of scenes with lots of shadows (Fig. 11.7). The positive versions of the pictures have white as illuminated regions, and black as regions in shadow. The negatives are reversed, though all the contours in the display are in exactly the same location. The outline versions replace each of the contours with a line, which physically is two contours close together. Vision can detect the structure of the scene in the positive, distinguishing the hollows from the hills and the margins of cast shadows from the terminators of attached shadows. The negative fares poorly (Cavanagh & Leclerc, 1989). But the outline is so poor that it fares worst of all (Kennedy, 1988a, 1989b; in preparation). Movies with outline chiaroscuro are also very poor in vision. Cavanagh and Anstis (personal communication), following discussions with Kennedy, prepared a movie with black-and-white patches with white regions showing illumination on moving objects (a face, shoe, model fly, and cube). We have prepared a negative version, in which the white regions show areas in shadow. An outline version, in which the lines replicated the contours of the movie's patches, was often unrecognizable, though the objects in the patchwork version were easily recognized. The outline version is even less recognizable than the negative version.

The evidence indicates chiaroscuro precedes outline depiction, that is shape-from-shading processing of static or moving arrays is completed before outline depiction arises in vision. This is a very powerful finding since outline, being made physically of black-and-white borders, must gain access

FIG. 11.7.   Positives, negatives and outlines. Each presents the structure of the
optic array from objects in illumination, with cast and attached shadows. The
outline drawings are even less amenable than the negatives to being processed
by the rules of shape-from-shading by vision. It is difficult in the outline figures
to make out the shapes of surfaces that vary in depth from the observer, if
there are no occluding edges. Examples include the eye regions and the mouth
regions in two of the figures here. Also, scission of a patch into foreground
and background regions is difficult in the outline figures. Examples include
fingers against the neck of a guitar, in the third figure here. Note that lines
are made of two contours, one of which replicates the contours of the positives. The other replicates the contours of the negatives.

to shape-from-shading processes. However, as Fig. 11.7 reveals, the percept
that results is a set of borders on a continuous surface, like a map of islands
in an archipelago. The chiaroscuro system of vision registers the brightness
differences in the picture as black marks on the picture surface (Fig. 11.8).
Once the black flat shapes are registered some extra feature that does not
play a role in brightness-difference processing can arise. As long as the feature is not a matter of brightness it cannot affect shape-from-shading. The
clearest case of this kind of feature is the axis of the line, defined as a
location—not a brightness border—midway between the two contours flank-
ing the line. At this stage in processing the visual system may also use the
contour of the line as a location rather than a brightness difference. The next
stage in perceptual processing may then use axes and contours, as locations
rather than matters of brightness, employing them as surrogates for surface
relief edges. As surrogates for boundaries of surfaces, they can activate the

Figure 8   Flow diagram of line depiction

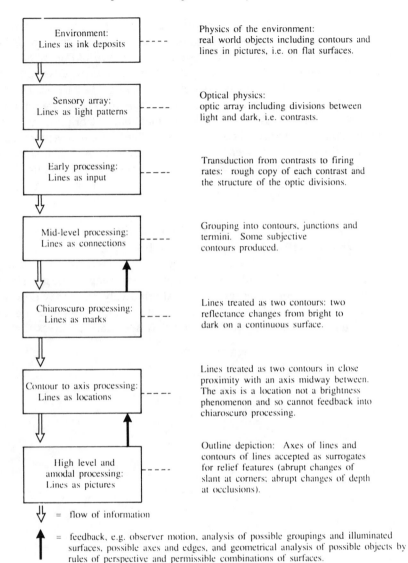

Environment: Lines as ink deposits	Physics of the environment: real world objects including contours and lines in pictures, i.e. on flat surfaces.
Sensory array: Lines as light patterns	Optical physics: optic array including divisions between light and dark, i.e. contrasts.
Early processing: Lines as input	Transduction from contrasts to firing rates: rough copy of each contrast and the structure of the optic divisions.
Mid-level processing: Lines as connections	Grouping into contours, junctions and termini. Some subjective contours produced.
Chiaroscuro processing: Lines as marks	Lines treated as two contours: two reflectance changes from bright to dark on a continuous surface.
Contour to axis processing: Lines as locations	Lines treated as two contours in close proximity with an axis midway between. The axis is a location not a brightness phenomenon and so cannot feedback into chiaroscuro processing.
High level and amodal processing: Lines as pictures	Outline depiction: Axes of lines and contours of lines accepted as surrogates for relief features (abrupt changes of slant at corners; abrupt changes of depth at occlusions).

= flow of information

= feedback, e.g. observer motion, analysis of possible groupings and illuminated
surfaces, possible axes and edges, and geometrical analysis of possible objects by
rules of perspective and permissible combinations of surfaces.

FIG. 11.8.   Flow diagram of line depiction in vision. Shape-from-shading processing
(or chiaroscuro) is complete before outline depiction occurs. Therefore outline drawing is not like high-contrast pictures. It cannot replicate successfully the chiaroscuro
patterns that give rise to apparent relief in directional illumination (Fig. 11.7). The
shape-from-shading component of vision registers outlines as black and white marks
on a continuous surface, like a map of islands. In the next stage, features used in outline depiction, such as axes of lines, are invoked. These features are independent of
brightness since they are processed as locations. Axes and contours, processed as locations, can be surrogates for abrupt change in surface relief. They are assessed by
an amodal geometry of surfaces with edges, available to touch as well as vision.

perceptual system's geometry for surfaces with edges. The surrogates and the geometry are independent of brightness matters, and so they can be amodal, available to touch as well as vision (the last step in Fig. 11.8).

In sum, pictures involving strongly directional illumination are difficult to decipher when they are traced as outline drawings. We hypothesize that chiaroscuro processing is complete in the visual pathways before outline picture analysis is undertaken. Outline uses location, not brightness.

In this conception of perception's use of outline, outline depiction depends on local brightness differences being used to define other local features such as axes of lines that are not brightness features. Accordingly, let us consider some important local features.

OUTLINE ACCESSES EDGES OF SURFACES, NOT JUST COMPLETE OBJECT SHAPES

Outline pictures might be interpreted by processes using whole gestalts, possible object shapes or coherent scenes. Alternatively, they may depend on local features such as edges and indicators of overlap. Presumably, both local and global factors are involved, but it is necessary to stress that local

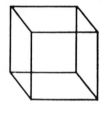

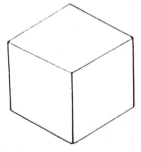

FIG. 11.9.   A wire cube and a solid opaque cube shown in outline. The picture of the wire cube uses contours of lines as boundaries of wires. Each contour stands for an occluding bound of a rounded surface. To depict corners, the picture of the opaque cube uses the axes of lines. These lie midway between the contours.

features are important, and to determine whether the kinds of local features outline uses in vision make sense to touch.

Consider drawings of a wire cube and an opaque cube (Fig. 11.9). The lines are depictions of long wires, occluding edges and convex corners. The Y-junctions made of three lines show the wires and convex corners meeting at the cube's apices. In the wire-cube drawing, X-junctions made of four lines show how one line occludes another. When lines depict wires, the lines act as foreground with background on either side. The contours of the line depict the occluding boundaries of the wire. In contrast, lines showing convex corners do not use their contours directly (cf. Kennedy, 1974, p. 144). Rather, the contours define the axis of the line, midway between the contours. It is the axis of the line that shows the locus of the convex corner. That is, the locus of the axis is seen as the locus of the change of slant between two surfaces. A Y-junction can appear as three wires, their contours defining the occluding boundaries of the wire. Or it can appear as the apex of a cube, where three surfaces meet. Where the three axes of the limbs of the Y meet is the apex.

An X-junction can induce extra contour. When it shows occlusion with one bar overlapping another, the top bar has its contours completed subjectively and the lower bar appears to extend underneath the subjective contours. That is, a slight break in the physical contours showing the top bar is filled in by extensions of the real contours on either side (Fig. 11.10). These extensions follow the direction of the inducing contour, as is common with subjective contours (Kennedy, 1988b).

An X-junction is two T-junctions back to back. When a T depicts a foreground surface occluding an edge of a background surface, the stem is subjectively separated from the crossbar. If the lines forming the T are thick enough, it is possible to discern that a subjective contour cuts off the stem of the T. The subjective contour can be impeded by replacing the contour defining the T with thin lines (Fig. 11.11). The lines have L-shapes at the junctions. The overall T-shape is still present in the display, but the local change usually keeps the stem from being cut off and the T appears to be all in one plane. The appearance of overlap is lost. In a complex outlined scene, shown by thick lines, replacing all the contours by lines has the striking effect (similar to presenting the display in equiluminance) of producing flatness at the junctions (Fig. 11.12). While apparent overlap is absent at the T- and X-junctions, foreground and background percepts are maintained alongside stretches of contour.

Do any foreground and background percepts arise in touch in connection with flat displays? Can a tactile line function as a foreground surface or as the axis of a depicted shape? While it seems possible that foreground, background and axis percepts could be engendered by lines, it is hardly credible that percepts that depend on subjective contours could be present in touch,

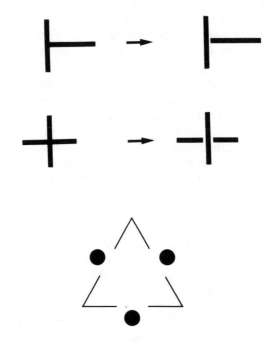

FIG. 11.10. A schematic indication of the result when overlap is seen at T-
and X-junctions of thick bars. The occluding bar has its contours completed
by purely subjective contours. The subjective contours are continuations of
real contours. The subjective contours cut off the occluded bar. This perceptual scission allows the occluded bar to be seen continuing under the occluding
bar. The third figure is a subjective contour display, wherein a subjective visual
division joins inducing elements. In the third figure, the black line inducers
often appear to be occluded by a subjective contour. The black circles usually
appear to lie on top of the subjective figure.

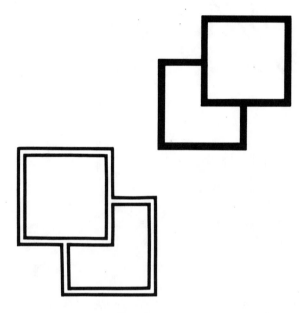

FIG. 11.11. Perceptual scission at T-junctions is impeded by turning the L-contours of the junctions into lines. The result looks flat. The local change at the junctions blocks the indication of overlap given by the whole form. If there is no perceptual scission at line junctions in touch, this may impede tactual perception of overlap in tactile pictures.

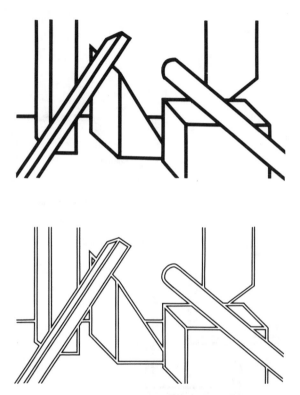

FIG. 11.12. A complex scene, with many examples of occlusion, is readily seen in the outline drawing. Each thick line is bounded by two contours. When the contours are replaced by thin lines, occlusion at the T-junctions is impeded. Note that in both versions of the display, the stretches of line between the junctions readily show foreground and background surfaces, with a step in depth between the surfaces.

except in the sense that touch takes samples of an edge to indicate a continuous edge. Research on these questions is in its infancy, but there are a few positive notes.

Kennedy (1980, 1982b, 1985b) reports blind people making outline drawings. His volunteers used lines for edges of objects, X-junctions for thin foreground objects occluding others (Fig. 8.6, p. 276, 1980; Fig. 4, p. 29, 1985b), T-junctions for a foreground surface occluding an object's edge (Fig. 8.7, p. 276, 1980) and Y-junctions for an apex of a cube (Fig. 9.8, p. 324, 1982b). However, no study aimed specifically at the perceptual effects of line junctions in touch has been attempted. Also, the features in the drawings occurred in the context of familiar shapes. Fujita (1989) studied foreground and background effects in touch directly, with real edges, and unfamiliar shapes, by using flat surfaces resembling jigsaw puzzle pieces laid on top of a flat surface. Subjects felt a flat surface with a zigzag edge, like a miniature mesa and a cliff edge, raised above the background flat surface. Then they were given the mirror-image mesa. This was the identical shape left–right reversed, like a pair of twins in profile facing each other. They were also given the patrix of the original mesa, a shape like a jigsaw puzzle piece that would have fitted with the original. It had concavities where the original had convexities. Subjects had little trouble recognizing the mirror image mesa had the same shape as the original, but they failed frequently to recognize the patrix had the same shape. The only change from the original to the patrix is in what is foreground and what is background. Evidently, as Rubin (1915) found in vision using pictorial stimuli, foreground–background impressions can control recognition in touch.

Rubin (1915) commented that closed line forms are generally seen as objects not holes. Kennedy and Campbell (1976) used tactile line forms resembling amoeba. The task for subjects was to recognize via touch flat solid objects, or holes in a flat surface, having the same shape as the amoeba. Subjects transferred from the line forms to the solid objects better than they did to the holes.

Wake, Shimuzu and Wake (1980) presented blindfolded, adventitiously blind and congenitally blind adults with simple raised-line patterns suggesting a square overlapping another square (like Fig. 11.11) a triangle overlapping a triangle, and so on. They also presented drawings of cubes, cylinders, and staircases in parallel projection. Unlike the sighted and adventitiously blind, who unanimously reported the patterns showed overlap, no congenitally blind person reported overlap or depth, the authors suggest. However, blind subjects did describe the overlapped forms as incomplete versions of complete forms, for example, "one square and another square with absence of left-bottom corner, both in the same plane." It would have been interesting to follow up these reports of incompleteness, to describe at least one of the overlap cases or parallel projection pictures as showing depth, and then to test whether the other displays were immediately interpretable in this manner. Evidently, this interpretation did not occur spontaneously to the congenitally blind. But what would the perceptual results be if blind subjects attempted this interpretation? Also, it is not clear what the demand characteristics of Wake's instructions were. We have not found unanimity in response from blindfolded undergraduate subjects, given tactile forms such as those of Wake et al. and nondirective instructions to describe the figures. About one-half of the subjects spontaneously report overlap after nondirective instructions.

Kennedy and Domander (1984) tested blind children on outline drawings resembling profiles. Each line could depict a profile facing left or facing right (Fig. 11.13). That is, it could be taken to depict foreground on either side.

FIG. 11.13. A profile shown by a line. The line can depict a face looking to
the left. In this case, the foreground surface is on the right of the line and the
background is on the left. The line can also depict a face looking to the right,
with the foreground on the left of the line. Raised lines like this were interpreted by blind children as faces looking to the left or the right. Switching the interpretation affected recognition of the raised-line display.

Kennedy and Domander asked their subjects to try to interpret the profiles
in this way. The results were that recognition of the line display was severely reduced by switching the depiction from foreground on the left to foreground on the right. Rubin (1915) reported the same effect in vision and attributed it to perceptual effects of foreground and background generated by
the line; there may be similar effects in touch.

Kennedy and Domander (1986a) tested lines standing as axes of human
figures with blind adults (Fig. 11.14). The task was to assign meanings to the
postures of the figures in a forced-choice task. The blind adults were slightly
more successful than blindfolded subjects, and comparable with sighted subjects inspecting the displays visually. The displays used by Kennedy and
Domander used an oval for the head, a single line for the body and a line
for the foot, no more. One pair of figures involved an X-junction showing
overlap. This provided no difficulty. It appears from the Fujita and Kennedy
studies that foreground and background effects may arise in touch from flat
displays, using simple lines or jigsaw-puzzle shapes without any need for extensive details. The Wake et al. study and our follow-up indicate the effects
may not arise sometimes without suitable suggestions. If some devices can
enable the line depicting a foreground edge at a T-junction to be tactually
distinct from the stem of the T, they would be especially significant. The crossbar could be more elevated, or be rougher, or have a different serrated pro-

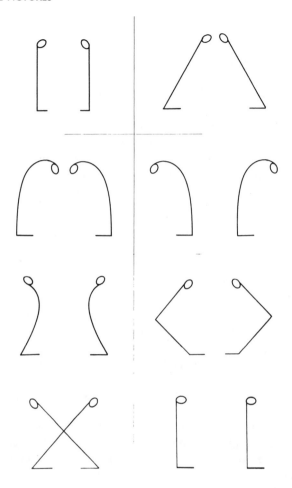

FIG. 11.14.   Schematic people shown as "twig figs." These are more abbreviated
than traditional stick-figure drawings of people. Blind people identified the drawings as pairs of people engaged in various scenarios. From top left: People talking, angry, old, sad, proud, polite, walking past each other, walking in single file.

file. These might trigger a tactile version of vision's ability to separate subjectively the crossbar and the stem, and apparent overlap might ensue.

THEORY OF TOUCH AND DEPICTION

Some theories of touch are quite pessimistic about the utility of tactile pictures. Others anticipate that some principles of visual pictures fit well with
"haptics," the principles of touch. We will describe three major contemporary

views, their implications for haptic use of pictures, and some studies bearing on the implications. The three views emphasize touch as contact, touch as procedures, and touch as distal or environmental.

Dunlea (1989) is the most recent of a line of commentators arguing that tactual perception requires direct contact with the object. Taken literally, this eliminates from touch the use of everyday tools, such as forks to test vegetables to see if they are cooked. This definition leads Dunlea to contend that many objects are inevitably inaccessible to touch. She mentions distant objects, large objects that "cannot be perceived in full (mountains, rivers and large buildings)" (p. 10), fragile objects, and minute objects. Dunlea believes touch is unlike vision in that vision alone allows summation of simultaneous spatial layout independent of time without struggling with information retrieval. She offers the thesis that the nonvisual senses have difficulty synthesizing a coherent sense of the environment and the observer's position in it. Dunlea's position has much in common with Revesz (1950) and Senden (1932/1960).

While it is true that touch always uses contact of some kind, it will not do to restrict tactile perception to momentary pressures. Touch uses patterns of pressures across time. But what kinds of patterns? If touch was a sense of immediate contact, and could not achieve a clear impression of simultaneous spatial layout, haptic pictures would be virtually impossible. Information about simultaneous layout is what they deliver. Further, if large and tiny objects were inevitably accessible to touch, one of the major uses of pictures would be lost, since we often use drawings to indicate what we know about such objects at a convenient scale. However, Dunlea leaves open the possibility that her definition of touch is too restrictive. She thinks, following Kidwell and Greer (1973), that blind people have a process that "pulls together" all the available sensory information into a haptic representation. On the face of it, here is a Trojan horse for her definition. If touch can pool information then surely touch can be used across time to gain information about shape. Touch can use the limbs, the legs and feet to get impressions of stairs while the arms and hands gain information about the railing. This kind of "ambulatory" touch is like vision, gathering a spatial sense of simultaneous layout by activities taking place across time. Consider a table, its place in a room, the room's position in a corridor, the corridor's location in a house, the house's location on a street, and the street's hills and grades. These are all accessible to ambulatory touch, across time. In principle, all the kinds of relief are accessible to touch, across time. Also, there are tiny and fragile forms we can feel but not see, such as minor perturbations on a smooth surface and strands of spiderwebs without highlights. In texture perception, touch is superior to vision for fine textures (Heller, 1989a).

Dunlea supposes vision can perceive a large object, such as a river, in full. But in most circumstances no one ever perceives a river in full visually. We have to take time to explore it. The blind and the sighted alike walk along the river, and learn about the river's shape. It is only when we hike through mountains, whether we are blind or sighted, that we will learn across time about the mountain's shape "in full." While skillful use of touch varies enormously from person to person, much as skillful use of vision does, in principle, touch has available to it information about big and small objects. In sum, the notion that touch is restricted to immediate contact seems inappropriate. Indeed, blind people are reported making drawings of boats, bridges, doors, and castles (Kennedy, 1980) none of which could be perceived in full, tactually, in one moment. Likewise, Heller (1989b) found one of the most easily identified pictures, so far as his early blind subjects were concerned, was a drawing of a human figure (correct on 5 of 11 trails in unconstrained identification, and 9 of 11 trails after 12 options were given). Other comparatively large objects Heller depicted successfully were a telephone, hanger, umbrella, and cane (5, 8, 6, and 9 identifications respectively when the 12 options were given.)

Klatzky and Lederman (1987; see also Lederman & Klatzky, 1987; Lederman, Klatzky, Chataway, & Summers, 1990) are very dubious about the value of haptic pictures. They argue touch relies heavily, though not exclusively, on "exploratory procedures." These are purposeful hand motions each one tuned to particular properties of objects. The procedures include running a finger along an edge to determine its shape, squeezing an object to establish its softness, and resting a finger on an object to discover its temperature. The observer is said to emphasize information about substance (hardness, thermal properties, and texture) when sorting objects. Pictures typically eliminate variation in substances. They provide planar shapes, all made of one substance. In many instances they also require careful attention to local contour segments, integrating them into a longer form. When the haptic system is forced to extract information sequentially, performance is poor, these theorists claim. To the extent that pictures rely on properties indicated in an optic array, such as linear perspective and occlusion, the haptic system will fail to make sense of the medium of pictures, they contend.

The Klatzky and Lederman thesis has much to commend it. It is likely that subjects can use distinctive properties of objects, such as the eraser at the end of a pencil, which has softness as well as shape to distinguish it from the other end. Furthermore, it is impossible to distinguish softness without pressure of some kind. That is, some exploratory procedures are *necessary* conditions for obtaining information. However, given suitable objects, a variety of motions can be used, and haptics can employ each of them. Touch is not dependent on invariant relationships between percepts and exploratory procedures. Touch can discover the shape of the torso inside a long-haired furry object by squeezing it lightly, using palpation (Katz, 1925). A static hand can discover the softness of an object that falls on it or pushes against it.

Touch can discern the temperature of an object via a hand held near the object, or while rubbing the object or squeezing it. To discover the consistency of a fluid, we can run our fingers through it, or have the liquid pouring through our passive fingers. Simultaneously we will discover its temperature. To feel a wave at the surface of a liquid, the normal way to act is passively, feeling the wave wash over us, the water level rising and falling. Touch can use hard tools to discern distal softness, and vice versa. The tool can tell us about the texture of the object at the far end of the the tool. Further, a table is a table whether it is made of plastic, wood, or glass. Shape is often quite independent of the material from which it is made. In short, Klatzky and Lederman's exploratory procedures do not cover the range of ways that touch operates.

Like Dunlea, Lederman and Klatzky conclude that the sequential examination of a display is difficult for touch, while the entire visual array is available in one view. This is a false dichotomy. Vision may assess an array more quickly than touch, but the process still takes time and it is never true that one view suffices to take in an entire optic array. The impression that vision delivers of a detailed and nonblurry scene is a product of many glances, and most of each glance except the central 2^0 is always ill-defined or out of focus. That is, vision relies on information available across a sequential examination just as touch does. Vision has become fast at taking in sequential information. There is no reason, in theory, why touch cannot do so too.Touch certainly improves in braille reading and in decoding vibrations indicating speech. Though touch may never fully equal vision's prowess, the key question is whether there are some matters that are spatial and pictorial but available to touch, through not being inherently visual. Likewise, music is certainly an auditory medium, but there are usable rhythms and distinctive octave relations in vibratory touch, even in the congenitally deaf (Kennedy, 1989b).

Are linear perspective and occlusion "visual"? Both of these are matters of direction. Linear perspective governs the angle subtended or "projected" by an extended object as it recedes from the observer's vantage point. If we try to point to the object's top and bottom or left and right side as it recedes, the pointing arm will traverse a smaller angle when the object is 20 feet away that when it is 5 feet away. This fact of direction is evident in pointing tasks undertaken by young and adult blind subjects (Kennedy, 1982b, 1983; Kennedy & Campbell, 1985). Blind adults occasionally make use of linear perspective in drawing pictures, using convergence or narrowing of sides to show a slanted surface (Kennedy, 1983). Occlusion depends on one object edge being in front of another object's surface in a given direction. Occlusion was present in Heller's (1989b) raised-line pictures of a telephone, scissors, and umbrella (recognized by 5, 4, and 6 blind observers out of 11, after being given a list of 12 objects). Kennedy and Fox (1977) also obtained recognition by 15 blind subjects of some pictures with occlusion, though at a low rate (12%). The rate at which the subjects identified pictures without occlusion— "imprints" in Kennedy and Fox's terms—was the same (12%). Loomis, Klatzky, and Lederman (1988) achieved recognition rates of 40–50% for tactile pictures, with blindfolded observers using both "narrow" (one finger pad, on the index finger) and "wide" (two finger pads, index, and middle fingers) methods of exploration. All of the 24 pictures except 1 involved T- or X-junctions, and hence decisions about possible occlusions. When vision was restricted to a small aperture, moved gradually and sequentially over the picture lines, visual rates of identification and response times were virtually identical to those in touch. Vision improves rapidly when given a wider field of view. For our purposes, the chief implication is that blindfolded subjects (and hence the late blind) can achieve considerable success with raised-line drawings when some involve occluding junctions.

Lederman et al. present evidence on seven blind observers identifying raised-line pictures of 2-D objects (e.g., comb) and 3-D objects (e.g., whistle), according to whether there were perspective cues or internal lines depicting edges. Interestingly, like Kennedy and Fox, they report identical recognition rates for the 2-D referents and the 3-D referents (10%). The absolute rates of identification are comparable with Kennedy and Fox (12%; 1977) and Heller 9%; 1989b) in a study on the congenitally blind. (Heller found the adventitiously blind scored 36%). Like Kennedy and Fox (1977), Lederman et al. found the sighted subjects identifying at a higher rate (30%; Kennedy & Fox, 27%). This is only to be expected since sighted people are highly familiar with pictures. The absolute identification rates are a matter of stimulus selection and criteria for accuracy in a particular study. High rates can be obtained for pictures of items such as a car, spectacles, boot, banana, telephone receiver, hand, pear, leaf, and knife. Further, context aids recognition dramatically. Kennedy (1980) found in a story context, simple pictures were almost always identified correctly by the blind (perfectly in 39 out of 41 stories, each with four or more illustrations). Lederman et al.'s results from the seven blind observers are therefore in line with reports from others, and offer some encouragement to the hypothesis that raised-line drawings employing perspective and internal occluding edges may be recognizable at a rate comparable with drawings showing 2-D referents. The low rates of identification need not be taken to be the maximum possible rate.

Occlusion of one object by another occurs as a result of the observer's vantage point: In drawing and identifying stick figures, blind subjects show some understanding of the configuration that results (Kennedy, 1980; Kennedy & Domander, 1986a), as we noted earlier in considering line junctions. Most blind adults and teen-agers acknowledge how individual shapes and arrangements of several shapes are affected by the vantage point being used in a drawing. They spontaneously report that an object is shown from above or from the side and realize what is hidden behind the side that is shown. In a variation of Piaget's three-mountains task, Heller and Kennedy (1989) used drawings of three objects. The objects are in a fixed arrangement, and can be drawn from various vantage points. Blind adults were asked to identify the vantage point from which the scene was drawn and to produce drawings using five different vantage points. The blind adults performed on a par with sighted subjects, and were superior to 14-year-old sighted subjects undertaking the drawing task visually. The only significant difference between congenitally blind, late blind, and blindfolded adults was that the congenitally blind required more time to respond. Notions such as convergence and occlusion are problems for sighted children drawing, not just for blind people.We suggest that they pose the same problems to the blind, and in coping with these problems the blind employ the same principles as the sighted. Both the blind and the sighted are trying to capture the same phenomenon: the direction of objects from a vantage point. This phenomenon governs touch as well as vision. We speculate that many blind people spontaneously think of pictures as showing the *shapes* of objects, not their *directions*. Sighted people have the same misconception. Once attention is drawn to the difference, many aspects of pictures that are initially puzzling may become clear to blind people. Much the same can be said about sighted people making drawings. They master perspective very slowly and often very imperfectly unless they are tutored. Sighted people often reject correct perspective drawings, and accept incorrect perspective drawings (Kubovy, 1986). We should not conclude that vision does not use vantage points, occlusion, and linear perspective because sighted subjects use these phenomena imperfectly in pictures, and the same holds for touch and the blind. It seems likely that the phenomena are ever-present in the normal environment, but only some aspects are readily translated into pictures. Which aspects, for which modalities, is at present disputable.

The definition of touch as a sense of immediate contact and exploratory procedures contrasts with a third conception of touch stressing the use of touch in an environment (Kennedy, 1982b, in press; Kennedy, Gabias, & Pierantoni, 1990).

In this third conception, touch discerns resistance (and temperature) varying across space *and time* and solves this as an equation with two roots: environmental relief (distal as well as proximal), and observer action. The relevant relief occurs at a wide range of scales, but always involves substances varying in hardness, offering surface layout with respect to a vantage point. The relevant action occurs in a variety of ways, so the distribution of resistance and the relief shape that is discerned are perceptually independent of any particular action that makes them known. Although there may be a favored action or best action, another can substitute. Passive touch can be equal or superior to active touch (Heller, 1989a; Magee & Kennedy,1980). A given object and its activities are tangible in many ways: A train can be felt directly, can transmit vibrations through the rails and platform, can provide a wind of passage, be encountered via a tool such as a long cane, and can radiate heat, or block off a cold wind. A rectangle is the same form, whether it is tiny and held in the palm, or large and grasped by both hands, or huge and needs to be walked around. The rules for joining surfaces are the same at all levels of scale. A form can be approached and examined from the side, or any other vantage point, whether it is tiny or huge. There is no preset time limit over which tactual exploration takes place. The layout that is perceived as simultaneously present is the distal surface layout in the environment. That is if the order of surfaces in the environment is 1 2 3 4 5 6 7 8 9, and touch meets first 23, then 567, then 12, 34, and then 789, the observer apprehends the distal array 1 2 3 4 5 6 7 8 9, not 2 3 5 6 7 1 2 3 4 7 8 9. The observer detects the *continuity* of 1 through 9 without ever needing to apprehend 1 through 9 in full as a unit (contra Dunlea) or needing to *image* 1 through 9 sequentially or simultaneously in his or her mind (contra Klatzky and Lederman). The information that something is complete is obtained without needing to perceive it completely all at once, or in sequential order. "Resistance" information, not acting actively or passively, is the basis of touch.

In this theory of distal touch in a large environment, the kinds of objects that can be discerned are sophisticated. As touch occurs across time, it makes known to the observer the actions of other objects including creatures. Patterns of actions distinguish inanimate objects from animate ones, ones with intentions from ones without, and ones that are reacting to the observer from ones that are unaware of the observer. That is, touch is concerned with communication, and types of objects, including ones revealing intention. In part, the fact that touch reveals knowledge of a vantage point, and another person's vantage points, is a basis for communication.

In this view of environmental touch, the domain for touch involves the geographical scale, the biological world, and indicators of mental states. In principle, it covers the same domain as vision. However, each sense has areas in which it is more acute, despite the fact that each sense uses the same principles as the others. Touch is better at detecting temperature, though vision can distinguish clear extremes, such as red hot and ice cold. Touch can also discriminate finer textures. Substance qualities such as rigidity and heat conductivity are better discerned by touch within some ranges. Touch can distinguish surface qualities such as stickiness and wetness better than vision; for example, snakes that are warm and dry can look clammy and moist. The viscosity of a muddy road is often discerned better by driving over it than by looking at it.

The environment of touch is governed by the same layout principles as vision. This has strong implications for tactile pictures. The sighted use a variety of projections to create pictures of an array. The use of these projections varies considerably in drawing development. These projections should be intelligible to the blind, if they arise in coping with the principles governing the layout that is in common to vision and touch. Also, the sighted use violations of correct shape to indicate metaphorically what cannot be depicted literally. The blind and the sighted understand the shapes of objects in much the same way, according to the theory of distal touch we are describing here. Hence, errors should be obvious to the blind as well as the sighted. Further, what appears to be an apt error to the sighted should also be apt to the blind. If so, pictorial metaphor could indicate the same to the blind as to the sighted. Accordingly, let us turn to some evidence on tactile pictures using a variety of projections, and to tactile pictures using a variety of shape transformations metaphorically.

PROJECTIONS OF AN OBJECT

As sighted children develop they draw using different projective systems (Caron-Pargue, 1985; Kennedy, in preparation; Willats, 1981). Kennedy (1983, 1984, 1985a) suggests that the blind make use of these projective systems, and proceed through the same developmental sequence. The hypothetical sequence is as follows: The earliest kind of drawing is a mark that represents a referent by fiat. Later, children draw using a mark that has a congruent shape to some aspect of the referent. At this stage, children may use several marks with shapes relevant to the referent, but they may not connect the marks. Later, the children make the marks connect to show how the parts of the object are joined. The drawing is a "folded out" version of the object. Later children restrict themselves to aspects of the object that face a vantage point. Later still, some aspects of projective convergence are used. In a less sophisticated version, squares are shown as rectangles, as though in parallel projection. In a more sophisticated version, convergence is used, as though in polar projection.

Gabias (1987) tested some implications of this developmental sequence with adult blind volunteers. In one study, blind adults were asked to judge two different *drawings* of a table, each one based on a different projection system. They were also asked to judge two different *descriptions* of a single drawing, each description based on a different projection technique. The first task involved a four-legged, square-topped table drawn as though folded out (a square, with two lines going up the page and two lines coming down) and also drawn from the side (a thin rectangle, with two lines coming down); see Fig. 11.15). Subjects were asked which drawing was likely to be drawn by an older person. The second task involved the table drawn like a star, as a rectangle with lines radiating symmetrically from the corners. This was described either as showing the symmetry of the table (folded out) or as show-

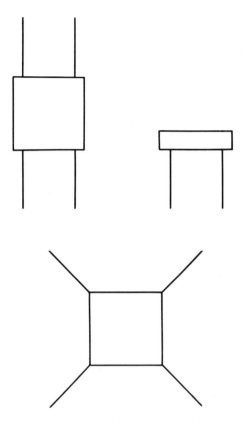

FIG. 11.15.   Drawings of tables. Drawings like these have been obtained from blind people. Blind adults were asked to determine which of the top two drawings would be more likely to be made by a younger person. One drawing shows the table as though it was folded out. The other shows a table from the side, and therefore uses a vantage point. The lower drawing shows a table in a star shape. Blind adults were given two different descriptions of the drawing. One described the table as though it were folded out. One used a vantage point, describing the table as drawn from underneath. The task was to judge which of the descriptions would be more likely to come from an older person. Accounts of the tables using vantage points were generally judged to indicate an older person was responsible for the drawing.

ing the table from underneath (vantage point). Again, subjects were asked which description would likely come from an older person. Eight of the congenitally blind volunteers consistently described the two drawings using a vantage point (from the side or underneath) as more likely to be from an older person. Only one consistently gave the opposite response ($p < .05$, with 6 ties).

Gabias's second study involved more projective systems, and a task in which subjects had to discern how different objects could be drawn using the same projective system. The "star" table was given, with the same description as before. Subjects were also given four drawings of a box. The foldout drawing used five squares (Fig. 11.16), which subjects were told showed the front of the box, the sides, the top, and the bottom. Another drawing showed two squares, described as the front and top of the box. Subjects were told only the parts "that face you" were shown. Another drawing showed a square topped by a thin rectangle. Subjects were told the top was drawn as a rectangle because the top "slants away from you." Another drawing showed two trapezoids, attached at the longest line. This line was said to represent the nearest edge of the cube, and the shorter sides parallel to the long line were said to represent edges farther away.

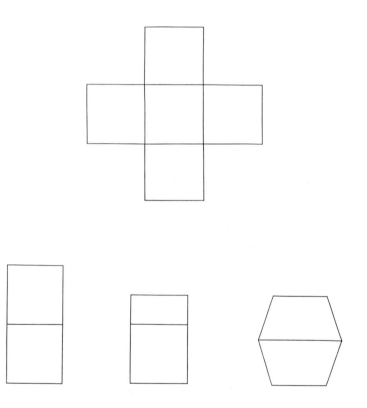

FIG. 11.16.   Four different ways of drawing a box. The five squares is a foldout drawing. The two squares show the sides that face the observer. The square and rectangle drawing shows the top by the rectangle, to indicate the top slants away from the observer. The two trapezoids indicate the nearest corner of the cube by the longest line.

Subjects were asked which drawing of the cube would most likely be drawn by someone who drew the star table and described it as drawn from underneath (vantage-point drawing). They were also asked to rank the other drawings of the cube as next most likely and least likely. They also were asked which drawing of the cube would most likely be drawn by someone who drew the star table and described it as drawn to show the symmetry (no vantage point).

Given the vantage-point description, the 24 congenitally blind volunteers ranked the cube drawings as follows: The two trapezoids drawing using convergence projection was most likely (rank 1.75), the square and rectangle using parallel projection was next most likely (2.4), then two squares (2.8) and finally the five-squares foldout system (3.0). Given the other description, the ranks reverse (the most likely is deemed to be the five-squares, rank 1.6; next the two squares, 2.3; next the square and rectangle, 2.8; and finally the two trapezoids, 3.3). Evidently, the blind volunteers distinguish the projection systems and recognize the relationships between the four. They can also tell which of the four is being used in a drawing of a different object. Further, the study with the table drawings indicates they may appreciate which drawing system is more juvenile and which is more advanced.

METAPHOR AND MOTION

Dent (1987), Kennedy (1982a, 1985c) and Kennedy and Simpson (1982) suggest pictures can involve metaphors. They offer pictorial examples of every kind of metaphor (e.g. allegory, hyperbole, personification, oxymoron). Consider drawing a picture of a bird swimming on a lake, with a wake stretching behind the bird. The wake is literal. If the wake is drawn behind a bird flying over the lake, to show the motion of the bird, it would be a metaphor. The transfer of apt properties to an inappropriate context is a basis for pictorial metaphors. Since blind people know about the true shape properties of objects, they may recognize pictorial anomalies as apt metaphors.

Kennedy and Domander (1986b) report blind adults making pictures of smelly garbage, a hammer hitting a table and making a loud noise, a hand in pain, a person shouting, and the wind. They found blind people deemed these referents to be impossible to depict in line drawings. That is, lines do not stand for the referents. This is an important judgment for the blind to make. It distinguishes relief from these referents, so far as naïve subjects are concerned. It indicates lines spontaneously stand for certain kinds of referents, but not others, in touch. Kennedy and Domander note that their volunteers indicated these referents could only be drawn *indirectly*. Hollins (1989) commented that lines are used rather indiscriminately by the blind for relief edges and intangible referents, and he argued outlines (and perspective) are visual conventions. In fact, blind adults are more selective than Hollins allows. They describe line drawings as suitable for some referents only. (Further, they appreciate and use some aspects of perspective).

Kennedy and Domander's 15 blind subjects volunteered a total of 185 devices for the five referents. The majority (121) of these devices showed the referents' context in a literal way, lines standing for edges. This shows that the blind people are judicious in their use of lines in pictures. Note that when the blind are asked to draw a chair they draw say a chair in profile (Heller, 1989b), not a chair's context, such as a table. But when they are asked to draw pain in a hand, they draw the hand, and demur about the pain. They resort to a context device, such as a pin pricking the hand, to suggest the pain.

Of the 185 devices, 40 were judged to be intended by the blind as metaphorical representations of the referent. Examples include an aura of pain around the hand, described as "an abstract" depiction and a shout shown by an especially thin line coming from the mouth of a person, using thinness to show the shout is "intangible." When each of the 40 devices was being drawn the blind person distinguished the use of line as unlike standard use of line, saying, for example, "I don't understand how you can draw something with no substance."

Kennedy and Gabias (1985) note that blind people drawing an object in motion may draw the object in an unrealistic fashion. For example, a wheel may be drawn with the hub off to one side to suggest that the hub is straining forward. The person making the drawing typically comments that the drawing is fanciful and imaginative. Similar comments have been made by blind people drawing a spinning wheel with curved spokes, or a single line of motion inside the circumference of the wheel, with no spokes shown.

If these devices are apt metaphors, they should be understood by blind and sighted observers. Kennedy and Gabias tested this conjecture with blind and sighted subjects. Five different drawings of wheels were given, each with distinctive spokes (Fig. 11.17). The lines of the spokes were curved, wavy, bent, dashed, and extended beyond the rim of the wheel. The 15 blind and 11 sighted volunteers rated the wheels according to how well they suggested a spinning motion. The blind and the sighted agreed on this ranking: Curved was best (rank 1.3) then bent, then wavy, then dashed, and finally extended (rank 4.5 for the blind and 4.7 for the sighted).

Other groups of blind and sighted subjects were asked to assign motion labels to the devices from a list of five choices. Eighteen blind and 18 sighted adults concurred in their interpretations. Curved means spinning, bent means jerky motion, wavy means wobbly motion, dashed means too fast to make out, and the extended lines mean brakes on.

FIG. 11.17. Five drawings of wheels in motion. The type of motion is indicated metaphorically by the shapes of the spokes. One of these is best for showing a wheel spinning, the blind and the sighted agree. The others show jerky motion, wobbly motion, motion too fast to make out, and a wheel with its brakes on, the blind and the sighted concur.

We speculate that some of the devices depend on a translation from temporal events to static patterns, a translation skill that is important and spontaneous for distal touch. The motion paths taken by a point on a steadily spinning wheel are curves. Similarly, jerky motion involves an abrupt change across time in speed or direction, like the bend across space in the bent spokes device. In wobbly motion, a wavy path or sinusoid is traced out over time.

The dashed spokes device is likely a translation from something perceived incompletely to a spoke drawn incompletely. The brakes on device is likely a matter of interpreting the five extensions of the spokes as brakes.

Kennedy, et al. (1990) tested a common device for translatory motion. Often, illustrators show a moving body by drawing rear profiles in a trail behind the body. The trail behind a ball resembles a line of C-shapes. Kennedy et al. drew the trail four times, once as evenly and densely packed Cs, once as evenly but widely spaced, once gradually becoming more densely packed the nearer the C-shapes were to the ball, and once gradually becoming more widely spaced the closer the C-shapes were to the ball. The majority (80%) of the blind and sighted adult volunteers agreed that the even dense Cs mean a speedy ball, even sparse Cs mean a slow ball, dense Cs close to the ball mean a ball accelerating, and widely separated Cs close to the ball mean a ball decelerating. Evidently, the represented speed varies in proportion to the density of the C-shapes. This is quite the opposite of stroboscopic pictures, we should note, so even the sighted adults (44 tested blindfolded, and 74 tested with a visual display) are not basing their interpretation on the one kind of common optical image that mechanically produces trails of profiles.

In sum, several studies find that devices present in static pictorial displays can be interpreted as kinds of motion by the blind and the sighted alike. Related devices are offered by blind people when asked to draw moving objects, or other referents deemed to be impossible to show in outline drawings by the blind. The blind describe these devices as imaginative and unrealistic. They distinguish them from use of lines to show relief edges. Kennedy and Domander note that, if asked, the blind themselves describe these devices as metaphorical. Since there is agreement among the blind and the sighted on the interpretation of these devices, they are not idiosyncratic. We suggest they are based on an understanding of the shape properties of objects that is common to the blind and the sighted. These devices are taken to be erroneous, as depictions of the object, but intentional. That is, they serve as communications, governed by intention, not just as replications of shape properties, for the blind and the sighted.

CONTENTIOUS ISSUES AND SPECULATION

Tactile pictures are a matter of controversy at present. Some commentators (e.g., Jansson, 1988) point to the length of time taken to explore a tactile picture, the low rates of identification in some studies and the inability of touch to discern as much detail in a picture as vision. Some argue that the use of lines to stand for relief features, including edges of objects, is necessarily indirect, consciously intellectualized, and very slow. They argue that when a display is examined line segment by line segment, any perceptual system, vision as well as touch, is slow.

We suggest there is considerable merit to these comments. It is not easy for novices to explore haptic pictures swiftly. However, much the same can be said for tactual exploration of unfamiliar objects, including small, irregular, three-dimensional solids (which some call "feelies") and visual exploration of pictures of objects from unfamiliar angles. Also, people from nonpictorial cultures are often slow to identify photographs on the first exposure to them. It is premature to conclude tactile pictures are not just slow at first but also inevitably slow. Further, the claim that tactile lines do not stand spontaneously for relief edges may be empirically false. Some blind people make line drawings as swiftly and competently as many sighted people, deploying the line to refer to the same features as sighted people. Like Warren (1984), Lederman et al. (1990) conclude "the blind can understand the medium of depiction in principle" (p. 63). It behooves researchers to find out how picture comprehension could be made more effective, as Millar (1975) pointed out, in reporting blind children can draw the human figure. Millar contends blind children have the same potential as sighted children.

We speculate that initially picture making is harder for novice sighted people than picture identification, but the reverse is true for the blind. Novice blind adults often make small, highly detailed drawings, too small to distinguish by touch, of referents such as bridges and airplanes that are too large to be discerned by a few hand contacts. We think this is because they intuitively understand the shape they wish to draw, and how to use lines for relief features. In making the drawing, they remain clearly aware of the shape they are producing and can guide the stylus appropriately, at a scale too small to be discerned by touch.

We also think that shape awareness of this kind may take considerable time and effort to develop, even in commerce with a real object. After some exposure to the real object, the result is, we suggest, detailed shape awareness. This is not an "image" of the shape all at once, but shape knowledge. It is a state like knowing you know the route home from work, which is not an image of the route "all at once." Likewise, we imagine that considerable commerce with a raised-line picture would lead to a detailed shape awareness. That is, the final product of exposure to the object and to the picture is not indirect or consciously intellectualized even if the process that got there was slow. We should not confuse the *process* and the *result*.

We also believe that when a class of objects has become familiar, exploration of a particular member of the class is relatively swift. If we know about tools, making out the details of a new screwdriver is swift: Is it a Phillip's head? A slot head? Is it sharp or worn? Is the grip rough or smooth? Is the shaft straight or bent? Short or long? Once we know the class, we know the relevant features to consider. Similarly, it may be expected that when tactile pictures are familiar, inspection of pictures of a well-known kind of object will be a swifter process. Blind children tested in Arizona (Kennedy, 1982b, in preparation) were proficient at tactile exploration, and identified tactile pictures at a rate exceeding blind children in Haiti, occasionally recognizing more than 50% of a sample of pictures. The Haitians could draw more effectively, possibly because manual skill in crafts and woodworking were stressed in their school.

We anticipate that tactile exploration of pictures, as it becomes more proficient, will allow larger chunks of the display to function as units, and to be grasped quickly. The role of junctions will become more evident. Ambiguities will be dispelled more rapidly. Alternatives will be sought more effectively and more quickly. Less time will be spent stuck on first impressions. In this connection, ultrasound pictures may be a helpful analogy. Initially these are incomprehensible to the sighted. To the expert, they reveal a great deal about the womb and the fetus within. Compare the line drawings replicating chiaroscuro structure in Fig. 11.7, which are mere ciphers as far as vision is concerned. No amount of experience, we predict, with outline versions of chiaroscuro structure will enable such displays to show vivid and comprehensible referents to human vision. They will never produce apparent shadow akin to the apparent depth in outlined relief. Outline depiction occurs, we contend, in perceptual pathways that are actuated after chiaroscuro has been analyzed and axes of lines registered. Like visual pictures, haptic pictures, the evidence indicates, are surrogates for relief. The question that demands a response is how extensive and comprehensive a pictorial facility can be built in touch on this foundation. In one sentence our response is: Form principles of depth and slant used by vision are also used by touch, and can stand on the foundation that lines depict relief corners and occlusions.

REFERENCES

Cabe, P. A. (1980). Picture perception in nonhuman subjects. In M. A. Hagen (Ed.), *The perception of pictures* (Vol. 2). New York: Academic Press.

Caron-Pargue, J. (1985). *Le dessin du cube chez l'enfant* [Children drawing cubes]. Berne, Switzerland, and New York: Peter Lang (European University Studies, Series 6, Vol. 166).

Cavanagh, P., & Leclerc, Y. G. (1989). Shape from shadows. *Journal of Experimental Psychology: Human Perception and Peformance, 15,* 3–27.

Cook, R. G., Wright, A. A., & Kendrick, D. F. (1987). *Determinants of categorization in pigeons.* Paper presented at the meeting of the Psychonomic Society, Seattle, Nov. 6–8.

Deregowski, J. B. (1989). Real space and represented space: Cross cultural perspectives. *Behavioral and Brain Sciences, 12,* 51–74.

Dent, C. (1987). Developmental studies of perception and metaphor: The twain shall meet. *Metaphor and Symbolic Activity, 2,* 53–72.

Dunlea, A. (1989). *Vision and the emergence of meaning.* Cambridge, England: Cambridge University Press.

Fukarai, S. (1974). *How can I make what I cannot see.* New York: Van Nostrand.

Fujita, N. (1989). *Left-right and foreground-background reversal in touch.* Paper presented at the preconference meeting on touch perception, Psychonomics Society, Atlanta, Nov. 16.

Gabias, P. (1987). *Drawing systems: Blind and sighed adults judge developmental priority.* Doctoral dissertation, New York University.

Gabias, P., & Kennedy, J. M. (1986). *Graphic texture indicates hardness to the blind.* Paper presented at a meeting of the Eastern Psychological Association, New York, April.

Gibson, J. J. (1979). *The ecological approach to visual perception.* Boston: Houghton Mifflin.

Goodman, N. (1969). *Languages of art.* Indianapolis: Bobbs-Merrill.

Hayes, A. (1988). Identification of two-tone images. *Perception, 17,* 429–436.

Heller, M. A. (1989a). Texture perception in sighted and blind observers. *Perception & Psychophysics, 45,* 49–54.

Heller, M. A. (1989b). Picture and pattern perception in the sighted and the blind: The advantage of the late blind. *Perception, 18,* 379–389.

Heller, M. A., & Kennedy, J. M. (1989). *Perspective taking, pictures and the blind.* Paper presented at the meeting of the Psychonomics Society conference, Atlanta, Nov. 17.

Hochberg, J. E., & Brooks, V. (1962). Pictorial recognition as an unlearned ability. *American Journal of Psychology, 75,* 624–628.

Hollins, M. (1989). *Understanding blindness.* Hillsdale, NJ: Lawrence Erlbaum Associates.

Jansson, G. (1988). *Criticisms of tactile pictures.* Paper presented at the preconference meeting on touch perception, Psychonomics Society, Chicago, Nov. 4.

Katz, D. (1925). *Der aufbau der taswelt* [The world of touch]. *Zeitschrift für psychologie, 11,* 1–270. (Ed. and translated by L. E. Krueger (1989), Hillsdale, N.J. Lawrence Erlbaum Associates.)

Kendrick, D. F., & Hardison, S. R. (1988). *Pigeon's concept of familiar versus unfamiliar scenes from their own experience.* Paper presented at the meeting of the Psychonomics Society, Chicago, Nov. 10–12.

Kennedy, J. M. (1974). *A psychology of picture perception.* San Francisco: Jossey-Bass.

Kennedy, J. M. (1980). Blind people recognizing and making haptic pictures. In M. A. Hagen (Ed.), *The perception of pictures* (Vol. 2). New York: Academic Press.

Kennedy, J. M. (1982a). Metaphor in pictures. *Perception, 11,* 589–605.

Kennedy, J. M. (1982b). Haptic pictures. In W. Schiff & E. Foulke (Eds.), *Tactual perception.* Cambridge, England: Cambridge University Press.

Kennedy, J. M. (1983). What can we learn about pictures from the blind. *American Scientist, 71,* 19–26.

Kennedy, J. M. (1984). How minds use pictures. *Social Research, 51,* 885–904.

Kennedy, J. M. (1985a). Arnheim, Gestalt theory and pictures. *Visual Arts Research, 11,* 23–44.

Kennedy, J. M. (1985b). Insights into blindness. *Encyclopedia Britannica Medical and Health Annual,* 154–165.

Kennedy, J. M. (1985c) Syllepse und Katachrese in bildern. *Semiotik, 7,* 47–62.

Kennedy, J. M. (1988a). *Outline and shape-from-shading: The little lines that can't.* Paper given at the Psychonomics Society, Chicago, Nov. 10–12.

Kennedy, J. M. (1988b). Line endings and subjective contours. *Spatial Vision 3,* 151–158.

Kennedy. J. M. (1989a). Universals of depiction, illusion as non-pictorial and limits to depiction. *Behavioral and Brain Sciences, 12,* 88–90.

Kennedy, J. M. (1989b). *Pictures to see and pictures to touch.* Invited address to Divisions 1, 3, and 10 of the American Psychological Association meeting, New Orleans, Aug. 13.

Kennedy, J. M. (in press). *Pictures to touch.* New Haven, CT: Yale University Press.

Kennedy, J. M., & Campbell, J. (1976). *Figure-ground coding of raised-line tactile displays.* Paper presented at a meeting of the Canadian Psychological Association, Toronto, June 9–11.

Kennedy, J. M., & Campbell, J. (1985). Convergence principle in blind people's pointing. *International Journal of Rehabilitation Research, 8,* 207–210.

Kennedy, J. M., & Domander, R. (1984). Pictorial foreground–background reversal reduces tactual recognition by the blind. *Journal of Visual Impairment and Blindness, 78,* 215–216.

Kennedy, J. M., & Domander, R. (1986a). Postures of twig figures: Reactions by the blind and the sighted. *International Journal of Rehabilitation Research, 9,* 63–66.

Kennedy, J. M., & Domander R. (1986b). Blind people depicting states and events in metaphoric line drawings. *Metaphor and Symbolic Activity, 1,* 109–126.

Kennedy, J. M., & Fox, N. (1977). Pictures to see and pictures to touch. In D. Perkins & B. Leondar (Eds.), *The arts and cognition.* Baltimore: Johns Hopkins Press.

Kennedy, J. M., & Gabias, P. (1985). Metaphoric devices in drawings of motion mean the same to the blind and sighted. *Perception, 14,* 189–195.

Kennedy, J. M. Gabias, P., & Pierantoni, R. (1990). Meaning, presence and absence in pictures. In K. Landwehr (Ed.), *Ecological perception research, visual communication, and Aesthetics* New York: Springer-Verlag.

Kennedy, J. M. & Ross, A. S. (1975) Outline picture perception by the Songe of Papua. *Perception, 4,* 391–406.

Kennedy, J. M., & Silver, J. (1974). The surrogate functions of lines in visual perception: Evidence from antipodal rock and cave art sources. *Perception, 3,* 313–322.

Kennedy, J. M., & Simpson, W. (1982). For each kind of figure of speech there is a pictorial metaphor: A figure of depiction. *Visual Arts Research, 16,* 1–11.

Kidwell, A., & Greer, P. (1973). *Sites, perception and the nonvisual experience.* New York: American Foundation for the Blind.

Klatzky, R. L., & Lederman, S. J. (1987). The intelligent hand. In G. Bower (Ed.), *The psychology of learning and motivation* (Vol. 21, pp. 121–151). New York: Academic Press.

Kubovy, M. (1986). *The psychology of perspective and Renaissance art.* Cambridge, England: Cambridge University Press.

Lederman, S. J., & Klatzky, R. L. (1987). Hand movements: A window into haptic object recognition. *Cognitive Psychology, 19,* 342–386.

Lederman, S. J., Klatzky, R. L., Chataway, C., & Summers, D. (1990). Visual mediation and the haptic recognition of two-dimensional pictures of common objects. *Perception & Psychophysics, 47,* 54–64.

Loomis, J. M., Klatzky, R. L., & Lederman, S. J. (1988). *Similarity of tactual and visual picture perception with limited field of view.* Paper presented at the preconference meeting on touch perception, Psychonomics Society, Chicago, Nov. 9.

Magee, L. E., & Kennedy, J. M. (1980). Exploring pictures tactually. *Nature, 283,* 287–288.

Marr, D. (1982). *Vision.* San Francisco: W. H. Freeman.

Millar, S. (1975). Visual experience or translation rules: Drawing the human figure by blind and sighted children. *Perception, 4,* 363–371.

Ratliff, F. (1971). Colour and contrast. *Proceedings of the American Philosophical Society, 115,* 150–163.

Revesz, G. (1950). *Psychology and art of the blind.* Toronto: Longmans Green.

Rubin, E. (1915). *Synsoplevede figurer.* Copenhagen: Gyldendals.

Salzhauer-Axel, E. (1989). *Art education for the blind.* Talk given in a symposium on the blind and pictures, Whitney Museum, New York, June 8.

Schiff, W., & Foulke, E. (Eds.). (1982). *Tactual perception.* Cambridge, England: Cambridge University Press.

Senden, M., von (1932/1960). *Raum—und Gestalt—auffasung bei operierten Blind geborenen vor und nach der Operation* (Translated by P. Heath as *Space and sight.* London: Methuen, 1960).

Steinberg, S. (1953). The eye is a part of the mind. *Partisan Review, 20,* 194–212.

Wake, T., Shimuzu, Y. and Wake, H. (1980). Perception of tactile three-dimensional information and visual aids for blind persons *Japanese Journal of Ergonomics, 16,* 27–36.

Warren, D. H. (1984). *Blindness and early childhood development* (2nd ed.). New York: American Foundation for the Blind.

Wartofsky, M. (1984). The paradox of painting: Pictorial representation and the dimensionality of visual space. *Social Research, 51*, 863–883.

Willats, J. (1981). What do the marks in the picture stand for? The child's acquisition of systems of transformation and denotation. *Review of Research in Visual Arts Education, 13*, 18–33.

Yonas, A., & Owsley, C. (1987). Development of visual space perception, In P. Salapatek, & L. Cohen (Eds.), *Handbook of infant perception* (Vol. 2). New York: Academic Press.

12

A Reversed Lag in the Recognition and Production of Tactual Drawings: Theoretical Implications for Haptic Coding

Susanna Millar
University of Oxford

INTRODUCTION

My thesis is that output factors are crucial in coding shape by touch. What I am proposing is that haptic representation is based on action plans. It is, of course, well known that movement is important in tactual perception. The very term "haptics" for active touch was coined to stress that fact. But it will be argued later that it is active movement that leads to the representation and tactual recognition of shape, rather than the other way about.

The thesis was originally motivated by a very simple but nevertheless surprising finding. Congenitally totally blind children produced reasonable drawings of the human figure more easily than they recognized such drawings. For sighted children, it is the other way about. Production lags behind recognition. Findings of this kind help us to understand the role of informational conditions in perception and representation.

It should be made clear from the outset that the question here is not about the *ability* of blind or of sighted children. There is no reason whatever to believe that the blind, because they are blind, differ in potential from the sighted. The point is that totally congenitally blind people provide important clues about the interplay between perception and cognitive skills. Studies are needed both for theoretical interpretation and for practical purposes, to understand precisely what information is missing without vision, and by what alternative routes that information can be acquired.

The view proposed here belongs broadly under the umbrella of information-processing theories. Such views should not be identified with naïve empiricism. They do not imply a disregard for genetic factors. No one doubts that newborn human infants differ in potential from the very brightest flea. But a naïve nativism will not do either. Not all knowledge of facts or knowledge of procedures is innately available to the human infant solely by virtue of developing into an adult. Information-processing theories are about the conditions under which knowledge of fact and of procedures is acquired, and how it is processed. Evaluating abilities, except if that is needed for a practical purpose, is rather like handing out medals for efficiency. It is in the main irrelevant to scientific inquiry. Information processing theories ask questions about what short and long-term information is available to a person in a given task, what alternative conditions can make it available, and how that affects heuristics and coding (representation). This applies also to the way in which haptic shapes are coded and represented.

The study that showed an apparent reversal between recognition and production will be reported in some detail because it highlights an informative paradox. It will then be set in the context of other findings and theoretical explanations of the development of drawing and their relevance to tactual shape coding. In order to do so, it is necessary first to distinguish different types of configurations that fall under the rubric of haptic shapes. Not all shapes are recognized in precisely the same way by active touch. For instance, the spatial frame and type of exploratory movement needed to recognize large three-dimensional objects are quite different than for a tiny raised-dot pattern, in touch. In other words, unlike vision, the additional information from other sources that is needed to complement touch, is not the same for all types of shape. The different categories of shape stimuli are briefly cataloged in order to pinpoint the type of shape coding with which this chapter is concerned.

CATEGORIES OF HAPTIC SHAPE
AND COMPLEMENTARY INFORMATION

In order to understand shape coding by touch, it is important to recognize how the senses normally operate together in space and time (Millar, 1981a). There are two main advantages in having several senses or sources of information about the same object or event. First, some of the information (for instance from vision and touch) overlaps. That makes for redundancy of information that is important in case of difficulty or failure. Second, the different senses provide additional information which complements the single source. To do so effectively, the sense modalities operate neither as totally separate systems that depend for cross-talk on learned translations; nor as a totally unitary system in which all sources supply exactly the same information. What does happen is that the information from different sources converges (Millar, 1981a). There is a good deal of evidence for this view, from physiological studies of shape recognition by touch (Sakata & Iwamura, 1978), from behavioral studies of hearing and seeing voices (e.g., McGurk, 1976), from vision and touch (Heller, 1982), and from studies of touch and movement (Millar, 1981a, 1988, 1990). The important implication here is that when one sensory source is missing, it is necessary not only to substitute other information, but also to restore the necessary complementarity and redundancy from other sources. Vision normally provides not only information about a given shape, but also a variety of other spatial cues or frames in the surround, which can be used to locate the shape and its features. Touch without vision has to get that complementary information from other sources. The point is that in touch the complementary information is not the same for all types of haptic shapes or tasks. At least five different categories have to be distinguished in terms of the complementary information that is needed for them. These will be discussed in turn.

The following five different types of tactual shape are: (1) vibratory stimuli, (2) the small, raised-dot characters of braille, (3) three-dimensional objects, (4) configurations described by ambulation or locomotion, and (5) raised-line configurations described by hand and arm movements.

Consider vibrotactile stimuli (Craig & Sherrick, 1982). Shape coding here depends on vibratory pulses delivered to the passive skin. In the Optacon, for instance, the finger remains stationary. Letters are perceived from the changing vibrations on the ball of the immobile finger. The main parameters of interest (e.g., acuity) are associated with distance between pins, and time interval between pulses (Craig & Sherrick, 1982). But the fact that the pins that deliver the vibrations form a rectangular array also has one great advantage for shape coding; namely that the array provides an invariant, rectangular spatial frame. Sensations on the finger can be referred to that frame in terms of relative locations (top/left; bottom/right). Shape coding in terms of spatial locations on the finger is thus facilitated. On the other hand, active movement is not essential.

When we turn to braille characters (Foulke, this volume), the important parameters are different. The fact that these characters are extremely small, that they lack redundancy because they are all derived from a six-dot matrix, and that no spatial frame surrounds the patterns, has important consequences for coding them as global shapes. The lack of an external spatial frame matters, because there is no stable spatial anchor in relation to which the constituent dots and gaps can be located reliably. Because the patterns lack redundancy, they also have few salient internal features that could serve as spatial anchor points. This does not greatly matter in discrimination tasks. Discrimination can be relatively easy because it does not need to rely on identifying shape, but can be based on texture differences (Katz, 1925; Millar,

1977, 1978, 1985a). Using texture differences redundantly certainly facilitates discrimination (Millar, 1986a; Schiff & Isikow, 1966). But identifying and recognizing the patterns as shapes if often very difficult. It is not, of course, by any means impossible as is sometimes suggested. But it tends to be slow, particularly early in learning. The typical unsystematic rubbing that characterizes the first recognition attempts by beginning readers makes this problem worse, because it loses track of the location of dots and gaps in a character still further. Active hand and arm movement becomes useful with proficiency. Fluent readers easily keep track of lines of text, using lateral movements in relation to body posture (Millar, 1987a). Braille teachers are well aware of the importance of relating the lateral (left to right) hand movements to an upright body posture to develop fluent reading. This suggests that convergent kinesthetic information from body posture and from active hand movements is important. With proficiency, hand movements also differ with the reading task (text reading or letter search), and the two hands can be employed divergently for spatial and semantic information, respectively (Millar, 1987a, 1987b). Higher-order cognitive skills as well as lower-order perceptual sources are thus involved. Nevertheless, active movement is not a sine qua non for recognizing braille. In principle, characters could be recognized from being passed under the stationary figure.

In contrast, coding the shape of large three-dimensional objects would be almost impossible without systematic active hand movements. We have a lyrical description of how the hands may build up the shape of an object by moving over its surface from the 19th-century physiologist, Weber (1978). The integration of complementary and overlapping information from touch, movement and other sources of kinesthetic (e.g., body-centered spatial axes) information seems to be the primary basis here in the absence of visual information (Laabs & Simmons, 1981; Millar, 1981b, 1985b). Physiological evidence suggests that touch and kinesthetic information converge in shape perception of this kind (Sakata & Iwamura, 1978).

In large-scale or geographic space, configurations can, in principle, be walked or danced. In visual conditions, updating cues for this are continuously available, and the environment provides a stable external frame to which current positions can be referred. Movements thus tend to be coded with reference to external spatial frames. In blind conditions, the primary source of convergent information in geographic space are sounds, either from external sources or self-produced, and cues from some other external sources (e.g., smell, air movements). Feedback from touch (landmarks that can be touched) tends to be intermittent, and except in familiar spaces, cannot be foreseen. Continuous updating of locomotion by reference to the relation between external planes is thus much less possible. Such conditions tend to elicit coding strategies based on sequential movement events (Byrne & Salter, 1983; Laabs & Simmons, 1981; Millar, 1975a, 1976, 1985b). It should be noted that this is a question of heuristics, not of efficiency. The same level of efficiency can be reached by quite different strategies (Hollyfield & Foulke, 1983; Millar, 1975a, 1976). The question of interest is rather how sequential (route) strategies are organized in terms of configurations, when such configurations are needed. Turning sequential information into configurations can make considerable demands on memory. Maps, drawings, and graphs are useful memory aids for that reason.

That brings us to the final category of shapes, namely small outline configurations, which can, in principle, be used to symbolize or represent three-dimensional objects or larger scale spaces. Typically, coding these involves hand and arm movements and feedback from touch. Systematic exploration is clearly important to familiarize flat shapes (Berla & Butterfield, 1977; Davidson, 1972). It is these small-scale configurations that are the focus of the present chapter, both in terms the proposed explanation and findings that prompted it.

A STUDY OF DRAWING, CONSTRUCTION AND RECOGNITION

Subjects, Tasks, and Findings

There are very few people who are actually totally blind from birth. The children who have taken part in my studies over the years are thus not a random selection of subjects whose sight happens to be impaired. They are children of varying ages (mainly as they come into the educational system) who know me well and who are well known to me because they are totally, or nearly totally blind from birth (ascertained by medical records from birth). As has been indicated, the reason for the interest is that their experience and performance is crucial to our understanding of the role which informational conditions have in tactual perception and representation.

The particular children who were available for the study that is reported here, were 21 congenitally totally, or near totally (see later) blind children. Their ages varied from 5 to 15 years, and they could be divided into three age bands of 7 children each with roughly equal mean intelligence (Williams, 1956) scores: Group I, mean age, 13 yrs., mean IQ, 100.3; Group II, mean age, 10 yrs., mean IQ, 107.6; Group III mean age, 7.1 yrs., mean IQ, 103.8. Table 12.1 shows the characteristics and causes of blindness of individual subjects. All except three children were totally blind from birth. Of the three others, one girl (Group I) had shown pupillary reaction to light shone directly into the eye in infancy; one boy (Group II) had light perception at 2 feet in exceptional (bright flash) conditions, and one girl (group III) had

TABLE 12.1
Characteristics of Individual Subjects in the Reported Experiment
on Drawing, Assembly and Recognition

Subjects	Sex	Age	I.Q.	Blind status from birth	Blind condition
Group I					
1.	f	14:9	104	Total	Optic disk hypoplasia
2.	f	13:4	99	Total	Retrolental fibroplasia no iris; corneal opacities
3.	f	12:11	87	Total	Bilateral anopthalmia
4.	m	12:10	98	Total	Retrolental fibroplasia
5.	f	12:9	113	Total now minimal LP early	Congenital bilateral cataract
6.	f	12:2	97	Total	Congenital retinal degeneration
7.	m	12:1	105	Total	Bilateral congenital cataract
Group II					
8.	m	11:3	107	Total	Bilateral cataract; Optic atrophy
9.	f	11:3	134	Total	Bilateral micropthalmos
10.	f	10:8	89	Total	Bilateral micropthalmos (clinically anopthalmia)
11.	m	9:11	105	Total	Primary optic atrophy
12.	m	8:7	109	Total	Retrolental fibroplasia
13.	m	10:1	89	LP (direct light only)	Primary pigmental retinal degeneration
14.	f	8:4	120	Total	Gross bilateral optic atrophy; Glioma
Group III					
15.	f	7:8	100	LP min peripheral	Retrolental fibroplasia
16.	m	7:7	116	Total	Anopthalmia (Bilateral micopthalmos)
17.	f	7:7	95	Total	Congenital retinal abnormalities
18.	m	7:2	98	Total	Retrolental fibroplasia
19.	m	7:0	90	Total	Retrolental fibroplasia
20.	f	7:0	120	Total	Bilateral anopthalmia
21.	f	5:6	100	Total	Retrolental fibroplasia

IQ From Williams (1956).
Blind status from birth (total from birth = total; minimal light reaction = LR min; light perception = LP), and blind condition.

peripheral light perception. None of these three had ever been able to see shapes, or even hand movements.

My original interest in drawing came about quite by accident many years ago, in the course of conducting a much more conventional study. But it led to studying drawings by blind as well as sighted children under controlled conditions. In a study conducted at the time (Millar 1975a), the totally congenitally blind children who took part then had never drawn anything before. The drawings of the human figure which these blind children produced on the very first occasion of drawing provided some exciting results. For one thing, the general body schemes used by some of the older blind children were remarkably similar to each other, and to those used by their (blindfolded) sighted cohorts, and indeed resembled conventional stick figures and outline drawing. But clearly, the blind children could not have copied from each other or from seeing pictures.

There were good reasons against regarding this as evidence for an innate ability to draw the human figure. Thus, not all children produced acceptable figures, and many younger blind mainly produced scribbles, when other equally blind older youngsters produced much the same scheme as the sighted.

The explanation suggested at the time (Millar, 1975a) for the similarity of the drawing schemes by older blind children and those of the sighted, was that the drawing task presents a set of problems. Thus, the request to draw objects must be regarded as demanding essentially a translation from three to two dimensions. It was proposed that blind as well as sighted children solve this task by using the "nearest" simple two-dimensional shapes as symbols for the body parts. Typically, heads are represented as circles, and arms and legs by lines. Clearly no head is a circle, either in vision or touch; and arms and legs are not sticks in either modality. But a circle is the simplest (two-dimensional) shape that captures, in the most general terms, the quality of movements needed to explore a head by touch. It can thus be used to symbolize these. It is also the simplest shape that captures the general shape of heads as perceived by vision. The hypothesis explains the fact that blind and sighted children used much the same conventional schema in drawing, although the blind subjects had never drawn before, and clearly had no opportunity to see conventional (or any other) drawings.

The study to be reported was initially motivated by the other question raised by the drawings; namely why the younger blind often produced scribbles, and did not solve the problem by appropriate configurations as the older blind did, although they had as little experience of drawing as the younger children. It was clearly not a question of familiarity with the human figure. There were lots of toys in the residential school where the children lived. The younger children played with dolls and with doll houses, as well as with other toys. They had collage "pictures" on the walls and often helped to produce them. The simplest explanation for the difference between drawings by older and younger children, neither of whom had drawn raised lines before, thus seemed to be that the younger ones lacked procedural drawing skills; in other words, that they did not know how to execute the drawing movements. If so, they should have much less difficulty in constructing a figure from simple constituent cardboard shapes.

The study to be reported was thus originally to compare drawing and assembly tasks to test the role of procedural skills in drawing by blind children. A recognition task was added as an extra control, because recognition is known to be usually much easier than any type of production or even reconstruction. There is a well-attested "lag" between recognition and production in drawings by the sighted (Maccoby & Bee, 1965). Thus, quite young sighted children are able to recognize pictures that they are unable to draw. Recognition was thus expected to be easier still than the assembly task, and was therefore added as a control task. The tasks were all randomly interspersed, and usually given on different days.

A standard (Sewell Raised-line Drawing) kit was used in the drawing and in the recognition tasks. The kit consists of a rubber pad on which sheets of plasticized paper are placed. Drawing with a biro on that paper produces raised lines that can easily be felt and discriminated. The kit was demonstrated, and the child was shown how to draw and feel lines on it. Similarly, prior to the assembly task, the child was shown the cardboard cutouts that were to be assembled, and was encouraged to feel them.

The representation of the human figure was of main interest, partly because that had been the subject of the previous study, and partly because it was possible to be sure that the children were familiar with the body and with body parts, from haptic experience of their own and other people's bodies, and from experience with dolls of various sizes. The question was how they would represent the figure. Geometric shapes (square, circle, cross, and triangle) were used as control objects.

For the recognition task, the drawings of the human figure shown to the children, were modeled deliberately on the two types of figure that blind children in an earlier study had produced spontaneously themselves (Millar, 1975b). One basic scheme that they, as well as sighted children, had used is like the conventional stick figure. The other, also used by sighted children, has an oval body, and is very similar to the scheme used in a subtest of a well-known (Terman & Merril, 1946) test for 4-year-olds. It was precisely because the very first drawings by congenitally blind older children had shown these two, apparently conventional schemes, which the sighted also used (Millar, 1975a), that they were here considered the ecologically most valid symbolic representations of the figure for the blind. They were consequently both used for the recognition task (Fig. 12.1, respectively). As an additional item, in recognition only, the picture of a house was used, in the "canonical" (Freeman, 1980) orientation (roof, four windows, door), which is typical in pictures for young children, and occurs also in the kind of collage that often festoons classrooms in schools for the blind. Each item for the recognition task (person, house and geometrical shapes) was drawn with the kit described earlier that produces raised lines.

Materials for the assembly task were cardboard cutouts, designed so that a picture of a person, (similar to either of the person stimuli for recognition) could be produced by assembling the pieces. The shapes consisted of four samples each of small (2-cm diameter) circles, four larger (4 cm) ovals, and four squares (4 cm), as well as long (4 x 4 cm) and shorter (2 x 0.2 cm) stick and curved (arc shaped shapes. In the examples in Figs. 12.2 et seq. the con-

FIG. 12.1 The two drawings of a person, shown in the recognition test.

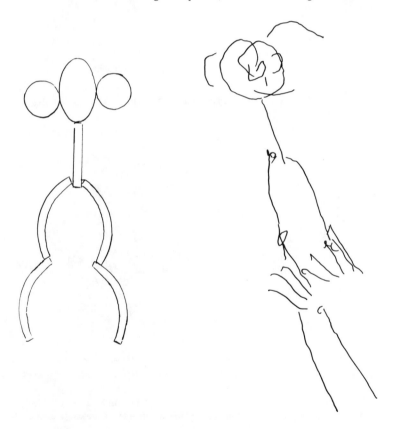

FIG. 12.2. Assembly (a, left) and drawing (b, right) by a 12-year-old (subject No. 5). No drawing experience as far as is known.

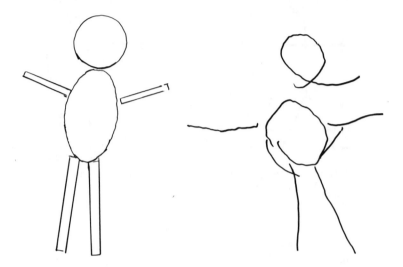

FIG. 12.3.   Assembly (a, left) and drawing (b, right) by an 11-year-old (subject No. 9). Little or no experience.

FIG. 12.4.   Assembly (a, left) and drawing (b, right) by an 8-year-old (subject No. 5). The child had some encouragement to experiment with drawing materials at home.

stituent cardboard cutouts are shown as used in by children in the assembly task.

The instruction for the drawing task was simply to draw the object (person or geometric figure) in any way the child wanted. The recognition task was simply to name each object (geometric shape or figure) as it was presented. It should be noted that the experimenter did not name the pictures at any time. For the assembly task, the child was encouraged to feel the constituent shapes, and was then asked to put them together (on a sheet placed on the drawing board) in such a way as to represent a person. He or she was told that more shapes of the same types were available if needed. When the child had finished, the experimenter drew around the shapes and noted their orientation, relative placement and proximity to each other, for subsequent assessment. As in the previous (Millar, 1975a) study, the children were asked to "think aloud" during all the tasks so that what they were doing could be recognized and noted, a request that these children understood well. Both drawing and assembly productions could thus be labeled and interpreted reliably.

Five independent observers rated the drawings and constructions (assembly) separately on a preset scoring system (2 points for each constituent part and each relative alignment, up to a total of 22 points), without being aware of the identity of the individual productions. The correlations between raters was extremely good (between $r = 0.96$ to $r = 0.81$, in both cases). Mean scores for drawing and assembly are shown in Table 12.2.

The statistical analysis (Anova) of scores of in terms of age and type of task did not support the hypothesis that lack of executive skill (lack of procedural knowledge) was the main factor in the poorer drawings. The hypothesis predicts that the younger blind would differ from older subjects much less on assembly than on drawing. The results showed, however, that although older subjects scored more highly overall, $(F (2,18) = 3.64; P < .05)$, assembly and drawing scores did not differ significantly. There was indeed a (nonsignificant) tendency for age to relate differently to the two tasks. But it was actually opposite to the predicted direction. It was the older children who were somewhat better on assembly than on drawing.

TABLE 12.2
Mean Scores for Drawing and Assembly by 3 Age Groups
of Blind Children

	Task	
Group	Drawing	Assembly
I	9.43	14.00
II	9.83	10.29
III	5.14	4.29

The findings implied that executive drawing skills were not the major factor in representations of the human figure here. That was also evident from comparing the productions in drawing and assembly tasks. Examples of good drawing and assembly solutions are shown in Figs. 12.2 to 12.4.

Looking at the productions in drawing and assembly tasks showed that subjects who used two-dimensional geometric shapes symbolically to represent the three-dimensional human figure, did so in both drawing and assembly. Similarly, children who did not use the shapes symbolically in one task, did not do so in the other task either. Children whose solutions to the drawing problem were undifferentiated scribbles, also produced assemblies (not shown here) in which disparate shapes were simply heaped together, without regard for the type shape he or she used. This is even more obvious from comparing the assembly and drawings also from poorer solutions, as shown in Figs. 12.5 and 12.6.

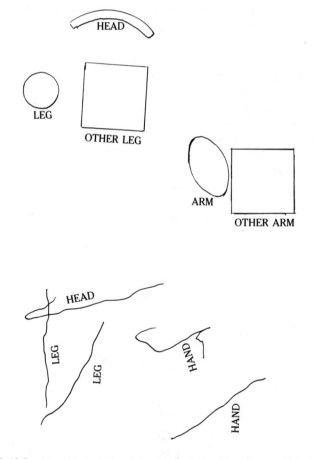

FIG. 12.5. Assembly (a, top) and drawing (b, bottom) by a 7-year-old (subject No. 18). No drawing experience as far as is known.

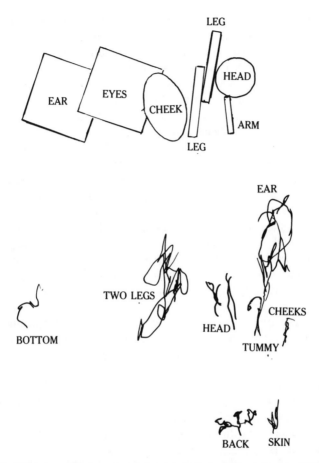

FIG. 12.6. Assembly (a, top) and drawing (b, bottom) by an 8-year-old (subject No. 12). This was the first time he had drawn a picture of anything.

Consider the assembly configuration in Fig. 12.5. The fact that an arc shape was used for the head may suggest that this 7-year-old boy was using shapes in a representative manner. But this is contradicted by the fact that he used a circle for one leg and a square for the other; and that he also represented the two arms by different shapes. The boy, of course, knew perfectly well that his legs were the same shape as each other, and that neither was a square. The point is that he was simply not using shape as relevant for representation. His drawing similarly did not differentiate the head from arms and legs by shape. A fairly typical example of earlier or simpler solutions, shown in Fig. 12.6, makes this point quite clearly. It is the first drawing by an 8-year-old boy with excellent musical skills. Asked to draw a man, or boy like himself, he was first puzzled. He then used a series of squiggles, naming each body part as he made a mark for it. Revealingly enough, the last-named item was the skin. That suggests that the boy was listing body parts in the order in which they occurred to him, but without thinking of them in terms of shape at all. The drawing consists of a list of body features, each one marked by a scribble as he named it. There was no attempt whatever to produce marks that bear some resemblance to shape. When asked to draw lines and circles (which would have sufficed as figural ingredients), he was able to do so.

It was also quite consistent that even those children who produced unrecognizable figures in drawing and assembly were able to draw lines and circles. Only triangles were relatively difficult. But the majority of all children could draw circles, even if not always perfectly closed, and lines, even if not always perfectly straight. Even those children who produced unrecognizable figures could therefore have used circles and lines to represent the human figure in their drawings. But they did not do so.

The findings thus suggest that to use simple flat shapes symbolically, in order to represent the three-dimensional figure, is a relatively sophisticated solution to the problem that drawing presents. To draw three-dimensional objects means to represent them in two dimensions. That explains why some young congenitally totally blind children when first asked to draw, produce scribbles. It does not mean that they intend scribbles, or that they could not use appropriate movements. When children's labels of their productions are considered, it becomes quite clear that the scribbles were intended as tokens for body parts. But it was also clear that they were not intended as outline shapes. In other words, they had not yet inferred that a solution in terms of flat shapes was possible.

Individual children vary in how they understand the request to draw. Some use an undifferentiated scribble while naming body parts. Others differentiate between head, chin, and abdomen on the one hand and arms and legs on the other, by using relative orientation of the lines to each other. Examples of these have been published previously (Millar, 1975a). Some children ask what they should use to portray the head, others spontaneously think of the solution to use two-dimensional shapes, for instance, a circle for the head (Millar, 1975a). Looking at individual productions, rather than at group results, suggests that shape solutions both in drawing and assembly were associated with the brighter subjects within each group. This is not perhaps surprising since "Draw-a-man" tests are known to relate to general intellectual ability (e.g., Goodenough, 1926; Harris, 1963). It is, of course, also the case that the brightest children tend to come from homes where they are encouraged to experiment (even very occasionally now with drawing materials). But in any case, as the overall intelligence level was at least average in each group, the association with IQ scores does not explain the lack of difference between assembly and drawing. What it does suggest is that the use of flat shapes to represent three-dimensional objects involves some form inference. But the more startling and revealing results were those for recognition.

The surprising finding came from looking at recognition of the human figure. Only 1 child out of the 21 subjects (less than 5%), recognized the stick figure drawing; and only one out of the 21 (less than 5%) recognized the other drawing of the human figure. Not a single child recognized the drawing of the house. The fact that overall intelligence was average, and several children were well above that, shows that the greater than 95% failure rate in recognition could not be due to lack of ability (see earlier). More important, the finding was contrary to the expectation that recognition would be the easiest task. By contrast, for the simple geometric shapes that were very familiar to the children, that was the case. Recognition was 100% correct for the circle, 91% for the triangle, 83% for the square, and 45% for the cross. This shows that recognizing simple geometric shapes of the kind that were constituent elements of the pictures of the figure and house was not the difficulty. The fact that the drawings of the human figure and house were more complex shapes could not be the sole explanation either. The children actually produced recognizable human figure drawings that were just as complex.

In order to get some measure of how recognizable the children's drawings actually were as human figures, they were assessed by independent observers. The drawings were traced without labels of any kind and presented on separate sheets in random order. Observers found that 39% of the drawings were definitely recognizable representations of the human figure. The difference in favor of drawing over recognition (less than 5%) by subjects is too large to require statistical calculation. It is the reverse of the well-known lag between recognition and drawing of pictures by the sighted (Maccoby & Bee, 1965).

Although the "reverse lag" was unexpected, it was remarkably consistent with finding that assembling the figure produced much the same results as drawing. The hypothesis of lack of executive skill alone would not explain that. All that was needed for the assembly task was to select reasonably appropriate geometric shapes for the body parts, and to position them with respect to each other. Given that they could recognize the constituent geometric shapes, the task should have been much easier than drawing. The hypothesis accounts even less for the fact that more than 95% of the children failed to recognize either of the two figure drawings, and that 100% failed to recognize the house, when an equally high percentage of subjects recognized the familiar geometric shapes that make up such figures. The probability that the figure was less familiar would make recognition more difficult, but that very fact should have had even worse effects on drawing; not the other way about.

The findings, and particularly the apparently reversed lag between recognition and production, suggest that using simple flat shapes and configurations as symbols for three-dimensional shapes and spaces is not an inevitable immediate response in haptic conditions. To understand this better, it is instructive to look at some of the theoretical explanations of early drawings. The findings are briefly discussed in relation to these later.

DEVELOPMENTAL THEORIES OF REPRESENTATION AND HAPTIC RECOGNITION OF SHAPE

There is little doubt that theories of perception and theories of drawing are predominantly concerned with vision. A major preoccupation in most accounts of drawing is with the portrayal of perspective, and the creation of visual illusions, or visually realistic scenes. The stereotyped nature of child art presents a problem for this, especially as it cannot be explained by the influence of culture and convention that affects adult art forms (Gombrich, 1970). Explanations differ mainly in emphasis on the process that is considered basic to this stereotypy. They are of interest here because drawings of the human figure by blind children (see earlier) exhibit some of the same stereotypy.

The common-sense view of drawing, which is shared by many blind children, is certainly that it is a peculiarly visual activity. Some researchers have also attributed children's "errors" in drawing to a failure in visual perception (Rice, 1930), or to failure in visual analysis (Maccobee & Bee, 1965). Mapping the optical array point for point as by a camera (Gibson, 1971) is another example of that view. A more sophisticated version is that thinking as well as vision is involved, and that the two are in fact 'indivisible' concepts (Arnheim, 1969). Clearly, the fact that congenitally totally blind children do produce recognizable drawings shows that vision is not a necessary condition for that. The fact that vision probably facilitates visually realistic representations is another matter.

Piaget's theory (Piaget & Inhelder, 1956), by contrast, considers immature logical–spatial development as the major factor in children's drawings. Luquet (1927) suggested that children draw what they know rather than what they see. Piaget's theory explains this by assuming that drawing directly reflects the child's cognitive (logical–spatial) immaturity. Children fail to portray visual information correctly because their mental representations of objects and spatial relations are prelogical, 'egocentric' and non-Euclidean. They therefore draw as if they could see aspects of objects that are actually occluded, fail to understand perspective, are unable to represent different viewpoints, and do not understand views that demand the use of Euclidean coordinates. However, although cognitive skills are involved in drawing (see earlier), Piaget's stages of logical jumps are unnecessary to explain such findings, and the theory does not account for spatial strategies by blind and blindfolded sighted children (e.g., Millar, 1979, 1981b, 1985b).

It is also quite unlikely that picture drawings reflect cognitive maturity solely or directly (Kosslyn, Heldenmeyer, & Locklear, 1977). Furthermore, recent studies have shown that apparently universal drawing "errors" can be altered by changing viewing conditions, or the aim and context of drawing, or verbal task instructions; and "errors" are reduced also when children merely need to recognize rather than to draw representations of objects (Cox, 1986; Freeman, 1980; Freeman & Cox, 1985). The alternative suggestion is that young children understand the spatial relations, but draw canonical (prototypical), or preferred views of objects (Cox, 1986; Freeman, 1980). However, the "preferred view" hypothesis does not explain the similarities between human figure drawings by congenitally totally blind and young sighted children.

A third type of explanation mainly implicates limitations in executive skill. One such theory (Goodnow & Levine, 1973) proposes an analogy with syntactic development, apparently suggesting an innate development of a grammar of action that involves rules for sequencing movements. Other analogies with language development emphasize ergonomic limitations of movements rather than rules in acquisition (e.g., Van Somers, 1984). A somewhat different suggestion is that children go through different stages of learning pictorial devices to handle external spatial relationships (Willats, 1977), presumably because easier devices are learned earlier. Whatever the formulation, there is no doubt that movement skills as well as knowledge of procedures are involved in drawing. But these could clearly not account for the finding (described earlier) that drawing was no worse than assembling constituent shapes, let alone for the fact that it was superior to recognition.

Finally, drawing has been explained as the acquisition of symbols that can represent three-dimensional objects and spatial relations in two dimensions (Goodnow, 1977; Millar, 1975b, 1986b). Drawing is seen as a problem (Goodnow, 1977) or as a series of problems (Millar, 1990) that the child has to solve. Goodnow attributes the limited "vocabulary" and stereotypy of young children's drawing mainly to limited executive ability, particularly in the sequencing of movements. But although limitations in drawing vocabulary and sequencing are contributory factors, they do not explain the present findings.

The very multiplicity of factors that have been implicated in different theories shows that we are not dealing with a unitary skill. Perceptual information, cognitive and inferential skill, movement-sequencing skills, knowledge of procedures, and using shapes symbolically, are all relevant to the task. Each of the subsidiary skills is relevant also to the findings reported in this chapter. Thus, the fact that blind children found triangles relatively difficult to draw although they could recognize them, is reminiscent of the difficulty young sighted children have in sequencing the lines and angles in drawing diamonds (e.g., Terman & Merril, 1946), although they can discriminate them from other forms. Here, as well as in assembling shapes, procedural knowledge or means of sequencing seem to be mainly involved. The task clearly also makes cognitive demands, and these are likely to be greater for blind than for sighted children. The fact that the general body schema produced by blind children is similar (albeit less elaborate) to the drawings by young sighted children (Millar, 1975a), is consistent with the notion of a limited drawing vocabulary in both cases. However, that clearly does not account for the puzzling fact that the children here failed to recognize such figures.

Analysis of the task, and the knowledge and skills that are needed minimally for solving it, suggests that the basic conditions that initially confront the blind and sighted child are quite similar. Thus, it is not often realized that the very fact of asking a child to draw actually conveys information. At the least, the very question shows the blind child that drawing is possible without vision. The sighted child is, of course, aware much earlier that he or she is expected to be able to draw. Further, the act of demonstrating the drawing kit, and how to make, and to feel marks on paper, gives information to the child about what drawing actually involves, beyond what he or she has heard, and conjectured (or previously experienced), from the talk of others. The sighted are likely to have had experience with drawing materials much earlier. In addition, the child has to understand that the marks he or she makes on paper are supposed to symbolize three-dimensional shapes and space. As a further requirement, he or she has to become aware, sooner or later, that the task includes the demand that the marks on paper should in some way resemble what is perceived in three dimensions. Looking at the basic problems which confront the child, it seems likely that the solutions are similar, to the extent that the task is the same. The fact that far fewer blind children draw recognizable figures as early as the sighted is easily explained by the fact that they generally do not get quite basic information about what to expect as early as the sighted. Furthermore, most sighted children see pictures from an early age. Although this is clearly quite insufficient to allow them to draw, the very fact provides the implicit information that flat shapes can used for this purpose. Young blind children are as yet still much less likely to have experience with (raised-line) pictures, or access to people who convey the information through description.

There is, however, one informational condition that does differ between haptic and visual conditions, and which is relevant to the reversal between recognition and production that was found in the study here. Visual conditions make it easy to see similarities in outlines across differences in size and depth. Perception is or feels more direct and the meaning of configurations is more immediate. That is the reason, for instance, why icons (pictures used as symbols for a theme) are used increasingly, especially in computer printouts. That is no mere fad. Icons convey a lot of information quickly. Tactual presentation and recognition of these is now under active consideration as aids for the blind. Learning to recognize tactual pictures is therefore increasingly important for blind children.

It should be quite clear that blind children can recognize raised-line pictures; and that haptic shape similarities can be understood in blind conditions. The question is not whether this occurs. The important question is about the conditions under which it occurs. Haptic shapes are less directly recognized initially than are visual shapes. It will be argued later that without vision, or precuing by naming (Heller, 1989), shape recognition depends initially on movement coding. That interpretation explains why recognition can be more difficult than production in haptic conditions.

THE ROLE OF MOVEMENT
IN HAPTIC SHAPE CODING

Production and Recognition

The advantage of production over recognition becomes intelligible if we consider the relation between arm movements and moving in geographical space (see earlier). The fact that blind children 'can' use haptic maps has been known for a long time (Herman, Herman, & Chatman, 1983; Leonard & Newman, 1967). To assume on such grounds that map use is an "unlearned ability" (Landau, 1986) is a question stopper rather than an explanation (Liben, 1988; Millar, 1988). Haptic maps, like drawings, use two-dimensional configurations to represent three-dimensional spatial relations. As we saw earlier, this is not a unitary process, but depends on a number of cognitive and perceptual processes and skills. The potential for acquiring all of these must obviously be assumed. But that tells us very little. The fact that sighted adults often find maps extremely difficult, while young children can solve some mapping problems, is a case in point. The question is what conditions provide the declarative and procedural knowledge that is needed to employ small, flat outline traces to symbolize three-dimensional objects and geographical spaces. Researchers should not assume that their subjects only use the information which the experimenter decides to convey. The effect that an apparently uninformative instruction had on the representation of a walk by a congenitally blind child, is shown in Fig. 12.7.

Fig. 12.7 shows representations of a square walk by two 8-year-old congenitally totally blind children. They had taken part in a study in which subjects walked several times around a square, guided by a rope that surrounded it. At each corner the child encountered a toy that was felt and identified. They were then asked to draw the walk and position of the toys (using the raised-line drawing kit as described earlier). Naïve subjects at this age typically represented the walk by a long line with toys marked at various distances on the way (Fig. 12.7a). The other drawing (Fig. 12.7b) was by another

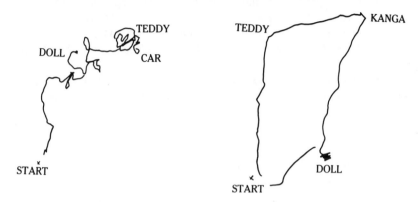

FIG. 12.7. Representations of a square walk by two congenitally totally blind 8-year-olds; (a, left) was drawn without comments from the experimenter; (b, right) was drawn with the comment by the experimenter to "show the turns" (see text). The findings are from an earlier study, and do not refer to subjects in the drawing and assembly experiment.

8-year-old who started her drawing in precisely the same way, using a straight line. She was beginning to continue it beyond the first corner (named toy), while saying "The rope is a long shape; it's got some turns." She was then told to show the turns on the page. That was sufficient. In other words, that very minimal instruction apparently conveyed the information that turns in walking can be shown by turns in hand movements. Many other young children, who were not specifically told to "show the turns," drew the walk as a straight line as illustrated in Fig. 12.7a. The child who drew the walk as shown in 12.7b, clearly knew that she had turned at the location of the toy, and clearly also knew how to make the relevant movement on the page. What she lacked, until she was told to "show the turns," was information from which to infer that she could and should map (symbolize, represent) body movements by hand movements.

The finding is instructive because it shows that the resemblance between body movements, or movements exploring a solid object, and movements describing an outline on the flat page, are not always immediate or direct in blind conditions. The point is that human learning has been regarded far too long as depending on a long, slow process of rewarded trials. What learning does require is information that is relevant to the child's previous knowledge of the situation. Here the child knew the procedure for "turning" on the page. She could execute that procedure, and did so, once she had realized that it was needed. But that realization depended directly on the instruction that she was to show the turns she had made in geographical space. The instruction thus incidentally, but importantly, implied that body turns could be shown by hand movements that make marks that she could feel. Older, brighter, more experienced and knowledgeable children presumably need fewer or no hints to make such inferences quickly. That explains incidentally where cognitive and inferential skills (see earlier) come in, and how they are relevant to the use of flat symbols for three dimensional objects.

A further point should be made. The relevant "match" made by the child in representing body movements on the page was initially with another movement (tracing on the page); it was not initially a match between the movement and a particular shape. This is important. The evidence is that recognizing familiar shapes depends on systematic movements (Berla & Butterfield, 1977; Davidson, 1972). Systematic movements are also needed to familiarize the shapes in the first place. They thus serve in the process of familiarizing haptic shapes. Further, it should be realized that for an exploratory movement to be systematic initially, that is to say, before the shape has become familiar, the movement must be guided by some prior cue, either from the context, from instruction, or from prior naming. Heller (1989) recently found a huge difference in haptic picture recognition by adults before and after the pictures had been named (9.1%, compared with 49.3%). That is entirely consistent with the results and argument here. Once a shape is familiar, recognition can be based on much less evidence; even a single feature can then be a sufficient cue for recognition. The evidence therefore suggests that movement information is at least as, or perhaps more, important than passive touch alone for coding shapes of this kind. Systematic movement thus underlies recognition of familiar shapes.

The reason why production can be easier than recognition in haptic conditions can therefore be explained by evidence from research on memory for movements (Laabs & Simmons, 1981). Thus movements that the subject selects or organizes himself or herself are remembered better than movements that are constrained or organized by the experimenter, unless the subject already understands the organization or is given prior clues to it (Diewert & Stelmach, 1978; Kelso & Wallace, 1978). While the reasons for better motor memory in these conditions are still controversial, some aspects of cognitive skill are probably involved. In any case, better memory for active movements that the subject selects or organizes, suggests that it is easier for subjects to educe similarities between what are otherwise quite different forms of active movement (e.g., arm movement and locomotion) which he or she produces, while an unfamiliar configuration constrains movements and lacks cues that could serve to access previous knowledge. It is intelligible that production is earlier and easier than recognition in these conditions.

The foregoing explanation is consistent with what we know of memory systems (Tulving, 1983). Thus, while recall is generally more difficult than recognition, this depends on the availability of retrieval cues. For recall and output skills generally, stored information has to be retrieved as well as accessed. Recognition is easier than production (recall) when the task provides retrieval cues. But when recognition is demanded in a context that provides no retrieval cues, and where there are no signs in common between stored knowledge and the perceptual context, access to that longer-term knowledge is difficult. In that case recognition becomes as difficult, or more difficult, than recall. It is contended here that this is the situation for unfamiliar haptic shapes. Actively selected movement production (recall) in that case has the advantage over recognition of unfamiliar configurations when there is no prior cue to priming that can serve as a retrieval cue.

The account proposed here suggests that the factors which theories of haptic coding have to take into account are not necessarily the same for every type of shape; but that for the configurations considered here, the role of information from active movement is primary.

SUMMARY AND CONCLUSION

The surprising finding that blind children were better at producing drawings of the human figure than at recognizing them, was considered in the context of an analysis of haptic shape information, and the multiple skills required in drawing.

It was argued that the problems in having to represent three-dimensional objects in two-dimensional space are in many respects the same for blind and sighted children. Initially, children do not use simple flat shapes to symbolize or represent three-dimensional objects on the flat page. Subsequently, both the blind and the sighted come to such solutions spontaneously. However, information in haptic conditions does impose differences that make recognition less direct. To recognize a shape as a symbol for a three-dimensional object by touch, the child has to infer a similarity between movements in geographic space and arm movements made in exploring two-dimensional outlines. The reason why production is easier than recognition in haptic conditions is that production involves self-produced movement. That provides cues for recognition when shapes are unfamiliar. If there are no prior cues (from context, naming, or production plans) to prime retrieval for haptic recognition, exploratory movements are constrained (rather than chosen) by the configuration. Constrained movements make inferences more difficult because they increase memory load. Familiar configurations, by contrast, have the usual advantage of recognition over production because previous exploration has established features that act as retrieval cues.

The explanation considered three main factors: (1) Recognition of familiar haptic shapes depends on features which are established initially by systematic movements and act as retrieval cues. (2) Memory for movements is better when movements are self-produced or organized, than when they are constrained by an unfamiliar display that provides no retrieval cues. (3) The relative difficulty of recognition and production (recall) is governed by the presence or absence of retrieval cues. Without prior cuing, production is thus easier than recognition. The thesis is that haptic recognition is indirect and has its basis in movement or output plans.

The argument and findings have implications for developmental theories of drawing and for theories of haptic coding. They underlie the fact that drawing is not a unitary skill, and suggest how the importance of subsidiary symbolic, procedural, inferential, perceptual, and output processes can vary with apparently small differences in task information. They also have practical implications for blind children. For theories of haptic shape coding, the findings imply first that models need to distinguish between different forms of haptic shape; and second, that for configurations of the kind discussed here, explanations have to include the conditions involved in movement processing and output plans as the basic information.

ACKNOWLEDGMENTS

The work to which the chapter refers was supported by a grant from the Economic and Social Sciences Research Council of Great Britain, which is gratefully acknowledged.

REFERENCES

Arnheim, R. (1969). *Visual thinking. Berkeley: University of California Press.*

Berla, E. P., & Butterfield, L. H., Jr. (1977). Tactual distinctive feature analysis: Training blind students in shape recognition and in locating shapes on a map. *Journal of Special Education, 11*, 336–346.

Byrne, R. W., & Salter, E. (1983). Distances and directions in cognitive maps of the blind. *Canadian Journal of Psychology, 37*, 293–299.

Cox, M. V. (1986). *The child's point of view. The development of language and cognition.* London: Harvester Press.

Craig, J. C., & Sherrick, C. E. (1982). Dynamic tactile displays. In W. Shiff & E. Foulke (Eds.), *Tactual perception: A source book.* Cambridge, MA: Cambridge University Press.

Davidson, P. W. (1972). The role of exploratory activity in haptic perception: Some issues, data and hypotheses. *Research Bulletin, American Foundation for the Blind, 24*, 21–28.

Diewert, G. L., & Stelmach, G. E. (1978). Perceptual organization in motor learning. In G. E. Stelmach (Ed.), *Information processing in motor control and learning.* New York: Academic Press.

Freeman, N. H. (1980). *Strategies of representation in young children.* London: Academic Press.

Freeman, N. H., & Cox, M. V. (Eds.). (1985). *Visual order: The nature and development of visual representation.* Cambridge, England: Cambridge University Press.

Gibson, J. J. (1971). The information available in pictures. *Leonardo, 4*, 27–35.

Gombrich, E. H. (1970). *Art and illusion.* Princeton, NJ: Princeton University Press.

Goodenough, F. (1926). *The measurement of intelligence by drawing.* Yonkers, NY: World Books.

Goodnow, J. J. (1977). *Children's drawing*. London: Fontana/Open Books.

Goodnow, J. J., & Levine, R. (1973). The grammar of action: Sequence and syntax in children's copying of simple shapes. *Cognitive Psychology, 4*, 82–98.

Harris, D. B. (1963). *Children's drawings as measures of intellectual maturity*. New York: Harcourt, Brace, & World.

Heller, M. A. (1982). Visual and tactual texture perception: Intersensory cooperation. *Perception & Psychophysics, 31*, 339–344.

Heller, M. A. (1989). Picture and pattern perception in the sighted and the blind; The advantage of the late blind. *Perception, 18*, 379–389.

Herman, J. F., Herman, T. G., & Chatman, S. P. (1983). Constructing cognitive maps from partial information: A demonstrative study with congenitally blind subjects. *Journal of Visual Impairment and Blindness, 77*, 195–198.

Hollyfield, R. L., & Foulke, E. (1983). The spatial cognition of blind pedestrians. *Journal of Visual Impairment and Blindness, 77*, 204–210.

Katz, D. (1925). *Der Aufbau der Tastwelt*. Leipzig, Germany: Barth.

Kelso, J. A., Scott, & Wallace, S. A. (1978). Conscious mechanisms in movement. In G. E. Stelmach (Ed.), *Information processing in motor control and learning*. New York: Academic Press.

Kosslyn, S. M., Heldenmeyer, K. H., & Locklear, E. P. (1977). Children's drawings as data about internal representations. *Journal of Experimental Child Psychology, 23*, 191–211.

Laabs, G. J., & Simmons, R. W. (1981). Motor memory. In D. Holding (Ed.), *Human skills*. New York: Wiley.

Landau, B. (1986). Early map use as an unlearned ability. *Cognition, 22*, 201–227.

Leonard, J. A., & Newman, R. C. (1967). Spatial orientation in the blind. *Nature, 215*, 1413–1414.

Liben, L. S. (1988). Conceptual issues in the development of spatial cognition. In J. Stiles-Davis, M. Kritchevsky, & U. Bellugi (Eds.), *Spatial cognition: Brain bases and development*. Hillsdale, NJ: Lawrence Erlbaum Associates.

Luquet, G. H. (1927). *Le dessin enfantin*. Paris: Alcan

Maccoby, E. E., & Bee, H. L. (1965). Some speculations conerning the lag between perceiving and performing. *Child Development, 36*, 367–377.

McGurk, H. (1976). Hearing lips and seeing voices. *Nature, 264*, 746–748.

Millar, S. (1975a). Translation rules or visual experience? Drawing the human figure by blind and sighted children. *Perception, 4*, 363–371.

Millar, S. (1975b). Spatial memory by blind and sighted children. *British Journal of Psychology, 66*, 449–459.

Millar, S. (1976). Spatial representation by blind and sighted children. *Journal of Experimental Child Psychology, 21*, 460–479.

Millar, S. (1977). Early stages of tactual matching. *Perception, 6*, 333–343.

Millar, S. (1978). Aspects of information from touch and movement. In G. Gordon (Ed.), *Active touch*. New York: Pergamon Press.

Millar, S. (1979). Utilization of shape and movement cues in simple spatial tasks by blind and sighted children. *Perception, 8*, 11–20.

Millar, S. (1981a). Crossmodal and intersensory perception and the blind. In R. D. Walk & H. L. Pick, Jr. (Eds.), *Intersensory perception and sensory integration*. New York and London: Plenum Press.

Millar, S. (1981b). Self-referent and movement cues in coding spatial location by blind and sighted children. *Perception, 10*, 255–264.

Millar, S. (1985a). The perception of complex patterns by touch. *Perception, 14*, 293–303.

Millar, S. (1985b). Movement cues and body orientation in recall of locations of blind and sighted children. *Quarterly Journal of Experimental Psychology, 37A*, 257–279.

Millar, S. (1986a). Aspects of size, shape and texture in touch: Redundancy and interference in children's discrimination of raised dot patterns. *Journal of Child Psychology and Psychiatry, 27*, 367–381.

Millar, S. (1986b). Drawing as image and representation in blind children. In D. G. Russell, D. Marks, & T. E. Richardson (Eds.), *Image 2*. Dunedin, New Zealand: Human Performance Associates.

Millar, S. (1987a). Perceptual and task factors in fluent braille. *Perception, 16*, 521–536.

Millar, S. (1987b). The perceptual "window" in two-handed braille: Do the left and right hands process text simultaneously? *Cortex, 23*, 111–222.

Millar, S. (1988). Models of sensory deprivation: The nature/nurture dichotomy and spatial representation in the blind. *International Journal of Behavioural Development, 11*, 69–87.

Millar, S. (1990). Imagery and blindness. In Peter Hampson, D. F. Marks, & J. T. E. Richardson (Eds.), *Imagery: Current developments*. London: Routledge & Kegan Paul.

Rice, C. (1930). The orientation of plane figures as a factor in their perception by children. *Child Development, 1*, 111–143.

Piaget, J., & Inhelder, B. (1956). The child's conception of space. London: Routledge & Kegan Paul.

Sakata, H., & Iwamura, Y. (1978). Cortical processing of tactile information in the first somato-sensory and parietal association areas in the monkey. In G. Gordon (Ed.), *Active touch*. New York: Pergamon Press.

Schiff, W., & Isikow, H. (1966). Stimulus redundancy in the tactile perception of histograms. *International Journal for the Education of the Blind. 16*, 1–11.

Terman, L. J., & Merril, M. A. (1946). *Measuring intelligence*. London: Harrap.

Tulving, E. (1983). *Elements in episodic memory*. Oxford, England: Clarendon Press.

Van Somers, P. (1984). *Drawing and cognition*: Descriptive and experimental studies of graphic production processes. Cambridge, England: Cambridge University Press.

Weber, E. H. (1978). *The sense of touch*. (De Tactu, 1834, transl. H. E. Ross, and Der Tastsinn und das Gemeingefuhl, 1846, trans. D. J. Murray, for the Experimental Psychology Society), London: Academic Press.

Willats, J. (1977). How children learn to draw. *Quarterly Journal of Experimental Psychology 29*, 367–382.

Williams, M. (1956). *Williams Intelligence Test for children with defective vision*. Windsor, England: N.F.E.R. Publishing Co.

13

CONCLUSIONS: THE FUTURE OF TOUCH

M. A. Heller
W. Schiff

Much progress has been made in the field in the past 10 to 15 years. We have seen a large increase in research on haptics and intermodal relations. We should point out that a great deal remains to be learned. Some theoretical problems have proven amenable to study, yet difficult issues persist. It is likely that we will see considerable progress in the field over the next decade. Some research will be prompted by concerns about application, as in robotic design, while other studies will stem from interests in fundamental theoretical issues.

What message should the reader of this book come away with? There are really many important themes described in this book, but two overriding points stand out. First, any adequate account of touch needs to consider the appropriateness of the level of analysis that is chosen. It is possible to approach a research problem from a sensory, perceptual, or cognitive perspective. All of these approaches are certainly valid. Some researchers have opted to investigate a particular problem from a sensory standpoint, and believe that sensory sorts of explanations may be most parsimonious. Others, however, have pointed out content areas where higher, cognitive processes must be invoked to explain the data. Millar, for example, has noted that it is important to consider a multiplicity of factors to explain the production and recognition of drawings, including the roles of representation, memory, and cognition. An adequate account of vibrotactile pattern recognition may require consideration of higher level cognitive functioning (see chapter by Sherrick, this volume). It is difficult to understand hemispheric laterality effects if we fail to consider the influence of language and spatial processes, with a left-hand (right cortex) advantage for some tasks that involve pattern perception, novel material, and little linguistic load. Even a task as ostensibly simple as reading letters drawn on the skin can depend on the provision of categorical information. That is, it may be difficult for someone to interpret a pattern drawn on the skin if he or she does not know whether to expect that the stimulus will be a letter, number, or geometrical shape. It is difficult to understand fully pain sensibility without recourse to cognitive sorts of variables, according to Rollman.

Developmentally, perception obviously occurs prior to some sophisticated cognitive skills, as can be seen in the work reported in the chapter by Bushnell and Boudreau. Babies respond to shape and pattern information long before they possess much linguistic or classificatory ability.

A second trend has also emerged from some of the work within this volume. Many of the authors demonstrate a concern with the relationship between touch and other senses. This reflects both an important research area and a traditional research strategy. Warren and Rossano have focused on the influence of vision on touch, while Bushnell and Boudreau considered the interaction between these two senses in infancy (also see Lederman, Thorne, & Jones, 1986). We should also point out that it is possible to interpret some of the results of studies of intersensory conflict in terms of "belief," a higher cognitive function. Thus, people may rely on the sense they have confidence in; however, confidence need not equal adeptness. Finally, Millar has observed that many perceptual tasks can be best accomplished with convergent input from more than one sense.

A promissory note was issued in the Introduction to the book. In the light of the evidence provided by the chapters, we offer some tentative solutions to the problems that were posed in the introduction. These views do not necessarily reflect those of every one of the authors of chapters within this volume, but represent those of the editors.

REPRESENTATION: VISUAL IMAGERY, COGNITION IN THE BLIND, AND TACTILE IMAGERY

Some researchers have argued that sighted people normally recode tactual impressions into visual images. However, the visual imagery issue is an interesting way to provide a nonexplanation for some phenomena. We really don't know what those visual or tactual images might be. The evidence clearly indicates that all of those "markers" for visual imagery also occur in the congenitally blind, for example, mental rotation, effects on memory, and so on. Thus, if images are to provide any sort of valuable scientific explanation, they really need to add something to our knowledge base. This doesn't mean that images don't exist. Images may exist, of course, and it is the job of researchers to demonstrate what difference the notion of imagery makes—and how it *adds* to our knowledge of phenomena.

One can make a much stronger case for the importance of *spatial reference information* for touch. This is important in *both sighted and blind people* when limited to touch (see chapter by Millar, this volume). Heller (unpublished experiment) has found, for example, that the effect of orientation on touch is robust with embossed letters, as well as braille. Visual guidance of tactual exploration helps sighted subjects identify tangible patterns. The aid provided by visual guidance mainly derived from spatial reference information (Heller, 1989). Visual imagery did not help sighted subjects cope with pattern tilt, even when light-emitting diodes allowed them sight of tactual scanning patterns in the dark.

Visual experience clearly matters, and it may be most influential in early childhood. However, the effects of visual experience may not be explicable in simplistic terms, that is, the visual imagery explanation.

We should bear in mind the aforementioned caveat about level of analysis. For example, it is clear that blind adults and children can make drawings of objects and animals (see chapters by Heller, Kennedy, and Millar, this volume; Heller & Kennedy, 1990). However, some studies have shown low identification of particular raised-line pictures (see Heller, 1989; Lederman, Klatzky, Chataway, & Summers, 1990). The problem seems to be recognition *and/or* naming of the drawings (see the discussion of pictures and blind people in the chapter on tactual perception in blind people, Heller). The difficulty then is an explanation of a number of failures to name correctly depictions of the objects. Logically, a naming failure can derive from the stimuli chosen, failure to perceive the shape depicted in a raised-line drawing, or a true recognition failure (the shape is perceived, but the individual doesn't know what it is), or a failure in *naming*, per se. It is clear that naming a pattern taps higher-level cognitive skills that go beyond perception.

To reiterate, some of the controversy in the field obviously derives from a failure to consider the level of analysis that is chosen. Experimental manipulations, for example, asking a person to name a tangible drawing, can be too coarse to explain many fundamental processes. A young sighted child, for example, may not know the name of something it sees, but this does not mean it does not perceive, say, a dog in the yard or a cat on a couch (Dretske, 1990). We need to distinguish naming from perception. This analysis also bears on *some forms* of the conflict that appears between ecological and nonecological approaches to perception. For example, it is not poor science to study "sensations," as long as one doesn't incorrectly identify some lower-level sensory process with higher, perceptual phenomena. The two may not always be causally related, and perception need not depend on "having sensations." In addition, the study of "higher" cognitive functions is also "legitimate," and there is no one "correct" research paradigm.

It is clear that some forms of perception don't require higher-level "enrichment," while other tasks may tap memory and prior knowledge. Examples of tasks that depend on higher-level cognitive skills include pattern recognition tasks using letters, braille, or reading braille text.

INTERSENSORY EQUIVALENCE

The evidence is abundant that some features of the environment can be perceived via either vision or touch. The evidence is even stronger if you consider the research with the blind, which supports the notion of "amodal" percepts for some attributes of objects—texture, aspects of form, and perhaps some other object characteristics. Transparency, for example, occurs in both vision and touch. We are able to feel an object through cloth, and the physician can palpate shapes through intervening flesh. There are some sensations, of course, that differ from one sense to the other. In addition, there are some qualities that don't easily translate: for example, shadows, color, and some odors. Thus, there may be *both* modality specific *and* amodal percepts.

ROLE OF RECEPTOR MOVEMENT:
ACTIVE VS. PASSIVE TOUCH

Perception depends on skilled movement. This doesn't necessarily imply top–down processing, in all cases. We can learn to attend to relevant features of objects, and need to explore systematically. Reading braille, for example, is a higher-level skill that taps top–down processes. Active touch is especially important during early phases of form perception tasks, and certain movements may be necessary for some types of information pickup (see Bushnell & Boudreau, this volume). This doesn't mean that passive touch can't work at all, but it does impede the acquisition of information. A large number of people, for example, fail at the Optacon. A component of this difficulty is due to problems with passive touch (Heller, Rogers, & Perry, 1990). Passive touch can be an effective strategy for known forms of limited set size (e.g., with categorical information in reading print-on-palm).

WHOLE VS. PART PERCEPTION AND SERIAL VS.
PARALLEL PROCESSING

We can force touch to process serially, by constructing large raised-line pictures and by using unskilled subjects. There is clear evidence, however, for parallel processing by skilled readers of braille and for small patterns. Skill is the key here, and the novice is more likely to function in a serial fashion. In addition, we should remember that vision can operate sequentially, since it samples spatial information over time, as when configurations are large.

DEVELOPMENT OF TOUCH

Infants clearly respond to texture and other tangible attributes of objects. There seems to be a shift in focus from the mouth to the hand, and Bushnell and Boudreau (this volume) have reported some interesting findings about the relative salience of thermal versus shape attributes in infants.

SENSORY DOMINANCE AND INTERMODAL RELATIONS

A great deal of progress has been made in this area. Vision is not invariably "dominant" over touch. Dominance relations depend on the attribute involved (form versus texture, etc.), with no visual dominance for some textures. In addition, dominance probably varies with the relative normalcy of our senses. The large and growing population of persons with low or poor vision, for example, is less likely to show visual dominance.

One may be justified in having doubts about the intersensory discrepancy paradigm in many of its forms. Much of the dominance literature (in adults) is overly dependent on the use of lenses, and intersensory relationships may change without this unusual manipulation of visual input. Distortion of visual information with lenses often does not allow for "correction," since we lose the context of the environment, and can't see the distortion. In addition, there are many cases in which we may not really have an "assumption of unity," that is, we expect to have different textures on different surfaces, as on the top and bottom of a table. Thus, the notion of visual dominance is a gross oversimplification, with much valuable experimental clarification coming in the past decade. For example, under normal viewing conditions, and with normal observers, we tend to rely on vision for judgments of form and location. However, judgments of location may be influenced by proprioceptive cues given a discrepancy between vision and touch, according to Warren and Rossano. We may then adopt a compromise judgment.

In a recent study, touch dominated vision in form perception when subjects were able to see their exploratory hand movements (Heller, 1990). Vision and touch were placed in conflict with the use of a mirror placed perpendicular to the letter display. This induced a discrepancy in both direction and form. Subjects touched the embossed, tangible letters p, q, b, d, W and M, while looking at them in a mirror, and were asked to identify the letters.

The upright mirror produced a vertical inversion of the letters, and visual inversion of direction of finger movement. Thus, subjects touched a "p," but saw themselves touching a "b" in the mirror. Most of the conflict subjects relied on touch, and only one showed visual dominance. The haptic stimuli were chosen on 52 out of 84 conflict trials, with only 18 correct visual judgments. A number of subjects showed a compromise between the senses, and sometimes based their judgments on vision and sometimes on touch. Other individuals showed a mixed pattern of responses, including left/right reversals.

Touch can be better than vision for many purposes, and this has frequently been overlooked by perception researchers. Any theory of perception must explain how people can feel splinters they can't see, or feel differences in fine textures that are not visible. We need to learn how to exploit the advantages of touch. One fundamental problem that needs some attention is the notion of the "normal observer." We know what this is for sight (i.e., visual acuity), but not for touch.

ILLUSIONS

This may be a very promising research area. Day and Over have both published numerous papers on tactile illusions in the 1960s and early 1970s (see Introduction, this volume; Day & Avery, 1970; Over, 1968). A number of studies suggest that there are differences in how naïve subjects "process" 2-D forms via touch as compared with vision. The horizontal/vertical illusion may disappear for touch if we orient the inverted T as on a CRT screen and eliminate tactile scanning movements toward the body. The illusion happens with the material flat on the table, because of radial/tangential effects—the radial movement toward the body is perceived as longer. Moreover, the illusion alters for touch when the inverted T-shape is arrayed in the frontoparallel plane, and placed alongside the observer or in front of him or her. Heller and his students have also studied this with raised-line drawings, and found that the effect depends on the *size* of the array, with little or no effect for smaller stimuli (1- or 2-in. patterns), even with the material flat on the table. The critical factor may be the size of the hand, with distortion more likely for patterns that are larger than that organ. The issue here is whether tactual space "works" in the same way as visual space. One complication, of course, is that no one is very skilled at reading raised-line drawings via touch. There is a "theoretical payoff" for work on tactual illusions, and we may also see some practical benefit for the production of tangible graphics. The key is to look for ways in which the hand can function well, rather than only look for ways to defeat the sense of touch and make it fail.

LATERALITY EFFECTS
AND HEMISPHERIC SPECIALIZATION

There are large individual differences here, but there is evidence for laterality. For example, there is a left-hand advantage in right-handed persons in identifying patterns with the Optacon (Heller et al., 1990) and in naming numbers printed on the palm at the body midline (Heller, 1986; O'Boyle et al., 1987). Laterality effects can interact with hemispace effects. In a presently unreported experiment, Heller and two students (Katrina Covington and Gail Rogers) found a substantial interaction between hand and hemispace when numbers were drawn on the palms of sighted subjects. It was much easier to read numbers printed on the left palm than the right when the hands were held at the body midline, or to the extreme left of the midline, but the hand effect vanished when the hands were kept in the extreme right hemispace. In the right hemispace, performance of the left hand dropped to the level of the right hand. The reader should note that crossing the body had no effect on performance with the right hand, only the left.

TECHNOLOGICAL CHANGE
AND THE FUTURE OF TOUCH

Knowledge has advanced in the field of touch, owing to some important technological innovations. The effects of instrumentation and technological advances have been most obvious in sensory physiology (see chapters by Cholewiak & Collins; Rollman; and Stevens), but other areas are also impacted (see chapter by Sherrick). For example, a 1985 NSF-sponsored conference on tactile stimulators recommended the development of dense, tactual arrays with close interpin spacing of stimulators (Craig, 1986). Presently, at Princeton, Roger Cholewiak is conducting research with the Multipoint Tactile Array System (MTAC), a tactile array with 256 closely spaced elements. The MTAC offers more precise control of stimulation than the Optacon, and may prove a valuable research tool. The Optacon is now more accessible to researchers who do not have programming skills since the development of commercially available software. InTouch software links the Optacon to Macintosh computers, and allows the user of the vibratory display to "read" material on the screen by way of the mouse or keyboard controls (Heller et al., 1990). Thus, the material at the cursor on the visual screen is tactually displayed on the vibrotactile Optacon array.

THE ECOLOGY OF TOUCH

Most of the research in science has not entailed inductive hypothesis generation (Popper, 1981). Inductive hypothesis generation involves following observation of phenomena with hypotheses that may be tested in a scientific manner. Most of the research on touch has followed the lead of the "hard" sciences, and researchers have been concerned about experimental control of variables. The typical research strategy entails generating a hypothesis and testing it. Precision in experimental control will allow one to come to conclusions about causal relations. However, there are some substantial risks that derive from precipitous experimental reductionism. The major problem is that by prematurely rejecting the study of many variables, we may control much of interest out of our research. In particular, we may fail to uncover substantial and important interaction effects.

Experimental control is a desirable and necessary aspect of research in touch. However, it is possible to begin studies of touch with naturalistic sorts of phenomena. Then, one may systematically engage in a process of subtraction of variables in an attempt to understand complex causal relations. Thus, one may start with rich behaviors, and multiple variables, progressively narrowing them down. Brunswik (1947, pp. 22–23) advocated the research technique of "fractional omission of factors." This is just one of many alternative, effective research strategies, that may have the advantage of eventually leading the researcher to understand interrelationships among those factors affecting touch (also see Sherrick & Craig, 1982, p. 77). Of course, some recent research in the area has been influenced by naturalistic concerns (e.g., Gordon & Cooper, 1975; Lederman, 1978; Klatzky, Lederman, & Metzger, 1985). We hope that we will see more efforts to seek answers in naturalistic settings.

Such theoretical concerns about research strategies is an important component of the ecological position presented by Schiff in the following section. This is fundamentally the same position about experimentation that was advocated by Brunswik (1947).

NATURALISTIC TOUCH

A gnawing concern with laboratory studies of touch is that there is little apparent connection between how we use touch in natural encounters with objects, surfaces, and substances, and how we respond when "stimuli" are delivered to subjects in laboratory studies. Aside from the early phenomenological descriptions emerging from David Katz's classical observations (e.g., see Katz, 1989; Krueger, 1982), there has really been no serious attempt to develop a "natural history" approach to the study of touching behaviors. Perhaps it is time for such an approach to emerge.

A naturalistic approach to touch and touching might be something like that of the European ethologists studying such animal behaviors as courtship, mating, nest building, care of young, aggression, predation, feeding, and the like. That is, it might bridge an apparent gap between the touch we study in controlled laboratory situations and touch occurring in various real-world settings in which we use touch to inform us of characteristics of objects and the conditions they are in at a particular time (e.g., the viscosity of food substances, or the dampness of towels). We are tempted to call for a "naturalistic" approach not because such approaches are, like motherhood or advanced academic degrees, inherently good, but because the study of touch, in spite of its intrinsic interest, seems to some observers somewhat sterile as an essential branch of what appears to be emerging as a functional perceptual psychology (e.g., Reed, 1988). Such a naturalistic approach is not meant to *replace* highly controlled laboratory research, but to provide a more meaningful context in which to interpret laboratory findings concerned with how and when we use our skin, muscle, and joint senses, and various haptic activities to obtain useful information about the world. Such an approach might also yield useful information while using various natural settings as field settings to test principles and micro theories, such as some of those broached in the chapters in the current volume.

One such realm might be called "Human Factors Haptics," that is, might lead to a better understanding of the person–machine haptic interface (e.g., see Norman, 1988 POET). How many of us have groped for sought-after controls on our VCRs, cameras, automobile radios, thermal control units, hi fi sets, all in the dark, only to have to turn on bright lights to push the correct button or lever? These are cases in which the visual system must be used to augment or replace touch because of human factors failures in designing machine controls commonly used in low-level illumination. We might improve our knowledge of touch, as well as our equipment by using an approach incorporating "critical incidents failures" of unaugmented and augmented touch.

Another naturalistic setting might be the baby nursery. We know far too little about how, when, and why caretakers touch their babies, what information they glean from such touching and palpations, and conversely what the babies gain from touching other people. While chapters in this volume examine legitimate concerns with infants' explorations of objects and surfaces, we have only an inkling of the aesthetic, social, diagnostic, and affectional roles of touch in this arena, and in others as well (although see Thayer, 1982).

Regarding haptic aesthetics, one might consider observing people in museums—especially those with collections of sculpture—to see what and how they touch, and how their conceptions of the art works emerge via touch as well as visual inspection. By cataloging touching behaviors and then following up with focused interviews of those who have done the touching, we might acquire a fuller knowledge of how various touching strategies and practices lead to various sorts of information networks concerning the important properties of objects. Such an approach is, of course, not limited to aesthetics, but could extend to the entire arena of touching behaviors.

Grocery stores might seem mundane as contrasted with the tactile laboratory, but anyone observing the tactile–haptic encounters at counters containing bananas, tomatoes, onions, carrots, and so on, must realize there is a great deal of tactile–haptic exploration and "testing" going on in such settings. Yet one cannot remember having read a thorough account of such behaviors, and the information they yield about foodstuffs. One may look forward to a dissertation with a title something like: "Vegetable Encounters of the Informative Kind."

Moving from fruit stands to department stores, consider the haptic behaviors of customers examining fur coats (or artificial versions thereof), sweaters, pillows, silk scarves, and so on. Their haptic behaviors, and the resulting decisions and impressions resulting therefrom should yield a rewarding set of data concerning how people feel such materials, and how they subsequently feel *about* those same items. The perceiver fondling a fur coat likely explores the softness, depth, and density of the fur with the fingers, just as the eye may caress the gloss, color, and visible texture. Pet shops are likely sources of valuable haptic information for fur still being worn by original owners! Manufacturers may know more about the haptics of consumer behavior than do perceptual psychologists—to wit, the weight of "fine" silverware and the heft of "better" chess pieces! The furniture and housewares department may hold several theses concerned with haptic behaviors and their consequences in judgment and decisions.

Auto repair shops may hold haptic mysteries, from the smoothness of reworked metals in body shops, to the locating of parts of the vehicle that cannot be viewed due to obscure location; anyone who has ever threaded a nut (or opened one) may testify to the naturalistic research possibilities here.

Hospitals should provide ready arenas as virtual emporiums of palpation, scanning, and stroking behaviors—mostly for obtaining information about tissue states, lump conditions (but see Adams et al., 1976; Bloom, Criswell, Pennypacker, Catania, & Adams, 1982), congestive conditions (via audition), and so on. Yet many studies concerned with touching in hospitals rarely record more than who touches whom, and for how long.

To conclude, students of touch and touching must consider ecological concerns if the future study of touch is to be related to the roles of touch in everyday life—life in the real world.

REFERENCES

Adams, C. K., Hall, D. C., Pennypacker, H. S., Goldstein, M. K., Hench, L. L., Madden, M. C., Stein, G. H., & Catania, A. C. (1976). Lump detection in simulated human breasts. *Perception & Psychophysics, 20,* 163–167.

Bloom, H. S., Criswell, E. L., Pennypacker, H. S., Catania, A. C., & Adams, C. K. (1982). Major stimulus dimensions determining detection of simulated breast lesions. *Perception & Psychophysics, 32,* 251–260.

Brunswik, E. (1947). *Systematic and representative design of psychological experiments.* Berkeley, CA: University of California Press.

Craig, J. C. (1986). *Science and technology to help the handicapped.* Final report of NSF sponsored conference, Bloomington, IN, May 9, 10, 1985.

Day, R. H., & Avery, G. C. (1970). Absence of the horizontal–vertical illusion in haptic space. *Journal of Experimental Psychology, 83,* 172–173.

Dretske, F. (1990). Seeing, believing, and knowing. In D. N. Osherson, S. M. Kosslyn, & J. M. Hollerbach (Eds.), *Visual cognition and action* (Vol. 2). Cambridge, MA: MIT Press.

Gordon, I. E., & Cooper, C. (1975). Improving one's touch. *Nature, 256,* 203–204.

Heller, M. A. (1986). Central and peripheral influences on tactual reading. *Perception & Psychophysics, 39,* 197–204.

Heller, M. A. (1989). Tactile memory in sighted and blind observers: The influence of orientation and rate of presentation. *Perception, 18,* 121–133.

Heller, M. A. (1990). *Intersensory conflict in form identification.* Paper presented at the annual meetings of the Psychonomic Society, New Orleans, Nov. 15.

Heller, M. A., & Kennedy, J. M. (1990). Perspective taking, pictures and the blind. *Perception & Psychophysics, 48,* 459–466.

Heller, M. A., Rogers, G. J., & Perry, C. L. (1990). Tactile pattern recognition with the Optacon: Superior performance with active touch and the left hand. *Neuropsychologia, 28,* 1003–1006.

Katz, D. (1989). *The world of touch.* L. E. Krueger, Trans. Hillsdale, N.J.: Lawrence Erlbaum Associates.

Klatzky, R. L., Lederman, S. J., & Metzger, V. A. (1985). Identifying objects by touch: An "expert" system." *Perception & Psychophysics, 37,* 299–302.

Krueger, L.E. (1982). Tactual perception in historical perspective: David Katz's world of touch. In W. Schiff & E. Foulke (Eds.), *Tactual perception: A sourcebook.* New York: Cambridge University Press.

Lederman, S. J. (1978). "Improving one's touch". . .and more. *Perception & Psychophysics, 24,* 154–160.

Lederman, S. J., Klatzky, R. L., Chataway, C., & Summers, C. D., (1990). Visual mediation and the haptic recognition of two-dimensional pictures of common objects. *Perception & Psychophysics, 47,* 54–64.

Lederman, S. J., Thorne, G., & Jones, B. (1986). Perception of texture by vision and touch: Multidimensionality and intersensory integration. *Journal of Experimental Psychology: Human Perception and Performance, 12,* 169–180.

Norman, D. A. (1988). *The psychology of everyday things.* New York: Doubleday.

O'Boyle, M. W., Wyhe-Lawler, F. Van, & Miller, D. A. (1987). Recognition of letters traced in the right and left palms: Evidence for a process-oriented tactile asymmetry. *Brain and Cognition, 6,* 474–494.

Over, R. (1968). Explanations of geometrical illusions. *Psychological Bulletin, 70,* 545–562.

Popper, K. (1981). The myth of inductive hypothesis generation. In R. D. Tweney, M. E. Doherty, & C. R. Mynatt (Eds.), *On scientific thinking.* New York: Columbia University Press.

Reed, E. S. (1988). *James J. Gibson and the psychology of perception.* New Haven: Yale University Press.

Sherrick, C. E., & Craig, J. C. (1982). The psychophysics of touch. In W. Schiff & E. Foulke (Eds.). *Tactual perception: A sourcebook.* New York: Cambridge University Press.

Thayer, S. (1982). Social touching. In W. Schiff & E. Foulke (Eds.), *Tactual perception: A sourcebook.* New York: Cambridge University Press.

AUTHOR INDEX

SUBJECT INDEX